The Politics of the Pharmaceutical Industry and Access to Medicines

The Politics of the Pharmaceutical Industry and Access to Medicines

World Pharmacy and India

Edited by
Hans Löfgren

Routledge
Taylor & Francis Group

LONDON AND NEW YORK

First published 2018
by Routledge
4 Park Square, Milton Park, Abingdon, Oxon OX14 4RN
and by Routledge
605 Third Avenue, New York, NY 10017

First issued in paperback 2023

Routledge is an imprint of the Taylor & Francis Group, an informa business

Publisher's Note
The publisher has gone to great lengths to ensure the quality of this reprint but points out that some imperfections in the original copies may be apparent.

Print edition not for sale in South Asia (India, Sri Lanka, Nepal, Bangladesh, Afghanistan, Pakistan or Bhutan).

British Library Cataloguing in Publication Data
A catalogue record for this book is available from the British Library

Library of Congress Cataloging in Publication Data
A catalog record for this book has been requested

ISBN 13: 978-1-138-10314-6 (hbk)
ISBN 13: 978-1-03-265292-4 (pbk)
ISBN 13: 978-1-315-13610-3 (ebk)

DOI: 10.4324/9781315136103

Typeset in Plantin 10/13
by Eleven Arts, Delhi 110 035

SOCIAL
SCIENCE
PRESS

For J. Manohar Rao

Acknowledgements

Early versions of some chapters in this volume were presented at a conference in Hyderabad in September 2010, organised jointly by the University of Hyderabad and Deakin University. I wish to acknowledge the role of J. Manohar Rao and other colleagues at both universities in the organisation of the seminar and early planning for this book. Its quality and readability owes much to the sub-editing by Alison Caddick, Crissene Fawcett, and Michael Leahy. I am also thankful to Esha Béteille and her staff at the Social Science Press for their support and professionalism.

Contents

List of Tables and Figures

TABLES

FIGURES

List of Contributors

Hans Löfgren is Associate Professor in Politics and Policy Studies, Deakin University, Melbourne, Australia.

Poduri Balaram is Vice President (India Operations), UAS Labs, Hyderabad.

Kajal Bhardwaj is a lawyer (HIV, Health and Human Rights) in New Delhi.

Christiane Fischer is a medical doctor working with BUKO Pharma-Kampagne, Bielefeld, Germany and the German ethical committee (DER Deutscher Ethikrat).

Deepak Kumar Jena is Head (International Business), UAS Labs, Minnesota, USA.

Claudia Jenkes is a journalist with BUKO Pharma-Kampagne, Bielefeld, Germany.

Narayanan Lalitha is a professor at the Gujarat Institute of Development Research, Ahmedabad.

André de Mello e Souza is a researcher at the Institute for Applied Economic Research, Brasilia, Brazil.

Anant Phadke has been involved since 1980 in advocacy for rational pharmaceutical policy, mainly through the All-India Drug Action Network (AIDAN).

Neelam Raaj is Senior Editor with *The Times of India*.

Philip Soos is a Masters research student in the School of Humanities and Social Sciences, Deakin University, Melbourne, Australia.

S. Srinivasan is associated with LOCOST, Vadodara, the All-India Drug Action Network (AIDAN), and the Medico Friend Circle (MFC).

Nguyen Thanh Tu is Deputy Director General, Department of International Law, Ministry of Justice, Vietnam.

G. Vijay is Assistant Professor in Economics, University of Hyderabad, Hyderabad.

List of Acronyms

ACTA	Anti-Counterfeiting Trade Agreement
ANDA	Abbreviated New Drug Applications
API	Active Pharmaceutical Ingredient
APPCB	Andhra Pradesh Pollution Control Board
ARV	Anti-Retroviral Drugs
AYUSH	Ayurvedic, Homeopathic, Unani
BIT	Bilateral Investment Treaty
CDSCO	Central Drugs Standard Control Organisation
CEP	Certificates of Suitability
CPCB	Central Pollution Control Board
CRAMS	Contract Research and Manufacturing
DCGI	Drugs Controller General of India
DMF	Drug Master Files
DPCI	Drug Price Control Order
DTAB	Drugs Technical Advisory Board
EC	European Commission
EFTA	European Free Trade Association
EIA	Environmental Impact Statement
EMR	Exclusive Marketing Rights
EPA	Environmental Protection Agency (USA)
EPTRI	Environmental Protection Training and Research Institute
EU	European Union
FDA	Food and Drug Administration (USA)

FDC	Fixed Dose Combinations
FDI	Foreign Direct Investment
FERA	Foreign Exchange Regulation Act
FIPB	Foreign Investment Promotion Board
FTA	Free Trade Agreement
GMP	Good Manufacturing Practice
HAART	Highly Active Anti-Retroviral Therapy
HAI	Health Action International
IMPACT	International Medical Products Anti-Counterfeiting Task Force
INN	International Non-proprietary Name
IPAB	Intellectual Property Appellate Board
IPR	Intellectual Property Rights
LDC	Least Developed Country
LMIC	Low and Middle-Income Countries
MCI	Medical Council of India
MHRA	Medicines and Healthcare Product Regulatory Agency (UK)
MNC	Multinational Company
MoEF	Ministry of Environment and Forestry
MPP	Medicines Patent Pool
MSF	Médecins Sans Frontières
NDDS	Novel Drug Delivery Systems
NGO	Non-governmental Organisation
NICE	National Institute of Clinical Excellence (UK)
NLEM	National List of Essential Medicines
NME	New Molecular Entity
OTC	Over-the-counter
PCB	Pollution Control Board
PHAR-MEXCIL	Pharmaceuticals Export Promotion Council of India
PIL	Public Interest Litigation
PPS	Public-private Partnership
R&D	Research and Development
SACC	South African Competition Commission
SLAPP	Strategic Lawsuits against Public Participation
TNMSC	Tamil Nadu Medical Services Corporation

TRIPS	Agreement on Trade Related Aspects on Intellectual Property Rights
TSDF	Treatment, Storage and Disposal Facilities
UNCHR	United Nations Commission on Human Rights
USPTO	United States Patent and Trademark Office
USTR	United States Trade Representative
WAP	Weighted Average Price
WIPO	World Intellectual Property Organization
WHO	World Health Organization
WTO	World Trade Organization

1

The Pharmaceutical Industry and Access to Medicines in India

Hans Löfgren

Pharmaceutical policy in India as elsewhere is shaped by conflicting economic and social interests and opposing values and priorities. Tensions can be understood as revolving around the contradiction between use value and exchange value in the production of medicinal drugs as commodities, as per Marx's original analysis. The use value of medicines—if safe and efficacious, of good quality, and prescribed and consumed appropriately—is the prevention, cure or alleviation of ill-health and disease. Health policy is—or should be—aimed at optimising the use value of medicines. For this purpose government agencies administer regulatory oversight of the manufacturing, marketing and distribution of medicines. Drugs made available to patients are expected to meet adequate safety, quality and efficacy standards, but regulation to ensure such standards is subject to controversy in most countries. This is a domain where definition and interpretation of scientific-technological principles and criteria is infused by partiality and bias grounded in social and material interests, as evidenced by recurrent debates about industry 'capture' of regulatory agencies, including the world's most reputable regulator, the US Food and Drug Administration (Angell 2005; Law 2006). In India, a Parliamentary Committee Report in 2012 depicted the Central Drugs Standard Control Organisation (CDSCO) as dysfunctional and influenced inappropriately by the exchange value perspective of manufacturers (Parliamentary Standing Committee on Health and Welfare 2012). The clash between use and exchange value perspectives is starkly illustrated by cases of products known to cause more harm than good, particularly common in poorly regulated markets such as India's, as shown by Srinivasan and Phadke.

Markets fail to generate socially adequate investments in basic research to discover new medicines and for this reason, governments are globally the principal funders and organisers of this type of research (Stevens et al. 2011). But the development of promising molecules into final products occurs largely under the auspices of multinational companies (MNCs) operating under the imperative of maximising exchange value. As a consequence, funding for research to develop drugs for diseases affecting mainly the poor in low and middle-income countries (LMICs) is dwarfed by funding of research focused on the diseases and conditions predominant in wealthy markets. In 2010, the MNCs contributed about $500 million to this type of R&D, out of total R&D spending by the top 50 global companies alone of more than $100 billion, and their participation requires special incentive mechanisms (Cacciotti, Jerry and Clinton 2012; Moran et al. 2011; World Health Organization 2010). There are also, in most countries, price regulation systems, and health insurance and reimbursement schemes, to enable affordable access to necessary medicines. Finally, the optimisation of use value requires not only safety, quality and efficacy regulation, and access to essential drugs for all, but also rational or 'quality use' of medicines. This requires measures to ensure the best possible use of medicines to improve health outcomes, including appropriate constraints and monitoring of services providers and prescribers (Srinivasan 2006, ch. 3).

India has yet to achieve either effective and reliable safety and efficacy regulation or universal access to essential medicines, and policy for quality use of medicines is rudimentary only (High Level Expert Group 2011; Parliamentary Standing Committee on Health and Welfare 2012). But the use value perspective has a strong presence in pharmaceutical policy debates, advocated for by activists and Left parties, professional groups and NGOs, and by academic analysts. Contributions to this volume demonstrate the impressive expertise and commitment of many Indian industry observers and public health advocates.

Indeed, India has a remarkable history of civil society engagement with drug policy and intellectual property rights (IPR), that is, the World Trade Organization's (WTO) 2005 Agreement on Trade-Related Aspects of Intellectual Property Rights (TRIPS), a recurring theme of this volume. From the 1980s, during the negotiations leading up to the formation of the WTO, a de facto coalition of public health advocates and domestic drug producers lobbied governments and mobilised public opinion against looming pharmaceutical patents (Sen Gupta 2010). Initially their efforts were directed squarely against the push by a group of US-based business associations and MNCs for IPRs to be brought under the trade umbrella in the global trade negotiations (Drahos, Peter and Braithwaite 2001). When TRIPS was a reality the focus shifted to damage limitation aimed at influencing the implementation of the agreement in national legislation (Rammana 2004; Tellez no year). The common objective of participants in the coalition was to ensure that amendments to the Patents Act, 1970 (enacted in 1999, 2002 and 2005) incorporated in full the 'flexibilities' available under TRIPS, as confirmed and extended in the declaration at the fourth WTO ministerial conference in Doha in 2001 on the TRIPS Agreement and Public Health, known as the Doha Declaration Agreement (World Trade Organization 2012). These flexibilities include the right of national governments to define patentability in domestic legislation, limits on data protection, pre- and post-grant opposition to patents, and provisions for the issuing of compulsory licensing, as explored by Narayanan Lalitha, Kajal Bhardwaj and others in this volume (Kerry and Lee 2007; Smith, Correa and Oh 2009).

Domestic firms had a stake in minimising IPR constraints on continued and expanded manufacturing and exports of generic drugs. The term generic drug refers to a copy of an original product whose patent has expired. In India, of course, all drugs were generics before 2005 in the sense that there were no product patents for pharmaceuticals. Obstacles to the market entry of generics in most instances are not technical, but derive from institutional arrangements, including the prescribing behaviour of doctors, brand loyalties, and regulatory and reimbursement systems, including retail pharmacy regulation and practices (Lofgren 2004). Generics can be marketed as branded products—that is, with a trade name belonging to the producer—or under the generic name of the active compound. In India and many LMICs, drugs are mostly marketed profitably as 'branded generics' at prices well above the cost of production. Moreover, as detailed by Chinu Srinivasan and Anant Phadke in this volume, because of lack of adequate regulation, in India too many of these products are irrational or marketed inappropriately. In contrast, in the US and Europe, generics are mostly low-profit commodity products. As patents expire, institutional arrangements ensure that prices come down radically. In the US, generics now constitute 80 per cent of the market by volume (Astra Zeneca 2011, p. 18). In the European Union and elsewhere, tender-based models of drug procurement guarantee a large market share for low-cost generics (Kanavos, Seeley and Vandoros 2009). These types of procurement systems can be found on a smaller scale in India and can potentially be expanded, as envisaged by the Planning Commission for the 2013–17 period (Bajal 2012)

To the extent that the large-scale domestic production of relatively inexpensive generic drugs makes possible the supply of affordable medicines in India and throughout the developing world, civil society groups could engage, at least until recently, in joint lobbying efforts with the local industry. Intense political conflict around these issues continued until enactment of the Patents (Amendments) Act, 2005 in April of that year (with retrospective effect from 1 January 2005). The parliamentary Left parties achieved significant last minute-changes from the Patents (Amendment) Ordinance of December 2004, including expanded scope for pre-grant patent opposition (Mueller 2007, pp. 529–30).

The upshot of the political struggles around pharmaceutical patents in the fifteen or so years leading up to the 2005 amendment is legislation that takes account—not in full, but more extensively than in probably any other country—of the flexibilities available under TRIPS. Indeed, the significance of India in global medicines production and supply make IPR and pharmaceutical policy in this country a matter of great import to people all around the world (see for example Christiane Fischer and Deepak Kumar Jena and Poduri Balaram in this volume). Post-2005, particular attention has focused on Section 3(d) of the Patents (Amendment) Act, 2005, intended to prevent the awarding of patents for new uses or slightly modified versions of known molecules, unless a 'significant enhancement of efficacy' can be demonstrated. The objective is to prevent 'evergreening', that is, unwarranted extension of monopoly pricing through patenting of trivial modifications. The conflicts around patentability and Section 3(d) are detailed by Narayanan Lalitha and by Kajal Bhardwaj, with particular reference to the infamous Novartis case. This saga, which has attracted global attention, commenced with the rejection in January 2006 of the patent on the cancer medicine imatinib mesylate (marketed by Novartis as Glivec) on the grounds that it represented a new form of a known substance and therefore was not patentable under Indian law. Novartis has since pursued all legal avenues of appeal and challenged the legitimacy of Section 3(d). (The outcome of the final Supreme Court hearing was not known at the time of writing.)

The coalition of public health advocates and domestic firms, which had opposed pharmaceutical patents, achieved, as noted, significant results in terms of Patent Act provisions enabling use of TRIPS flexibilities but their interests increasingly diverged as firms adapted to the new IPR regime. In this respect, CIPLA is the outstanding exception, as explained in the chapter by Neelam Raaj. But ultimately, family-owned domestic generics manufacturers and the MNCs equally operate under the commercial imperative of capital accumulation. Most scientists and industry executives undoubtedly aspire to contribute to better health—it is just that corporate survival requires that exchange value be maximised (Harvey 2010). In this perspective, public health benefits are purely incidental; there is little reason for disquiet, for example, if new drugs add little to already available therapies, as is too often the case (Angell 2005, chs. 4–5). Nor is irrational prescribing or the proliferation of irrational combination drugs or the lack of therapeutical value of many top-selling products, as detailed by Chinu Srinivasan and Anant Phadke, a concern from a business perspective. The 10:90 divide, whereby less than 10 per cent of medical research is devoted to diseases accounting for more than 90 per cent of the global disease burden, is a glaring manifestation of the primacy of exchange value (Matlin 2005).

Yet, the significance of medicines to human welfare is such that capital accumulation as principal impetus for R&D, production, pricing and distribution is under unremitting challenge. This challenge has broadened and intensified to the point where there is now a global debate on alternatives to patents as mechanism for funding of medical R&D, as explained in the chapter by Philip Soos and Hans Löfgren (see also e.g. Pogge, Rimmer and Rubenstein 2010). In global policy discourse, and in pharmaceutical debates in India, the aim of access to essential medicines for all has increasingly come to be accepted, at least rhetorically, by all participants. The Doha Declaration is often viewed as the breakthrough point for an international 'access to medicines' norm, in the sense of 'shared expectations about appropriate behaviour held by a community of actors' (Finnemore 1996, p. 22). Yet despite positive developments, such as new funding through philanthropic foundations and public-private partnerships, 'access to medicines' remains an ambiguous policy objective, meaning different things to different actors.

As detailed in this volume, we find in India a domestic industry which, in over four decades, has accumulated impressive technological capabilities and huge production capacities. Its expansion from a low base post-1972 is generally understood to have been a relatively autonomous process consistent with the broader policy of self-reliance, unfolding in partial confrontation with the MNCs (this story is told most comprehensively in Chaudhuri 2005). G. Vijay in his chapter raises doubts about aspects of this analysis, pointing to a link between enhanced environmental regulation in the USA and the expansion of 'dirty' chemical and pharmaceutical manufacturing in India. Vijay highlights MNC outsourcing of environmentally destructive manufacturing to poorly regulated sites such as locations close to Hyderabad where Active Pharmaceutical Ingredients (APIs) manufacturing is clustered. (APIs are active chemicals with therapeutic value in powder form used for production of formulations.)

The Indian pharmaceutical industry is often described as the 'pharmacy of the global South'. But large production volumes and relatively low prices have not resulted in reliable access to essential medicines of good quality for all. As Srinivasan (2011, p. 43) sees it, it is the 'irony, and the tragedy ... that [the] success [of the domestic pharmaceutical industry] has not translated into availability or affordability of medicines' for the people of India. If anything, the balance may be shifting precariously in the opposite direction with the market entry of new, patented drugs. The industry's orientation towards developed country markets—as suppliers of APIs and generics, and of outsourcing services—and the recent wave of acquisitions of Indian firms by MNCs, does not bode well for the future of production of low-cost essential drugs for the developing world (Chaudhuri 2012). This chapter proceeds with an account of industry dynamics and policy regimes in the three major periods in the recent history of the Indian pharmaceutical industry:

The colonial and the early post-independence era when the policy framework was tailored to the needs of the MNCs.

The period of rapid domestic industry growth between 1972 and 2005 when only process patents were allowed.

The post-2005 era of TRIPS compliance, including product patents, in which firms are becoming increasingly integrated into the global innovation and production networks of the MNCs.

THE PRE-1972 PRODUCT PATENT PERIOD

From the mid-nineteenth century to independence and after, the Indian market provided foreign companies with an outlet for high-priced drug products developed and manufactured elsewhere. Patent legislation (based on the British Patent Law of 1852) was first introduced in 1856. The purpose, according to an authoritative source, was 'to enable the English Patent holders to acquire control over Indian markets' (Narayanan 1998 cited in Mueller 2007, p. 506). The legislation was renewed in 1859 and amended in the 1870s and 1880s. The Patents and Designs Act, 1911, which replaced all previous legislation, provided for patents in all product categories, including pharmaceuticals, for sixteen years from date of filing, and patent administration was brought under the management of the Controller of Patents (Mueller 2007, pp. 507–8;, see also Basheer 2005, 311–12). Product patents resulted in monopoly pricing but had a 'negligible effect in terms of spurring domestic pharmaceutical (or other) innovation' throughout this long period (Mueller 2007, p. 508).

India's first allopathic drug firm, the Bengal Chemical and Pharmaceutical Works, is reported to have been established in Calcutta in 1901 (Ramachandran and Rangarao 1972, p. M-27). Other firms emerged in subsequent decades and both World Wars provided an impetus to local manufacturing (Chaudhuri 2005, p. 22). CIPLA was established in 1935, and the story of this important company is told by Neelam Raj in a subsequent chapter. From the 1960s onwards, other private firms were established which emerged later as significant players, including Ranbaxy (1961), Lupin Laboratories (1972), Torrent Pharmaceuticals (1972) and Dr Reddy's Laboratories (1984). Still the MNCs dominated the domestic market and Indian-owned firms remained marginal until well into the 1970s.

Analysts such as Chaudhuri (2005) and Rao (2007), and industry figures like CIPLA's Dr Hamied (2005), present a picture of unimpeded market exploitation by the MNCs before 1972. The 'interests [of the MNCs] appeared to be in conflict with the national objective of providing drugs at low costs' to the Indian population (Ramachandran and Rangarao 1972, p. M35). Foreign firms such as Glaxo, Parke Davis and Burroughs Wellcome did not engage in R&D or API manufacturing nor was technology transfer of any significance. 'It was far more profitable ... to import the bulk drugs and late drug intermediates from their parent companies, often at monopoly prices that had no relation to the ruling international prices, and formulate them into finished dosage packs sold under popular brand names' (Bhagat 1982, p. 58). There were 'long delays in introducing the newer drugs marketed abroad' (Ramachandran and Rangarao 1972, p. M-31) and India was 'well-known for having relatively high drug prices' (Lall 1974, p. 163).

The mainstream economic theory rationale for IPRs is as incentives for innovation, and patents are thought to be particularly important for bringing new pharmaceutical products to market (DiMasi, Hansen and Grabowski 2003). Yet, as already noted, this effect was negligible in the case of the Indian pharmaceutical industry pre-1972. However, patents give rise to another incentive, significant in this period (and again post-2005), 'the incentive to invest in changing the rule to gain even more protection (the *protectionist incentive*)' (Drahos, Peter 2011, p. 36, italics in original). Historically, product patents made it possible for the MNCs to exploit Indian consumers through supply of high-priced, not very up-to-date drugs, with no offsetting benefits in terms of domestic innovation. Contrary to neoliberal public policy theory, dynamism and innovation emanated from the government sector. Cheaper, essential medicines were supplied by state-owned companies established in the 1950s and 1960s with assistance from the WHO, UNICEF and the Soviet Union, and the production of APIs was pioneered in the public sector. Two significant public sector companies were established; Hindustan Antibiotics Ltd (HAL) in 1954 and Indian Drugs and Pharmaceuticals (IDPL) in 1961, both of which generated major technological and entrepreneurial spill-over effects, as did the laboratories of the Council of Scientific and Industrial Research (CSIR) (Chaudhuri 2005, ch. 2).

Domestic firms lobbied from the 1940s for a more supportive policy environment, but it took two major inquires and parliamentary deliberations over many years for the Patents and Design Act 1911 to be replaced with an IPR regime more attuned to the needs of consumers and domestic companies. At independence, Nehru's government had pragmatically recognised that self-reliance could not be pursued immediately in the pharmaceutical sector; local firms were in no position to replace the MNCs as suppliers of necessary medicines. However, in January 1948 the government appointed the Tek Chand committee to 'review the patent laws in India with a view to ensure that the patent system was more conducive to the national interest'. The Chand report, issues in 1950, recommended an 'efficient machinery ... to tackle the issue of abuses [of patents]' including provisions for compulsory licensing (cited in Mueller 2007, p. 511). A patents bill based on this report was introduced in Parliament in 1953 but thereafter lapsed. The government appointed a second committee in 1957 chaired by Justice Rajagopala Ayyangar. In its 1959 report the committee found that most Indian patents were held by foreigners and most were not worked in India. It concluded that 'the system was being exploited by foreigners to achieve monopolistic control over the market' (Adelman and Baldia 1996, p. 518). At long last, these reports resulted in the enactment of the Patents Act, 1970. Elite and popular opinion against pharmaceutical product patents, which had been building over several decades, culminated in this legislation, which was framed deliberately to build an environment more conducive to the domestic manufacturing of low-cost generic drugs. Indira Gandhi gave expression to these sentiments in 1981: '[m]y idea of a better ordered world is one in which medical discoveries would be free of patents and there would be no profiteering from life or death' (cited in Mueller 2007, p. 496). Neelam Raaj in this volume cites Dr Hamied's account of a meeting with Indira Gandhi a decade earlier: 'We said to her that this drug is life-saving, and why should millions be deprived of it just because the patent holder doesn't like the colour of our skin? She passed the bill within a week' (Jack 2008).

THE PROCESS PATENT ERA 1972–2005

The Patent Act 1970 (implemented in 1972) formed the centrepiece of a new policy regime that, as noted, had as explicit purpose the promotion of a self-reliant indigenous drug industry. Patents for pharmaceutical (food and agrochemical) products were disallowed and only one production process could be patented (for a maximum of seven years). Moreover, the Foreign Exchange Regulation Act (FERA) allowed new investments only for companies with a foreign equity holding of 40 per cent or less, and the MNCs were obliged to dilute their ownership of local operations. The drug price control system, first implemented in 1963, peaked in 1979 in terms of market share subjected to price controls and has since been progressively watered down (Malhotra 2010, p. 112). More radical measures were also contemplated in the 1970s; the so-called Hathi committee recommended in 1975 the wholesale nationalisation of the drug industry and that generic names should be used for all new single-ingredient products. This was 'the high-point of social justice and pharmaceutical nationalism ... which made the little Indian's access to medicinal justice the focus of state policy' (Krishna Iyer 2002). Intense industry protestations ensued and most of the committee's recommendations were not implemented.

No new significant pharma subsidiaries were established after 1972 and some MNCs abandoned the country altogether (Chaudhuri 2005; Rangnekar 2006). For their part, domestic firms grasped the opportunities provided by the new policy regime 'with both hands and proved dramatically that its reverse engineering skills were second to none in the world. [This also] resulted in the birth of affordable medicine' (Reddy 2004). Indian firms, often in collaboration with public sector research organisations such as the Central Drug Research Institute (Lucknow) and the Indian Institute of Chemical Technology (Hyderabad), developed alternative processes for the production of a wide range of APIs and generics, drawing on a strong chemical engineering tradition and the availability of skilled, low cost labour.

This array of policy initiatives produced a domestic drug industry which within twenty years made India self-sufficient in the production of most basic medicines. According to Lanjouw (1998, p. 4), Indian firms in 1991 supplied 70 per cent of the APIs and 80 per cent of formulations for the Indian market. The absence of product patents meant that every drug was a generic, and firms developed processes to manufacture at low cost a wide range of bulk and finished drugs. There was, as yet, virtually no corporate spending on discovery research but large-scale manufacturing of generics enabled the accumulation of significant technological know-how. Importantly, there was a sharp decline in the price of medicines in the domestic market and growth in exports meeting developing country and later US and European demands for affordable, quality medicines.

From the mid-1990s, the politics of pharmaceuticals centred on interpretations of TRIPS-compliance. As noted, the coalition between public health advocates and domestic firms weakened as major firms such as Ranbaxy and Dr Reddy's reconsidered their critique of product patents as they commenced discovery research activities, albeit on a small scale. Within the group of leading Indian-owned firms opposition to product patents abated—CIPLA being a major exception—as prospects seemed to be opening for their own patenting, and as business models premised on collaborations with the MNCs became more attractive. At the same time, the broader process of liberalisation, in conjunction with the changes to the Patents Act, brought about the piecemeal dismantling of the policy regime put in place in the 1970s which had made possible the emergence of a large domestic generics industry. The sector was opened up to foreign direct investments and the drug price control policy was weakened. Hereafter, there has been a diversity of domestic industry perspectives on IPRs and government pharmaceutical policy, and there is no longer a clear-cut dividing line between domestic firms and the MNCs. Still, several firms other than CIPLA also remain critical or at least ambivalent about TRIPS compliance. The chief operating officer of Natco Pharma, issued in March 2012 with India's first compulsory licence, declares:

If it was not for India, I do not think there would be affordable generics in the world. Indian companies play a role as finished dosage or chemical suppliers internationally, and have contributed significantly, either directly or indirectly, to a reduction of healthcare expenditure worldwide. I am a defendant of the fact that innovation needs to be rewarded, but we do also need to take into account the economic situation of countries like India, where we need to address certain peculiarities that are inherent to the country. Going forward, the biggest challenge will remain the public policy challenge. We need to find ways to reward innovation, while at the same time take care of the needs of the general public. Both the MNCs as well as local Indian players need to address this challenge together. (Anonymous, 2011)

FULL TRIPS-COMPLIANCE FROM 2005

India was obliged to achieve full TRIPS compliance within ten years of the formation of the WTO in 1995 and final legislation for this purpose was passed by parliament in 2005. The result was the re-introduction of the basic elements of the policy regime which prevailed before 1972; after an interlude of 34 years, patents could again be issued for pharmaceutical products (and for foods and chemicals). The successful business model of reverse engineering became irrelevant since Indian companies could no longer manufacture or market patented drugs without licence from the patent holder. The 2005 amendment had been preceded by changes to the Patents Act in 1999 and 2002, each accompanied by intense debates centred on their implications for domestic firms and access to affordable essential medicines. It was again argued by many critics of the Presidential Ordinance of December 2004, which foreshadowed the final legislation, and of the Patents (Amendment) Act, 2005, that more medicines would become unaffordable to a large proportion of the world's population (e.g., see special issue of *Combat Law*, vol. 4, no. 2, 2005 http://www.combatlaw.org/?p=848). In the words of CIPLA's chairman, Dr Y.K. Hamied:

I have no doubt that [the 2005 Patent Act amendments] will deprive the poor of India and also third world countries dependent on India, of the vital medicines they need to survive. It will divide the human race into those who can afford life saving drugs and those who cannot. It will lead to a systematic denial of drugs to the three billion in the poorer nations, an act tantamount to selective genocide by the year 2015 (Hamied 2005).

By this stage, it seemed as if the MNCs long campaign for a global IPR regime, detailed by e.g. Sell (2003) and Drahos and Braithwaite (2001), had achieved full success in India. Yet, since 2005, political and social tensions around IPRs in the pharmaceutical sector have if anything escalated in India and internationally. It is no longer considered acceptable in global policy discourse to argue openly that patents should override public health considerations (Schroeder and Singer 2011). Proponents of pharmaceutical patents are careful to put their case in terms of ostensible innovation benefits also for populations of LMICs, and the MNCs seek credit for providing compensation for monopoly pricing through public-private R&D partnerships, differential pricing arrangements, donation programs and other forms of philanthropy (Jack 2012). But there is evident frustration on the part of the MNCs and the governments in the countries where they are headquartered over ostensibly excessive use of TRIPS flexibilities and unexpectedly ineffective TRIPS enforcement. Many free-trade agreements (FTAs) have included TRIPS-plus provisions, extending monopoly pricing beyond the legal requirements under TRIPS, but the push by the US for strengthened IPRs has faced strong resistance, for example in negotiations for the Trans-Pacific Partnership Agreement (AFTINET 2012). Arguably, the success of the MNCs in putting in place a global intellectual property rights regime has been 'curtailed by the skilful yet subtle attempts by negotiators from less developed countries to inject ambiguities, flexibilities, limitations, and exceptions into the TRIPS Agreement' (Yu 2011, p. 493).

The 2001 Doha Declaration reinforced the momentum for a global public health agenda. Of particular significance is that the Declaration confirmed that '[e]ach member [country] has the right to grant compulsory licences and the freedom to determine the grounds upon which such licences are granted' (World Trade Organization 2001). A compulsory licence authorises a third party to manufacture and sell a product without the consent of the patent holder in return for adequate compensation. The US and other pro-MNC governments exercise strong pressures for compulsory licences to be considered only in circumstances of national emergency, and developing countries have not made extensive use of such licences. Between January 1995 and June 2011 there were only in the order of 24 compulsory licensing episodes in 17 nations, mostly for HIV/AIDS medications (Beall and Kuhn 2012, p. 1). Notwithstanding these pressures, and obstacles built into many FTAs (Joint United Nations Programme on HIV/AIDS 2012), compulsory licences are on the policy agenda in many countries and can be an effective threat in negotiations, as explained by André de Mello e Souza in this volume.

India's first compulsory licence for production of a medicinal drug is of great importance. On 12 March 2012, the Hyderabad-based generic company Natco Pharma gained a licence for the production and supply of its brand of the patented anti-cancer drug sorafenib, marketed by Bayer as Nexavar. The price of Bayer's version of this drug was Rs 280,000 a month, an astronomical figure for almost all Indian households. Natco committed to selling the same drug at 3 per cent of this price, while paying a licence fee and still expecting to make a profit. The licence was issued essentially on the grounds that Bayer's price was exorbitant. Bayer also did not manufacture the drug in India and imported in such small volumes that only a tiny fraction of potential patients could benefit. The Controller General of Patents, Designs and Trademarks, P.H. Kurian, concluded, just prior to retiring from the office, that the drug 'was not bought by the public due to only one reason, that is, its price was not reasonably affordable to them'. This decision sets a very significant precedent for compulsory licences on other patented products sold at unaffordable prices (Srinivasan 2012).

The foremost issue of contention since 2005 has been that of patentability as defined in Section 3(d) of the legislation, a topic addressed by N. Lalitha and Kajal Bhardwaj in this volume. Section 3(d) is intended to prevent the awarding of patents for slightly modified versions of known molecules, unless a 'significant enhancement of efficacy' can be demonstrated. The extension of monopoly pricing through the patenting of trivial product modifications is a form of rent seeking known as evergreening, in corporate parlance an important 'life cycle management' technique (Hess and Litalien 2005). The purpose is to delay the market entry of cheaper generic brands. Evergreening is a manifestation of the anti-competitive 'protectionist incentive' effect generated by IPRs. Patenting of this type does not stimulate innovation but causes social welfare losses through the stifling of competition (Drahos, Peter 2011, pp. 36–7). The removal of Section 3(d), as sought by Novartis in its drawn-out legal battle for a patent on a marginal modification of an out-of-patent product, would be a heavy blow to patients in India and the developing world. It would also be detrimental to domestic firms where business model remain premised on the low-cost manufacturing of generics.

Yet some analysts, particularly in the trade press, view TRIPS compliance as a positive development which is making Indian firms more innovation oriented (Anonymous 2011). In the new IPR regime, these firms are said to engage increasingly in patenting of their own discoveries, including patenting of new chemical compounds. A few leading companies such as Dr Reddy's and

Ranbaxy have invested in discovery research since the 1990s. Lacking the huge resources required to develop a compound all the way to commercialisation, their strategy was to patent promising new drug candidates and licensing them out to large MNCs for development and commercialisation in exchange for royalties. For a period around 2005 sections of the domestic industry claimed that a process of catching-up in innovation with established pharma MNCs was underway. The research director of Nicholas Piramal asserted: 'The big pharmaceutical companies say it costs them at least $800m to develop a new drug ... Well, we can do it for $50m ... We are going to develop a cancer drug to prove it' (Dyer 2004). If this strategy was ever seriously pursued, it has now been abandoned and R&D efforts are reported to have stagnated (Joseph 2011). The information available does not point to a significant shift towards discovery R&D; in 2011 'at least 10 Indian companies engaged in basic research, while 32 NCEs are in early stages of development' (Anonymous 2011). This compares with 12 New Zealand discovered NCEs in clinical development in 2008, and 189 compounds discovered in Australia in clinical development in 2007—countries that rate barely a mention in the specialised literature on the global pharmaceutical industry (Lockhart, Babar and Garg 2012, p. 2). The flagship company 'Dr Reddy [has] removed the line "discovery led global pharmaceutical company" from its grandiose vision statement and replaced it with "the viable vision" to transform the company into an "ever flourishing company"' (Joseph 2011, p. 10). Product development in this sector requires huge resources. Top-tier Indian firms remain small by international standards; a 2011 ranking of the world's fifty top prescription drug suppliers does not include a single Indian firm (Cacciotti, Jerry and Clinton 2011).

Undoubtedly the industry has reached a scale and scientific-technological sophistication which make Indian firms important global players, as shown by Deepak Kumar Jena and Poduri Balaram in this volume. With marketing infrastructure, production plants and R&D facilities in Europe and North America, and a long-standing presence in many developing countries, several companies have become MNCs in their own right. This group of industry leaders have adapted their business strategies to the new IPR regime. While most already marketed generic medicines will continue to be available, the new regime prevents the production and exports of generic versions of new patented drugs, for example, new second and third line HIV/AIDS medications, unless compulsory licenced, or voluntarily licenced by the patent holder. In the new policy environment, many firms find alliances with the major MNCs commercially attractive. Growing markets for contract research and manufacturing services ('CRAMS') offer opportunities for these companies to become part of global innovation and production networks. The recent wave of MNC acquisitions of domestic firms provides a conspicuous manifestation of this trend, which does not bode well for the future of production of low-cost essential drugs for the developing world (Chaudhuri 2012).

FINANCIAL AND ECONOMIC CRISIS AND ACCESS TO MEDICINES FOR ALL

India's pharmaceutical industry comprises more than 10,000 manufacturing units. Around 80 per cent of these produce final drugs, around 20 per cent APIs or bulk drugs. About a third of the global manufacturing of medicines is in facilities in India (Ministry of External Affairs 2012). Indian firms, as detailed by Christiane Fischer and others in this volume, have made an enormous contribution to making affordable essential medicines available in Africa and globally. CIPLA is now the world's largest supplier of antiretroviral drugs. That CIPLA's CEO, Dr Hamied, continues to criticise the patent system epitomises the best sentiments within the domestic industry sector. The pharmaceutical production capacity and the scientific-technological skills in India could sustain the supply of even larger volumes of medicines at a very low cost, if 'only' the use value perspective could be fully reflected in pharmaceutical policy in India and globally. The principal obstacles to access to affordable essential medicines for all are not technical, but caused by institutional and political arrangements and entrenched economic interests and privileges. The patent system, which has been extended globally through TRIPS and associated norms, rules, institutions and policies and practices, including TRIPS-plus provisions in many FTAs, as explored in several chapters, results in monopoly pricing which deprives hundreds of millions of people from access to essential drugs. Patents also distort the R&D process to the detriment of all consumers but the poor in India and other LMICs in particular. While all (or almost all) pharmaceutical sector stakeholders pay lip service to the proposition that people everywhere, irrespective of economic and social circumstances, should have access to affordable essential medicines, the reality is that progress has been limited and that gains made, for example in the supply of low-cost HIV-AIDS medications, are precarious.

The unfolding of the global economic and financial crisis, which commenced in 2008, reinforces volatilities and apprehensions. Informed analysts envisage, at best, an extended period ahead of stagnation in the global economy with dire implications for workers and the poor everywhere (Bellamy Foster and McChesney 2012). This crisis puts downwards pressures particularly on growth in developed pharma markets, possibly such that these 'will contract for the first time in history' (IMAP 2012, p. 1). In response, the business strategies of the pharma MNCs have shifted to focus more on LMICs, particularly India and China; '[t]here is consensus that future growth in the Pharma Industry will mainly come from emerging markets' (IMAP 2012, p. 1). As noted, this creates commercial opportunities for sections of the Indian pharma industry, but incorporation of domestic firms into the supply chains of the MNCs, or the outright acquisitions of Indian firms, give rise to real concerns about the future supply of affordable generics. It is also evident that the Indian economy and society is under severe stress, both as a consequence of the global economic and financial crisis and as a consequence of internal tensions in its political economy. At the time of writing, it is widely suggested that the period of high if uneven growth from the late 1990s has stalled, with a likely negative impact on access to medicines. Yet, colossal health inequities in India and in the global system have created a momentum for arguments and policies grounded in a use value perspective. Encouragingly, it is widely accepted in pharmaceutical policy discussions that medicines are not commodities to be produced principally for the purpose of maximising exchange value.

There is a huge volume of journal articles, reports and web publications on the Indian pharmaceutical industry and access to medicines policy. This volume adds to a rather more sparse monograph literature (but see Chaudhuri (2005), Malhotra (2010) and Rao (2007)). The chapters which follow are for the most part framed from a use value perspective on medicines; in this respect, the book fits within the tradition of advocacy and mobilisation for access to essential medicines for all. Several chapters place the Indian experience in an international context. Tu Thanh Nguyen explores an avenue for enhancing affordability that is less commonly discussed, namely the role of competition law and the interface between this type of legislation and the IPR system. André de Mello Souza provides an astute analysis of the politics of AIDS treatment in Brazil, another large emerging economy with a history of struggle for access to medicines that in some respects parallels that of India. The central theme, however, in most chapters is the extent to which India will maintain its tradition of making use of available scope for manoeuvrability within the global IPR system. The different perspectives on medicines—as use values for better health, or as exchange value to sustain capital accumulation—come to the fore in these long-standing debates about product patents and the direction of India's pharmaceutical industry.

References

Adelman, M.J. and Baldia, S., 1996. 'Prospects and Limits of the Patent Provision in the TRIPS Agreement: The Case of India', *Vanderbilt Journal of Transnational Law*, vol. 29, pp. 507–33.

AFTINET 2012. *Australian Fair Trade and Investment Network*, <http://aftinet.org.au/cms/>.

Angell, M., 2005. *The Truth About the Drug Companies: How They Deceive Us and What to do About it*, Random House, New York.

Anonymous 2011. 'India: Good Endings, Good Beginnings!', *Pharm.Exec. com*, retrieved 1 June 2012, <http://www.pharmexec.com/pharmexec/article/articleDetail.jsp?id=739265>.

Astra Zeneca 2011. *Annual Report and Form 20-F Information*, http://www.astrazeneca-annualreports.com/2011/documents/pdfs/annual-report-pdf-entire.pdf

Bajal, V., 2012. 'India Weighs Providing Free Drugs at State-Run Hospitals', *New York Times*, no. 5 July, <http://www.nytimes. com/2012/07/06/business/India-may-provide-free-drugs-at-state-run-hospitals.html?pagewanted=all>.

Basheer, S., 2005. '"Policy Style," Reasoning at the Indian Patent Office', *Intellectual Property Quarterly*, vol. 3, pp. 309–23.

Beall, R. and Kuhn, R., 2012. 'Trends in Compulsory Licensing of Pharmaceuticals since the Doha Declaration: A Database Analysis', *PLoS Med*, vol. 9, no. 1, p. e1001154.

Bellamy Foster, J. and McChesney, R.W., 2012. 'The Endless Crisis', *Monthly Review*, vol. 64, no. 1, pp. 1–28.

Bhagat, M., 1982. *Aspects of Drug Industry in India*, Centre for Education and Documentation, Mumbai.

Cacciotti, J. and Clinton, P., 2011. '12th Annual Pharm Exec 50', *Pharmaceutical Executive*, no. 1 May, retrieved 21 June, <http://licence. icopyright.net/user/viewFreeUse.act?fuid=MTYzMjkzNjk%3D>.

Cacciotti, J. and Clinton, P., 2012. 'Pharm Exec 50: Growth from the Bottom Up', *PharmExec.com*, retrieved 1 August, <http://www. pharmexec.com/pharmexec/Top+Feature/Pharm-Exec-50-Growth-from-the-Bottom-Up/ArticleStandard/Article/detail/773562>.

Chaudhuri, S., 2005. *The WTO and India's Pharmaceuticals Industry: Patent Protection, TRIPS, and Developing Countries*, Oxford University Press, New Delhi.

Chaudhuri, S., 2012. 'Multinationals and Monopolies: Pharmaceutical Industry in India after TRIPS', *Economic and Political Weekly*, vol. 47, no. 12, pp. 46–54.

DiMasi, J.A., Hansen, R.W. and Grabowski, H.G., 2003. 'The Price of Innovation: New Estimates of Drug Development Costs', *Journal of Health Economics*, vol. 22, pp. 151–85.

Drahos, P., 2011. 'Six Minutes to Midnight: Can Intellectual Property Save the World?', in K Bowrey, M Handler and D Nicol (eds), *Emerging Challenges in Intellectual Property*, Oxford University Press, Melbourne, pp. 30–45.

Drahos, P. and Braithwaite, J., 2001. 'Intellectual Property, Corporate Strategy, Globalisation: TRIPS in Context', *Wisconsin International Law Journal*, vol. 19, pp. 451–80.

Dyer, G., 2004. 'A Laboratory for Globalisation: How India Hopes to Reshape the World Drugs Industry', *Financial Times*, 18 August, Comment and Analysis, p. 9.

Finnemore, M., 1996. *National Interests in International Society*, Cornell University Press, Ithaca, New York.

Hamied, Y.K., 2005. 'Address to the Sixty-Ninth Annual General Meeting', CIPLA, retrieved 2 July 2006, <http://www.cipla.com/corporateprofile/financial/cm69.htm>.

Harvey, D., 2010. *The Enigma of Capital: And the Crises of Capitalism*, Oxford University Press, Oxford [England]; New York.

Hess, J. and Litalien, S., 2005. 'Battle for the Market: Branded Drug Companies' Secret Weapons that Generic Drug Makers Must Know', *Journal of Generic Medicines*, vol. 3, no. 1, pp. 20–9.

High Level Expert Group 2011. *Report on Universal Health Coverage for India*, Planning Commission of India, New Delhi.

Planning Commission of India 2011. *Report on Universal Health Coverage for India*, by High Level Expert Group.

IMAP 2012. *Global Pharma and M&A Report 2012*.

Jack, A., 2008. 'The Man Who Battled Big Pharma', *Financial Times Magazine*, no. 28 March, retrieved 19 June, <http://www.ft.com/intl/cms/s/0/bd8dccee-f976-11dc-9b7c-000077b07658.html#axzz1yD7xObBC>.

Jack, A., 2012. 'Pharmaceuticals: Philanthropy and Business Join Forces', *Financial Times*, no. 23 April, retrieved 21 June 2012, <http://www.ft.com/intl/cms/s/0/0d2b135a-887b-11e1-a727-00144feab49a.html#axzz1yNe2fpOq>.

Joint United Nations Programme on HIV/AIDS 2012. *The Potential Impact of Free Trade Agreements on Public Health* UNAIDS, Geneva.

Joseph, R.K., 2011. *The R&D Scenario in Indian Pharmaceutical Industry*, Research and Information System for Developing Countries (RIS), New Delhi.

Kanavos, P., Seeley, L. and Vandoros, S., 2009. *Tender Systems for Outpatient Pharmaceuticals in the European Union: Evidence from the Netherlands, Germany and Belgium*, European Commission Brussels.

Kerry, V. and Lee, K., 2007. 'TRIPS, the Doha declaration and paragraph 6 decision: What are the remaining steps for protecting access to medicines?', *Globalization and Health*, vol. 3, no. 1, p. 3.

Krishna Iyer, V.R., 2002. 'Patent Issues: The Doha-Delhi Odyssey', *Frontline*, vol. 19, no. 6.

Lall, S., 1974. 'The International Pharmaceutical Industry and Less-Developed Countries, with Special Reference to India', *Oxford Bulletin of Economics and Statistics*, vol. 36, no. 3, pp. 143–72.

Lanjouw, J.O., 1998. 'The Introduction of Pharmaceutical Product Patents in India: Heartless Exploitation of the Poor and Suffering'?, Working Paper No. 6366, National Bureau of Economic Research, Cambridge, Mass.

Law, J., 2006. *Big Pharma: How the World's Biggest Drug Companies Control Illness*, Constable, London.

Lockhart, M.M., Babar, Z.U.D. and Garg, S., 2012. 'Drug Development and Research in New Zealand: Policies Affecting the Industry', *Drug Development Research*, vol. 73, no. 1, pp. 1–10.

Lofgren, H., 2004. 'Generic Drugs: International Trends and Policy Developments in Australia', *Australian Health Review*, vol. 27, no. 1, pp. 39–48.

Malhotra, P., 2010. *Impact of TRIPS in India: An Access to Medicines Perspective*, Palgrave Macmillan, Basingstoke, Hampshire.

Matlin, S., 2005. 'Introduction: Poverty, Equity and Health Research', in S. Matlin (ed.), *Global Forum Update on Research for Health Volume 2*, Pro-Brook Publishing, London, pp. 9–13.

Ministry of External Affairs 2012. 'Overview of Pharmaceutical Industry', Government of India, retrieved 7 June 2012, <http://www.indiainbusiness. nic.in/industry-infrastructure/industrial-sectors/drug-pharma.htm>.

Moran, M., Guzman, J., Abela-Oversteegen, L., Liyanage, R., Omune, B., Wu, L., Chapman, N. and Gouglas, D., 2011. *Neglected Disease Research and Development: Is Innovation Under Threat?*, Policy Cure, Sydney.

Mueller, J.M., 2007. 'The Tiger Awakens: The Tumultuous Transformation of India's Patent System and the Rise of Indian Pharmaceutical Innovation', *University of Pittsburgh Law Review*, vol. 68, no. 3, pp. 491–641.

Narayanan, P., 1998. *Patent Law*, 7, 3rd edn, Eastern Law House, Calcutta.

Parliamentary Standing Committee on Health and Welfare 2012, 'The Functioning of the Central Drugs Standard Control Organisation (CDSCO)', Government of India, New Delhi.

Pogge, T.W.M., Rimmer, M. and Rubenstein, K. (eds), 2010. *Incentives for Global Public Health: Patent Law and Access to Essential Medicines*, Cambridge University Press, Cambridge, UK; New York.

Ramachandran, P.K. and Rangarao, B.V., 1972. 'The Pharmaceutical Industry in India', *Economic and Political Weekly*, vol. 7, no. 9, pp. M27-M36.

Rammana, A., 2004. *Interest Groups and Patent Reform in India*, Indira Gandhi Institute of Development Research, Mumbai.

Rangnekar, D., 2006. 'No Pills for Poor People: Understanding the Disembowelment of India's Patent Regime', *Economic and Political Weekly*, vol. 41, no. 5, pp. 409–17.

Rao, M.J., 2007. *Globalization, Technology, and Competition: IPRs, Indian Pharmaceutical Industry and WTO*, Serials Publications, New Delhi.

Rao, S., 2012. "'Irrational" combination drugs flood Indian mkt', *The Financial Express*, no. 14 June, retrieved 14 June, <http://www.financialexpress.com/news/irrational-combination-drugs-flood-indian-mkt/918017/#>.

Reddy, A.K., 2004. 'Address to Pharmacophore 2004: International Symposium', Hyderabad.

Schroeder, D. and Singer, P., 2011. 'Access to Life-Saving Medicines and Intellectual Property Rights: An Ethical Assessment', *Cambridge Quarterly of Healthcare Ethics*, vol. 20, no. 2, pp. 279–89.

Sell, S.K., 2003. *Private Power, Public Law: The Globalization of Intellectual Property Rights*, Cambridge University Press, Cambridge, U.K.

Sen Gupta, A., 2010. 'B.K. Keayla: A Personal Reminiscence', *Economic and Political Weekly*, vol. 45, no. 51, pp. 25–6.

Smith, R.D., Correa, C. and Oh, C., 2009. 'Trade, TRIPS, and pharmaceuticals', *The Lancet*, vol. 373, no. 9664, pp. 684–91.

Srinivasan, S., 2006. *(The Revised) Lay Person's Guide to Medicines*, LOCOST, Baroda.

Srinivasan, S., 2011. 'Medicines for All', the Pharma Industry and the Indian State', *Economic and Political Weekly*, vol. 46, no. 24, pp. 43–50.

Srinivasan, S., 2012. 'The Compulsory Licence for Nexavar: A Landmark Order', *Economic and Political Weekly*, vol. 47, no. 14, pp. 10–3.

Stevens, A.J., Jensen, J.J., Wyller, K., Kilgore, P.C., Chatterjee, S. and Rohrbaugh, M.L., 2011. 'The Role of Public-Sector Research in the Discovery of Drugs and Vaccines', *The New England Journal Of Medicine*, vol. 364, no. 6, pp. 535–41.

Tellez, V.M., 'Patent Reform in India: The Campaign to Protect Public Health', <http://www.ipngos.org/NGO%20Briefings/Patents%20Act%20amendment.pdf>.

World Health Organization 2010. *Research and Development Coordination and Financing: Report of the Expert Working Group*, WHO, Geneva.

World Trade Organization 2001, 'Declaration on the TRIPS Agreement and Public Health', WT/MIN(01)/DEC/2 20 November 2001 edn.

World Trade Organization 2012. *The Doha Declaration Explained* World Trade Organization,, retrieved 25 April 2012, <http://www.wto.org/english/tratop_e/dda_e/dohaexplained_e.htm>.

Yu, P.K., 2011. 'TRIPS and its Achilles' Heel', *Journal of Intellectual Property Law*, vol. 18, pp. 479–531.

2 Challenges of Regulation of Medicines in India

S. Srinivasan and Anant Phadke[1]

A major component of health care in developing countries is medicines. In India, the costs of medicine are between 50 and 80 per cent of the total cost of treatment. The Indian pharma industry is seen as a success story in terms of self-reliance in the manufacturing of a wide range of essential medicines at relatively low costs. In comparison with most developing economies, with the possible exception of China, this industry is indeed a success story, selling more than Rs one trillion worth of Active Pharmaceutical Ingredients (APIs) and their formulations annually. It is often called the pharmacy of the third world,[2] and most developing countries now wish to emulate the Indian model. The success can be attributed to, among other factors, India's process-patent-only-regime for medicines in the Indian Patent Act 1970, until its abandonment in 2005, replacing it with product patent regime for medicines, because of TRIPS obligations.

The irony, and the tragedy, is that this success has not translated to availability or affordability of medicines for all (Selvaraj and Anup 2012). Medicines in India are overpriced and unaffordable, a glaring silent violation of human rights. It causes severe financial and mental stress to majority of patients, often leading to their impoverishment and penury.

In addition, there are an enormous number of 'branded generics', many of them irrational. This adds to the cost of health care unnecessarily. Many medicines are promoted in unethical ways.

There is no code for marketing, nor a law to discourage unethical drug promotion. Decisions taken by the regulatory authorities are not transparent. Adding to this chaotic scenario is the arrival of product patents and the need for regulating new biotech drugs. The introduction of new vaccines in the Indian public health system needs to be regulated on a scientific basis as currently new vaccines are sought to be introduced without any population based studies, and without assessing cost-efficacy. Poorly regulated clinical trials have proliferated because India is viewed as a 'destination' for carrying out drug-related clinical trials. In the context of this background, this chapter addresses the regulatory challenges to India's booming pharma industry. It examines how the functioning of this industry can be made ethical and its products rational and affordable for the country's citizens.

PRICE REGULATION

The key features of the pharma market in India are fairly well established as regards pricing:

The same medicine is sold at a range of prices, also by the same company.

The brand leader is often also the price leader (the costlier brands of the same medicine sell more, with some exceptions).

Doctors tend to prescribe the costlier versions. Patients are vulnerable and there is no consumer resistance. It is the patient who mostly pays out-of-pocket for the full cost of medicines unlike in the developed countries.

The profit margins are anywhere between 100 to 4000 per cent (see Tables 2.1 and 2.2 below).

Competition therefore does not automatically result in lowering prices.[3]

Medicine prices are fixed in accordance with what the perceived target market for the brand can take.

Markets are distorted by unfair and unethical marketing practices of pharma companies, further adding to the end-consumer costs.

Table 2.1: A Comparison of Medicine Prices

(prices in Rupees)

Generic Name of Drug (1)	Unit (2)	Chittorgarh Tender Rate (3)	MRP Printed on pack/strip (4)	TNMSC Prices (5)	(Column 4/ Column 5) (6)
Albendazole Tab 400 mg	10 tablets	11.00	250.00	4.55	54.94
Alprazolam Tab IP 0.5 mg	10 tablets	1.40	14.00	0.51	27.45
Amlodipine Tab 2.5 mg	10 tablets	2.30	23.00	0.41	56.01
Atorvastatin Tab 10 mg	10 tablets	9.90	65.00	2.10	30.95
Cetrizine 10 mg	10 tablets	1.20	35.00	0.49	71.42
Diazepam Tab 5 mg	10 tablets	1.40	18.00	0.55	32.72

Note: TNMSC (Tamil Nadu Medical Services Corporation) prices are from its website, http://www.tnmsc.com/tnmsc/notification/Drugs232.pdf, for 2011–12. Chittorgarh prices are of well-known companies and are at http://chittorgarh.nic.in/Generic_new/generic.htm. Column (6) gives an idea of how many times the retail market MRP is in comparison to the TNMSC procurement price—the latter being near the cost of production.

Several government committees have underscored the need of regulation of medicine prices. For instance, the Report of the Standing Committee on Chemicals and Fertilizers, 2005–06, Fourteenth Lok Sabha observed:[4]

... there is a provision that strict watch will be kept on the movement of the prices and the Government may determine the ceiling levels beyond which increase in prices would not be permissible, [but] this provision has seldom been applied. ... The Committee are unhappy over this unsatisfactory state of affairs and desire that the situation should be remedied forthwith. They therefore, recommend that for the category of medicines for the same therapeutic use, the Government should determine a reasonable ceiling beyond which increase in prices may not be allowed.

Table 2.2: Data on Relationship of Bulk Medicine Price in Relation to Price of Formulations of Market Leaders

(prices in Indian Rupees)

Name/Strength/ Use	1. Bulk Drug Price per Kg	2. Cost of Active ing-redients per 1000 Tabs	3.Total RM Cost per 1000 Tabs	4. Mfg Cost	5. Total Cost per unit	6. Price of Market Leaders per unit	7. Market Leader's Price/ Total Cost per Unit (as percent)
Albendazole Tabs 400 mg Anti-hookworm	1260	504	564.17	282.38	0.85	17 (Glaxo)	2000
Amlodipine Tabs 5mg Anti-hypertensive, anti-anginal	2982	21	34.98	58.27	0.10	2.45 (Cipla)	2450
Amoxy 500 Caps Antibiotic	1583	931	1017.71	272.23	1.30	8.00 (Ranbaxy)	615
Atenolol Tabs 50 mg Anti-hypertensive, anti-anginal	1173	59	67.64	79.59	0.15	2.85 (Nicholas Piramal)	1900
Cephalexin Caps 250 mg Antibiotic	2791	698	841.53	361.71	1.20	7.00 (GSK)	583
Cephalexin Caps 500 mg Antibiotic	2791	1396	1612.83	370.12	1.99	13.00 (GSK)	653
Cetrizine Tablets 10 mg Antiallergic	3510	35	44.65	68.45	0.12	3.10 (CIPLA)	2583
Diazepam Tabs 5 mg Sedative	2850	14	20.69	85.89	0.11	2.20 (Ranbaxy)	2000
Enalapril Maleate Tabs 5 mg							

(contd...)

(Table 2.2: contd...)

Name/Strength/ Use	1. Bulk Drug Price per Kg	2. Cost of Active ingredients per 1000 Tabs	3.Total RM Cost per 1000 Tabs	4. Mfg Cost	5. Total Cost per unit	6. Price of Market Leaders per unit	7. Market Leader's Price/ Total Cost per Unit (as percent)
Congestive Cardac Failure, hypertension Fluconazole Caps 150mg	5954	30	48.69	66.89	0.12	3.00 (Cadilla)	2500
Candidiasis, opportunistic infections in AIDS Fluoxetine caps 20 mg	5836	884	978.33	265.55	1.25	34.51 (CIPLA)	2760
Depression, psychiatric problems Glibenclamide Tabs 5mg	2496	57	180.59	280.38	0.47	4.00 (Cadilla)	851
Anti-diabetic Metformin Tabs 500mg	2341	12	19.10	73.25	0.10	0.90 (Aventis)	900
Anti-diabetic Paracetamol Tabs	218	109	125.83	142.92	0.27	1.00	370
Pain, fever Pyrazinamide Tabs. 750 mg	227	113	123.96	152.98	0.28	1.80 (Crocin)	642
TB	966	743	752.28	248.38	1.00	6.30 (Lupin)	630

Source of Mfg and Bulk Drug Costs: LOCOST Vadodara. Market leader prices from MIMS India March 2011

The Department-related Parliamentary Standing Committee on Health and Family Welfare Forty-Fifth Report, August 2010, had this to recommend inter alia:

... 36. The Committee is, however, of the considered view that given the current ground realities in the country where more than 80 per cent population is dependent on private medical care and nearly 45 crore people live below the poverty line, the most effective and direct approach would be to put a blanket cap on profit margins of all medicines across the board. Medicines are the only item where the decision to buy is not taken by the purchaser but by a third party, i.e., doctor. Therefore, if prescribers and producers join hands and take advantage of a patient's helplessness, only (the) state can stop them.

The government has, however, chosen to ignore the above recommendations when it comes to implementation. The 1979 Drug Price Control Order (DPCO) controlled the prices of a majority of medicines in the market (approximately 80 per cent by value). The number of medicines under Price Control has been reduced from 347 in 1979 to 74 in the DPCO of 1995 (which is still in force). Thus currently, only a handful of medicines are under price control. The cost-plus formula elaborated in the Drug Price Control Order, 1978 is based on turnover-based, marketshare criteria to decide which medicines ought to be within or out of price control. This flawed method[5] has resulted in anomalies such as:

Most essential and useful medicines are kept out of price control.

Non-essential and harmful medicines such as analgin, phenylbutazone, Vitamin E, sulphadimidine, mebhydrolin, diosminepanthonate and panthenols, bacampicilin are under price control.

Most of the Essential Medicines including those for HIV/AIDS, cancer, hypertension, coronary artery disease, multidrug resistant tuberculosis, diabetes, iron deficiency anemia, ORS, tetanus, filariasis, vaccines (new) for rabies, hepatitis B, sera for use in tetanus, diphtheria, Rh isoimmunisation, anticonvulsants and antiepileptics, diptheria, snake bite, suspected rabid dog bite/rabies, etc. fall outside price control.

Price control, since it is based on market share criteria, produces only partial regulation. Chloroquine for malaria would be under price control but not equally important other anti-malarials.[6] This is true for leprosy medicines and analgesics as well.

Of the 300 top selling brands in the ORG Nielsen list of October 2003, only 36 (that is only 12 per cent) were price controlled. The remaining 88 per cent were not.[7]

The National Pharmaceutical Pricing Authority is under the Department of Pharmaceuticals of the Ministry of Chemicals and Fertilizers, and does not fall under the Ministry of Health, that administers health and related issues. This serious dichotomy directly impacts the common people and their access to medicines.

To rectify some of these problems, a more recent report of the Planning Commission appointed High Level Expert Group (HLEG, 2011) has recommended the following—(HLEG 2011, pp. 119–40):

Increase public spending on drug procurement to 0.5 per cent of the GDP and provide free essential medicines to all.

Enforce price regulation and apply price control on all formulations in the Essential Drug List.

Ensure drug and vaccine security by strengthening the public sector and protecting the capacity of Indian private sector companies to produce low cost drugs and vaccines needed for the country.

Strengthen institutional mechanisms for procurement and distribution of allopathic and Ayurvedic, Unani, Siddha and Homeopathy (AYUSH) drugs.

Promote rational use of drugs through prescriber, patient and public education.

Strengthen Central and State regulatory agencies to effectively perform quality and price control functions.

Protect the safeguards provided by the Indian patents law and the TRIPS Agreement against the country's ability to produce essential drugs.

Transfer the Department of Pharmaceuticals to the Ministry of Health.

The Draft National Pharmaceuticals Pricing Policy (NPPP-2011) which came out around the same time—and which itself was prompted by the Supreme Court in an ongoing drug pricing

PIL—has also recommended price regulation of all medicines in the National List of Essential Medicines (NLEM 2011). However in the case of the NPPP-2011, the devil is in the details. It recommends as price ceiling the Weighted Average Price (WAP) of the top three selling brands (by volume) of each of these medicines. We have shown elsewhere that such a procedure actually legitimizes high prices and, is in effect, a price decontrol policy (Srinivasan 2011b; Selvaraj et al., 2012).[8] Alternatives for determining ceiling price have been proposed, for example: as Weighted Average Price (WAP) of the *cheapest* three brands, or as a multiple (say 4 or 5) of procurement prices of efficient public procurement systems like the Tamil Nadu Medical Services Corporation (TNMSC).

WEEDING OUT OF IRRATIONAL MEDICINES: A NECESSARY COMPLEMENT TO PRICE CONTROL

Any move to regulate prices of medicines in India has to be complemented by a radical move to completely weed out irrational medicines and irrational Fixed Dose Combinations (FDCs). Marketing of these irrational medicines, which probably account for more than 60 per cent of retail sales, results in unnecessary costs to patients. HLEG (2011, p. 134), previously alluded to, discussed at some length the prevalence of irrational combinations and observed that 'there is a clear need to phase out hazardous, nonessential and irrational medicines and irrational "Fixed Dose Drug Combinations". Recent reports on "superbug" nosocomial infections indicative of anti-microbial drug resistance in India merely add to the need to end the irrational drug prescription and dispensing practices.'

Weeding out or 'phasing out' of these irrational medicines would need to be top priority and a prerequisite for promoting rational prescriptions by doctors. Mere price control of essential medicines, and mere discouraging of non-essentials through ceiling prices, is not enough.

The Drugs Controller General of India (DCGI) is hesitant to remove irrational combinations, something which can be only attributed to lack of political will if not plain corruption and/or lack of intellectual clarity, or a failure of imagination; or a wariness of the hostile response that it would trigger from pharma companies, the medical profession and the pharma trade. Companies circumvent the ceiling price by adding to the formulation an extra API, which is itself out of price control, so that the new formulation is rendered out of price control. This additional scientifically unnecessary ingredient is sometimes harmless but sometimes harmful one. To close such escape hatches, the Pronab Sen Task Force Report proposed: 'For formulations containing a combination of a drug in the NLEM and any other drug, the ceiling price applicable to the essential drug would be made applicable.' The HLEG Report, as well as the draft NPPP-2011, could have taken note of this recommendation. These documents could also have endorsed a related recommendation by the Pronab Sen Committee: debrand, that is remove brand names, to ensure true competition among generics. In addition, medicines of the same class—for instance all gastric acid suppressants (omeprazole, rabeprazole, lansoprazole, pantaprozole, etc.), all ACE inhibitors used to lower blood pressure (enalapril, lisinopri, ramipril, perindopril etc)–should have the same ceiling price unless superiority is demonstrated by a particular medicine.[9]

A closely allied matter is that the current list of essential medicines, NLEM 2011, includes only 348 medicines. In reality, there are additional medicines in use for the care of HIV positive patients which are also rational and essential. Any essential drug listing process needs to be flexible to accommodate such specific, genuine medicine needs of special groups.

Weeding out already "well-established" irrational medicines as well as irrational FDCs is a huge problem in itself. But over and above that, how does a regulatory authority continue to approve new combinations such as the ones listed in Table 2.3 below? Is there no consideration of the science of pharmacology—or evidence base—before taking these shocking regulatory decisions for the manufacture/marketing of these new medicines?

Obviously evidence-based medicine is not the basis of these drug approvals. The DCGI's response in the last couple of years has been to set up a list of about a dozen expert committees—each pertaining to a medical specialty—which will be consulted for future approvals, especially to consider the rationality and

Table 2.3: Medicines Approved for Marketing In India:
Lack of Evidence-based Process

S. No	Product Name	Claimed Indication	Date of Approval
	List of Approved Drug From 01.01.2010 to 31.12.2010		
204	Cerebroprotein Hydrolysateinjection (Lyophilised) ... 1050mg/2100mg (approx) equivalent to nitrogen ... 30mg/ 60mg respectively.	Cranial injury, cere-bro-vascularcerebro-vascular pathological sequelae and aprosexia *(abnormal inability to sustain attention)* in dementia.	04/11/10
49	Citicholine 500mg + Piracetam 400mg Tablets	Acute stroke	16/03/2010
1	Ferrous ascorbate 100mg + Folic acid 1.1 mg tablet and Omega-3-fatty acid 200mg capsules combikit	Iron, folic acid and omega-3-fatty acid deficiency	08/01/2010
67	Atorvastatin10mg + Ramipril 5mg + Aspirin (EC pellets) 75mg/150mg + Metoprolol (ER tablets) 25mg Capsules	Certain cases of Ischemic heart disease	05/04/2010
23	Pregabalin SR 75/ 150/300mg + Methylcobalamin 1500mcg tablets	Adult patients with peripheral neuropathy	09/02/2010
51	Mecobalamin 750 mcg + Pyridoxine 1.5mg + Nicotinamide 45 mg + Benfotiamine 150mg Tablets	Diabetic neuropathy in adults	16/03/2010
37	Methylcobalamin 750mcg + Pregabalin 75/150mg + Vitamin B61.5mg + Folic acid	Painful diabetic neuropathy in adults	05/03/2010

(contd...)

(Table 2.3 contd...)

| | List of Approved Drug From 01.01.2010 to 31.12.2010 | | |
S. No	Product Name	Claimed Indication	Date of Approval
	0.75mg + Benfothia-mine7.5mg capsules		
123	Methylcobalamin 1500mcg +Pyridoxine 100mg +Nicotinamide 100mg injection	Diabetic neuropathy in adults	23/06/2010
189	Pregabalin 150mg/75 mg +Methylcobalamin 750mcg +Alpha lipoic acid 100mg +Pyridoxine 3mg +Folic acid 1.5mg capsule	Painful diabetic neuropathy in adults only	12/10/10
32	Cefixime 100mg/200mg + Cloxacillin 500mg/ 500mg tablets	Adult patients with upper and lower respiratory tract infections, skin and soft tissue infections	12/02/2010

Notes to the table

1.The CDSCO (Central Drugs Standard Control Organization) has approved two medicines to be used in patients with cerebrovascular disease which lack any evidence base of their efficacy. Cerebroprotein hydrolysate is a Chinese medicine of unknown efficacy prepared from fresh porcine brain. How was it approved for marketing in India? A search on PUBMED did not reveal any records of its efficacy. Similarly the use of citicholine and piracetam in acute ischemic stroke lacks an evidence base.

2. A plethora of preparations has been approved for treatment of diabetic neuropathies, without any rationale.

3. An inappropriate combination of two antibiotics has been approved, of which one requires twice a day administration while the other needs to be administered 4 times a day.

4. An irrational preparation containing iron, folic acid, and omega-3 fatty acids has been approved for treatment of 'iron, folic acid and omega-3 fatty acid deficiency'. This particular, selective combination of deficiencies does not exist in the scientific literature. The addition of omega-3 fatty acid is entirely irrational.

5. The CDSCO is approving combinations of two antihypertensives, a cholesterol lowering agent, with aspirin with the remark for 'secondary prophylaxis of ischemic heart disease in patients where use of such combinations in appropriate'. This combination has not been recommended in scientific literature.

Source: Table and commentary, courtesy Anurag Bhargava, July 2011, personal communication

evidence-base of the medicines concerned. The performance and effectiveness of these committees is yet to be evaluated. However a special commission to eliminate irrational drugs and irrational Fixed Dose Combinations needs to be set up to clear the backlog of eliminating thousands of irrational medicines/irrational Fixed Dose Combinations.

There is a need for an agency in India that is independent of the office of the Drug Controller General of India (DCGI), such as the National Institute of Clinical Excellence (NICE) in the UK, to create a scientific basis for the decisions of the CDSCO/DCGI with respect to vaccines and medicines. Such an organisation could be empowered to undertake independent appraisal/comparator studies, and make market approval recommendations on new and existing medicines (and also treatments and procedures) on the basis of risks, benefits, costs and efficacy. In November 2009, NICE refused to approve sorafenib, the medicine for which India's first compulsory licence was awarded, for use in the National Health System in UK on the basis that increasing survival in liver cancer by six months did not justify its high price—around £2,500–3,000 per patient per month.[10] We do not have a legally empowered organisation in India which could reject medicines on such grounds even when its advantages over existing alternatives are marginal or non-existent.

LAW ON BANNING IRRATIONAL MEDICINES

Section 26A of the Drugs and Cosmetics Act, 1940, empowers the Central Government to prohibit in public interest the manufacture, sale or distribution of a drug if there is no therapeutic justification for it. There is a substantial need for strengthening and clarifying this law on the power of the government to ban medicines so that legal challenges by vested interests among drug manufacturers—who are not worried too much about rationality at the best of times—do not succeed. We make this comment in the light of the recent attempts to weed out some harmful medicines—nimesulide (below 12 years age), cisapride, phenylpropanolamine (PPA), human placenta extracts, and silbutramine and R-silbutramine. The ban order on these products was stayed and successfully challenged in the Chennai and Delhi High Courts, the latter court even substantially modifying the ban order on placental products.[11]

On 30 May 2011, based on the recommendations of an expert committee constituted by the Centre at the direction of the Delhi High Court, a relaxation was given by an amended gazette notification allowing the use of human placental extract for topical application for healing wounds and injections for pelvic inflammatory disease. Why does the Court not accept the recommendations of the government-appointed expert committee rather than that of the Court-appointed expert committee? We wonder how one committee of experts is superior to another.

The questions raised by the decision on placental products include:[12] What is the sanctity of the DCGI's decision and its impact on public health if decisions taken under section 26A can be appealed against in a Court of Law and reversed? What if the government had appealed against the order of the Delhi High Court?

The Chennai High Court rejecting the government's ban order on PPA using its powers under judicial review decided—inter alia—that due consultation with the Drugs Technical Advisory Board (DTAB) had not been undertaken—although, in this case, an expert committee was consulted—and that satisfaction envisaged in Section 26A necessarily involves consultation of the DTAB. On the other hand, it can be asked that when a drug is approved, the DCGI does not consult the DTAB, then why is it necessary to consult the DTAB while banning a drug. There is no clear mandate, in the opinion of the authors, in the Drugs and Cosmetics Act that Section 26A has to be read together with Section 5.

Even as we write this, in early June 2012 a judgment of the same Chennai High Court has given a contrary opinion. We quote a newspaper report:[13]

The Centre need not consult Drugs Technical Advisory Board (DTAB) before exercising its power under Section 26A of the Drugs and Cosmetics Act 1940 to regulate, restrict or prohibit manufacture, sale or distribution of a drug or cosmetic if it is otherwise satisfied that those medications are likely to cause risk to human beings or animals, the Madras High Court has held.

Rejecting the argument of a group of pharmaceutical companies that such consultation was mandatory, Justice V. Ramasubramanian said that the Court could not be forced to introduce a clause which had been deliberately omitted by the legislature. He pointed out that only other provisions of the Act, except for Section 26A, had made consultation with the DTAB obligatory. ...

... It created a sense of urgency for the committee to look into the aspect of quality control and it appointed a sub-committee which in its report made a vital observation that 'in the case of drugs, a little latitude shown to a manufacturer may spell all the difference between life and death,' the judge said and took this as a cue to reject the technical argument of pharmaceutical companies on mandatory consultation with DTAB.

He went on to state: 'Since public accountability of executive and legislative authorities is far greater than that of courts (at least as on date), this court is expected to avoid a path that angels fear to tread. Otherwise, courts themselves are likely to be used as a tool even by the other wings, to achieve what they wish to achieve, by arriving at right decisions through a wrong process of reasoning.

Suffice it to say, there is a case of review for powers of ban under Section 26A if the government is serious about weeding out irrational and harmful drugs en masse. Public interest and safety ought to take precedence and we need to avoid a situation where such orders are sought to be reversed by recourse to courts as a matter of routine. That is not to deny anybody's right to appeal. Reversal of ban orders has to be the exception rather than the rule.

Notwithstanding legal issues, there is a need for a capable, adequate mechanism that would review periodically, and routinely, the rationality and safety of the medicines marketed in India and to eliminate irrational drugs and irrational Fixed Dose Combinations. Such a review is required to achieve the objective of promotion of generic medicines and of 'medicines for all'. Initially, to address the backlog, an expert committee could be appointed to formulate detailed criteria for weeding out irrational drugs and irrational Fixed Dose Combinations.[14] This committee would also need to formulate, after due consultation with legal experts, the appropriate legal mechanisms for implementation of such reviews.

Periodic review of medicines market in India will require good pharmacovigilance. The existing mechanism needs to be strengthened through nationally connected computerized system of data collection and vigilance.[15] A related area is mechanisms for audit of prescriptions which will, in the long run, inhibit poly pharmacy—it is common for doctors to unnecessarily prescribe many medicines when lesser number would suffice. Routine prescription audits and publishing of results of such audits may limit the irrational use of medicines, especially antibiotics, and possibly bring down resistance to anti-infectives including antibiotics. There are reports of plans of the Ministry of Health 'to set up mandatory "drug control committees" in all hospitals in line with the existing "infection control committees" with the objective of identifying and clearing the prescription of expensive and unwanted medicines' (Francis 2012b).

TOWARDS ETHICAL MARKETING AND PROMOTION OF MEDICINES

India's pharma companies indulge in unethical promotion of medicines. Most doctors are misled, and let themselves be misled by pharma company representatives, about the indications, therapeutic benefits, side-effects and contraindications: a willing suspension of critical faculties aided by (until recently) the lack of provision for mandatory Continuing Medical Education for re-certification of medical degrees. Doctors and their organizations are indirectly bribed to make them party to irrational, excessive use of costly medicines.[16] Though the Medical Council of India (MCI) has now put stricter restrictions on doctors about accepting gifts and favours from the pharma companies, MCI has no mandate over hospitals. Hence curbs are required on companies to prevent misleading, unethical promotion. MCI has now mandated 6 credit points per year of Continuing Medical Education for renewal of registration. But since AYUSH doctors are registered with their respective Councils, this directive of the MCI does not apply to the AYUSH doctors though most of the AYUSH doctors use allopathic medicines. AYUSH doctors constitute about half of the 1.5 million doctors registered in India.

Lay persons are bombarded with hugely exaggerated claims about the benefits of Over-the-Counter (OTC) medicines and have no idea about their contraindications and side effects. This misleading promotion also needs to be strictly restricted. (The definition of 'OTC medicines' needs to be clarified to the public so that there is no room for doubt. In fact OTC medicines are not defined in the Drugs and Cosmetics Act. It is to be inferred as drugs not specified in Schedules H, G, and X and now probably Schedule HX list of antibiotics). The voluntary codes by the pharmaceutical industry have been in existence for decades. However there is so far not even one complaint or action taken recorded on the website of the association of pharmaceutical companies. Given that many issues have surfaced over the years in the media, this clearly suggests a need to safeguard the interests of consumers more effectively.

The USA and many other countries have moved to legally enforceable regulation of promotional practices as voluntary codes have failed abysmally. A mandatory code on the lines of the template prepared by Health Action International (HAI), covering promotion both to medical professionals and general consumers, should replace the existing voluntary code.

In January 2011, under the aegis of the Chennai-based Consumer Action Group (CAG), members of several civil society groups including the All India Drug Action Network, Medico Friend Circle, LOCOST, Federation of Medical Representatives Association of India, and the Lawyers Collective, developed a draft code that could form part of the Drugs and Cosmetics Rules. A widely and easily accessible mechanism for redress against misleading advertisements is also necessary. If consistently and widely advertised across all media, consumers could participate in the process of enforcement. But curiously the DCGI has never considered curbing unethical drug promotion part of his mandate—indeed how could he without legislation for this purpose.

PROMOTING TRANSPARENCY AND DECLARATIONS OF CONFLICT OF INTEREST

A civil society group in 2010 filed a Right to Information (RTI) appeal seeking the protocols used by the PATH-Merck 'observational study' in the HPV vaccine project. The information sought was denied under the grounds that it constituted a trade secret. But why is the study design or protocol of a demonstration project that sought to gain experience and build evidence for the future introduction of HPV vaccination into the public health system in India considered a 'trade secret'? Surely all information on a public service should be public knowledge and should be in the public domain (Sarojini et al. 2010). This example is symptomatic of the larger malaise of 'confidentiality' which makes it possible for individuals and institutions to evade responsibility and prevents accountability when things go wrong.

Drug regulation in India is notoriously non-transparent. There is no transparency in the process of approval of new drug formulations for manufacture and marketing, nor easy public access to research data used in approval of new medicines or data related to clinical trials.

Accountability would need to be ensured by, among other things, declaration of conflict of interests in all medicine-related policy making agencies followed by withdrawal/recusal from decision making by those declaring such conflict of interests. For instance, those who have been legal counsel for big pharma companies in the last 20 years in the Supreme Court should ideally not be involved, at the highest levels, in pharma policy formulation such as price regulation. Presently lawyers and senior legal counsel and even cabinet ministers are routinely playing a game of musical chairs. There is no formal time frame for which retired government officials should stay out of positions in private bodies that they were in a position to benefit when in service. Similarly ethics committee members in clinical trials are often friends of those conducting the trials. Elsewhere, to make decision making transparent it is necessary for a competent cell to be constituted to make public the relevant, necessary information (decisions, reports of Committees, minutes of the meetings etc.) on the relevant agency website. Even as we write this there is a bill in the Parliament called the Prevention and Management of Conflict of Interest Act, 2011, waiting to be passed.[17]

The process of approval of new medicines in India needs to be made evidence-based, transparent, and oriented to public health needs. Only medicines which have established safety, efficacy, and cost effectiveness ought to be approved. The website of the Central Drugs Standard Control Organization (CDSCO) could provide summary and detailed information on the evidence base reviewed before approval of medicines. The letter of approval for a new drug to be marketed in India, its approved indications, contraindications, patient information material, ought to be available from the CDSCO website. The approval of any new medicines as well as FDCs must be based on a rigorous, transparent process of evaluation of evidence of therapeutic synergism, and convenience of administration.[18]

GENERAL REVIEW OF ALL LEGISLATIONS

Some of the more important laws and legislations pertaining to medicines are listed in the box. Many of them were formulated in the decade following India's independence, a few even earlier.

Laws Pertaining to Drug Production and Use in India

The following Acts and Rules made there under govern the manufacture, sale, import, export and clinical research of drugs and cosmetics in India:

The Drugs and Cosmetics Act, 1940 and Drugs and Cosmetics Rules 1945

The Pharmacy Act, 1948

The Drugs and Magic Remedies (Objectionable Advertisement) Act, 1954

The Narcotic Drugs and Psychotropic Substances Act, 1985

The Medicinal and Toilet Preparations (Excise Duties) Act, 1956

The Drugs (Prices Control) Order 1995 (under the Essential Commodities Act)

The Trade and Merchandise Marks Act, 1958

The Patents Act, 1970

Source: Adapted from, Central Drugs Standard Control Organization at http://www.cdsco.nic.in/index.html

---

There should be a comprehensive review of all relevant legislation considering the increased complexity of the pharma sector and the enormous growth of the industry. We have already pointed to the need to curb unethical drug promotion. In fact, there is a need for the DCGI to be empowered to take action on misleading advertisements and promotional literature—current legislative provisions are clearly inadequate—we specifically refer to provisions in Sections of the Drugs and Magic Remedies (Objectionable Advertisements) Act, 1954, and Rules (1955), provisions of the Drugs and Cosmetics Act (Section 17 and 18 on misbranded, adulterated and spurious drugs), and Schedule J of the Rules to the Drugs and Cosmetics Act. These all need to be harmonized such that it will deter misleading advertisements as well as fancy claims in respect of drugs and devices. Nevertheless, the Drug Commissioners have not made sufficient use of such powers that do exist (for instance drugs for baldness, a specified proscribed condition in the said provisions, are routinely advertised with impunity); the laws are toothless in preventing fairness creams presumably because this is not a specified condition in the Schedule to the Drugs and Magic Remedies (Objectionable Advertisements) Act and is neither in the list of items in Schedule J of the Rules to the Drugs and Cosmetics Act nor is it claimed in the labels or cartons for action under the provisions of the Drugs and Cosmetics Act (Section 17 and 18 on misbranded, adulterated and spurious drugs). Courts have clarified that the definition of drug in the Drugs and Magic Remedies (Objectionable Advertisements) Act includes devices but we have seen little action in preventing the fantastic claims in advertisements routinely appearing in the media. Schedule Y dealing with clinical trials and/or manufacture of new drugs also needs substantial plugging of loopholes in the light of laissez faire in the trials conducted by contract research organisations and individual medical doctors.

OTHER ISSUES

Whistleblower Scheme

There are no punishments awarded to officials within the DCGI's office or its equivalent in states for misdemeanors. The CDSCO website (http://www.cdsco.nic.in/Whistle per cent 20Blowe per cent 20 per cent 283 per cent 29.pdf) refers to a reward scheme for whistleblowers for spurious and fake drugs. But there is no provision for the protection of whistleblowers including whistleblowers from within on issues that are other than spurious and fake drugs, for example on decisions that involve unethical compromises. Whistleblowers need to be encouraged so that the DCGI's office and its State equivalents are above suspicion, armed as they are with tremendous powers to licence drugs.

At the same time, staff numbers and expertise at CDSCO and at State level Drug Commissioners' offices need to be increased manifold because of the present lack of capacity to cope with the challenging tasks of reviewing increasing mounds of data submitted for clinical trials and drug approvals. Ongoing surveillance and safety studies require even more qualified human resources. (We understand that the 12th Five-Year Plan is provisioning for a significant increase in staff at CDSCO including drug inspectors and quality control laboratories.)

GMP and Schedule M and Quality

July 2005 was set as deadline for Schedule M, a quality standard for production of medicines. The DCGI's office went to the extent of sending a G.O. (government order) that no public procurement agency should ask for WHO GMP and only Schedule M will suffice. Indeed in Gujarat, the Drugs Commissioner went about closing companies that did not meet the July 2005 deadline for Schedule M. However as of April 2012, we have the DCGI and Government of India talking of promoting WHO GMP and schemes for financial aid to many drug companies to comply with WHO GMP. This is characteristic of the confusion prevailing in the pharma sector. Yet, because of export requirements, India has the highest number of companies with USFDA certification and WHO GMP outside of the USA.

For most companies in the small and medium sector, confusion continues to prevail. There are only broad general guidelines available and no clear advice on what is specifically required in each department of a manufacturing unit to comply with GMP or even Schedule M.[19]

This is partly because the regulatory authorities are not themselves clear on these issues, which results in significant transaction costs for middle and small manufacturing units. We suggest merging Schedule M and WHO GMP as an initial step, leading to clear guidelines for quality and good manufacturing practices that do not require second guessing by manufacturers hereafter.

Quality also means quality at the level of manufacturing of a medicine—the pharmaceutics and the behavior during a formulation's life span. If the regulatory authorities are aware of, for example, problems in the formulation of specific drugs in specific presentations, why not share this knowledge at the time of licence approval and save proliferation of badly made medicines or medicines that do not stand up to the quality standards during say, the 2-year life of a product. In fact, we would suggest that like Standard Treatment Guidelines for prescription of medicines, the Drug Controller's office could make available Standard Manufacturing Process sheets for each drug—most such knowledge is not patented, and though in public domain in theory, is not easily accessible for small manufacturers. We would similarly ask that the regulatory authorities provide advice on standard storage practices to be followed along with the Standard Manufacturing Process. This would result in fewer occasions of drug 'failures' in the market by otherwise honest and ethical manufacturers.

Regulating Vaccines and Biotech Products

The current trend in India's medical policy establishment is to advocate vaccines for many health problems facing the developing world. Indeed vaccines are one of the most cost-effective of modern medicines and a good tool for overcoming infectious diseases. But if with public sanitation, safe disposal of excreta and provision for safe drinking water, cholera infective hepatitis, typhoid, polio and some diarrhoeas can be prevented, why resort primarily to vaccines to overcome these diseases? If vaccine manufacturers had their way, there is a list of 54 vaccines that would enter the National Immunization Programme in India. However our performance with our National Immunization Programme itself is very poor. Full immunization—BCG, DPT3, OPV3, Measles—in 2008 was at the most 66 per cent, probably significantly lower.[20] Doctors are paid high margins for vaccines[21] and it is no wonder that many medical professionals recommend all sorts of vaccines, even though their role and cost-efficacy is typically not well established in India.

A national workshop of academicians and concerned health activists was held in June 2009 and a draft national vaccine policy, by civil society groups, was prepared (Madhavi et al. 2010). As this draft policy points out, 'The choice of which vaccine to give (or not to give), target population, and mode of administration,(dosage, schedule, interval between doses, intramuscular or intra dermal, etc.), are important policy decisions that must be guided by a strong scientific rationale, after wider scientific debate in the country, with rigorous inputs from multi centric field epidemiology, irrespective of whether it has been proven in populations abroad ... Combining any UIP (Universal Immunisation Program) vaccine with any non-UIP vaccine needs rigorous scrutiny and public debate. Other combinations must be proven to be equivalent to or more effective and safer than single vaccines before adoption.'

These concerns are not merely theoretical, and have been a subject of a recent debate in the context of the HPV vaccine (Sarojini et al. 2010, 2011; Phadke 2012).

We now have an official vaccine policy of the Government of India which has ignored the suggestions of the above mentioned draft vaccine policy of civil society groups. (There has been a rethink since however—see note 22.)

Biotech Products

It is debatable whether the optimism regarding the category of biotechnology-based drugs is justified or for that matter their high prices. '... the hype (in the Western biotech industry) would have us believe that it is a roaring success. Financially this is certainly not the case. The top 2 or 3 companies account for most of the revenues, and just a few years ago it was estimated that the industry as a whole has lost $100 billion since its inception in the 1970s (*Profitless prosperity,* 2006). Are these disastrous financial figures compensated for by overwhelming medical success? It does not appear so. One of the most well-known biologics is Avastin, used to treat various cancers, which had revenues of $5.7 billion in 2009 (Allison, 2010). This extends life by a couple of months (Shaffer, 2010). Medically speaking, one might well describe Avastin as a qualified success and yet it is one of the block busters of the industry. Undoubtedly there are biologics that do a lot of good for particular patient groups (and for certain companies) but that that is not the whole picture.'[23]

In any case, there is no logic in keeping these biotech drugs out of the purview of the Drugs and Cosmetics Act. All biotech drugs are overpriced and there is no price regulation. In fact, the regulation of biotech drugs is sought to be moved to the Department of Biotechnology thus moving it out of the purview of Drug Price Regulation too which is currently under the Department of Pharmaceuticals, Ministry of Chemicals and Fertilisers.[24]

Counterfeit Medicines

Contrary to current international discourse especially from the EU, the Indian law does not define counterfeit medicines to include drugs violating IP rights. In fact Indian laws do not define or use the term 'counterfeit' in the discussion on medicines. Section 17, 17A and 17B of the Drugs and Cosmetics Act define misbranded drugs, adulterated drugs and spurious drugs. Section 27 of the Drugs and Cosmetics Act defines penalties extendable up to life imprisonment.

Recent discourse at the World Health Organization, the World Customs Organization, WIPO, the EU and elsewhere conflate issues of quality with intellectual property. The WHO in 2006 formed a global coalition of stake holders named the International Medical Products Anti-Counterfeiting Task Force (IMPACT) to address the issue of counterfeiting of medical products. IMPACT comprises major anticounterfeiting players, including international organisations, NGOs, enforcement agencies, pharmaceutical manufacturers' associations and drug and regulatory authorities.

In a move parallel to the WHO-led IMPACT, the United States, Australia, Canada, Japan, Morocco, New Zealand, Singapore, South Korea and countries of the European Union—31 countries in all by January 2012—signed the Anti-Counterfeiting Trade Agreement

(ACTA). Despite the name, the agreement is designed to address not only counterfeiting, but a wide range of intellectual property enforcement issues. ACTA would curtail the rights and freedoms of citizens around the world, including freedom from warrantless search and seizure and the right to privacy.[25] India's medicine exports with destinations marked for Brazil and African continent have been seized several times while transiting Amsterdam even before ACTA was formally signed. Specifically, ACTA's provisions would make it very difficult for access to generics for developing countries. On 4 July 2012 however the European Parliament voted '478 to 39 to reject the Anti-Counterfeiting Trade Agreement, a move that means it cannot come into force anywhere within the EU. In doing so, it followed the advice given to it by five parliamentary committees and heeded the massive public protests that were sparked by the treaty earlier this year.'[26] In principle however, ACTA could nevertheless come into force outside the EU, between the United States and a number of smaller countries like Australia, Canada, Japan, Morocco, New Zealand, Singapore and South Korea—countries where the treaty is widely supported—unless of course the US Senate rejects it too.

It is important that India's Drugs and Cosmetics Act be not amended to include definitions of counterfeit as coterminous with infringing (as per local laws) IP status, conflating 'counterfeit' with substandard, spurious and adulterated medicines. IP issues should be separated from issues of quality, safety and spuriousness. Not doing so 'strengthens the agenda of entities interested in IP enforcement since they can legitimately use quality and safety issues as a front to push for the adoption of an IP enforcement framework. The extensive links between IMPACT and organisations promoting an IP enforcement agenda suggests that the resulting effect will be public health concerns being addressed through an IP enforcement lens' (Third World Network 2010).

Patent Linkage

The patentability of a medicine, especially when its patent is questioned post or pre-grant, can take a long time to determine in India. Meanwhile, patients especially among the poor can be denied life-saving medicines at much lower prices. Patent status is the jurisdiction of the Patents Controller whereas licensing for manufacture and marketing and adhering to quality norms are the domain of the Drug Controller's office. IP status of a medicine should not be a determining factor for approval of a medicine by the DCGI. (For more on the Patent Linkage, see Bharadwaj in this volume.)

CONCLUSION

This chapter has tried to outline some of the major challenges in medicine regulation in India from a scientific point of view. At the core of the challenge is the promotion of scientific, evidenced based medicines—both in terms of licensing for manufacture and marketing, and in terms of prescribing by the medical profession—in a milieu where therapeutic anarchy prevails. Unethical behavior at all levels from licensing to manufacture and marketing as well as prescription needs to be actively prohibited—the unethical must become difficult if not illegal. A parallel level of challenge is promotion of good quality at the level of production, marketing and storage. Here strict and fair exercise of the law would be useful even as we are against capital punishment as a deterrent. The law should be an enabler as regards quality.

Just as we go the press, a Parliamentary Committee Report[27] has made strong indictments on the state of regulatory anarchy in the CDSCO (Central Drugs Standard Control Organisation) whose head is the DCGI (Drugs Controller General of India). It has commented on issues related to drug approvals and withdrawal of medicines, banned and ought to be banned, as well as certain structural issues. It has put its finger on the root issue by interrogating the self-declared mission of the CDSCO which was/is to 'meet the aspirations ... demands and requirements of the pharmaceutical industry.' A case of priorities gone awry: 'For decades together it has been according primacy to the propagation and facilitation of the pharma industry, due to which, unfortunately, the interest of the biggest stakeholder i.e. the consumer has never been ensured.' (Para 2.2 of the Parliamentary Committee Report.)

The requirement is simple: medicines that are available in India have to be of quality; and decision making as to what medicines to licence and which ones ought not to be marketed have to be based on some accepted canons of modern medicine drawing upon related disciplines of pharmaco-therapeutics. That is decisions taken have to be evidence-based and the evidence is to be weighed critically in the light of the science of modern medicine. Therefore the business of CDSCO is to facilitate licensing, production and marketing of medicines keeping relevant legal provisions, scientific evidence and policy objectives in mind and not the bottom line of pharma companies. It also follows that the medicines available in India should be able to treat/prevent illnesses in the most cost-efficacious manner. In a sector rife with market failure, the challenge is to ensure that medicines are affordable and accessible even as pharma companies must be encouraged to flourish with ethical compliance and evidence-based medicine promotion in an atmosphere of innovation and genuine competition (Srinivasan 2004).

Notes

1. This chapter draws on existing published/unpublished material by the authors. Excerpts from the following have been consulted and reproduced in part.

a) Srinivasan, S., 2011. '"Medicines for All", the Pharma Industry and the Indian State.' *Economic and Political Weekly*, 11 June, XLVI: 24.

b) Srinivasan, S., 2012. 'Medicines for All: Unexceptionable Recommendations.' *Economic and Political Weekly*, 25 February, XLVII: 8.

c) Phadke, Anant and Srinivasan, S., 2011. 'Draft Recommendations of the Subgroup on Drug Regulation.' Unpublished discussion paper for the subgroup convened by the Ministry of Health and Family Welfare, for inputs to the 12th Five-Year Plan. 4 July.

2. For some reasons not analysed sufficiently, India dominates the formulations market internationally and China dominates the API market.

3. Competition works in bringing down prices when a branded generic is initially introduced. After other players enter into the market, the same branded generic is available at a range of prices with often the costlier

versions selling more and in many cases the brand leaders tend to be price leaders.

4. Recommendations/Observations of the Committee, Para 10, in *Availability and Price Management of Drugs and Pharmaceuticals*. Seventh Report, Standing Committee on Chemicals and Fertilizers, 2005–06, Fourteenth Lok Sabha, Lok Sabha Secretariat, New Delhi, September 2005.

5. See Chapter 1, LOCOST/JSS, 2004 for problems with market share methodology.

6. The price control on drugs of any category is partial at best, with only one or two drugs of a category being represented in the price controlled list. For example, in the case of NSAIDS only ibuprofen, aspirin, and phenylbutazone are represented in the previous DPCO list while in the market under the category of NSAIDS 21 drugs are available. This partial representation of drug categories seriously dilutes the efficacy of the DPCO in making essential drugs available, especially by shifting demand from a price-controlled drug to alternative drugs not under price control.

7. The aforementioned survey of the 300 top-selling brands (as per the ORG/IMS list) with sales of $3.75 billion, revealed that they included medicines of uncertain efficacy, safety, such as ginseng, liver extract, Vitamin E, and nimesulide; irrational combinations of antibiotics, which lack therapeutic justification; and expensive congeners. Out of the top 300 top selling brands only 115 brands were of drugs included in the National List of Essential Medicines 2003; i.e. 62 per cent of brands were of drugs, which were not considered relevant by experts to be included in the National List of Essential Medicines (2003). These include more expensive alternatives of essential drugs, irrational combinations, and irrational drugs. For details, see LOCOST/JSS, 2004. There is no reason to believe the situation in 2012 would be different.

8. For critique of market share based criteria in price regulation, see Chapter 1, LOCOST/JSS, 2004.

9. At present there is a wide variation in their retail prices. Usage of a particular member of the drug class is supplier driven and the price of the latest entrant is usually higher. A generic version of enalapril 5 mg costs Rs 5 per strip of 10 tablets; its branded version costs around Rs 25. In contrast, the branded versions of lisinopril, ramipril and perindopril for equivalent dose are priced at Rs 38, Rs.67 and Rs79 respectively per strip. (Price data, *MIMS India,* Dec 2011).

10. For the gut wrenching questions this move produces, see http://news.bbc.co.uk/2/hi/health/8367614.stm.

11. For details of the gazette order of the Government of India, see http://cdsco.nic.in/html/GSR_418 per cent 28E per cent 29.pdf

12. The revised order allows use of placental products for pelvic inflammatory disease (PID) and topical application for wound healing and also that meticulous details traceability of the donors of the placenta be kept so as to ensure so that the placenta is collected from donors who are free from HIV, HBsAg, HCV and other viruses. For related Gazette Notification, see http://www.cdsco.nic.in/GSR_418 per cent 28E per cent 29.pdf

13. See 'Centre need not consult DTAB before banning drugs, says High Court' at http://www.thehindu.com/todays-paper/tp-national/article3485400.ece. Accessed 11 July 2012.

14. A very large number of medicines in India do not have any generic name; they are available only as brand names. Many of these brands are top-selling, irrational Fixed Dose Combinations, and are not recommended by standard medical textbooks/authorities and hence have no generic name. Unlike rational FDCs like oral contraceptive pills or co-trimexazole or Oral Rehydration Salts, these irrational FDCs have only brand-names. Hence 'promotion of generic drugs' implies elimination of these irrational FDCs.

15. The Government of India has started a five-year 'roadmap' of pharmacovigilance programme for India. (See http://www.cdsco.nic.in/pharmacovigilance.htm). We hope the program attains its objectives in due course. 'Even after launching the pharmacovigilance programme two years ago, the progress of setting up adequate number of centres to collect clinical data is far from satisfactory. In the first phase of the programme, the target was to set up 40 ADR centres, but just 22 were set up. Although 60 more centres were planned last year at an investment of Rs 60 crores, only 40 more added subsequently. There is no doubt that the country requires a massive capacity building for this programme and the number of centres should have been expanded to at least 100 by now. The union health ministry has sought a financial allocation of Rs 250 crores for the national pharmacovigilance programme mainly to set up more ADR centres and increasing the manpower during plan period. Funding may not be a constraint for the government considering the seriousness of the project but the question is how seriously the programme will be implemented in the coming years.' (Francis 2012a).

16. See for instance "Sponsored' doctors under scanner' at http://newindianexpress.com/nation/article563870.ece, accessed 22 July 2012.

17. For a text of the bill see, http://164.100.24.219/BillsTexts/RSBillTexts/asintroduced/conflict-E.pdf. Accessed 20 July 2012.

18. Fixed dose combinations of drugs add therapeutic value in certain patients with infectious diseases and in some chronic diseases. For this reason the WHO List of Essential Medicines includes around 30 recommended combinations. On the other hand, in India a single drug like Paracetamol is available in 46 combinations. The presence of highly priced combinations of dubious efficacy is crowding out the cost-effective single ingredient essential medicines of proven value. The multiplicity of combinations and the sheer number of formulations which results from this make any attempt at quality assurance extremely difficult if not impossible.

19. This experience is based on inter alia that of LOCOST, a non-profit generic manufacturer. Both the authors have been associated with LOCOST over two decades.

20. See for immunization coverage figures for 2008: http://www.searo.who.int/vaccine/LinkFiles/EPI2008/India08.pdf. Accessed 29 April 2011.

21. Lodha, Rakesh and Anurag Bhargava (2010): 'Financial incentives and the prescription of newer vaccines by doctors in India', *Indian Journal of Medical Ethics*, January-March, VII: 1.

22. Available at http://mohfw.nic.in/WriteReadData/1892s/1084811197NATIONAL per cent 20VACCINE per cent 20POLICY per cent 20BOOK.pdf. Responding to criticism of civil society groups and others, the new official vaccine policy has again been labeled as *Draft Vaccine Policy*. For comments of All-India Drug Action Network (AIDAN) on this relabeled New Draft Vaccine Policy, see *mfc bulletin,* Issue No 351, Feb-June 2012, p. 12–13. Also available at www.mfcindia.org

23. Personal Communication from industry observer and researcher Gayatri Saberwal, April 2011 and April 2012.

24. The Draft Biotechnology Regulatory Authority of India (BRAI) Bill 2011 also has the by now infamous clause, Section 62, that proposes imprisonment and fine for anyone who 'without evidence or scientific record misleads the public about safety of GM crops.' For a critique of the bill, see Bhargava, 2011.

25. See the May 2011 version at http://trade.ec.europa.eu/doclib/docs/2011/may/tradoc_147937.pdf and/or http://acta.ffii.org/?p=633

26. See http://www.zdnet.com/acta-rejected-by-europe-leaving-copyright-treaty-near-dead-7000000255/

27. Rajya Sabha Secretariat: Department-Related Parliamentary Standing Committee on Health and Family Welfare. Fifty-Ninth Report on the Functioning of the Central Drugs Standard Control Organisation

(CDSCO). New Delhi (May 2012). For a commentary on the Standing Committee Report see Srinivasan, 2012b.

References

Allison, M., 2010. 'Avastin's Commercial March Suffers Setback', *Nature Biotechnol.* 28, pp. 879–80.

Bhargava, P.M., 2011. 'Unconstitutional, unethical, unscientific', *The Hindu,* 28 December.

Francis, P.A., 2012a. 'Progress of Pharmacovigilance', Editorial, Pharmabiz. com, 14 March.

Francis, P.A., 2012b. 'Auditing Prescriptions', Editorial, *Pharmabiz.com*, 6 March.

HLEG 2011. *Report on Universal Health Coverage for India*, High Level Expert Group, Planning Commission of India, http://uhc-india.org/

LOCOST/JSS. *Impoverishing the Poor: Pharmaceuticals and Drug Pricing in India*. Vadodara/Bilaspur. 2004. See Chapter 4, 'Pharma Pricing in India: A Failure of the Markets?'. Also available at http://www.scribd. com/my_document_collections/2879052

Madhavi, Y., et al., 2010. 'Evidence-based National Vaccine Policy', *Indian J Med Res*, May, 131: 617–28.

Madhavi, Y. and N. Raghuram, N., 2012. 'National vaccine policy in the era of vaccines seeking diseases and governments seeking public private partnerships', *Current Science*, 102(4): 557–8. Also at http://cs-test.ias. ac.in/cs/Volumes/102/04/0557.pdf. Accessed 4 April 2012.

NLEM, 2011. 'National List of Essential Medicines.' Available at http:// pharmaceuticals.gov.in/NLEM.pdf.Accessed 23 August 2012.

Phadke, A. and Srinivasan, S., 2011. 'Draft Recommendations of the Subgroup on Drug Regulation.' Unpublished discussion paper for the subgroup convened by the Ministry of Health and Family Welfare, for inputs to the 12th Five-Year Plan.

Phadke, A., 2012. 'Polio eradication, a dubious claim', *The Hindu Business Line,* 27 January.

'Profitless Prosperity' 2006. *The Economist*, 379, 63 (22 April).

Pronab Sen Task Force Report. 2005. Report of the Task Force to Explore Options other than Price Control for Achieving the Objective of Making Availabl Life-Saving Drugs at Reasonable Prices. Sept. 20. Submitted to the Department of Chemicals & Petrochemicals. Government of India.

Available at http://www.pharmaceuticals.gov.in/ Also called Pronab Sen Committee Report.

Sarojini N.B., Srinivasan, S., Madhavi Y., Srinivasan S. and Shenoi, Anjali, 2010. 'The HPV Vaccine: Science, Ethics and Regulation', *Economic and Political Weekly,* 45(48): 27–34.

Sarojini, N., Shenoi, Anjali., Srinivasan, S., and Jesani, A. 2011. 'Undeniable Violations and Unidentifiable Violators', *Economic and Political Weekly*, 46(24): 17–19.

Selvaraj, S. and Karan, Anup K., 2009. 'Deepening Health Insecurity in India: Evidence from National Sample Surveys since 1980s', *Economic and Political Weekly*, XLIV: 40, 3 October, 2009.

Selvaraj, S. and Karan, Anup K., 2012. 'Why Publicly-Financed Health Insurance Schemes are Ineffective in Providing Financial Risk Protection' *Economic and Political Weekly*, 47(11): 60–8.

Selvaraj, S., et al. 2012. 'Pharmaceutical Pricing Policy: A Critique', *Economic and Political Weekly*, 28 January, 47(4): 20–3.

Shaffer, C., 2010. 'Pfizer explores rare disease path', *Nature Biotechnology*, 28, 881–2.

Srinivasan, S., 2011a. '"Medicines for All", the Pharma Industry and the Indian State', *Economic and Political Weekly*, XLVI: 24 June 2011.

Srinivasan, S., 2011b. 'Pharma industry gets away lightly', *Hindu Business Line,* 8 November.

Srinivasan, S. 2012a. 'Medicines for All: Unexceptionable Recommendations', *Economic and Political Weekly*, XLVII: 8, 25 February 2012.

Srinivasan, S. 2012b. 'A Stinging Indictment of India's Drug Regulation Authority', *Economic and Political Weekly*, XLVII: 25, 23 June 2012.

Third World Network 2010. 'WHO's 'Counterfeit' Programme: Legitimises IP Enforcement Agenda, Undermines Public Health', TWN Briefing Paper 2, 63rd World Health Assembly, http://www.twnside.org.sg/title2/briefing_papers/nontwn/Briefing.paper.on.WHO.Counterfeits.pdf

3   CIPLA: Patients before Patents

Neelam Raaj

India faces huge healthcare challenges at home but there is no denying its place as the medicine factory of the world. The starring role in this has been played by CIPLA, India's first major pharmaceutical company,headquartered in Mumbai, which is today the world's largest supplier of anti-retroviral medicines.

The turning point came in 2001 when CIPLA offered to supply quality HIV/AIDS drugs at a fraction of the price quoted by multinational companies. Other Indian firms followed CIPLA's model and today India produces 80 per cent of HIV/AIDS medicines used by patients in developing countries, according to Médicins Sans Frontières (MSF). In 2012, the Yusuf Hamied-helmed firm, one of India's top four pharmaceutical companies by sales value, cut prices of cancer drugs. This was another significant milestone in the battle for access to affordable medicines. The war is far from won but this chapter tells the story of CIPLA's contribution to this struggle.

Dr Yusuf K Hamied, the chairman and managing director of Indian pharmaceutical firm CIPLA, has been called all manner of names—pirate, copycat, pain in the neck, robin hood, generic genius, and even god. It is invective or praise, depending on which side of the patent row you're on and where you're living. 'In Africa, CIPLA is a temple and Dr Hamied is God.' Ajit Dangi, former head of Johnson and Johnson's drug unit in India,* in an interview to Kamath 2012.

*The quotes of Dr Yusuf Hamied in this chapter are from newspaper and television interviews given between 2001 and 2012 and from phone interviews conducted by the writer over two sessions in February and May 2012.

But it is the 'P' word (or 'pirate') that has become a favourite with multinational drug companies for whom Hamied has been quite a headache and one which cannot be readily cured with a cheap generic pill from CIPLA's well-stocked medicine cabinet!

Asked by the *New York Times* how it felt to be dubbed a pirate, Hamied narrated an anecdote about an American friend who visited India and paid for his trip by buying 1,000 Voltaren tablets, made by Ciba-Geigy, for his mother's arthritis. The price in America was $2,000. In India, because of stiff competition from imitators, Ciba-Geigy sold the same product for 5 cents a tablet, so he paid $50. 'Somebody had been pirated,' Hamied said. 'And in this case, it was not by the Indian' (McNeil 2000). It is perhaps this reasoning that's behind the rock-bottom pricing of CIPLA.

MODEST BEGININGS

However, the firm—which has become quite a thorn in the side of the multinational pharmaceuticals—had a modest start. The father of the present chairman, Khwaja Abdul Hamied, was the man behind it. K.A. Hamied, who was a follower of Mahatma Gandhi, was sent to study chemistry in England in 1924. Instead, he changed ships and went to Germany, then the world's leader in chemicals, where he got his doctorate. On a Berlin lake, he met a Lithuanian Jew and the two fell in love. The couple fled when Germany was shifting into Nazi hands, came back to Bombay and founded the Chemical, Industrial and Pharmaceutical Laboratories, later known as CIPLA. He gave the company his patent and proprietary formulas for several drugs and medicines, without charging any royalty. On 17 August 1935, CIPLA was registered as a public limited company with an authorized capital of Rs 600,000 (CIPLA Ltd 2012).

The search for suitable premises ended at 289, Bellasis Road (the present corporate office) in Mumbai, where a small bungalow with a few rooms was taken on lease for 20 years for Rs 350 a month. At that time, India didn't have a single domestically-owned pharmaceutical company of significance.

CIPLA was officially inaugurated on 22 September 1937 when the first products were ready for the market. In his autobiography, CIPLA's founder K.A. Hamied (who has a square named after him in Mumbai) recounted how even his friends needed 'great persuasion' to buy shares. At one time, the company ran out of money to pay salaries and the prospect of a shutdown was imminent. It was only income from sale of 'Okasa', a tonic for male impotence that somehow kept it afloat though the tough times lasted for years (Hamied 1972).

The outbreak of the Second World War and the consequent disruption in shipping lanes proved to be a blessing for CIPLA, as doctors and hospitals had no choice but to rely on indigenous products and not European formulations. CIPLA also had to churn out medicines for the war effort. As demand for medicines from the Indian army surged, and supplies from European manufacturers collapsed, CIPLA provided quinine to treat malaria, emetine injections for dysentery and nikethamide tablets for trauma (Jack 2008).

YUSUF HAMIED LIVING UP TO HIS LEGACY

Yusuf Hamied says his father never pushed him to carry on his legacy but he went to Cambridge to study chemistry anyway. After completing his doctorate, he flew back to India in the mid-sixties to take up a job at the family firm as officer in charge of research and development.

But he soon realized the constraints of the business. 'Every major drug we wanted to manufacture was covered by patents—a monopoly granted to the innovator for 20 years. The MNCs controlled 85 per cent of the domestic market and exports of drugs from India were negligible,' he says. An archaic British Patent Act of 1911 meant that prices of drugs were higher in India than Europe!

The following year, Hamied helped form the Indian Drug Manufacturers' Association with the aim of weakening the patent regime to help local producers. The breakthrough came a decade later, when its members presented their case to Indira Gandhi, then prime minister. At the time, a blood pressure drug by British pharmaceutical company ICI called propranolol—the first beta blocker—was too expensive for Indians. 'We said to her that this drug is life-saving, and why should millions be deprived of it just because the patent holder doesn't like the colour of our skin? She got the bill passed within a week.'

INDIA'S PATENT LAW 1972

The colour argument may not have had much validity since the company was probably more worried about profits than race but the prime minister bought it and India's patent law came into force in 1972. Patents now applied not to the chemical compounds themselves but to the processes used to manufacture them. To put it simply, India would grant only process, not product patents. This allowed Indian companies to take up a medicine, unravel it and work backwards to develop its own process—a method called reverse engineering.

The law ushered in what Hamied describes as the start of a golden era for India's generic companies including CIPLA. But the going was not easy.

THE THREE DRUG COMBINATION: POTENT COCKTAIL

At the start of the 1990s, the Indian Council of Medical Research asked him if he could make a version of Glaxo Wellcome's AZT, the first AIDS medicine. Within two years, it was on sale at one-fifth of the western price. But even then few Indians could afford it, and, to his chagrin, the authorities said their budget would be allocated to prevention of AIDS. 'I lost my shirt, and closed down manufacturing,' said Hamied (Jack 2008).

In 1997, his interest was sparked again when he came across the HAART (Highly Active Anti-Retroviral Therapy) Medical Report. It claimed that a cocktail of three drugs was effective in controlling and managing HIV/AIDS. The three-drug combination could vary but essentially consisted of a minimum of 6 pills to be taken daily. At the time, these were only produced individually by different MNCs—Bristol-Myers Squibb of the United States, Boehringer-Ingelheim of Germany, and GlaxoSmithKline of the United Kingdom—and the combined price was around $10,000 to 15,000 per patient per year. This was simply unaffordable particularly in the poor sub-Saharan countries where AIDS was rampant.

'We decided that, under the circumstances, the best cocktail consisted of Stavudine, Nevirapine and Lamivudine. The three drugs in question were separately being produced by three different MNCs. They could not combine them into one tablet, but legally we in India could,' says Dr Hamied.

CIPLA's product Triomune was born. Along with Triomune, CIPLA developed other fixed dose combinations, of importance being Duovir-N containing zidovudine, lamivudine and nevirapine in one tablet.

A LIFE-SAVING OFFER

In September 2000, at the European Union before a big audience, CIPLA offered its Triomune to the international community at a special rate of $800 per patient per year as against the then prevailing price of over $10,000. Dr Hamied told *The Wall Street Journal* that he worked for days on his speech, which he delivered in Brussels to African health ministers, international organizations and big drug companies (Pearl and Freedman 2001). 'Friends, I represent the Third World,' he began. There should be 'no monopolies for vital, life-saving and essential drugs,' he said. Then he listed CIPLA's discounted prices. He also offered, free of cost, know-how and technology to any third world government that wished to produce its own ARV drugs. 'A collective gasp could be heard across the room,' recalls Bill Haddad, former *New York Post* investigative journalist who has worked closely with Hamied.

It was a watershed moment for international activists fighting for access to affordable AIDS drugs. One of these was James Love, then head of the Ralph Nader-founded Consumer Project on Technology. James Love, had been trying for years to persuade governments in developing nations to wrest control of AIDS-drug policy and pricing from the multinationals. 'It shocked everyone and blew up in smoke the idea that the pharmaceutical companies were making donations,' Love said in an interview (Lindsey 2001). 'It was a third of the best prices you could get out of the branded guys in what they thought were donations.'

But there were more shocks to come. Love met with Hamied to persuade CIPLA to better its earlier offer. In an email interview to this writer, Love, who is now director of Knowledge Ecology International, a Washington group involved with patents and human rights, said, 'I met Hamied after asking Bill Haddad if he could make the introduction. We first met in London in I think August of 2000. I kept in touch with Dr Hamied, and negotiated the final deal via email, in January/February of 2001. I found Hamied very easy to deal with if you bothered to listen and understand what he was saying.' The negotiations were successful and Hamied ended up quoting $350, the lowest cost ever for a three-drug anti-HIV cocktail. This offer made to Médecins sans Frontiéres (MSF) clinics was less than one-thirtieth of the price of existing HIV medicines. The only proviso was that it be distributed free to patients. The three-drug combination offered at $350 annually, would work out to be less than a dollar a day. This received widespread media attention, with a front-page article in the *New York Times* (McNeil 2000).

Not surprisingly, the pharmaceutical industry was not overjoyed. The then GlaxoSmithKline CEO Jean-Pierre Garnier described CIPLA as price-undercutting 'pirates' at a healthcare forum in Boston. 'They are pirates. That's about what they are. They have never done a day of research in their lives', he said. (CIPLA dismisses Glaxo 'piracy' allegation' 2001).

Michelle Childs, Director of Policy/Advocacy of MSF's Access Campaign, points out that CIPLA's fixed dose combination ('FDC')—combining three pills into one—is still not available from the originator companies. 'FDCs make it easier for drug treatments to be managed and for people to adhere to treatment, as instead of a handful of pills, they can take one pill in the morning and one pill at night.' Ease of treatment is particularly important in low-resource countries as patients can then remember their doses easily and not take the wrong one. The drugs were also available in heat resistant forms, which proved extremely valuable for use in the developing world, where often there is scarce access to refrigeration facilities (AVERT 2012).

Childs describes Hamied's offer as a pivotal moment because at the time, the price of the same drug cocktail from multinational pharmaceutical companies was around $10,000 per patient per year. 'This was in the early days of the HIV epidemic. There were questions about whether you could treat people living in Africa with HIV at all and even if you could, it was felt by many to be too expensive to do so and people were being left to die. MSF had for the previous two years been running a campaign to get the MNCs to lower their prices but prices were only coming down moderately and were still unaffordable for most,' she says.

Dr Mark Cotton, currently director of Children's Infectious Diseases Clinical Research Unit (KID-CRU) at University of Stellenbosch in Cape Town, South Africa, says that access back then, was entirely dependent on how wealthy the patient was and whether he or she had medical insurance (Getz 2001). Even that covered only about 5 to 10 per cent of those who needed it, says Dr Cotton, who worked extensively with pediatric HIV patients. So what happened to the other 90 per cent? They effectively got nothing.

CIPLA's offer succeeded in shaking many things up. Companies such as GlaxoSmithKline and Merck and Co slashed the price of their AIDS cocktails to $600 a year from about $10,000. At the end of April 2001, 39 pharmaceutical companies withdrew a suit they had filed in a Johannesburg court against generic companies like CIPLA.

But one more hurdle remained to be crossed—approval from the World Health Organization. There were still questions about the medical efficacy of this generic fixed dose combination. The MSF gathered evidence and published a clinical study in *The Lancet* establishing the medical efficacy of this generic fixed-dose combination. On 1 December 2003, the WHO prequalification project approved the CIPLA product. This then meant that the donor could purchase it. Almost three years later, on 17 November 2006, the FDA also granted it tentative approval under 'expedited procedures for the President's Emergency Plan for AIDS Relief (PEPFAR). By 2006, 75 per cent of developing countries were using this drug combination (produced by CIPLA and other manufacturers) in their national treatment protocols.

CIPLA continued to win orders, in the process helping create new international systems for drug procurement and regulation. Hamied put his feelings into words. 'It gives us tremendous satisfaction. Every year, I tell our shareholders they should be very happy they are contributing to a humanitarian cause' (Jack 2008).

SUCCESS STORY

But if his move was good for patients, it was also good for the company's bottom line. CIPLA is now the world's largest antiretroviral drugs supplier and the publicly listed company is valued at nearly $5 billion, while business magazine *Forbes* puts Hamied's personal fortune at $1.75 billion. CIPLA is currently India's fourth largest pharmaceutical company by sales, after Dr Reddy's Laboratories, Sun Pharma and Lupin. Its revenues are Rs 6,433 crore (as on March 2011) with exports contributing 52 per cent. In fact, Hamied puts it this way: 'If you look at CIPLA's volume of production and multiply it by the prices [at which the drugs we make are available] in America, it will show you CIPLA as a $40 billion to $50 billion company.'

The 2,000 products it makes span more than 65 therapeutic categories treating ailments from asthma to AIDS, and find customers in 180 countries (Datamonitor 2012). In the respiratory segment, it is a leader in the Indian market.

Hamied notes there are several other things he did to help grow the industry. In the 1960s, there was little raw material manufacture in India. 'That is something I started because my background was ideal to develop local capacity to produce active pharmaceutical ingredients (APIs). I pushed all the Indian companies to take on the multinationals and start producing APIs in-house, which was a revolutionary step at the time'(Ghaswalla 2011).

Not just the AIDS crisis, Hamied made waves again in 2009 when global fears of a bird flu pandemic spiked demand for oseltamivir, the only drug thought to be effective against the disease. Its maker, Switzerland-based Roche Pharmaceuticals, said it couldn't produce enough. Hamied stepped in, without a licence from Roche, and started manufacturing the drug. The outbreak didn't take on the proportions that everyone feared and CIPLA's stockpile of the drug proved to be of no use.

THE ROAD AHEAD

Now, bigger challenges stare at CIPLA. Since 2005, the Indian government brought its patent laws in line with those of the developed world. Indian companies can keep making certain knockoffs, but they cannot copy drugs patented after 1995 without a licence.

Hamied paints a grim picture post 2015 when drugs invented after 1995 will enter the market. 'Currently, in the Third World, older drugs don't die. They coexist with newer ones. As patents expire, we acquire the legal right to manufacture off-patent drugs, making it a continuous process.' But after 2015 that cycle will stop. 'Even people like you and me will not be able to afford drugs,' he says.

Internally too, the company is facing several challenges. One of which was leadership which was addressed recently to some extent. The vacuum left by former joint MD Amar Lulla, who succumbed to cancer in December 2010, has been filled by S Radhakrishnan, a CIPLA veteran of 25 years and former Chief Financial Officer (CFO).

Two Hamied scions—Kamil, 31 and Samina, 36—in 2012 formed part of its senior management team. Both Dr Hamied and his younger brother, joint MD MK Hamied (father to Kamil and Samina), are in their 70s.

'Their induction has put to rest the debate on CIPLA's succession plan,' ChiragDagli, analyst, ICICI Securities, was quoted as saying (Kamath 2012). Kamil, a mass communications graduate from New York University, has been with CIPLA for over six years and is handling key functions. SaminaVaziralli, a post-graduate from the London School of Economics who has worked with Goldman Sachs in London and New York, handles HR and administration.

There has also been an attempt to hire talent from outside. Key examples are Sanjay Bhanushali, formerly at Dr Reddy's, joining the exports team; Chandru Chawla, earlier with Lupin, handles corporate strategy and development; while VS Mani, ex-Wockhardt has taken over as CFO from Radhakrishnan. The biggest challenge of this team is to revitalise exports since the focus is clearly on overseas sales.

When asked about a succession plan, Hamied tries to dispel doubts. 'When you talk about succession, it means you are writing me off. Don't do that just yet. And anyway I have brought in professional managers to run the company.'

CIPLA has also been drawing criticism from some quarters over its stand on issues like the medicines patent pool. Medicines Patent Pool (MPP), an independent organization based in Geneva, aims to bring together two entities which have perpetually been at loggerheads—Big Pharma (which wants to protect its patents) and generic companies (which copy patents) so that the supply of cheap HIV drugs to poor countries continues.

The MPP, which was set up in 2010, asks companies to contribute their HIV patents. Generic companies can then copy some HIV drugs while avoiding long and expensive legal battles with innovator companies. And innovator companies can retain some control over royalty, and maintain a balance between profitability and their societal responsibilities.

One of CIPLA's critics over this stand is James Love, who thinks pooling can get more drugs to Africa: 'CIPLA made a strategic mistake in trying to tear down the Medicines Patent Pool (MPP). I hope it reverses course and becomes a supporter.'

Hamied told this writer that the concept was good but the question was making it work. 'We have offered 10 patents on ARVs to the patent pool but they are yet to decide on it. We have not imposed any restrictions on the countries where the drugs can be sold as long as CIPLA gets 4 per cent royalty on sales.'

The problem, he says, is that the MPP has been focusing only on the 'big boys'. 'Indian firms also have patents on ARVs. Why not ask them to contribute to the pool?'

Criticism or not, few doubt CIPLA's role in the continuing war on AIDS, chiefly in Africa, which is home to 22 million of the 33 million people worldwide who are infected with the human immunodeficiency virus (UNDP statistics).

India is still the pharmacy of the developing world, points out Childs from MSF. 'While a number of African countries are seeking to produce ARVs themselves, including in Uganda in a joint venture with CIPLA, the majority of ARVs, are still from India. Over 80 per cent of the AIDS medicines MSF uses to treat 170,000 patients across the world are generics from India. More than 80 per cent of all donor-funded HIV medicine purchases for developing countries from 2003–08 were for generic drugs from India' (Waning, Diedrichsen and Moon 2010).

The biggest challenge ahead is generic versions of the new medicines. Said Childs, 'This is a real concern for us, not just in India, but in all developing countries that produce generic drugs. We fear a return to 2000 when treatments were priced out of reach. As HIV is a lifelong disease people will need to switch to newer treatment regimes. A number of these newer treatments are under patent in India such as etravirine and raltegravir and company discounts are not affordable for developing countries. Without generic competition to bring prices down, a potential third line regime containing these drugs could thus be available for the poorest countries for the prohibitive price of $2,766 per person per year at best. This price applies to Africa and least developed countries only, with middle income countries paying substantially more. To put it more clearly, the cost of third-line drugs is 23 times that of first-line and seven times that of second-line drugs. The most affordable second-line drug is $465—three times more than the most affordable first-line drug.'

Waning, Diedrichsen, and Moon (2010) voice similar apprehensions. 'Among many concerns around the future of global ART scale up are higher prices for new WHO-recommended, first-line regimens that utilize zidovudine or tenofovir in place of stavudine. As of 2008, the Indian generic global median price for newly recommended tenofovir-based regimens ranged from $246 to $309 per person per year, notably 3.3 to four times higher than the price of the most commonly used older regimen (3TC/NVP/d4T30). Identical regimens, comprised of non-Indian generic and innovator ARVs, are considerably more expensive than the Indian generic versions'.

Childs fears that if action is not taken to rein in these drug costs then for people already failing on their second line combination, this unaffordable price will mean they almost certainly face death once again.

Ellen t'Hoen, former director of the Medicines Patent Pool, noted that because TRIPS implementation will affect both producers in key manufacturing countries and countries that depend on these manufacturers for raw materials, prices will remain high and access to new medicines will become more problematic for populations in the developing world (t'Hoen 2009). Generic producers will also be blocked from developing fixed-dose combinations or paediatric formulations until the relevant patents on the individual components of the combinations expire.

One of CIPLA's focus areas is drugs for paediatric use. Earlier too in 2000, CIPLA had offered to supply free worldwide, the single dose drug nevirapine capable of stopping the transmission of HIV from mother to child. In November 2010, the company developed a first-of-its-kind 'Mother-Baby Pack' to reduce the incidence of mother-to-child transmission of the disease. Developed in collaboration with UNICEF, this color-coded, take-home kit contained the entire range of ARVs and antibiotics required by an HIV-infected mother—starting from the 14th week of pregnancy until the sixth week after delivery.

In February 2011, a Ugandan pharmaceutical company part-owned by CIPLA announced a $30 million project to expand capacity at generic AIDS and malaria-drug plants in Kampala followed by a $50 million investment in a new production line for pharmaceutical ingredients (Khisa 2011). This will further reduce the cost of treatment and improve drug delivery in Uganda. In addition to improving drug access, partnerships like this one could help bypass increased restrictions on intellectual property.

Durban-based CIPLA Medpro Ltd., a CIPLA subsidiary, is also one of the fastest growing pharmaceutical companies in South Africa and an important domestic provider of ARVs. Expanded, local generic production has the potential to further reduce ARV prices in South Africa and across the region (GHSi 2012).

But will the good work continue? Childs notes that there is an additional threat since Indian companies are increasingly investing in off-patent generics for the profitable Western market and may no longer find it worthwhile or safe to invest in development of new drugs for HIV or other diseases where the primary market is in poor countries. 'It is not yet clear what strategy CIPLA will ultimately take,' she says.

There are also worrying reports that CIPLA is reducing production of AIDS drugs. Asked about this in an interview, Hamied said, 'Let me quote you a statistic from the National Institutes of Health: India produces 92 per cent of all AIDS drugs that are sold in the world but they are worth only $1 billion. The balance 8 per cent account for $16 billion! We don't want to reduce production but these drugs are sold under tenders where the winner takes all. We've not been getting tenders of late as other Indian firms are undercutting our prices' (Karmali 2012) .

Another major threat to Indian generic production is that an increasing number of firms are being bought up by multi-national companies and/or entering into close agreements with such companies. Daiichi Sankyo, a Japanese drugmaker, bought India's Ranbaxy in 2008 for $4.6 billion. Smaller deals followed, such as Reckitt Benckiser's purchase of ParasPharma. Abbott bought Piramal's generic business for a whopping nine times its annual sales. 'CIPLA stands out today as one of the last truly independent Indian firms, ready to challenge the practices of MNC and to challenge intellectual property rules that undermine generic production. There are worries that CIPLA's independence could also come under threat,' feels Childs.

Hamied, however, is unequivocal about not selling. Money, he says, is not his driving force. 'I don't want to make money off these diseases which cause the whole fabric of society to crumble. India alone will have 35 million HIV cases by 2015, and it is something we can't afford.' CIPLA is not against strategic partnerships and alliances but selling is not on the horizon, he declared.

Taking on MNC pharma companies still is. In May 2012, he slashed prices on three major anticancer drugs by up to 75 per cent.

Interestingly, CIPLA's decision to slash prices came only months after India's patent authority forced Germany's Bayer to grant a compulsory licence (CL) to another Indian generic drug producer—Hyderabad-based Natco Pharma Ltd—for its kidney- and liver-cancer medicine Nexavar.

CIPLA already has been selling sorafenib, the generic version of Nexavar, since 2010, after Bayer's legal attempts in India to block the drug failed. Bayer then brought a patent infringement case against CIPLA in India, which is continuing.

In its CL order of March 2012, India's patent office stipulated that Natco price the drug at Rs 8,880 for a pack of 120 tablets (a month's dosage) and pay 6 per cent of net sales as royalty to Bayer.

Bayer's patented medicine costs Rs 280,000 ($5,234) for a month. Now, CIPLA has cut the price of its generic version of Nexavar to Rs 6,840 ($128) for a month's supply.

Asked about the timing of the move, Hamied said the CL had set a new benchmark price. 'Natco was going to sell the drug for Rs 8,880 and donate free supplies of the medicine to 600 patients each year. So the price we've quoted roughly works out to the same.'

So is he against compulsory licensing? In an interview in April 2012, Hamied said: 'I think what is necessary is that the Indian government should take a major positive step forward and introduce a pragmatic compulsory licensing policy that means I do not have to apply to the drug control for permission, there should be an automatic licence of right and we pay the patent holder a 4 per cent royalty. Canada had this bill S91 which the Indian government should examine and I hope that people listening in will ask the government to follow the Canadian bill S91 which was in force from 1969 to 1992. If it was good enough for Canada during that period I sincerely believe that it is good enough for the developing world and the world to follow' (CIPLA Launches Anti-Malarial Drug in India 2012).

CIPLA also slashed the cost of its copies of AstraZeneca PLC's lung-cancer drug Iressa by almost 60 per cent. Retail prices have come down from Rs 10,200 to Rs 4,250, the official said.

The third drug that CIPLA has dropped prices on is on brain tumour drug temozolamide. Schering makes the original drug. On the 20-mg pack of five, CIPLA has brought down the price from Rs 1,875 to Rs 480; on the 100-mg strength, prices are down from Rs 8,900 to Rs 2,400 and on the 250-mg—it is down from Rs 20,250 to Rs 5,000.

Hamied described the move as an attempt to bring cheap cancer medicines to the world, just as the company became a champion of HIV patients in Africa a decade ago. 'We had taken the lead to provide affordable medicine for AIDS and I think the time has now come—10 years later—when we do a similar thing for cancer,' he said in an interview (Kumar Sharma 2011).

CIPLA plans to later sell these low-price cancer drugs in other developing countries, he added. 'Wherever there are no intellectual-property restrictions, we'll launch these drugs. Wherever there are intellectual-property restrictions we'll abide by the law of the land.'

By slashing the prices of its cancer products, experts say the company intends to play the volume game in the oncology drug market. Currently, the oncology portfolio contributes a meagre 1 per cent to the company's total revenues. This is likely to increase with the 75 per cent price cut initiated by the company.

Deepak Malik, pharma analyst at Emkay Global, told *The Financial Times* that CIPLA's price cut might not have a huge effect on its bottom line but would likely cause others to follow suit. 'CIPLA has very little stake in oncology, only $3 million of sales comes from this class of drugs, so it is not a very big hit on their numbers,' he said. 'So they will only gain. They may be able to garner better market share in cancer drugs ... and other players will be forced to lower their prices in order to compete' (Munshi 2012).

But can the world reconcile the pirate and the Robin Hood? James Love has the last word: 'Dr Hamied is not a pirate, he is a businessman, and a pretty good scientist, who is not intimidated by big pharma, the US government, or anyone else. He is partly, but not entirely motivated by profit. He does have a conscience, and he is also willing to take some risks. If it was not for Dr Hamied doing what he did in early 2001, we might not have had the global fund. His actions were quite important then, and they are still today, as he puts pressure on the India government and others to protect supplies of inexpensive drugs.'

References

AVERT 2012. 'AIDS, Drug Prices and Generic Drugs', <http://www.avert.org/generic.htm>.

CIPLA dismisses Glaxo 'piracy' allegation, 2001. Rediff.com, 13 March, <http://health.rediff.com/money/2001/mar/13cipla.htm>

CIPLA Launches Anti-Malarial Drug in India, 2012. moneycontrol.com, <http://www.moneycontrol.com/news/business/cipla-launches-anti-malarial-drugindia_696688.html>.

CIPLA Ltd 2012. *Company website*, <http://www.cipla.com/index.htm>.

Datamonitor 2012. *Cipla Limited: Company Profile*, London.

Ghaswalla, A., 2011. 'Y. K. Hamied: Changing the Dialogue', *Pharmaceutical Executive*, no. 1 October, <http://www.pharmexec.com/pharmexec/Global/Y.K. Hamied. Changing-the-Dialogue/ArticleStandard/Article/detail/744321>.

Getz, A., 2001. 'Questions And Answers: On The Aids Front Line', *Newsweek*, no. 8 March.

GHSi 2012. *Shifting Paradigm: How the BRICS Are Reshaping Global Health and Development*, Global Health Strategies initiatives (GHSi), New York.

Hamied, K.A., 1972. *K.A. Hamied: An Autobiography; A Life to Remember*, Lalvani Publishing House, Bombay.

Jack, A., 2008. 'The Man Who Battled Big Pharma', *Financial Times Magazine*, no. 28 March, retrieved 19 June, <http://www.ft.com/intl/cms/s/0/bd8dccee-f976-11dc-9b7c-000077b07658.html#axzz1yD7xObBC>.

Kamath, G., 2012. 'Don't look now, CIPLA just might be changing, says CIPLA chairman and MD Dr Yusuf Hamied', *Economic Times*, no. 19 January.

Karmali, N., 2012. 'Indian Tycoon Slashes Costs Of Cancer Drugs, Claims More Humanitarian Impact Than Gates, Buffett Combined', *Forbes*, no. 6 June, <http://www.forbes.com/sites/naazneenkarmali/2012/06/12/ciplas-new-battle/>.

Khisa, I., 2011. 'CIPLA Uganda Venture to Invest $80m in Expansion', *Daily Monitor*, <http://www.monitor.co.ug/Business/Commodities/-/688610/1102808/-/cc5i02/-/index.htm>.

Kumar Sharma, E., 2011. 'Hamied's Tough Options', *Business Today*, no. 21 August, <http://businesstoday.intoday.in/story/ciplas-chairman-yk-hamied-on-challenges-ahead/1/17549.html>.

Lindsey, D., 2001. 'The AIDS-Drug Warrior', *Salon*, <http://www.salon.com/2001/06/18/love_9/>.

McNeil, D.G.J., 2000. 'Selling Cheap 'Generic' Drugs, India's Copycats Irk Industry', *New York Times*, 1 December, <http://www.nytimes.com/2000/12/01/world/selling-cheap-generic-drugs-india-s-copycats-irk-industry.html?pagewanted=all&src=pm>.

Munshi, N., 2012. 'CIPLA's Enlightened Self-interest', *Financial Times*,

8 May, <http://blogs.ft.com/beyond-brics/2012/05/08/ciplas-enlightened-self-interest/#axzz1yp8XIxvz>.

Pearl, D. and Freedman, A., 2001. 'Altruism, Politics and Bottom Line Intersect at Indian Generics Firm', *Wall Street Journal*, 3 December.

t'Hoen, E.F.M., 2009. *The Global Politics of Pharmaceutical Monopoly Power: Drug Patents, Access, Innovation and the Application of the WTO Doha Declaration on TRIPS and Public Health*, AMB Publishers, Diemen.

Waning, B., Diedrichsen, E. and Moon, S., 2010. 'A Lifeline to Treatment: The Role of Indian Generic Manufacturers in Supplying Antiretroviral Medicines to Developing Countries', *Journal of the International Aids Society*, vol. 13:35.

4

Systemic Failure of Regulation: The Political Economy of Pharmaceutical and Bulk Drug Manufacturing

G. Vijay

The 2009 report *Industry and Economic Update: Pharmaceuticals and Bio-technology* (CIS 2009) presents the great promise of the pharmaceutical industry in India. This science-based industry is estimated to be worth over Rs 680 billion, contributing 1 per cent of India's total GDP. The industry is highly fragmented with about 300 large-scale and about 8000 small-scale units, producing around 350 different bulk drugs and several thousand formulations. About seventy-five bulk drugs or active pharmaceutical ingredients (APIs) are subject to price regulation by the National Pharmaceutical Pricing Authority, under the Drug Price Control Order, 1995. Products based on APIs in this category mostly experience intense price competition and relatively low profitability. It is the supply of bulk drugs and formulations to external markets that holds the key to higher profitability. The change in India's intellectual property rights regime since 2005 is said to have resulted in increased foreign direct investment (FDI) in research and more subcontracted manufacturing for international corporations by Indian manufacturers.

FDI inflows in the pharmaceutical sector since the year 2000 are valued at Rs 65.5 billion (about 1.67 per cent of total FDI inflows for all sectors), and are largely directed at production for exports. FDI inflows were estimated at Rs 11 billion in both 2007 and 2008. The CIS (2009) report states that of the 300 organised manufacturers in India, 200 control 75 per cent of the market.

Of the 160 companies tracked in this report, 25 per cent have their registered offices in South India, where, in the main, manufacturing commenced only in the past twenty-five years (CIS 2009: 3).

Although the report observes that '[t]he average research and development (R&D) expenditure of Indian pharmaceuticals companies is low at 5 per cent of total revenue as compared to about 15 per cent internationally', it is optimistic about the industry and holds that 'drugs and pharmaceuticals exports account for over 40 per cent of industry sales ... despite slowdown in exports in the other sectors, [the] drugs and pharmaceuticals industry is expected to maintain its 3 per cent share in total exports in FY2010 as it has done in FY2009' (CII 2009: 18). The CII report explains that the industry's global advantage

arises from factors like a competent work force, proven track record in cost effective chemical synthesis, a well-established legal framework, growth of the information technology sector and a general acceptance of the principles of globalisation. Although the United States and Europe account for a large share of the overseas drugs and medicines markets, many Indian companies have diversified their international market base in recent years by starting marketing or manufacturing facilities in other regions like Asia, CIS, Russia, and Africa. (CII 2009: 4)

To the extent that comparative advantage in the production of pharmaceuticals and bulk drugs is not based on R&D and innovation, it can be logically surmised that it is derived from cost-cutting and cost-shifting strategies. These include precarious and unsafe employment conditions, lenient regulation of treatment, storage and disposal facilities (TSDF) and effluent treatment services; dependence on research carried out by publicly funded institutions; poorly regulated drug trials on ill-informed and vulnerable people; and dumping of toxic and hazardous effluents onto public lands or common property and into community-owned water bodies. All of these costs remain unaccounted for. The evaluation of the pharmaceutical industry and its contribution to public welfare would be incomplete without an analysis of these factors.

This chapter challenges the myth of pharmaceuticals constituting a Sun Rise industry of great potential for the future of the nation (Vijay, 2009b). This notion has come to assign a privileged status to such production, which in turn has contributed to regulatory agencies treating manufacturers as life-savers and nation builders, and de facto above the law. Firms in this sector have been allowed to violate rules and regulations, while the rest of society carry the costs of this growth in the 'national interest'. This chapter highlights an important category of hidden costs borne by society at large, which provides the pharmaceuticals industry with competitive advantages in international markets. It explains a pattern of systemic regulatory failure resulting in the bad manufacturing practice of pharmaceuticals and bulk drugs manufacturers dumping untreated toxic and hazardous effluents into the environment, with a focus on Patancheru, Bollaram, Gaddapotharam and Kazipally villages in the Medak district, located in the Telangana region of Andhra Pradesh. I argue that treating manufacturers in this sector as privileged actors nullifies independent monitoring by regulatory institutions, permits violation of environmental standards and exaggerates the benefits of pharmaceuticals for economic development.

THE REGULATION OF INDUSTRIAL POLLUTION

We need to analyse the theory and practice of the regulatory framework to understand its role both as a manifestation and a cause of systemic underestimation of costs shifted onto society at large by dirty industries.

Conventionally, economics analyses environmental pollution as an externality problem whereby the activity of one actor imposes involuntary costs on another, leading in turn to problems of pricing and allocation. The dominant approaches see environmental goods as public goods requiring governments to enforce marginal pricing in the form of taxes where markets fail to generate socially desirable outcomes (Baumol and Oates 1988). Alternatively, they are viewed as essentially reciprocal costs emanating from lack of property rights over environmental resources. Here the role of the government is seen as ensuring a well-defined property rights and zero transaction cost regime. The assumption is that there should be a market for rights, leading to efficient allocation of environmental resources in favour of those that value the resources the most by compensating the original owners adequately (leaving them no worse-off) (Coase 1960).

These approaches, however, view pollution as a partial equilibrium or localised problem, in which the effect or consequence of an externality is assumed to be limited to the specific actors and commodities that are part of the immediate externality problem. It is thus that payment of a tax by the polluter, or compensation through bargaining for the victim, is considered to solve such externality problems. However, approaches to the problem of pollution from outside the field of economics, such as environmental science, and especially toxicology, have conceptualised it differently, for example, in terms of 'exposure pathways of pollution'.

Exposure pathways of pollution are defined as the 'channels followed by pollutants from their source via air, soil, water, and food, to humans, animals, or their environment' (BusinessDictionary.com 2012). In this perspective, while the act of polluting may be a localised occurrence, pollutants are carried in the soil, air, water and food with adverse impacts on plants, animals and human beings, beyond the immediate environment. It is only by considering pathways of pollution of dirty goods like pharmaceuticals and bulk drugs that actual costs can be assessed. A similar analytical structure is found in economic development research focused on 'global value chains', which describes pathways of value generation and distribution.

The value chains literature discards the notion of production occurring within vertically integrated firms for linked production structures stretching beyond the firm. In the context of globalization, the production of commodities is seen not as a singular system but as multiple chains of interlinked processes of adding value to a commodity—from the raw material stage to an intermediary one, to the final product—so that the division of labour, or labour process, can be disaggregated and dispersed or decentralised. Disaggregated production processes may then be located in different regions, depending on where a particular value-addition process can be undertaken most cheaply (Gereffi, Humphrey and Sturgeon 2005).

Disaggregation of the production process introduces the question of global differences in regulation regimes. With pathways of exposure to pollution suggesting that the effects of pollution spill over from local circumstances, and with global value chain analysis showing that value creation is similarly not an isolated process, but an interconnected network of processes dispersed globally, it becomes clear that the production process involves sequential externalities affecting other products and economic actors in the countries in which production processes are carried out. Assessing the value of an industry to society requires that all the interconnected effects of a production process be taken into account. In this context, it is also insufficient for an understanding of the regulatory system to consider only formally legislated standards. Daniel Berkowitz, Katharina Pistor and Jean-Francois Richard (2000) argue that rules or standards are likely to be more effectively implemented in nations when they evolve internally rather than being transplanted from outside. This is conceptualised as a 'transplantation effect'. Thus harmonisation of regulatory standards may not actually lead to their effective implementation. Where cost-cutting or cost-shifting strategies form the basis of profit making, social relations are often rigidly constrained by functional and institutional limitations, such as incomplete information, institutional capture, missing and imperfect markets, and structural limitations like dependence, hegemony, prejudice, stigma, insecurity, vulnerability, lack of freedom and even threats, violence and physical coercion. However sophisticated the formal institutions, the processes that cause such problems give rise to systemic failures. The observations of the first head of the US Environmental Protection Agency (EPA), William D. Ruckelshaus (1970), are pertinent in this context:

[W]e thought we had technologies that could control pollutants, keeping them below threshold levels at a reasonable cost, and that the only things missing in the equation were national standards and a strong enforcement effort. All of the nation's early environmental laws reflected these assumptions and every one of these assumptions was wrong ... the errors in our assumptions were not readily apparent in EPA's early days because the agency was tackling pollution in its most blatant form. The worst problems and the most direct ways to deal with them were apparent to everyone.

As the realisation dawned on the EPA that technological solutions did not exist to control all pollution, TSDFs were established in areas that were predominantly inhabited by Black, Hispanic and other poor and marginalised groups. This 'institutional innovation', however, eventually led to the rise of environmental justice and anti-racism movements, which in turn led to the creation of the 'Superfund' program to clean up hazardous wastes and prevent damage to citizens' health (Cleaning up the Nation's Hazardous Wastes Sites 2012). It was this social calibration that pushed the United States to outsource dirty goods production to other countries, and which therefore makes the United States the largest importer of pharmaceuticals, bulk drugs and other dirty goods (Foster 2002; Shrader-Frechette 2002).

Regulation policy in different societies assigns different weights to pristine nature as against accumulation. Martinez Alier (2002) argues that there are two concepts of sustainability: weak and strong. The weak concept of sustainability holds that all environmental resources can be assigned an appropriate monetary value. The concept of strong sustainability holds that qualitatively different values are non-commensurable, and therefore money cannot be an appropriate measure for all types of value. Alternatively, independent physical indexes of measuring environmental quality have been developed. Democratic deliberation that gives scope for the expression of different values beyond but also including the market as one of the valuation frameworks is seen as an appropriate mechanism of valuation.

The development of the environmental regulation regime in India has been diabolical. While a robust Environmental Protection Act (EPA1986) was framed in the post-Bhopal disaster era (with stringent standards for industrial emissions), simultaneously the United States was developing into the largest importer of bulk drugs, pharmaceuticals and other dirty goods produced in India. The EPA framework is not based on the assumption that ecological problems and social costs can be solved merely by assigning an appropriate price or by compensation. Not only has the EPA enforced stringent standards, it has created the Pollution Control Board (PCB). The PCB has independent laboratories for testing ambient standards[1] through environmental impact assessments (EIA) and effective executive powers to close down economic activities which breach legally prescribed standards. The industries in turn are expected to be equipped with in-house treatment facilities or to ensure that their effluents are processed in effluent treatment plants (ETPs) so as to meet legal ambient standards before releasing waste or disposing of it as sludge in the prescribed manner via authorised TSDFs. In addition to the PCB, in 1992 an independent body called the Environmental Protection Training and Research Institute (EPTRI), a registered society not directly controlled by government, was formed to create awareness about environmental pollution and to act as an independent third party institution to monitor the regulation by the PCB. Following a 1995 amendment to the EPA, EIAs of industrial activities are to be heard publicly before environmental clearance is granted. They have been made mandatory as a participatory and deliberative democratic mechanism for the social regulation of economic activities. In addition to these regulatory mechanisms, local governments, or *panchayats*, are vested with powers to close down polluting industries. The Constitution also provides citizens with a right to organise collective action to put pressure on the system to deliver justice. Thus in terms of legal provisions and institutional structures, India's environmental regulatory framework is quite robust. How, then, can we explain that pharmaceuticals and bulk drugs manufacturing units resort systematically to cost-shifting strategies to gain competitive advantage? The anatomy of regulatory failure can be located in the broader political economy. On the basis of a political economy perspective, I present empirical evidence to show that the failure to effectively regulate the pharmaceuticals and bulk drugs industries in India is systematic and not an anomaly.

STRUCTURE AND METHODOLOGY

There is a concentration, dating from the late 1970s, of around 320 pharmaceuticals and bulk drugs producers in the Industrial Development Areas of the Medak district of Andhra Pradesh (Greenpeace 2004). Appendix 4.1 lists industries in these polluted areas including the sites of this study. The Ministry of Environment and Forestry (MoEF) estimates the total number of polluting industries at 170. Some of the largest Indian manufacturers and exporters, including Dr Reddy's, Aurobindo, Hetero Drugs, Matrix, Virchow, and SMS, along with a number of medium- and small-scale manufacturers, have plants located in these critically polluted regions. In all, twenty-two villages—more than 21,000 people—have been affected by industrial pollution. Around fifty-three village water bodies, including nine rainwater reservoirs, two village ponds and fifty-two open wells and bore wells, have been completely polluted by the dumping of toxic effluents (Vijay 2009b). In addition to the twenty-two villages affected directly by the dumping of toxic wastes by pharmaceutical firms, several villages located elsewhere have also suffered as a consequence of a new 'regulatory' intervention, explained by the Andhra Pradesh Pollution Control Board as follows:

... 18 km pipeline was laid by Hyderabad Metro Water Supply and Sewerage Board (HMWS and SB) for transportation of treated effluents from the outlet of PETL to K&S main sewer which is connected to the newly constructed sewage treatment plant (STP) at Amberpet, finally discharging the treated waste water into the river Musi. Initially, 25% (500 KLD 9 (kilo litres per day) of the treated effluents of PETL were connected to an 18 km pipeline on 7.07.2009, 50% (1000 KLD) from 9.08.2009, 75% (1500 KLD) from 7.10.2009 and 100% (2000 KLD) on 26.03.2010 (APPCB, 2010).

It is pointed out elsewhere in the same document that

there is a flow of 150 MLD of wastewater into the Musi river and ... it can assimilate the discharge of industrial waste. There is a massive increase in the irrigated area for agriculture in 23 villages alongside the stream of the Musi river. There is a four-fold increase in the area under cultivation, from 25 thousand odd acres to 99 thousand acres in official figures and in reality it is much more than what official statistics can reveal. (Ramana Murthy and Reddy 2003)

The Writ Petition 1056 of 1990[2] accuses a large number of the pharmaceuticals and bulk drugs producers in the region of not complying with legal emissions standards. A report submitted by the District and Sessions Judge Justice Sangareddy in 1999 identified some of the affected villages and provides details of the land affected. The total agricultural land affected is over 10,000 acres. This, however, is an underestimate which does not include several affected villages. Despite the fact that certain important concerns are addressed by the judiciary, even in the legal approach the fallacy of the framework that understands pollution as a local problem re-emerges. Even in the immediate context there are other victims, apart from farmers with legal entitlements to agricultural lands, whose livelihoods are based on water-dependent activities and who suffer a loss of income as a consequence of pollution. Washermen households, fishermen households and households engaged in livestock rearing, for example, have not been considered for compensation.

Apart from this incompleteness in addressing the problem by the judiciary, the costs of pollution extend further into spaces outside the ambit of the immediate actors. It is these processes that magnify the costs and bring into question the feasibility and magnitude of the cost of identifying and resolving the problem of pollution and, ultimately, the whole rationality of encouraging dirty goods industries in the name of development. The fundamental thesis of this chapter is that this omission is structural and systemic, owing to the bias built into the development model emanating from a particular kind of political economy. This bias determines the nature and functioning of institutions in a way that favours the dirty goods industries as against other economic agents and raises the fundamental question of who gets to control ecological resources that have economic value. Examining sequential regulatory failure in the value chain of the dairy industry, I will illustrate a pathway of exposure to pollution.

STRUCTURES OF THE VALUE CHAINS IN THE RURAL ECONOMY

The twenty-two pollution-affected villages located in the immediate vicinity of the industrial development areas where pharmaceuticals and bulk drugs manufacturing units are located, and the twenty-three villages along the Musi River and several other villages located along the streams carrying pollutants, are engaged in primary economic activities. A number of food crops are produced, including paddy rice, maize, pulses, poultry and eggs, sugarcane, horticultural crops such as mango and guava, aqua-culture products like fish, and livestock production, including goats and buffalos. As these commodities become inputs, they affect other activities; for instance, maize as poultry feed, and products used in restaurants, hotels, and bakeries. Sugarcane is used to produce sugar. Commodities and economic activities such as these are, in turn, connected to the tourism and entertainment industries. Thus we find that rural economy value chains are like an octopus—with a central mantle and head producing valued commodities that branch off in different directions as related value chains.

One such value chain is that of the buffaloes reared in this region for the dairy industry. Buffalo milk is either sold informally, directly to households, or to local hotels, restaurants, bakeries and sweet shops, or to the diary industry. The dairy industry has become increasingly formalised and profitable, encompassing private players such as Reliance, Heritage and Jersy, and cooperative undertakings such as Amul and Vijaya Dairy. There are recent reports of the dairy industry expanding in value terms to $1.3 billion or Rs 73 billion (using current exchange rate) and growing exports to Europe, the United States and the Middle East (NAAS 2003). The value chains-based analytical framework gives us an idea of how commodities with a low value at their site of production through value chains enter a variety of highly valued commodities and services. This interaction becomes especially significant when commodities like milk and milk products become carriers of toxic pollutants generated by the pharmaceutical industry. Consequently, carriers of pollution do not merely affect their own value adversely but end up devaluing the high cost commodities of which their products are a part. They affect, then, not only existing value, but may deny potential value realisable in domestic as well as international markets through reputational impact.

PATHWAYS OF POLLUTION IN THE DAIRY INDUSTRY

The pharmaceuticals and bulk drugs manufacturing industries have resorted to several strategies of dumping toxic and hazardous wastes to avoid the cost of treating effluents: pumping effluents into streams, using water tankers to dump effluents on open lands, dumping effluents into bore wells and so on. It has been pointed out elsewhere that treatment of effluents and their safe storage and disposal involves high costs. Globally, these costs are very high in the rich countries but relatively low in developing economies. However, despite the relative advantage of developing or poor countries, given the nature of dirty goods producers operating in these countries they find these costs high in relation to their own returns and opportunity costs. They much prefer to use their returns for reinvestment into production rather than cleaning up pollution. Once effluents are dumped into the environment, pollutants containing highly toxic materials, such as arsenic or cadmium, get into the soil and water, which in turn, are absorbed by the plants that grow in the polluted environment (Chandra Shekar et al. 2003). The polluted water and plants carrying pollutants are consumed by livestock, such as the buffaloes. Through buffaloes, the toxic substances then find their way into milk, which then enters the market as food for the larger society. At this stage we can say that there has been an inter-sectoral spill-over of costs both in terms of the products produced by another sector and in terms of the costs borne by consumers. The pathways of exposure to pollution in this case is summarised in Table 4.1.

Although capitalist systems operate on the basis of atomistic individual decisions, there is an important role assigned to basic institutions that ensure that individual and social valuation coincide. Scholars like Douglass North (1990) and Richard N. Langlois (1989) have emphasised the importance of institutions in reducing uncertainties in this sense. By setting standards and ensuring that

Table 4.1: Pathways of Exposure to Pollution: A Model Process Chart

Exposure pathway	Source	Release mechanism	Transport Mechanism	Potential receptors at risk	Exposure route	Likelihood of complete pathway in the case of pharmaceuticals and bulk drugs dumping in Medak	Circumstances leading to complete pathway
Food chain	Pharmaceuticals and bulk drugs industries resorting to:	Since dumping is rampant the release is more prone to be through direct uptake into food chain	Uptake of contaminants by plants from water, livestock through grazing, poultry through water and fodder or fish through water (through multiple forms of dispersion)	Destination of produced meat, milk, eggs or fish (households, restaurants, sweetshops etc.)	Ingestion of food items, including the intake of water	Shown to exist based on the evidence provided by K. Chandrashekar et al. 2003	Dumping of effluents by pharmaceuticals and bulk drugs industries on land and in water used by food producers which has gone unchecked due to non-existence or failure of standards and monitoring

(contd...)

(Table 4.1: contd...)

Exposure pathway	Source	Release mechanism	Transport Mechanism	Potential receptors at risk	Exposure route	Likelihood of complete pathway in the case of pharmaceuticals and bulk drugs dumping in Medak	Circumstances leading to complete pathway
Surface water	Open dumping using water tankers and contaminated soil	Deposition of dust could be relevant to those regions located at a distance		Households consuming food crops and fruits cultivated in pollution-affected areas			
Ground water	Pumping effluents into open streams or into rain-water or dumping effluents using bore wells, contaminating			Households engaging in self-consumption of agriculture or horticulture produce or livestock, milk, poultry, eggs or			

(contd...)

(*Table 4.1: contd...*)

Exposure pathway	Source	Release mechanism	Transport Mechanism	Potential receptors at risk	Exposure route	Likelihood of complete pathway in the case of pharmaceuticals and bulk drugs dumping in Medak	Circumstances leading to complete pathway
	surface and groundwater sources			fish			
Soil	Uncovered waste and decomposing waste in landfill site run by Ramky						
Air	'Treated' water let out by effluent Treatment Plants run by government as well as by industrial cooperatives						

Model Source: A. Redfearn and D. Roberts (2002)

social actors conform to standardised procedures and objective indicators of verification, regulatory institutions play a critical role of technical calibration of social valuation.

REGULATORY CHECKS ON PATHWAYS IN VALUE CHAINS

I will proceed to investigate just one segment of the process of inter-sectoral spill-over of the costs of pollution from pharmaceutical and bulk drug manufacturing. This representative study holds for all commodities produced in the polluted villages. Considering the case of the dairy industry, I show that if an industry is protected from detection of ecological dumping at the site of production, this by default extends to all stages of the value chains into which pollutants enter. The chain of regulatory institutions in this case, from the source of pollution to the final incidence, can be divided into primary, secondary and tertiary effects, as presented below.

Table 4.2: Chain of Regulatory Institutions

	Classification of regulatory institution	Regulatory institution
1.	Primary regulators	(a) Ministry of Environment and Forests (b) Central Pollution Control Board (c) Andhra Pradesh Pollution Control Board (d) Judiciary—State High Court and Supreme Court

2.	Secondary regulators	(a) Effluent Treatment, Storage and Disposal Facilities
		    (i) Jedimetla Effluent Treatment Plant
		    (ii) Bollaram Central Effluent Treatment Plant
		    (iii) Patancheru Effluent Treatment Plant
		    (iv) Ramky Environmental Technologies
		(b) Environment Protection Training and Research Institute
		(c) Veterinary hospitals

3.	Tertiary regulators	(a) Milk procurement centres (b) Milk chilling centres (c) Milk processing units

Source: field study

Primary Regulatory Institutions

The pharmaceuticals and bulk drugs industries in this study have been operating for almost one and a half decades without holding the public hearing or achieving environmental clearance from the Central Pollution Control Board (CPCB) that are mandatory (according to the 1995 amendment to the EPA, 1986). It was only after public interest litigation (PIL) was launched by the Goa Foundation that the Supreme Court ordered the CPCB to take the necessary action. As a result, public hearings were held in different parts of Medak district on 11 and 12 April 2005. During these hearings, the industrialists presented EIA reports by private laboratories, which stated that industrial discharges were consistent with legal standards. However, several victims of pollution made presentations to the committee charged with overseeing the hearings, and many villagers registered their protest and asked for closure of the polluting industries.

Having seen the proceedings go against them, a section of the industry's representatives manhandled and threatened a Greenpeace activist involved in the protest, Bidan Chandra Singh. Following this altercation, an angry group of villagers attacked some of the industry representatives, which resulted in police beating up the protestors and disruption of the public hearing. When Singh sought to register a complaint about the assault and the threats he had received to the local police station, he was assaulted again, by Circle Inspector of Jinnaram Police Station, along with another participant (this author). Subsequently, while the manufacturers received environmental clearance certificates, the activists were charged with assaulting a police officer, rioting and damaging public property. For the next four years the accused had to present themselves before Narasapur Court for examination, after which the case was struck down. Each visit to the court cost the accused villagers Rs 500 in commuting costs, as well as lost wages and disruption to their agricultural activities. This was a classic case of what has been called Strategic Lawsuits Against Public Participation (SLAPPs) This entire episode stands as testimony to the role of un-civility as a social mechanism of accumulation. It nullifies social calibration through the use of crude force and institutionalised harassment of an 'emerging civil society'.

To present yet another instance of institutional failure, consider the case of SMS, a large-scale manufacturing unit accused in the Public Interest Litigation WP No.19661 of 2002, High Court of Andhra Pradesh. SMS has a long history as a chronic violator of environmental laws.

On 4 September 2004, the PCB taskforce identified SMS as culprit(s) responsible for releasing mercaptin gas and closed down this manufacturing. While it was lobbying to reopen its functions, on 8 September 2004, the SMS unit was caught again, burning solid toxic wastes outside its premises. A sum of Rs 25 lakhs was collected by the PCB from SMS as a precautionary deposit for allowing them to resume production. The SMS industry after having acquired another small firm, Konar Organics Ltd., in the industrial development area of Gaddapotharam, was caught by the PCB taskforce on 24 November 2004 for illegally dumping effluent into open streams. On 15 February 2005, again villagers caught the SMS industry releasing effluent into the open streams. In spite of this poor record, SMS has been awarded the WHO-GMP (World Health Organization Good Manufacturing Practice) Certification by the Drugs and Copyright, Drugs Control Administration, Government of Andhra Pradesh.

Systemic failure of regulatory institutions is shown by the practice of private laboratories providing EIAs to pharmaceutical firms. While the regional office and field technicians of the Andhra Pradesh Pollution Control Board (APPCB) have compiled indisputable evidence of pollution based on water sample tests, soil tests and photographs, none of this evidence seems to have been examined or provided during the course of the inquiry. There is massive evidence produced by independent researchers from Jawaharlal Nehru Technological University, Indian Institute of Chemical Technology, National Geophysical Research Institute, National Institute of Nutrition and by foreign scholars from Goteborg University, Sweden, which establish the presence of toxic and hazardous effluents in alarming quantities in the village water bodies (Chandra Shekar et al. 2003).

Rao et al. (1999) found that when water is affected by industrial pollution, the pollution spreads through seepage and waterflow to a much larger area. In more recent work on the level of pollution, Larsson, de Pedro and Paxeus (2007: 753) observe that 'the discharge load of Ciprofloxacin corresponds to approximately 45 kg of ... API ... per day, which is equivalent to the total amount consumed by Sweden (population of nine million) over an average 5 day period'.[3]

How it is possible, given standardised scientific protocols for examining water and soil samples for the presence of pollution, that what is observable in alarming levels for some scientists evades the private laboratories that provide EIA reports for the industry? Remarkably, while on the one hand regulatory bodies provide environmental clearances, on the other hand, other regulatory authorities publish reports expressing full awareness of violations of environmental regulations.

The OECD notes that '[a]ccording to the CPCB, as of June 2006, 73 per cent of the 2672 units under 17 categories of highly polluting industries were in compliance, which is a decrease from 2004, when the rate was 84 per cent ... The major non-complying sectors are chloralkali (29%), thermal power (27%), copper (25%), iron and steel (24%), *and pharmaceuticals (23%)*' (my emphasis, OECD 2006: 11).

The Comptroller and Auditor General of India's (CAG) report of 2008 points out:

Monitoring and enforcement of the Rules by Andhra Pradesh Pollution Control Board (APPCB), the regulatory authority to enforce implementation of the Rules has so far restricted its efforts to mere issue of notices and *not penalized the defaulters* though stiff penalties were provided for by the legislature. Thus, the legislative intent has not been translated into effective compliance.

In a more recent report the Ministry of Environment and Forests states that

there are about 36,000 hazardous waste generating industries in India which generate 6.2 million tonnes out of which land fillable hazardous waste is about 2.7 million tonnes (44%), incinerable hazardous waste is about 0.4 million tonnes (7 %) and recyclable hazardous waste is about 3.1 million tonnes (49%). *Indiscriminate and unscientific disposal of wastes in the past has resulted in several sites in the country becoming environmentally degraded.* There are 141 hazardous waste dumpsites that have been primarily identified in 14 States/UTs out of which 88 critically polluted locations are currently identified. Gujarat (about 29%), Maharashtra (about 25%) and Andhra Pradesh (about 9%) are the top three HW generating States. (my emphasis, MoEF 2010: 50)

Secondary Regulatory Institutions

It is a legislative requirement that firms engaged in manufacturing involving emissions of toxic or hazardous wastes must have in-house treatment facilities. These technologies must provide primary treatment of effluents and bring down the pollution, as measured on the basis of PH level, Total Suspended Solids (TSS), Total Dissolved Solids (TDS), Biological Oxygen Demand (BOD) and Chemical Oxygen Demand (COD), to legally determined ambience standards. For carrying out further treatment, two common effluent treatment plants (CEPTs) were established at Patancheru and Bollaram industrial development areas in the early 1990s. At that time, the polluting industries decided strategically to make the Andhra Pradesh Industrial Infrastructure Corporation (APIIC) the regulatory agency overseeing effluent treatment since neither the technologies nor the capacity enhancement to handle effluent treatment had been developed.

As part of the record of proceedings of the Supreme Court pertaining to the Writ petition 1056/90 in 1996, the District Judge observed that:

It is unfortunate that the State owned APIIC which is in charge of day to day operations of the CEPT, in an utter disregard of the provisions contained in the Environment (Protection) Act, 1986 and its rules, is discharging such partially treated effluent into the stream Nakkavagu. The industrialists have very cleverly entrusted the management to the state owned APIIC in order to escape themselves from the penal provisions of the Environment Protection Act, 1986 and its rules.

A report submitted to the Supreme Court by District Judge Justice Jagpal Reddy observed that the CETPs at Bollaram and the Patancheru ETPs were accepting effluent from industry far exceeding the legally prescribed standards. Whereas the capacity of the Bollaram treatment plant was 120 tankers of effluent per day, it was receiving 200.

Finding that government-managed treatment plants had low capacity and were inadequately equipped, the manufacturers took this as an opportunity and constituted themselves as a cooperative society, starting yet another treatment plant, at Jeedimetla. This plant was outside of direct state control. The PCB pointed out that the Jeedimetla effluent treatment (JETL) plant was violating standards. It responded by claiming it was doing a better job than both of the government-controlled treatment plants. In this way the JETL came into existence as a 'regulatory' institution controlled and administered by functionaries appointed, with salaries paid by, the polluting industries themselves. Soon enough, the Patancheru effluent treatment plant which was under the APIIC was taken over by the manufacturers, who constituted themselves as a private enterprise called Progress Effluent Treatment Limited. The government and the PCB, which were in direct control of secondary effluent treatment with the establishment and an unstated ratification of the JETL and PETL models of effluent treatment, became mere overseers. The autonomy of the regulatory body in effect ceased as the polluters became the owners of the effluent treatment plants.

The private treatment, storage and disposal facilities business is an extension of the process described above. In September 2010, participants at an international conference in Hyderabad (including this writer and the editor of this volume) visited an industrial development area where pharmaceuticals and bulk drugs manufacturing is clustered. They witnessed the conditions of the treatment, storage and disposal facility run by Ramky Enviro Engineering Pty Ltd. There is conspicuous, visible seepage of toxic and hazardous waste all around the land-fill site, which supposedly uses Australian technologies. On 19 January 2009 there was a major fire accident at the Ramky treatment and storage site at Dundigal. Several environmental groups raised questions about whether the accident was planned—whether it was meant to burn the hazardous sludge that had been accepted in excess of the site's capacity. But far from holding Ramky responsible for the risks generated through irresponsible management of hazardous waste, the government in March 2010 provided Ramky Enviro Engineering with occupational health and safety assessment certification (Series 18001, OHSAS 18001) as part of the 39th National Safety Day Celebrations organised by the Department of Factories of Andhra Pradesh and the National Safety Council, Andhra Pradesh Chapter.

In this case, conflict continued between the effluent treatment plants and TSDFs owned by private companies and the PCB, necessitating a third party arbitrator to independently validate or refute claims and counter-claims. EPTRI started to function with a onetime grant from the central government of Rs 66 lakhs, and from the state government to the tune of Rs 2,13.3 lakhs. The nature of employment of many of those working for EPTRI is informal and insecure. The ongoing employment of these employees, including the technicians conducting laboratory tests on water, soil and other samples, is linked to the decisions of the administration, which has industry representatives. Further, the EPTRI is largely dependent on income from consultancy, laboratory testing and other services provided to firms in this sector for its own running costs, including salaries.

Recently EIAs, laboratory sample tests and consultation services have been provided by private laboratories such as Ramky Enviro Engineering Ltd and Bhagavati Anna Consultants Pty Ltd, which have recognition from the National Accreditation Board for Testing and Calibration Laboratories (under the federal Department of Science and Technology). This legal recognition gives such laboratories authority to issue certifications legally admissible in a court of law and eligible as evidence before government regulatory bodies. Companies are free to choose the organisation they wish to pay for EIAs and for other consultation services. The manufacturers may nominate a laboratory or decide to choose a consultant based on open tendering. EPTRI then has to compete with the private laboratories. Bids and offers made by EPTRI, with government officials in its employ, are under greater scrutiny than are those of the private laboratories offering similar services. EPTRI officials, under condition of anonymity, have informed the author during interviews that the EIAs and other consultation services are offered by private laboratories at prices insufficient to meet even the material costs of conducting tests. Thus the competition with private laboratories is not only intense but predatory, a huge dilemma for EPTRI which cannot meet its operating costs without revenue from services to the industry.

The desperation of EPTRI becomes clear in financial statements which the author has secured under Right to Information. When EPTRI offers services to industry, such as EIAs, it usually enters into a memorandum of understanding in which it is agreed that companies using EPTRI's services make 50 per cent of the payment before procuring the report and 50 per cent after. EPTRI officials have stated in interviews that those industries that have received adverse EIAs, and therefore, cannot secure environmental clearances, have defaulted on their payment of the full amount for the services provided. EPTRI, instead of pursuing the outstanding receipts, has decided to write them off. EPTRI officials state that the writing-off of outstanding receipts is done so EPTRI can avoid conflict with the industry. Thus the structure of the so-called third party process is skewed in the direction of writing favorable reports because these are likely to secure more paying clients and higher income. The process shows just how dependent EPTRI is on the polluters the agency is supposed to regulate.

At the secondary level of regulation, the toxic and hazardous waste dumped by the pharmaceuticals and bulk drugs industries directly, by effluent treatment plants or by TSDPs, finds its way into the water and the soil through flow and seepage into the local vegetation. Toxic and hazardous wastes are then ingested by livestock reared in pollution-affected areas. A farmer whose cattle suffer from health-related problems could easily report the matter to the regulatory institutions, for example, the PCB, or approach the court for compensation. But to do so effectively, the farmer requires the evidence that establishes a connection between the ailments suffered by his animals and the pollution generated by pharmaceuticals manufacturing. As part of the environmental economics course taught at the University of Hyderabad, household-level surveys were conducted by students in 2008, 2009 and 2010 in Kazipally, Gandigudem, Sultanpur, Dyara, Kistareddypet, Arutla, Chiduruppa villages. A total of 360 households were interviewed out of a total of approximately 1400. The findings suggest that, on average, two to three cattle per household have died from consuming polluted water. The data pertaining to the cases reported at the veterinary hospital in Patancheru were analysed using the registry of cases for 2006, 2007, 2008 and 2009. Interestingly, not a single case of an ailment or death of a buffalo due to pollution has been recorded. The veterinary hospitals located in polluted areas are not equipped with diagnostic or laboratory facilities. The ailments affecting cattle have to be deduced from problems reported by their owners and through clinical diagnosis on that basis. While there is a lack of systematic reporting of cases, cattle that are carriers of industrial toxins and hazardous wastes often suffer from or die as a result of the consumption of polluted water or of grazing on polluted lands. In such cases an autopsy on the animal has to be performed at the veterinary hospital in Hyderabad. However, in cases where it is proven that the cause of death is industrial pollution, again a systemic 'correction' is made.

Over the years, the pharmaceutical manufacturers have created a mechanism to circumvent this possibility. No sooner does a farmer get a tentative report from the local veterinary hospital that the death of an animal has occurred possibly due to pollution, than the manufacturers association (the Model Industrial Association) or individual industrialists offer to pay compensation to the cattle owner on condition that the farmer will not pursue the case further. Although this may compensate the farmer for his immediate loss, it is at the cost of spill-over of pollution, with the sequential externalities going unidentified and thereby causing increased costs further along the pathway.

Tertiary Regulatory Institutions

Beyond the primary institutions, the pathways of pollution initiated by pharmaceuticals and bulk drugs manufacturers have already extended into the food chains. The pollutants have led to inter-sectoral intrusion, destroying or adversely affecting rural primary and tertiary sector activities, including agriculture, horticulture, fisheries, livestock and other water-dependent activities. The secondary institutions, such as the agriculture department, providing extension services; local water administration; horticulture extension services; fisheries extension services; veterinary hospitals; and the like, must rectify this so that the carriers of pollution do not actually end up in the food consumed by human beings. In cases where the secondary regulatory institutions also fail, there is a third level of regulatory institution that oversees food safety.

The focus here is on the specific chain of regulatory institutions concerned with milk and milk products. Milk procurement was originally undertaken by milk cooperatives developed during the white flood of 1970–79. There are now private sector procurement centres at the village level. While prior to the growth of the private sector the milk was tested using relatively crude methods for presence of fat, and solids but not fat (SNF), milk vendors employed different types of adulteration. After the entry of the private sector, more sophisticated milk analysers have been introduced. They are equipped to identify adulteration such as water, salt, sugar and urea more accurately than the presence of toxic chemicals or heavy metals. Thus in the first stage of regulation, such pollutants evade detection. From the procurement centres at the village level, the milk is transported by tankers to chilling centres at the town level. The chilling centres are more like transit points between the village procurement centres and the urban processing centres. Every tank is tested for the above stated parameters, thus preserving traceability to the point of origin of the milk. The milk is then pasteurised and kept chilled by passing liquid ammonia through pipes that pass through the containers filled with the pasteurised milk. This process helps kill harmful bacteria and preserve the milk. The milk is transported in milk tankers to the processing units. Thus even at the second level, toxic chemicals and heavy metals evade detection. When the milk reaches the processing unit it is tested to reconfirm the same set of parameters (fat, SNF and bacteria) and re-pasteurised. During the course of pasteurisation milk with different levels of fat and SNF is segregated into different categories of milk. Some milk is sent to aseptic plants where a process referred to as ultra-high treatment is employed. This process involves downloading the milk from the tankers from the chilling units into a bacto-fridge, after which the milk is pasteurised at 75 to 85 degrees Celsius and then cooled to 4 to 6 degrees. It is then homogenised and heated again to 138 degrees, cooled, then vacuum packed into pillow packs, which can retain the milk for 90 days, and brick packs, which can retain the milk for 120 days. In the processing unit, some tests are performed on the milk by an attached laboratory.

Laboratory officials at the milk processing unit have informed the author that milk is a highly perishable commodity and there is no time to perform tests on the milk samples for toxins and heavy metals. However, since this is mandatory, once every six months, milk samples are sent to private laboratories for testing. Curiously, as if to complete the system of pathways of sequential externalities at the final point—consumption of the milk—the private laboratory that tests the milk samples is the same private laboratory that provides the EIA clearances to polluting pharmaceuticals and bulk drugs manufacturing industries: Bhagavathi Anna Laboratories. The milk and milk products that could have toxins and heavy metals are especially dangerous as they may be carcinogenic.

FINAL OBSERVATIONS

Two different objections can be mounted in relation to the inadequate testing and regulation of milk products. The first is that unchecked pollution by pharmaceuticals and bulk drugs producers violates environmental laws and the right to health as part of the fundamental right to life. The second is a cost-benefit analysis of the production of milk products and pollution pathways, and manufacturers' economic rationale for their unwillingness to meet regulatory standards, if not collusive practices to avoid regulation. However, any conclusion we might reach as a result of this study of existing institutions remains indeterminate.

On the production side, pollution destroys basic characteristics of natural resources which as a consequence cannot be used for alternative purposes. According to agriculture and irrigation experts, the polluted lands in the affected areas under study cannot be used for agriculture for another fifteen years, and that is if no additional effluents are added to the existing levels of pollutants. This will cause rigidities in the flow of resources if relative prices change in favour of other activities such as food, fodder or fiber, relative to the prices of polluting products. On the consumption side, polluted goods are likely to be consumed by a host of consumers, causing enormous costs,[4] the value of which is unknown. These may include also the owners of the polluting industries who could find themselves as consumers of the polluted food. This suggests that anarchy prevails in the production of value and its accumulation and that we are observing destruction or subversion of the regulatory institutions established to facilitate the growth of Sun Rise industries, such as the pharmaceuticals and bulk drugs industries. Indian pharmaceuticals and bulk drugs industries are not innovative. They are predominantly intermediaries in a structure of accumulation dominated by big global capital. In these structures of accumulation, global firms engage in cost shifting through externalisation of costs onto third world societies in order to provide comparative advantage and control of international markets. The value contributed by polluting industries in countries such as India is fictitious to the extent that the cost of environmental destruction is not accounted for. Yet the increasing fictitious significance of these industries provides the necessary, if illusory, grounds for lobbying for further policy sweeteners and incentives, deregulation and a privileged status that permits polluting firms to violate laws. Statisticians and economists are very much a part of this game of policy manipulation.

One possible explanation for systemic regulatory failure lies in the orientation of the development process, which seems to promote exports and foreign earnings to meet unsustainable import-driven consumption patterns of the affluent classes. Future research must focus on connecting the unsustainable consumption patterns of the affluent to the evolution and behaviour of production and regulation structures and to the changing nature of social relations and their political ecology.

Acknowledgement

I wish to thank Professor Hans Löfgren, who has encouraged me to pursue my research. I also wish to thank all my colleagues at the Department of Economics, especially Professor Manohar Rao, Professor A.V. Raja, Professor R. Vijay and Professor Vamsi, whose valuable comments have enriched my understanding. Thanks are due also to the students from the environmental economics course who carried out the village-level surveys, and to all the officials and functionaries of the organisations that have provided data. I wish to acknowledge the cooperation of G. Shyam Sunder and friends at Mogiligidda village.

Notes

1. Ambience standards are scientifically determined safety limits for the presence of potentially hazardous substances in the air, water and soil.

2. Writ Petition filed by the Indian Council for Enviro Legal Action as a Public Interest Litigation in 1990 with the Supreme Court of India. Details are available on the official websites: http://cpcbenvis.nic.in/newsletter/legislation/ch15dec02a.htm   and http://www.cpcb.nic.in/divisionsofheadoffice/ess/Patancheru-Bollaram.pdf

3. Ciprofloxacin is an antibiotic drug used as an anti-bacterial. Unnecessary consumption of such drugs is known to cause drug resistance, see http://www.drugs.com/pro/ciprofloxacin.html. That pathways of antibiotic drugs through food animals (intentionally or unintentionally) to humans cause drug resistance is also a well-established finding, see see http://www.nrdc.org/health/files/raisingresistance.pdf

4. Conventionally these include direct and indirect costs such as direct expenditure on health related costs and the value of person-days of productive labour lost respectively. This may not be a comprehensive set of costs, since there could be loss of quality of life, psychological costs incurred and contiguous costs borne by household members due to interdependent welfare functions, which cannot be as easily converted into monetary equivalents. The costs could further increase if the diseases are contagious or if the cure involves subsidized public health insurance or other services, thus translating into collective or social costs.

References

APPCB, 2010. 'Final Action Plan for Improvement of Environmental Parameters in Critically Polluted Areas of 'Patancheru-Bollaram Cluster', Andhra Pradesh, November, <www.cpcb.nic.in/divisionsofheadoffice/ess/Patancheru-Bollaram.pdf>.

Baumol, W.J., Oates, W. and Wallace, E., 1988. *The Theory of Environmental Policy*, 2nd edn, Cambridge University Press, Cambridge.

Berkowitz, D., Pistor, K. and.Richard, J.F., 2000. 'Economic Development, Legality and Transplant Effect', CID Working Paper No. 69, <http://www.cid.harvard.edu/cidwp/039.pdf>.

BusinessDictionary.com 2012 Business Dictionary: http://www.businessdictionary.com/definition/exposure-pathway.html

Chandra Sekhar, K., Chary, N.S., Kamala, C.T., Venkateswara Rao, J., Balaram, V., and Anjaneyulu, Y., 2003. 'Risk Assessment and Pathway Study of Arsenic in Industrially Contaminated Sites of Hyderabad: A Case Study', *Environment International*, 29(5): 601–11.

Cleaning up the Nation's Hazardous Wastes Sites 2012 http://www.epa.gov/superfund/

Coase, R.H., 1960. 'The Problem of Social Cost', *Journal of Law and Economics*, 3, October: 1–44.

CIS, 2009. 'Industry and Economic Update: Pharmaceuticals and Bio Technology', Confederation of Indian Industry Southern Region, Quarterly Update, October–December.

Comptroller and Auditor General of India (CAG), 2008. 'Performance Audit on Management of Waste in India', Report No. P.A. 14 of 2008, <www.cag.gov.in/html/reports/civil/2008_PA14_SD.../chap_1.pdf>.

Foster, J.B., 2002. *Ecology Against Capitalism*, Monthly Review Press, London.

Gereffi G., Humphrey, J., and Sturgeon, T., 2005. 'The Governance of Global Value Chains', *Review of International Political Economy*, 12:1, February.

Greenpeace India 2004. State of Community Health in Medak District, <http://www.greenpeace.org/india/Global/india/report/2004/10/state-of-community-health-at-m.pdf>

Grossman, G.M. and Krueger, A.B., 1994. 'Economic Growth and the Environment', NBER Working Paper 4634. National Bureau of Economic Research, Cambridge, MA.

Bugge, H.C., 1996. 'The Principles of "Polluter Pays" in Economics and Law', in E. Eide and R. van den Bergh (eds), *Law and Economics of the Environment*, pp. 53–54, Oslo, Jurdisk Forlag.

Shrader-Frechette, K., 2002. *Environmental Justice*, Oxford University Press, Oxford.

Langlois, R.N., 1989. *Economics as a Process; Essays in New Institutional Economics*, Cambridge University Press, Cambridge.

Larsson, D.G.J., De Pedro,C. and Paxeus,N. 2007. 'Effluent from Drug Manufactures Contains Extremely High Levels of Pharmaceuticals', *Journal of Hazardous Materials*, 148: 751–5.

Lewis, J., 1988, 'Looking Backward: A Historical Perspective on Environmental Regulations', *EPA Journal*, United States Environmental Protection Agency (EPA), <http://www.epa.gov/aboutepa/history/topics/regulate/01.html>

Martinez-Alier, J., 2002. *The Environmentalism of the Poor: A Study of Ecological Conflicts and Valuation*, Edward Elgar, Cheltenham UK.

Ministry of Environment and Forests, 2010. Report of the Committee to Evolve Road Map on Management of Wastes in India, New Delhi. <http://moef.nic.in/downloads/public-information/Roadmap-Mgmt-Waste.pdf>

National Academy of Agriculture Sciences (NAAS), 2003. 'Export Potential of Dairy Products', Policy Paper 23, December.

North D.C., 1990. *Institutions, Institutional Change and Economic Performance*, Cambridge University Press, Cambridge.

OECD, 2006. 'Environmental Compliance and Enforcement in India: Rapid Assessment, Organisation for Economic Cooperation and Development', Paris, www.oecd.org/dataoecd/39/27/37838061.pdf

Ramana Murthy, R.V., and Muthyam Reddy, K., 2003. 'In search of Sustainable Development: Musi 'Green Belt' Blues', Annual Conference Proceedings, Andhra Pradesh Economic Association.

Ramky Enviro Engineering, 2010. 'Ramky Awarded by the Department of Factories Government of Andhra Pradesh and National Safety Council Andhra Pradesh Chapter', Media Release, <http://www.ramkyenviroengineers.com/PressRoom.html>

Rao, V.V.S.G., Subrahmanyam, K., Yadalah, P. and Dhar, R.L., 1999. 'Assessment of groundwater pollution in the Patancheru Industrial Development Area and Its Environs, Medak District, Andhra Pradesh, India', in *Impacts of Urban Growth on Surface Water and Groundwater Quality,* Proceedings of IUGG 99 Symposium HS5, Birmingham, IAHS Publ. no. 259. http://iahs.info/redbooks/a259/iahs_259_0099.pdf

Redfearn, A. and Roberts, D., 2002. 'Health Effects and Landfill Sites', in R.E. Hester and R.M Harrison (eds), *Environmental and Health*

Impact of Solid Waste Management Activities; Issues in Environmental Science and Technology, pp. 103–40, The Royal Society of Chemistry, Cambridge.

Ruckelshaus, W.D., 1970. 'The First Administrator on Establishment of EPA', EPA Press Release, http://www.epa.gov/aboutepa/history/org/origins/first.html

SMS Pharmaceuticals Ltd, 2005. Public Issues Draft Prospectus, Stock Exchange Board of India, <www.sebi.gov.in/dp/**sms**pharma.pdf>.

Stewart, R.B., 1993. 'Environmental Regulation and International Competitiveness and the Law', *The Yale Law Journal*, 102(8): 2039–106.

Supreme Court Proceedings on Writ Petition (Civil) No. 1056 of 1990, Petitioner Indian Council for Enviro Legal Action versus Union of India and Others.

Vijay, G., 2009a. 'Defragmenting "Global Disintegration of Value Creation" and Labour Relations', *Economic and Political Weekly*, 44:22, 30 May.

Vijay. G., 2009b. 'Cemicals and Pharmaceuticals in South India; Sun Rise Industrialisation or Global Cost Shifting of Dirty Goods Manufacturing', in H. Lofgren and P. Sarangi (eds), *The Politics and Culture of Globalisation; India and Australia*, Social Sciences Press, New Delhi. pp. 158–80.

Appendix 4.1: List of Industries in Criti cally Polluted
Industrial Development Areas (IDA) of Medak District

Industries Under Polluti on Control Bord Regional Office, Sangareddy[1]

S. No	Name of the Industry and Address
1.	M/s. NSL (Presently M/s. Pennar Industries Ltd), IDA, Patancheru, Medak dist
2.	M/s. Hitesh Chemicals, IDA, Patancheru, Medak dist
3.	M/s. TFL Quinn India Ltd., IDA, Patancheru, Medak dist
4.	M/s. Roopa Industries Lt, IDA, Patancheru, Medak dist
5.	M/s. Rallis India Ltd, IDA, Patancheru, Medak dist
6.	M/s. Arch Pharma Labs Ltd., (formerly Merven Drugs), Gundla Machnoor Village Hatnoor Mandal, Medak Dist
7.	M/s. Arabindo Pharma Ltd, Unit-1, Borpatala Village, Hatnoor Mandal, Medak
8.	M/s. Arabindo Pharma Ltd, Unit-V, IDA Pashamailaram, Patancheru Mandal, Medak dist.

(contd...)

(Table Appendix 4.1: contd...)

S. No	Name of the Industry and Address
9.	M/s. Arabndo Pharma Ld, Unit-VIB, Chitkul Village, Patancheru Mandal Medak dist.
10.	M/s. Arabindo Pharma Ltd, Unit-IX, (Formerly Rnit-III/Vamsi), Gundlamanchnoor Village, Hatnoor Mandal, Medak dist.
11.	M/s. Cirex Pharmaceuti als Ltd., Gndlamanchnoor Village, Hatnoor Mandal, Meak dist.
12.	M/s. Deccan Leathers Ltd., IDA, Patancheru, Medak dist
13.	M/s. Everest Organics Ltd., Aroor village, Sadaivpet Mandal, Medak dist.
14.	M/s. Hyderabad Chemicals Products Ltd., IDA Pashamailaram, Patancheru Mandal, Medak dist.
15.	M/s. Nestro Pharmaceuti cals Ltd., IDA Pashamailaram, Patancheru Mandal, Medak dist.
16.	M/s. Neuland Laboratories Ltd., Unit-II, IDA Pashamailaram, Patancheru Mandal, Medak dist.
17.	M/s. Nitya Laboratories Ltd., IDA Pashamailaram, Patancheru Manda, Medak dist.
18.	M/s. Pennar Industries Ltd., Isnapur village, Patancheru Mandal, Medak dist.
19.	M/s. Rantus Pharma Pvt. Ltd., IDA Pashamailaram, Patancheru Mandal, Medak dist.
20.	M/s. Venkar Chemicals Pvt. Ltd., IDA Pashamailaram, Patancheru Mandal, Medak dist.
21.	M/s. Alpex Internati onal Ltd (Formerly Global Bulk Drugs), Digwal village, Kohir Mandal, Medak dist.
22.	M/s. Arabindo Pharma Ltd, Unit-VI-A, Chitkul Village, Patancheru Mandal Medak dist.
23.	M/s. Avon Organics Ltd., Yawapur village, Sadasivpet Mandal, Medak dist.
24.	M/s. Biological E Ltd., IDA, Patancheru, Medak dist
25.	M/s. Covalent Laboratories Ltd., Gundlamanchnoor Village, Hatnoor Mandal, Medak dist.
26.	M/s. Inventa Chemicals Ltd., Unit-III, Pati Village, Patancheru Mandal Medak dist.
27.	M/s. ion Exchange (India) Ltd., IDA, Patancheru, Medak dist
28.	M/s. Jupiter Bio Science Ltd., Cheriya (V), Sangareddy (M), Medak dist
29.	M/s. Matrix Laboratories Ltd., Unit-VII, IDA Pashamailaram, Patancheru Mandal, Medak dist.
30.	M/s. MSN Laboratories Ltd., Rudraram Village, Patancheru Mandal, Medak dist.

(contd...)

(Table Appendix 4.1: contd...)

S. No	Name of the Industry and Address
31.	M/s. Nicholas Piramal India Ltd., (Formerly Global Bulk Drugs, Unit-II) Digwal village, Kohir Mandal, Medak dist.
32.	M/s. Venkataram Chemicals Ltd., Kardanoor Village, Patancheru Mandal, Medak dist.
33.	M/s. Biological E Ltd., Unit-II, IDA, Patanchru, Medak dist
34.	M/s. ITW India Ltd., (Steel Strapping Division), Rudraram Village, atancheru Mandal, Medak dist.
35.	M/s. MSN Pharmachem Pvt. Ltd., IDA Pashamailaram, Patancheru Mandal, Medak dist.
36.	M/s. Indian Chemphar Ltd., IDA, Patancheru, Medak dist
37.	M/s. Nicholas Piramal (I) Ltd., Unit-III (Formerly Canere Acti vities and Fine Chemicals Ltd.), Digwal village, Kohir Mandal, Medak dist.
38.	M/s. Arene Life Sciences Ltd., (Formerly Jayeinth Drugs and Pharmaceuti cals Pvt. Ltd, Phasell, IDA Pashamailaram, Patancheru Mandal, Medak dist.
39.	m/s. Virchow Petrochemicals Pvt. Ltd., (Formerly Ambhuja Petrochemicals) Plot No. 17A, IDA, Patancheru, Medak dist
40.	M/s. Reliance Cellulose Products Ltd., IDA, Patancheru, Medak dist
41.	M/s. Gulf Oil Corporation Ltd Phase-II, IDA Pashamailaram, Patancheru Mandal, Medak dist.
42.	M/s. Suven Life Sciences Ltd., (Formerly Suven Synthesis Ltd., M/s. Lordvin Labs Ltd), Phase-II, IDA Pashamailaram, Patancheu Mandal, Medak dist.
43.	M/s. SS. Organics Ltd., Aroor village, Sadasivpet Mandal, Medak dist.
44.	M/s. Dulichand Silk Mills Ltd., Unit-II, Sy. No. 305 and 306, Plot No. 4, Industrial Park, Indrakaran Village, Sangareddy Mandal, Medak dist.
45.	M/s. Parle Agro Pvt. Ltd. Plot No. 58–63, IDA Pashamailaram, Patancheru Mandal, Medak dist.
46.	M/s. SNF India Pvt. Ltd, Plot No. 19/B, Phase-II, IDA Patancheru, Medak dist.
47.	M/s. Sawaria Pipes Ltd, Sy. No. 257, Nandigama village, Patancheru Mandal, Medak dist.

Industries Under Polluti on Control Board Regional Office, Sanareddy[2]

48.	M/s. Harika Drugs Ltd., Gummadidala village, Jinnaram Mandal, Medak District
49.	M/s. Reddy's Laboratories Ltd., Unit-I IDA Bollaram, Jinnaram Mandal, Medak Dist
50.	M/s. Reddy's Laboratories Ltd., Unit-II, IDA Bollaram, Jinnaram Mandal, Medak Dist

(contd...)

(Table Appendix 4.1: contd...)

S. No	Name of the Industry and Address
51.	M/s. Reddy's Laboratories Ltd., Unit-III, IDA Bollaram, Jinnaram Mandal, Medak Dist
52.	M/s. Mylan Laboratories Ltd Unit-I (Formerly Matrix Laboratories Ltd., and earlier M/s. Vorin Laboratories Ltd., IDA Gaddapotharam, Jinnaram Mandal Medak Dist[3]
53.	M/s. Astrix Laboratories Ltd., (Formerly M/s. Matrix Laboratoires Ltd., Unit-II) IDA Gaddapotharam, Jinnaram Mandal, Medak Dist
54.	M/s. Glochem Industries Ltd., IDA Bollaram, Jinnaram Mandal, Medak Dist
55.	M/s. Pragathi Organics Ltd., IDA Bollaram, Jinnaram Mandal, Medak Dist
56.	M/s. Erythro Pharma Pvt. Ltd., IDA Gaddapotharam, Jinnaram Mandal, Medak Dist
57.	M/s. Lee Pharma Ltd., IDA Gaddapotharam, Jinnaram Mandal, Medak Dist
58.	M/s. Arabindo Pharma Ltd., Unit-VIII, IDA Gaddapotharam, Jinnaram Mandal, Medak Dist
59.	M/s. Yagmag Labs Pvt Ltd., IDA Gaddapotharam, Jinnaram Mandal, Medak Dist
60.	M/s. Senor Organics, IDA Gaddapotharam, Jinnaram Mandal, Medak Dist
61.	M/s. Virupaksha Organics Pvt., Ltd., IDA Gaddapotharam, Jinnaram Mandal, Medak Dist
62.	M/s. Symed Labs Pvt. Ltd, Bonthapally, Jinnaram Mandal, Medak Dist
63.	M/s. Fleming Laboratories Ltd., Nawabpet village, Shivampet Mandal, Medak Dist
64.	M/s. Sai Advanti um Pharma Ltd., (Formerly Prasad's Drugs Ltd), IDA Bollaram, Jinnaram Mandal, Medak Dist
65.	M/s. Plant Organics Ltd., IDA Bollaram, Jinnaram Mandal, Medak Dist
66.	M/s. Saraca Laboratories Ltd., IDA Gaddapotharam, Jinnaram Mandal, Medak Dist
67.	M/s. Apex Drugs and Intermediaries Pvt., Ltd., IDA Gaddapotharam, Jinnaram Mandal, Medak Dist
68.	M/s. Hartex Rubbers Ltd., IDA Bollaram, Jinnaram Mandal, Medak Dist
69.	M/s. Island Veer Chemic Pvt. Ltd, IDA Bollaram, Jinnaram Mandal, Medak Dist
70.	M/s. Kalvik Laboratories Pvt., Ltd., IDA Bollaram, Jinnaram Mandal, Medak Dist
71.	M/s. Kekule Pharma Ltd., (Formerly Kekule Chemicals Pvt., Ltd), IDA Khazipally, Jinnaram Mandal, Medak Dist

(contd...)

(Table Appendix 4.1: contd...)

S. No	Name of the Industry and Address
72.	M/s. Neo Medichem Pvt. Ltd, Bonthapally, Jinnaram Mandal, Medak Dist
73.	M/s. Gayathri Drugs Pvt. Ltd., Bonthapally, Jinnaram Mandal, Medak Dist
74.	M/s. Sigachi Laoratories Ltd., Bonthapally, Jinnaram Mandal, Medak Dist
75.	M/s. Vayajayanthi Drugs Pvt., Ltd., Bonthapally, Jinnaram Mandal, Medak Dist
76.	M/s. Biotech Pharma Ltd., IDA Gaddapotharam, Jinnaram Mandal, Medak Dist
77.	M/s. sheethal Chemicals Pvt. Ltd., IDA Bollaram, Jinnaram Mandal, Medak Dist
78.	M/s. Techbond Laboratories Pvt. Ltd., Anantharam Village, Jinnaram Mandal, Medak Dist
79.	M/s. Zyden Gentec Ltd., (Formerly M/s. Sree Venkateshwara Medichem Labs Pvt. Ltd.), IDA Bollaram, Jinnaram Mandal, Medak Dist
80.	M/s. Prabhava Organics Pvt. Ltd., IDA Bollaram, Jinnaram Mandal, Medak Dist
81.	M/s. Enpiar Pharma Pvt. Ltd., IDA Bollaram, Jinnaram Mandal, Medak Dist
82.	M/s. Hygro Chemicals harmatek Pvt. Ltd., IDA Bollaram, Jinnaram Mandal, Medak Dist
83.	M/s. Parsin Chemicals Ltd., Anrich Industrial Estate, IDA Bollaram, Jinnaram Mandal, Medak Dist
84.	M/s. Twin Star Laboratories Ltd., Bonthapally, Jinnaram Mandal, Medak Dist
85.	M/s. Warner Laboratories Ltd., Laxmakkapally village, Mulug Mandal, Medak Dist
86.	M/s. Konar Organics Ltd., IDA Khazipally, Jinnaram Mandal, Medak Dist
87.	M/s. Mylan Laboratories Ltd (Formerly Matrix Laboratories Ltd., (R&D), Anrich Industrial Estate, Bollaram Village, Jinnaram Mandal, Medak Dist.
88.	M/s. Rampex Labs Pvt. Ltd., IDA Bollaram, Jinnaram Mandal, Medak Dist
89.	M/s. Yenkey Drugs and Pharmaeuti cals Ltd (Formerly known as M/s. Yenkey Medico Drugs Pvt. Ltd) Sy. No. 14, IDA Gaddapotharam, Jinnaram Mandal, Medak Dist
90.	M/s. Sibra Pharmaceuti cals Ltd, (Formerly known as M/s. Paks Veterinary Drugs Mfg. Co. Ltd) Sy. No. 3–72, IDA Gaddapotharam, Jinnaram Mandal, Medak Dist
91.	M/s. Neuland Laboratories Ltd., (R&D Center), Bonthapally, Jinnaram Mandal, Medak Dist

(contd...)

(Table Appendix 4.1: contd...)

S. No	Name of the Industry and Address
92.	M/s. Neuland Laboratories Ltd., Bonthapally, Jinnaram Mandal, Medak Dist
93.	M/s. Granules India Ltd., Bonthapally, Jinnaram Mandal, Medak Dist
94.	M/s. Virchow Drugs Pvt. Ltd., Bonthapally, Jinnaram Mandal, Medak Dist
95.	M/s. Mylan Laboratories Ltd Unit-VI (Formerly Matrix Laboratories Ltd., Unit-VI, earlier Fine Drugs and Chemicals Ltd.,) IDA Gaddapotharam, Jinnaram Mandal, Medak Dist.
96.	M/s. TPS Laboratories Pvt. Ltd., IDA Gaddapotharam, Jinnaram Mandal, Medak Dist
97.	M/s. Divis Pharmaceuti cals Pvt. Ltd., IDA Gaddapotharam, Jinnaram Mandal, Medak Dist
98.	M/s. Siris Crop Science Ltd, Gummadidala village, Jinnaram Mandal, Medak Dist
99.	M/s. KRS Pharmaceuti cals Pvt. Ltd., IDA Gaddapotharam, Jinnaram Mandal, Medak Dist
100.	M/s. Sri Krishna Drugs Ltd., (M/s. Arandy Laboratories Ltd.), IDA Bollaram, Jinnaram Mandal, Medak Dist
101.	M/s. Prudenti al Pharmaceuti cals Ltd., IDA Bollaram, Jinnaram Mandal, Medak Dist

1. Available at www.oecd.org/dataoecd/39/27/37838061.pdf
2. Source: http://www.saiindia.gov.in/cag/ap-2008-civil-chapter-3
3. Source: http://www.moef.nic.in/downloads/public.../Roadmap-Mgmt-Waste.pdf
4. See Forum for Better Hyderabad—Annual Report for 2008-09 at: www.hyderabadgreens.org/images/Annual%20Number08-09.pdf
5. http://ramkyenviroengineers.com/PressRoom.html

5 TRIPS Flexibilities and Access to Patented Medicines in India

Narayanan Lalitha

The flexibilities contained in the TRIPS Agreement are intended to improve access to patented medicines. Especially in developing countries like India, the effectiveness of flexibilities depends on how they are incorporated into national legislation. Countries in which the pharmaceutical industry is a leading or major contributor to innovations naturally seek maximum gain from the patent status of innovations and restrict opportunities for the exploitation of flexibilities. In contrast, countries that have a vibrant generics industry operating in domestic and export markets seek to ensure that adhering to TRIPS does not jeopardise the interests of this industry or its consumers. Thus, in designing patent legislation, developing countries should adopt a pro-competitive strategy tilted towards 'second comers' rather than distant patentees.

Known as the 'pharmacy of the third world', India produces generics of many pre-1995 molecules. In the post-2005 era this advantage seems to have been weakened since, firstly, new drugs patented since 2005 cannot be produced through reverse engineering and, secondly, patent protection can be sought for improvements to, or new processes introduced into, existing pre-1995 molecules. This may have a serious impact on access to affordable medicines. For instance, second-line anti-retroviral drugs (ARVs) under patent would be twenty-six times costlier in developing countries than first-line ARVs available as generics (Grace 2005: 31). This is a cause for concern in India, which has the second largest population of people living with HIV/AIDS. Structural changes—in the form of mergers and acquisitions, and strategic sales alliances—may preclude measures to adopt TRIPS flexibilities. Also, the experiences of countries that have adopted free trade agreements (Guennif and Lalitha 2007) suggest that adopting TRIPS along with other measures actually curtails the ability of these countries to take advantage of flexibilities. This chapter focuses on the flexibilities adopted by India and concludes with several options that would better enable India to gain access to new medicines in the future.

USE OF TRIPS FLEXIBILITIES

Having recognised that developing countries would require more time than developed countries to introduce patents for pharmaceutical products, TRIPS Article 65.4 provided for a transition period with specific time limits. Between 1995 and 2000 member countries were required to demonstrate minimum compliance in respect of patentability: twenty-year patent protection for products from the time of submitting an application, and protection for products and processes in all technological fields.

Countries that had not previously provided product patents in the field of agro chemicals and pharmaceuticals were required to do so over the period 2000–04. This also meant establishing the machinery for receiving patent applications and the granting of exclusive marketing rights (EMR) for those applications that had already received patent and marketing approval in another WTO country, as per Article 70.8. India adhered to the required minimum compliance within the transition period and amended its national patent laws to provide for access to medicines, as illustrated below.

EXEMPTIONS FROM PATENTABILITY

Article 27.1 makes it clear that the criteria for patentability are novelty, inventive step and industrial applicability, yet the terms 'novelty' and 'inventive step' are not defined. Advantageously, they are left for interpretation under national laws. In developing and least developed countries it is important that the scope of patentability is in line with the country's public health policies and that governments are aware that unduly expanding the concept of patentability distorts competition and reduces access to medicines (Correa 2007).

As the pipeline for new drug has begun to dry up and new molecules fail Stage 3 clinical trials (Grabowski2008), the number of new molecules approved by the US Food and Drug Administration (FDA) has fallen significantly: to twenty-one (fifteen new chemical entities (NCEs) and six new biologicals) in 2010, below the twenty-four and twenty-five NCEs approved in 2008 and 2009 respectively (Mullard 2011).[1] Pharmaceutical companies are therefore increasingly looking for ways to extend patent protection and build on patents already in use. This may take the form of incremental innovations that could lead to better therapeutic effectiveness than the original innovation and wider consumer acceptance (WHO 2006), which makes claims of 'ever greening' more difficult to sustain.

T.C. James (2009) argues that critics of Section 3(d) of the Indian Patents Act 1970 generally do not mention Section 54, which provides for additions to existing patents when improvement and new uses of an existing innovation can be demonstrated. The reason that multinational corporations prefer Section 3(d) over Section 54 is that the former extends the life of the patent while under the latter the term of the additional patent, together with that of the main patent, ends on the same day. Keeping a public health perspective in mind, the Indian government has restricted patentability to NCEs alone, and has defined those inventions that are not patentable under Sections 3 and 4 of the Act. Although controversial, Section 3(d) was included to ensure that secondary patents would not be granted unless they were therapeutically effective, thus preventing granting of patents to 'me too' inventions. Similarly, India allows new patents subject to the condition that they are not merely a discovery of a new property or new use of a known product.

Realising that the patentability of second indications extends protection to cases where no new products have been developed, several countries have rejected patent claims over such innovations

(Wanis 2010; Correa 2007). In the United States and the European Union, which offer protection on second indications, data exclusivity is also provided. Many developing countries have not restricted patentability on new use of known products. Of the forty-nine countries reviewed by Musungu and Oh (2005), only 20 per cent excluded the second indication criterion. If a provision like Section 3(d) of the Indian Patents Act is not available, generics producers cannot count on producing generics of the molecules patented before 1995 because minor variations are likely to result in new patent claims, which stalls the entry of generics.

Although India does not (unlike Brazil,[2] which used to) seek prior consent from its health ministry before approval of a drug-related patent, it has, through Section 25, introduced checks in the form of pre- and post-grant opposition to patent applications. A written pre-grant opposition—which satisfies the eleven grounds specified in the Patents Act—can be lodged by anyone, free of charge without their having to fill out a form. The application must be completed within six months of publication by the patent controller. Post-grant opposition, however, is restricted to the category of 'person interested'[3] and must be submitted within a year from the date of publication of a patent having been granted. Except for the period 2006–08, more than one hundred pre-grant oppositions have been sought annually (see Table 5.1). In no one year, however, has the percentage exceeded one per cent. Filing pre-grant opposition requires objectors to have sufficient technical expertise to monitor published patent applications and analyse the relevant precedents on which to base objections; to date, effective pre-grant opposition has

Table 5.1: Number of Pre-grant Patent Oppositions during 2005–10

Year	Number of published applications	Number of pre-grant oppositions
2005–06	23,398	156 (0.66%)
2006–07	19,310	44 (0.23%)
2007–08	60,506	64 (0.10%)
2008–09	40,749	153 (0.37%)
2009–10	34,305	103 (0.30%)

Source: Government of India (2010b: 11)

only come from pharmaceutical companies, and a few civil groups assisted by people with expert knowledge of patent application processes. The small number of pre-grant oppositions could also be interpreted as, perhaps there were other applications that did not match the capable generics manufacturers' business interests and hence were not opposed.

The patent ordinance introduced in December 2004 to meet India's commitment to introduce TRIPS-compliant legislation by 1 January 2005 excluded grounds for pre-grant opposition, but this was reinstated in the third amendment of the Patents Act (Grace 2005). Both Section 3(d) and pre-grant opposition have proven useful for the generics pharmaceutical industry.[4] In 2009–10, of the 103 pre-grant oppositions, thirty-two were taken further, and of a meager total of twenty-eight post-grant oppositions, only four were pursued (Government of India 2010b). Successful use of pre-grant opposition has resulted in the exclusion of patents for some lifesaving drugs. Some of the controversial rejections are discussed below.

The Case of Gleevac

During the transitional period, Novartis was granted EMR in India for Gleevac (imatinib mesylate), which is used to treat chronic myeloid leukaemia. An infringement case against the nine generic companies that produced Gleevac for the domestic market[5] by Novartis resulted in different verdicts in two courts. The Madras High Court ordered six of the companies to stop the manufacture, sale, marketing and export of imatinib mesylate, while the Mumbai High Court refused to provide an interim injunction against three of the generics manufacturers.[6]

Based on the pre-grant opposition filed against Novartis by the generics manufacturers, in 2006 the Chennai patent office rejected Novartis's application. One of the reasons for the rejection of the patent was based on Section 3(d), which stated that Gleevac lacked novelty and inventive step, and also failed to show increased efficacy compared to the earlier form of imatinib, a pre-1995 molecule.

Novartis's counter-argument was that the use of the expressions 'enhancement of known efficacy' and 'differ significantly in properties with regard to efficacy' without accompanying guidelines specifying their scope makes Section 3(d) ambiguous and grants the patent controller absolute discretion (Banerjee and Roy 2009). The case was transferred from Madras High Court to the Intellectual Property Appellate Board (IPAB). The IPAB also held that Novartis was not entitled to a patent on imatinib mesylate, as the product did not meet the requirement of increased therapeutic efficacy. Novartis then has appealed this decision in the Supreme Court of India. At the time of writing, the case is still pending.

The Case of Valganciclovir

Valganciclovir, used for organ transplants and eye infections in AIDS patients, is sold by the innovator Roche as Valcyte, and by CIPLA as Valcept. The patent office in Chennai granted a patent to Roche for this product in 2007, but this was challenged by the Lawyers Collective, an Indian NGO, which filed a pre-grant opposition (allegedly not followed up by the patent office). According to the Lawyers Collective, Valcyte is a pre-1995 molecule that lacks inventive step and hence should not have been granted a patent. While the Madras High Court remanded the case back to the Chennai patent office, Roche decided to appeal to the Supreme Court. Meanwhile, CIPLA launched its generic version in 2008, which was challenged by Roche in the Mumbai High Court, with Roche alleging patent infringement and trademark violation. In March 2009, the Supreme Court ruled in favor of Roche, but asked Roche not to pursue the patent violation case against CIPLA until the Chennai patent office had re-examined the case.

In May 2010, the patent office in Chennai refused the patent on valganciclovir on the grounds that the ester, gancyclovir, was already on the market and being administered intravenously for HIV infections and hence did not meet the criteria of patentability. Owing to problems with intravenous administration, an oral dosage with increased bio-availability was developed from the L-valinate ester of gancyclovir, a combination with hydrocholoric acid, resulting in valgancyclovir hydrocholoride (Roche's Valcyte).

Two interesting aspects of these cases are the vigilance of the Lawyers Collective, which resulted in revocation of the patent, and the court's verdict regarding the lack of inventive step, as compared to the IPAB's contentious decision about Gleevac's lack of therapeutic efficacy (Spicy IP blogspot 2005).

The Case of Tenofovir

In September 2009, the patent office in New Delhi refused a patent, on the grounds of evergreening, for the Aids drug Tenofovir Disoproxil Fumarate (TDF) filed by US company Gilead Sciences (*Business Standard* 2009). This drug was also refused patent in the United States, but the company's strategy before the award decision in India is worth noting. Tenofovir is highly recommended by the WHO for the treatment of HIV/AIDS. In developing countries, Gilead's patent-protected Tenofovir sold for $5,718 per patient, per year. In 2007 Gilead entered into an agreement with eleven Indian companies to manufacture and sell Tenofovir in ninety-five countries, using Gilead's technology. Local producers could produce Tenofovir subject to payment of royalties, and on the condition that the drug would not be sold in certain countries, for example, Brazil and China (IDMA 2009). Licensed sellers of Tenofovir were also required to buy the active ingredients from Gilead's affiliated licensed suppliers. Concerned by these restrictive clauses, CIPLA refused Gilead's licensing offer and filed a pre-grant opposition on the grounds of evergreening and that granting the patent would lead to non-affordability of the drug worldwide (International drugmart.com 2010). As a pre-existing molecule—TDF is created by the addition of a salt (fumaric acid) to the existing compound, tenofovir disproxil—Tenofovir should not have been eligible for patent. Civil society groups had also filed pre-grant oppositions, joined for the first time by a foreign advocacy group—the Brazilian Interdisciplinary AIDS Association—since India's granting of a patent would have affected access to Tenofovir in Brazil as well. In September 2009 the Delhi patent office refused the patent on Tenofovir, which meant that consumers could purchase the generic version at approximately $700 a year.

Although the cases highlighted here demonstrate that Section 3(d) has been used effectively, the drawback is that 'it puts much of the onus on the patent examiners (through pre-grant oppositions) or through courts' (Gehl 2006: 713). Further, of great concern is the low number of patents granted by Indian patent offices, which appears to relate to a shortage of examiners, shown in Tables 5.2 and 5.3 (Government of India 2010b). In 2005–06 and 2009–10, 10 per cent of total patent applications were related to pharmaceuticals (Government of India 2010b: 34). Between 2004 and 2009 fifty-five patent examiners left the organisation, while in January 2009 forty-seven became assistant controllers—which explains the reduction in the number of patent applications examined and granted in 2009–10, arguably putting the remaining examiners under enormous pressure (Government of India 2010b: 6). The possibility of lapses cannot be ruled out, particularly regarding examination of therapeutic efficacy claims; as Gopakumar (2010a)

Table 5.2: Status of Patent Applications in India 2003–10

	2003–04	2004–05	2005–06	2006–07	2007–08	2008–09	2009–10
Filed	12,613	17,466	24,505	28,940	35,218	36,812	34,287
Examined	10,709	14,813	11,569	14,119	11,751	10,296	6069
Granted	2469	1911	4320	7539	15,316	16,061	6168

Source: Government of India(2010b: 6)

Table 5.3: Technical Field of Specialization of Working Examiners as on 31 March 2010.

Broad field of specialisation	Number of examiners
Biochemistry	5
Biotechnology	9
Chemistry	20
Civil engineering	2
Computer science	6
Electrical and electronics engineering	13
Metallurgy	2
Mechanical engineering	6
Physics	3
Microbiology	12
Textile engineering	2
Total	80

Source: Government of India (2010b: 26)

points out, a minor amendment can readily satisfy the requirement of 'enhancement of efficacy'. Since patent offices, are not equipped with labs to examine whether the properties of claimed inventions differ significantly with regard to efficacy, there is ample scope for evergreening, which may lead to lengthy litigation. Further, the pre-grant opposition cases highlighted above represent cases where generics manufacturers and civil society groups were confident about the nature of the patent and their claims. More significantly, the granting of these patents would have affected the interests of generics manufacturers.

Automatic Licences

While drugs patented before 1995 can continue to be produced by the domestic industry, production of those patented since 2005 is subject to the innovator's approval. Hence the Indian government has had to look for a strategy, in the form of Section 11A(7), for drug applications that were filed during the transition period but for which production by the Indian pharmaceutical industry had already commenced. Section 11A(7) states

provided also that after a patent is granted in respect of applications made under sub-section (2) of section 5, the patent holder shall only be entitled to receive reasonable royalty from such enterprises which have made significant investment and were producing and marketing the concerned product prior to 1.1.2005 and which continue to manufacture the product covered by the patent on the date of grant of the patent, and no infringement proceedings shall be instituted against such enterprises.

This important provision has enabled the generics industry to continue production of these drugs. Potential conflicts can arise, however, in interpreting the terms 'significant investment' and 'reasonable royalty'.

Gopakumar's analysis (2010b) shows that of the 301 new molecular entities (NMEs) approved by the US FDA between 1995 and 2004, the Central Drug Standards Control Organisation of India (CDSCO), under the Section 11A clause, provided approval for the manufacture of 128 generic versions of those entities. His analysis

Table 5.4: NMES and Implication for Access
to Medicines in five Major Diseases.

Disease	No of FDA approved NME 1995–2004	No of NMEs invented prior to 1995	Number of generics manufacturers	Number of generics manufacturers with 11A immunity
Diabetes	13	12	9	9
Hyper tension	17	13	13	6
Cardiovascular	9	9	5	5
Cancer	33	26	22	16
HIV/AIDS	15	14	12	5

Source: Compiled from information in Section VI of Gopakumar (2010b)

of NMEs for five major diseases, approved in the United States and for which marketing approval in India was sought, demonstrates that Section 11A provides better access to medicines than any other flexibility option (see Table 5.4).

Compulsory Licensing

A compulsory licence—also referred to as a non-voluntary licence—is a very useful tool. Under certain circumstances and subject to procedural safeguards, it provides a third party with the right to manufacture a patented product without the authorisation of the patent holder. While Article 31 of the TRIPS Agreement notes the circumstances under which a compulsory licence can be used, member countries can also introduce clauses into their own national legislation that give them wider opportunities. Countries which had not analysed the impact of the different TRIPS' clauses would end up adopting the TRIPS text in to their national law which could be detrimental to the access to medicines. For example, by adding the clause, 'second invention must show significant technical progress and be of technical and economic importance compared to the first invention' (Kongolo 2004: 191), Egypt has placed more hurdles in utilizing compulsory licensing and generics production.

The experience of compulsory licensing in several African, Asian and developed countries has been the subject of detailed analysis (Bartelt 2003; Varella 2004;Musungu and Oh 2005; Oh 2006, Ling 2006; Chokevivat 2007) showing that in a majority of cases—and particularly in African countries—it has been used to gain access to anti-retroviral drugs. The United States and Canada have both used the compulsory licensing option to gain access to non-pharmaceutical and pharmaceutical products to counteract anti-competitive tendencies.

Accessing compulsory licensing, however, is not easy, as is evident in the experiences of South Africa and Brazil (Varella 2004), and in Malaysia, where pressure tactics aimed at preventing the use of compulsory licensing have been adopted including the withdrawal of production facilities, reduction of foreign direct investment and suing of governments. Even if a compulsory licence is obtained, successful production and supply requires access to the active pharmaceutical ingredients and the technology needed to manufacture the patented drug. Compulsory licensing is discouraged by innovator companies since a product produced under this option equips the licencee with the technology and know-how, thus enabling the first mover to launch a generic version of the drug after the patent expires.

Although TRIPS Article 31 allows for production of the patented invention 'without the authorization of the right holder', concern over the provision that 'any such use shall be authorized predominantly for the supply of the domestic market of the member authorizing such use', has resulted in adoption of Paragraph 6 of the 2001 Doha Declaration. Paragraph 6 recognises the concerns of those WTO members who are unable to obtain compulsory licences because of lack of or inadequate manufacturing facilities.

In view of this, a decision was made in 2003 and adopted in the form of waiver of Article 31(f) in December 2005. According to this waiver, a country can issue a compulsory licence on the basis of public health need, either for domestic use or for export. Once two-thirds of member countries have formally accepted this amendment, it will be incorporated into the TRIPS Agreement and replace the 2003 waiver. The permanent amendment will allow any member country to export pharmaceutical products made under compulsory licensing and will require countries to change their own national laws. The deadline for ratifying the change was first extended from 31 December 2009 to 31 December 2011 and now been extended further to 31 December 2013 (WTO 2011).

Like most countries, India provides for compulsory licensing in its patent amendments. As per Section 84 of the Patents (Amendment) Act 2005, any interested person can seek a compulsory licence at any time after the expiration of three years from the date of grant of a patent, on the following grounds:

that reasonable requirements of the public with respect to the patented invention have not been satisfied

the patented invention is not available to the public at a reasonably affordable price

the patented invention is not produced in the territory of India.

Section 91 of the Act provides for the issue of compulsory licences for related patents, while Section 92 provides for the export of patented pharmaceutical products under exceptional circumstances and Section 100 allows the issue of compulsory licence for government purposes. In the wake of the Doha Declaration, the Patents (Amendment) Act 2005 introduced a new provision under Section 92A for the grant of a compulsory licence for the export of patented pharmaceutical products[7] to countries without manufacturing facilities.

Under Sections 84 and 91, compulsory licences can only be issued by the patent controller three years after the granting of a patent. Under Section 92, the controller can issue a compulsory licence only after the government issues a notification, and under Section 92A, the controller can only act after the importing country has issued a CL (Government of India 2010b; Government of India 2010c).[8] The industry's inability to produce the product and lack of a market may be among the reasons for limited use having been made of Section 84.

In August 2011, Natco Pharma filed an application for a compulsory licence—the first in India for the drug Nexavar, produced by Bayer—on the grounds that Nexavar was not manufactured in India, cost $51 per tablet, amounting to $6150 for a month's course, and was available only in a few pharmacies in particular metropolitan cities. As Nexavar reaches only 1 per cent of patients, 99 per cent face death because the drug is unaffordable (BioSpectrumAsia Edition 2011). In a sensational decision, the patent controller granted India's first compulsory licence to Natco Pharma in March 2012, under the Section 84 of Indian Patents (Amendment) Act 2005. Natco submitted evidences to the fact that Nexavar was available to only 2 per cent of the patients, the prices were unaffordable and the product was not worked in India. In return of the compulsory licence, Natco would make the drug available at Rs 8,880 and pay a royalty at the rate of 6 per cent of the sales to Bayer. Though this is a land mark decision that paves the way for access to expensive patented medicines, there are hurdles on the way. Bayer has already appealed against the order in the higher courts and it is possible that the compulsory licence order is reversed in favour of Bayer. While that may or may not happen, the conditions of the patent controller for Natco to utilize the compulsory licence is not clear. The patent controller has ordered that (1) Natco's product has to be distinctively different than Bayer's and (2) Bayer shall provide no legal, regulatory, medical, technical, manufacturing, sales, marketing or any other support to licencees, which are not specified in the Patents Amendment Act (Srinivasan, 2012). While the first condition could be a precaution that the product produced under compulsory licence looks different than the innvator's packaging, the second clause if it is uniformly made applicable for all the subsequent compulsory licences could prove to be problematic. Because Nexavar is a special case, where Natco already has the technology to produce both the active pharmaceutical ingredient and the formulation. But if this class is enforced in cases where the licencee does not have the knowhow, then the licencee has only the licence in paper and can not exploit the patent at all.

India is yet to derive the full benefit of the compulsory licensing provisions, that leaves room for interpretations to suit the patent holder (Chaudhuri 2005; Chaudhuri 2010; Gopakumar 2010a). The 'three year patent cooling period' stipulated in Section 84, is unwarranted as it is a requirement under the Paris Convention, not under TRIPS (Grace 2005). Chaudhuri (2005: 91) observes that the wording of the grounds for granting compulsory licences in Section 84 is not amenable to easy interpretation and is not operationally useful and the procedure specified is cumbrous. The procedure is open-ended, without any time limit imposed for the grant of the compulsory licences.

Section 86 of the Patents Act goes a step further, stating that if the

controller is satisfied that the time which has elapsed since the sealing of the patent has for any reason been insufficient to enable the invention to be worked on a commercial scale to an adequate extent or to enable the invention to be so worked to the fullest extent that is reasonably practicable, he may by order, adjourn the further hearing of the application for such period not exceeding twelve months in the aggregate as appears to him to be sufficient for the invention to be so worked. (Patents Act 1970, 2010: 53).

Gopakumar (2010a) observes that governments' use of CLs has been restricted to non-commercial use. Consequently, when disputes arise it is likely that courts will restrict the sale of the medicines to public sector hospitals only.

Payment of royalties for the use of a compulsory licence is another important issue. Under Section 90, the controller is responsible for ensuring that the royalty takes into account any expenditure incurred by the patentee in making or developing the invention, or obtaining a patent and keeping it in force, together with other relevant factors. This clause could severely constrain research, and subsequent patents, particularly if they depend on an earlier patent, but also in the so-called automatic licence cases. In the case of government use of a patent, however, Section 100(3) states that the 'patentee shall be paid not more than adequate remuneration in the circumstances of each case, taking into account the economic value of the use the patent' (The Patents Act, 1970, 2010: 59).

Even if these uncertainties about compulsory licensing are sorted out, very few firms are likely to come forward to produce drugs under Section 92A (Gehl 2006; Basheer 2007) because of the smaller returns from production on this basis, as compared to those expected from the sizeable investments firms usually make to produce these drugs. The returns might also be smaller because compulsory licensing would be focused on exports to poorer countries that have an inadequate manufacturing base.

Exceptions to Patent Rights

TRIPS Article 30 provides limited exceptions to the exclusive rights of the patent holder in certain cases. Exceptions should not unreasonably conflict with the normal exploitation of the patent or affect the legitimate interests of the patent owner, and should take into account the legitimate interests of third parties. The much emphasised common exceptions are:

the early work done on innovations prior to their approval by a regulatory authority
research use and individual prescriptions
parallel importation.

Section 47 stipulates that, during the protection period, a patented invention can be used purely for experimental research or for teaching purposes.

Patent Linkage

Most countries provide exceptions for research and the early working of innovations, also referred to as Bolar provisions. It is notable that developing countries with production capacity such as India, Thailand and Malaysia have provided the early working of patented innovations. Section 107A (The Patents Act 1970: 65) states that

any act of making, constructing, using, selling or importing a patented invention solely for uses reasonably related to the development and submission of information required under any law for the time being in force in India, or in a country other than India that regulates the manufacture, construction, use, sale or import of any product

would not be considered an infringement. During the period of patent protection, generics manufacturers can develop the process and have them ready to manufacture and enter the market when the patent expires.

Patent linkage prevalent in China, Canada and the United States allows innovator companies to delay the entry of generics,. Through the Section 107A provision, India has effectively de-linked the patent and the marketing approval process for generics.

Presently two separate regulatory authorities operate in India, namely, patent offices, which grant patents, and the Drug Controller General of India (DCGI), where marketing approval is given. Section 107A has provided relief to CIPLA, a major Indian generics producer, in a case filed by, Bayer in the Delhi High Court against the Union of India, DCGI and CIPLA for granting marketing approval for the generic version of Sorefenib Tosylate, on which Bayer has a valid patent until 2020. Sorefenib Tosylate is used for treatment in kidney cancer and costs approximately $5937.5 for a month's supply of 120 tablets. Bayer claimed that the DCGI should consider the patent status of Sorefenib Tosylate before granting approval to any generics company, which resulted in the court ordering an interim injunction stopping the DCGI from granting approval to CIPLA. The Cancer Patients Aids Association intervened; pointing out that because of the High Court's order the DCGI had ceased accepting applications for marketing approval. The court then altered its interim injunction to refer only to Sorefenib Tosylate. In August 2009, the Delhi High Court rejected Bayer's appeal and refused to sanction patent linkage, which enabled CIPLA to pursue the development of a generic version of Sorefenib Tosylate.

Parallel Imports

Parallel imports incorporate the 'first sale doctrine' wherein a patent holder loses their right over a sale, import and resale of a patented product once the first authorised sale has been made. The rationale is that the patent holder has already been rewarded through the first sale and should not be allowed to profit repeatedly on the same good by controlling its use, resale or distribution (Basheer and Kochupillai 2008). The exhaustion of rights may be national, regional or international.[9] India, Taiwan, Japan, New Zealand and Australia recognise the principle of international exhaustion (Basheer and Kochupillai 2008). International exhaustion can be an important tool, as countries can take advantage of the differences in the prices prevailing in different international markets for the same patented product. In India, the 2002 amendment had permitted importation of patented products from the person authorised by the patentee to sell or distribute the product, omitting the option of importing drugs produced under compulsory licence. This omission was corrected in the 2005 amendment, which stated that importation could occur via a person duly authorised to produce and sell or distribute the product. However, clarity of the terms used is still required: 'In the strict sense, it means parallel importation cannot be done from a person, who is legally authorized only to sell and not to produce' (Gopakumar 2010a: 344).

Basheer (2007) notes that if production facilities are established by Indian generics manufacturers in Bangladesh (which has until 2016 to adopt product patents) they could legally produce patented medicines and India could import them under the parallel import clause. Here again, procedural measures are needed to guard against possible abuse of the provision to take advantage of differential pricing, and a parallel 'grey market' of patented products.

Prices

It has been estimated that 10 to 15 per cent of drugs are affected by patents (Grace 2005), yet the TRIPS Agreement does not prevent developing countries from putting a ceiling on the price of patented drugs. In India, where there are differences even in the prices for regulated generic drugs (GOI 2010d), an agency like the Patented Medicines Price Review Board of Canada, which controls and reviews the prices of patented drugs, should be considered (Lalitha 2005).

Although the presence of generics offers substantial price reductions, such as for Gleevac, Valganciclovir and Tenofovir, prices remain beyond the reach of many poor consumers. India, therefore, must think seriously about revising its essential drugs list to include newer drugs, and bring these drugs under strict price control.

Some clauses in the bilateral trade agreements into which India is presently venturing, such as with the European Union, may create obstacles (see Bhardwaj in this volume). For instance, under the investor-state arbitration mechanism clause in that agreement, if implemented, the Indian government can be sued for putting price controls on patented products produced by EU-based companies (MSF 2011a). Given that multinationals from the United States, Germany and Switzerland (that also have production facilities in EU countries) dominate the patents filed and granted in India (Gopakumar 2010b), the investor-state arbitration mechanism would work against India's interests, preventing the imposition of price ceilings.

Data Exclusivity

TRIPS Article 39.3 requires member countries to provide protection for undisclosed information or test data submitted for approval against 'unfair commercial use'. The United States and the European Union have interpreted this clause as providing for data exclusivity, meaning regulators cannot rely on protected data to provide approval for similar products. Provision of data exclusivity, as well as the patent term, would delay competition as many countries provide data protection from the time a product is introduced into the market. A drug patent granted in 2010 would expire in 2030; supposing a product entered the market in 2025, a ten-year data exclusivity would result in monopoly for the product until 2035.

The United States offers five years of data protection for pharmaceuticals, a further three years for new indications of existing drugs, ten years for agro chemicals and seven years for orphan drugs. The European Union offers ten years for both pharmaceuticals and agro chemicals, and one extra year for new indications of existing drugs. Canada offers protection for eight years, while Japan and China offer six years. India protects agrochemical-related test data for three years but pharmaceutical data are not protected (Government of India 2007). Although most developing and least developed countries refrain from providing data exclusivity, those that have negotiated FTAs with the United States have been required to provide data exclusivity, broadening the scope of protection and restricted access to medicine (Cullen 2007). In its 2006 report, the Commission on Intellectual Property Rights, Innovation and Public Health (WHO 2006: 144) recommends that

A public health justification should be required for data protection rules going beyond what is required by the TRIPS Agreement. There is unlikely to be such a justification in markets with limited ability to pay and little innovative capacity. Thus, developing countries should not impose restrictions for the use of or reliance on such data, in ways that would exclude fair competition or impede the use of flexibilities built into TRIPS.

The FTAs that India has negotiated or is currently negotiating loom as an impending threat to access to medicines. Researchers who have analysed the FTAs between the United States and countries such as Thailand, Jordan and Morocco discuss the 'TRIPS plus' nature of the conditions that effectively thwart the countries' ability to provide access to patented medicines (Kuanpoth 2006; Rossi, 2006; Roffe and Spennemann 2006; Guennif and Lalitha 2007), and indicate the introduction of the data exclusivity clause through the FTAs. Fortunately India has announced in the 'UN high level meeting on HIV/AIDS that it will not accept data exclusivity as part of the FTA currently being negotiated with the EU. This announcement at the AIDS summit now means that both EU and India have officially confirmed data exclusivity will not be part of the FTA text'.[10]

FUTURE OPTIONS

An analysis referred to in James (2009) points out that of all the new drugs analysed between 1981 and 2000, 63.23 per cent were superfluous and did not add to the clinical possibilities offered by other products. Section 3(d) places enormous responsibility on patents offices and the courts, yet patents offices appear severely stressed in present circumstances. In 2009–10, only twenty examiners were available to examine 3,070 drug applications (Government of India

2010b: 35). In other words, each examiner had 153.5 applications to attend to. Assuming they worked all year, examiners would have had 2.4 days to spend on each application. It needs to be borne in mind that examining a patent application under the Section 3(d) requires case-by-case examination of the patent application. Thorough scrutiny would also help to ensure that generics manufacturers were able to continue under the Section 11A clause.

The discussion in this chapter shows that providing for measures that facilitate access to medicines depends on individual governments' foresightedness. The presence of a vibrant domestic pharmaceutical industry also helps in visualising the shape of things to come. According to the available information, there are 4,198 working patents in India (Government of India 2010b: 25). The Indian Ministry for Health should undertake an enquiry to establish the number of granted pharmaceutical patents and working patents. This data should be analysed for price, availability of generics and how patents match with the demand for newer drugs, following which the government could apply for compulsory licensing under the Indian territorial clause or affordability criterion. The territorial clause, which has been used a number of times in Thailand, should similarly be employed in India. Importantly, the decision on the Nexavar compulsory licence could open the floodgates for compulsory licensing of other cancer and AIDS drugs that are priced prohibitively. Compared to the nearly 4,000 product patents granted for pharmaceuticals in India, only a small number of patents have been challenged using the post-grant provision, perhaps because not all that is patented might be of interest for the generic manufacturers taking into consideration the constraints on manufacturing knowhow and capacity.

Another concern is that even if all the complexities surrounding compulsory licensing options were sorted out, developing country manufacturers might still have limited interest in pursuing that option for economic reasons. Hence, if the government decides to use the compulsory licensing under government use option or under Section 92A (compulsory licence for export of patented pharmaceutical products in certain exceptional circumstances), financial incentives may be needed to persuade generic manufacturers.

As more companies plunge into biologics, there could be strong pressure on countries like India to provide for data exclusivity in pharmaceuticals either directly or through free trade agreements, possibilities that need to be monitored closely.

Overall, by improving patent examination procedures and provision of personnel, using the compulsory licensing option as Thailand does, and strict enforcement of price control, India may gain access to new medicines.

Notes

1. According to this news item, by July 2011 the FDA had approved twenty new drugs. www.fiercebiotech.com/story/woodcock-new-drug-approvals-reach-20-year-high/2011–07–08.

2. See Basso Maristela (2006) for a discussion on this.

3. The Patents Act 1970 defines a 'person interested' as a person engaged in or promoting research in the same field as the one to which the invention relates.

4. Between 2005 and 2008, twenty out of the twenty-five patent applications were rejected on the grounds of Section 3(d). See www.livemint.com/2009/09/07234455/3-provisions-helped-India-cull.html?h=A1.

5. Gleevac is a lifelong medicine. As manufactured by Novartis, patients pay $2500 per year, whereas the generic version would cost $166.6.

6. The Madras High Court considered that Novartis's program of free patient access to Gleevac satisfied the public interest criteria. The Bombay High Court noted that the validity of the EMR was challenged by the generic manufacturers, and that Gleevac was expensive. The fact that Novartis was importing and supplying Gleevac triggered fears about the sustainability of its supply (Basheer 2008).

7. Section 92A of the Patents (Amendment) Act 2005 stipulates the conditions under which this can be used: '(a) the compulsory licence shall be solely for manufacture and export of patented pharmaceutical products; (b) the export should be to a country having insufficient or no manufacturing capacity in the pharmaceutical sector, to address public health problems; and (c) a compulsory licence should have been granted by that country, or that country should have by notification or otherwise,

allowed importation of patented pharmaceutical products from India'
(Khader 2007: 732).

8. In the year 2008–09, two applications were received under Section
92A and both were rejected (Government of India 2008–09: 21). added

9. Under national/domestic exhaustion, the resale of patented products
would be confined to areas that are not served by the authorised agent.
Under regional exhaustion, patented products sold in one of the countries
in the regional bloc can be imported and sold in another country within
the region. Under international exhaustion, after the patented product is
legitimately placed in one country it can be imported from that country
and sold in another country.

10. http://www.msfaccess.org/media-room/press-releases/press-release-
detail/?tx_ttnews[tt_news]=1700&cHash= 2f6721d292, accessed 30 June
2011.

References

Banerjee, M., and Yajnaseni, R., 2009. 'Patentability of Incremental
    Innovation Vis-à-vis S3(D) of the Indian Patents Act: Striking a Balance',
    NUJS Law Review, October–December, 2(4): 607–36.
Bartelt, S., 2003. 'Compulsory Licences Pursuant to TRIPS Article 31 in
    the Light of the Doha Declaration on the TRIPS Agreement and Public
    Health', *The Journal of World Intellectual Property*, 6(2): 286–310.
Basheer, S., 2007. 'India's New Patent Regime: Aiding "Access" or
    Abetting "Genericide"?',*International Journal of Biotechnology*, 9(2):
    122–37.
——— 2008. 'The Efficacy of Indian Patent Law: Ironing out the Creases in
    Section 3(d)', *Scripted*, 5(2): 232–66, electronic copy available at http://
    ssrn.com/abstract=1086254, accessed from SSRN.com on July 2011
Basheer, S., and K. Mrinalini, 2008. 'ExhaustingPatent Rights in India:
    Parallel Imports and TRIPS Compliance', *Journal of Intellectual
    Property Rights*, 13(5): 486–97.
Basso Maristela (2006),'Intervention of Health Authorities in Patent
    Examination, The Brazilian Practice of the Prior Consent', *International
    Journal of Intellectual Property Management*, 1(1 and 2): 54–74.
BioSpectrum Asia Edition., 2011. 'Compulsory licence plea filed', www.
    biospectrumasia.com/content/020911IND17008.asp,
Business Standard, 2009. 'India Refuses Patent Protection for AIDS drugs
    of US Company', 2 September, www.business-standard.com/india/news/
    india-refuses-patent-protection-for-aids-drugus-company/368821/.

Chaudhuri, S., 2005. *The WTO and India's Pharmaceutical Industry: Patent Protection, TRIPS, and Developing Countries*, Oxford University Press, New Delhi.

―――― 2010. 'The Indian Pharmaceutical Industry After TRIPS' in K. Bharadwaj (ed.), *Five Years into the Product Patent Regime: India's Response*, United Nations Development Programme, New York, www. undp.org/poverty, Accessed on 4 March 2011.

Chokevivat, V., 2007. 'Facts and Evidences on the 10 Burning Issues Related to the Government Use of Patents in Three Patented Essential Drugs in Thailand: Document to Support Strengthening of Social Wisdom on the Issue of Drug Patent', Ministry of Public Health and the National Health Security Office, Thailand, www.moph.go.th/hot/White%20 Paper%20CL-EN.pdf.

Commission on Intellectual Property Rights (CIPR), 2002. 'Integrating Intellectual Property Rights and Development', Commission on Intellectual Property Rights, London, www.iprcommission.org/papers/ pdfs/final_report/CIPRfullfinal.pdf.

Correa, C., 2007. 'Guidelines for the Examination of the Pharmaceutical Patents: Developing a Public Health Perspective', WHO, ICTSD, UNCTAD working paper, available at www.iprsonline.org.

Cullen, D., 2007. 'Data Protection: The New IP Frontier: An Overview of Existing Rules and Regulations', *Journal of Generic Medicines*, 5(1): 9–25.

European Aids Treatment Group, 2011. 'India says "no" to policy that would block access to affordable medicines', www.msfaccess. org/media-room/press-releases/press-release-detail/?tx_ttnews[tt_ news]=1700&cHash= 2f6721d292,

Gehl, P., 2006. 'India's Product Patent Protection Regime: Less or More of "Pills for the Poor"', *Journal of World Intellectual Property*, 9(6): 694–726.

Gopakumar, K.M., 2010a. 'Product Patents and Access to Medicines in India', *The Law and Development Review*, 3(2): 325–68.

―――― 2010b. 'The Landscape of Pharmaceutical Patents Applications in India: Implications for Access to Medicines' in K. Bharadwaj (ed.), *Five Years into the Product Patent Regime: India's Response*, United Nations Development Programme, New York. www.undp. org/poverty,

Government of India, 2007. 'Report on Steps to be Taken by Government of India in the Context of Data Protection Provisions of Article 39.3

of TRIPS Agreement', Department of Chemicals and Petrochemicals, Ministry of Chemicals and Fertilisers, New Delhi, http://chemicals.nic.in/DPBooklet.pdf.

_____ 2009, Annual Report 2008–09, Annual Report of Office of the Controller General of Patents, Trademarks and Geographical Indications, New Delhi, http://ipindia.gov.in/cgpdtm/AnnualReport_English_2008_2009.pdf

_____ 2010a. Annual Report 2009–10, Department of Pharmaceuticals, Ministry of Chemicals and Fertilisers, Government of India, New Delhi, http://pharmaceuticals.gov.in/AnnualReportEnglish.pdf.

_____ 2010b. Annual Report 2009–10, The Office of the Controller General of Patents, Trademarks and Geographical indications, Ministry of Commerce and Industry, Department of Industrial Policy and Promotion, Government of India, New Delhi.

_____ 2010c. Discussion Paper on Compulsory Licensing, http://dipp.nic.in/ipr-feedback/CL-DraftDiscussion.doc.

_____ 2010d. 'Forty Fifth Report on Issues Relating to Availability of Generic, Generic-Branded and Branded Medicines, Their Formulation and Therapeutic Efficacy and Effectiveness', Parliament of India, New Delhi,http://164.100.47.5/newcommittee/reports/EnglishCommittees/Committee%20on%20Health%20and%20Family%20Welfare/45th%20report.pdf.

Grabowski, H., 2008. 'Follow-on Biologics: Data Exclusivity and the Balance Between Innovation and Competition', *Nature Reviews Drug Discovery*, 7(6): 479–87.

Grace, C., 2005. 'A Briefing Paper for DFID: Update on China and India and Access to Medicines', DFID Health Resource Centre, London, www.dfid.gov.uk/aboutdfid/organisation/accessmedicines.asp.

Guennif, and Lalitha, N., 2007. 'TRIPS Plus Agreements and Issues in Access to Medicines in Developing Countries', *Journal of Intellectual Property Rights*, Vol. 12 (5), 471–79.

IDMA 2009. 'India Overturns HIV Drug Patents', *IDMA Bulletin*, 34(xl): 35–36. Internationaldrugmart.com 2010. 'CIPLA's generic HIV drug tenofovir receives USFDA approval'.

James, T.C., 2009. 'Patent Protection and Innovation:Section 3 (d) of the Patents Act and Indian Pharmaceutical Industry', www.nipoonline.org/section-report.doc.

Khader F.A., 2007. The Law of Patents-With a Special Focus on Pharmaceuticals in India, LexisNexis Butterworths, New Delhi.

Kongolo, T., 2004. 'Compulsory Licence Issues in African Arab Countries', *Journal of World Intellectual Property*, 7(2): 185–99.

Kuanpoth, J., 2006. 'TRIPS Plus Intellectual Property Rights Rules:Impact on Thailand's Public Health', *Journal of World Intellectual Property*, 9(5): 573–91.

Lalitha, N., 2005. 'Review of the Pharmaceutical Industry of Canada', *Economic and Political Weekly*, 40(13): 1355–62.

Lawyers Collective, www.lawyerscollective.org.

L.C. Yoke., 2006. 'Malaysia's Experience in Increasing Access to Antiretroviral Drugs: Exercising the "Government use" Option', Intellectual Property Rights Series 9, Thirdworld Network, Malaysia, www.twnside.org.sg, accessed on 10 August 2008.

Medicins Sans Frontières (MSF), 2011a. Investment Chapter of the EU-India FTA :Implications for Health, at www.msfaccess.org/fileadmin/user_upload/medinnov_ accesspatents/LONG_The_Intellectual_Property_and_Investment_Chapters_of_the_EU-India_FTA___Implications_for_Health.pdf, accessed on 30th June 2011.

Mullard, A., 2011. '2010 FDA Drug Approvals', *Nature Reviews Drug Discovery*, 10(February 2011): 82–85.

Musungu, S. and Oh, C., 2005. 'The Use of Flexibilities in TRIPS by Developing Countries: Can they Promote Access to Medicines, Study 4c', Commission on Intellectual Property Rights, Innovation and Public Health, World Health Organisation, Geneva.

Oh, C., 2006. 'Compulsory Licences: Recent Experiences in Developing Countries', *International Journal of Intellectual Property Management*, 1(1 and 2): 22–36.

Patents Act, 1970, 2010. *Universal's Bare Acts and Rules*, Universal Law Publishing Co. Pvt. Ltd, New Delhi.

Roffe, P. and Spennemann, C., 2006. 'The Impact of FTAs on Public Health Policies and TRIPS Flexibilities', *International Journal of Intellectual Property Management*, 1(1–2): 75–93.

Rossi, F., 2006. 'Free Trade Agreements and TRIPS Plus Measures', *International Journal of Intellectual Property Management*, 1(1–2): 150–72.

Spicy IP blogspot, 2005. 'Breaking News: Roche Loses Valcyte Case', http://spicyipindia.blogspot.com/2010/05/breaking-news-roche-loses-valcyte-case.html.

Srinivasan S., 2012. 'Compulsory Licence for Nexavar: A Landmark Order', *Economic and Political Weekly*, 67 (14): 10–13.

Varella, M., 2004. 'The WTO, Intellectual Property and AIDS-Case Studies from Brazil and South Africa', *Journal of World Intellectual Property*, 7(4): 523–47.

Wanis, H., 2010. 'Agreement on Trade Related Aspects of Intellectual Property Rights and Access to Medication: Does Egypt have Sufficient Safeguards Against Potential Public Health Implications of the Agreement', *Journal of World Intellectual Property*, 13(1): 24–46.

World Health Organisation (WHO), 2006. 'Public Health, Innovation and Intellectual Property Rights', Report of the Commission on Intellectual Property Rights, Innovation and Public Health, Geneva.

_____ 2011. 'Overview: the TRIPS Agreement', www.wto.orghttp://www.wto.org/english/tratop_e/trips_e/amendment_ e.htm.

6 India's Free Trade Agreements: Implications for Access to Medicines in India and the Global South

Kajal Bhardwaj

INTRODUCTION

India was not always the pharmacy of the developing world. Between achieving independence in 1947 and the 1970s, India was dependent on imports of highly priced medicines as a result of patents on medicines that were granted in India. India inherited its patent regime from the British and applied the Patents and Designs Act, 1911 which provided for high patent protection. A US Senate report in 1961 examined the Indian experience with patents and access to medicines and noted that, 'India, which does grant patents on drug products, provides an interesting case example. The prices in India for the broad spectrum antibiotics, Aureomycin and Achromycin, are among the highest in the world. As a matter of fact in drugs generally, India ranks among the highest priced nations of the world—a case of an inverse relationship between per capita income and the level of drug prices.'[1]

In 1959, the 'Report on the Revision of the Patents Law' submitted by Justice N. Rajagopal Ayyangar to the government[2] outlined detailed recommendations for the overhaul of India's patent regime including the recommendation that patents on medicines should be restricted to process patents. Based on these recommendations, the government enacted the Indian Patents Act of 1970. The law continued to allow companies and others to apply for patents but identified food and pharmaceuticals as areas where these monopoly rights would be limited. Only process patents could be granted under this law for medicines. What this meant was that the medicine itself, i.e. the product, could not be patented, and that manufacturers were free to come up with different processes to manufacture the same medicine (a process sometimes referred to as reverse engineering). Even these 'process' patents were granted for periods of only five or seven years.[3] The Indian government also put in place industrial policy measures and public sector research institutions to collaborate with the local industry. The result: a strong and vibrant Indian generic industry featuring large, medium and small scale companies. And an industry that over the next several decades was able to provide safe, effective and affordable medicines to much of the global South.

The impact of the growth of India's indigenous generic capacity to produce safe, effective and affordable generic medicines was felt beyond the Indian borders by the 2000s; most dramatically in the case of antiretrovirals (ARVs) used in the treatment of HIV. By the mid-1990s, effective treatment for HIV in the form of triple combination therapy (i.e. three medicines taken at the same time) was known to the world though it was largely available only in developed countries.[4] United Nations led efforts to collaborate with the multinational pharmaceutical industry at the time to get lower priced ARVs to developing countries were largely unsuccessful.[5] The best discount available from multinational pharmaceutical companies that held the patents on these ARVs was $10,549. And donation programmes were able to reach only a fraction of those in need of treatment. During the same period, the potential of local production of ARVs and its impact on lowering the cost of treatment was revealed by Brazil which produced its own ARVs and started supplying them locally at a cost of approximately $2700 per person per year (see de Mello e Souza in this volume).

But the real turning point for access to treatment in the developing world came in 2001 when an Indian generic company, CIPLA, made an unimaginable offer to provide first line triple combination AIDS medicines at $350 per person per year. Today competition from and between Indian generic producers has resulted in price reductions for first line AIDS medicines from as much as $15,000 in 2000 to less than $120 per person per year for the current preferred first line triple combination in 2012.[6]

In addition, the lack of product patents on each separate medicine allowed Indian generic manufacturers to combine the three different ARVs in one single pill. The availability of these generic fixed-dose combinations simplified HIV treatment in resource-limited settings and resulted in government treatment programmes across the developing world. Over 8 million people living with HIV are now on treatment in developing countries.[7] A 2010 study which examined the purchase of donor-funded HIV medicines found that as of the end of 2009, 'among paediatric ARV and adult nucleoside and non-nucleoside reverse transcriptase inhibitor markets, Indian-produced generics accounted for 91 per cent and 89 per cent of 2008 global purchase volumes, respectively.'[8]

TRIPS Compliance: Using the Doha Declaration in India

In 2005, however, India had to amend its patent law to fully comply with its obligations under the World Trade Organization's (WTO) Agreement on Trade Related Aspects of Intellectual Property Rights (TRIPS).[9] As opposed to the 1970s patent regime, TRIPS required India to start granting 20 year product patents on medicines. Product patents give patent holders exclusive rights over the manufacture, sale, use, offer for sale and import of the patented medicine. This allows them to exclude competitors or generic companies from producing the medicine and the lack of competition results in high prices and restricted availability. The impending change in India's patent regime and its impact on the continued production and supply of generic ARVs in India attracted significant national and international concern from public interest groups and the United Nations.[10] It was also the subject of intense debates in the Indian Parliament. In their quest to balance public interest with India's WTO obligations, the Indian Parliament turned to the 2001 Doha Declaration on TRIPS and Public Health. Signed by all WTO members, the Doha Declaration states categorically that, TRIPS 'can and should be interpreted and implemented in a manner supportive of WTO members' right to protect public health and, in particular, to promote access to medicines for all.'[11]

The Indian Parliament included multiple health safeguards in the amendments to India's patent law including compulsory licences, patent oppositions, the bolar and research exceptions, parallel imports, automatic licencing for medicines produced before 2005 and ensuring that the medicine registration system was separate from the patent regime. An additional key health safeguard was a provision restricting evergreening i.e. the practice of pharmaceutical companies to extend their exclusive rights on a medicine by making minor or obvious changes to the medicine and applying for additional patents. Section 3(d) of India's patent law prohibits patents on new uses of known medicines. It also prohibits patents on new forms of existing medicines unless the patent applicant can show a significant increase in efficacy.[12] The law also allows challenges to patent applications (pre-grant) and to patents (post-grant) by a broad range of actors. People living with HIV, cancer and hepatitis-C have used these provisions to ensure that frivolous patents are not granted on key medicines in India.

Impact of TRIPS Compliance

Despite all these efforts and the health safeguards in the Indian patent law, nearly 4000 patents have been granted in India related to medicines.[13] And the impact of patents on key medicines is beginning to be felt. *Pegylated interferon*, a medicine needed by those living with hepatitis C has been patented and a course of treatment (usually 48 weeks) can cost nearly Rs 7,00,000 (approximately $12,000).[14] This does not include the cost of other medicines, doctors' fees, diagnostics or other healthcare costs for the treatment of hepatitis C. A newer HIV medicine known as *raltegravir* is also patented in India by Merck and Co. and priced at $2500 per patient per year,[15] and costs four times the Indian price in other developing countries.[16] This is the price for just one medicine and a comparison with the price of the currentlypreferred first line of HIV of three medicines at less than $120 per patient per year presents a sobering picture.

The high prices and decreased availability of newer medicines has meant that within seven years of the change in India's patent regime, compulsory licensing has had to be invoked. In March 2012, the Indian Patent Office issued India's first compulsory licence[17] on *sorefanib tosylate*, a drug used in the treatment of kidney and liver cancer which is patented in India by the multinational German company, Bayer Corporation. Bayer was selling the drug at Rs 2,88,000 or approximately \$5200[18] per person per month. The generic equivalent made by Natco Pharma Limited which applied for and received the compulsory licence is sold at Rs 8,800 or \$160 while the version made by another Indian generic company, CIPLA Limited (that has chosen to challenge Bayer's patent instead of pursuing the compulsory licence route) is priced at Rs 6780 or \$124.[19] Bayer filed an appeal against the compulsory licence that was scheduled to be heard in September 2012.

The safeguards in the Indian law are also facing an onslaught from several MNCs. Bayer unsuccessfully sued the Indian government in its attempt to enforce patent linkage in India; something Bayer does not even enjoy under EU law.[20] Roche has unsuccessfully used litigation in an attempt to enforce higher standards for the granting of temporary injunctions in patent infringement cases.[21] The most critical litigation for the health safeguards in the Indian law is the one filed by Swiss MNC Novartis AG in the Indian Supreme Court to weaken Section 3(d), reported to be close to final resolution at the time of writing. Developed countries like the US are also using bilateral pressure though the US Special 301 law and lobbying. In a deposition before a US Senate committee, a United States Patents and Trademark Office (USPTO) official highlighted the level and extent of such lobbying noting that many of their activities in developing countries were aimed at, for example, preventing the issuance of compulsory licences.

The new TRIPS compliant law in India is also having an impact on the business models and commercial considerations of Indian generic companies. Several top Indian companies have been acquired by MNCs or have tie-ups with them. The promoters of the Indian companies, it must be said, are not worse for wear in this situation as MNCs have made offers that are several times the valuation of the generic companies. Those who have not sold and continue to operate are tying up with MNCs for deals of all shades and scales.[22] Their improved share prices are their rewards. For improving and increasing access to treatment, however, the situation is grim. These buy-outs and tie-ups mean that these companies are now unlikely to challenge patents, launch new medicines and take on MNCs in legal battles.

For instance, in 2006, patent oppositions were filed by public interest groups and generic companies against the patent applications filed by US MNC Gilead Sciences related to the HIV medicine *tenofovir*. Within a week, Gilead offered voluntary licences to the generic companies for the production and supply of *tenofovir* in a limited number of developing countries. Several generic companies took these licences even though Gilead had no product patents on *tenofovir* as yet and as a condition of taking those licences withdrew their patent oppositions. As public interest groups and at least one generic company persisted with their oppositions, these product patent applications were later rejected by the Indian patent office. Later in 2011, Gilead issued fresh licences to four generic companies as well as through the Medicines Patent Pool again with a limited number of countries for these companies to supply to. And again in a situation where Gilead has no product patents in India and only has one patent in one of the countries (Indonesia) included in the 2011 *tenofovir* licence. Despite the health safeguards in the Indian law and the restrictions on their ability to manufacture and supply medicines in key developing countries, generic companies have continued to sign similar voluntary licences on other medicines as well.[23]

While India's first compulsory licence was based on an application from a generic company there are fears that with increasing tie-ups and takeovers, there would be few generic manufacturers who would either apply for or fill future compulsory licence orders.

INDIA'S FTA NEGOTIATIONS: AN OVERVIEW

Even as India struggles to work within the WTO framework to provide access to affordable medicines domestically and abroad, MNCs through lobbying or litigation and developed countries through trade agreements, are hard at work to get developing countries to adopt provisions on intellectual property far in excess of what is required by the TRIPS regime—what are known as TRIPS-plus measures.

The primary method to pressure India into adopting even greater intellectual property protection and other measures that negatively impact access to medicines is through free trade agreements (FTAs). Also known as regional trade agreements (RTAs), Economic Partnership Agreements (EPAs), etc., FTAs are used by developed countries to win greater trade liberalization commitments from the South than they could achieve through the WTO. As they are negotiated country by country (or sometimes by regional blocks), Southern countries have decreased bargaining power to resist these agreements as opposed to the multilateral forum which, by comparison, offers developing countries a platform to jointly negotiate on and is more transparent. FTAs cover a broad range of subjects including trade in goods, services, competition, government procurement, and impact many industrial and services sectors.

If TRIPS represented the first wave of globalised intellectual property rules, FTAs negotiated by the United States of America (US) such as the Central American Free Trade Agreement (CAFTA) and a host of other US FTAs negotiated with developing countries represent the second wave. The third wave is where the EU in a stark departure from its traditional model of trade negotiations is now demanding wide ranging TRIPS-plus measures of developing countries as is Japan. The US, after a brief hiatus, has also re-started its FTA project with the ambitious Trans-Pacific Partnership Agreement (TPPA). The Anti-Counterfeiting Trade Agreement (ACTA), negotiated in secret by several developed countries and some of their developing country allies focuses purely on TRIPS-plus IP enforcement. Bilateral Investment Treaties (BITs) signed by several developing countries with developed countries since the 1990s have also become a cause for concern with increasing evidence of the use of these treaties by MNCs to challenge government policies related to health.

Although India has been negotiating FTAs with countries in the North and the South, TRIPS-plus measures are a feature of North-South FTAs. The key FTA negotiations that will be examined in this chapter relate to those with the European Union (EU), the European Free Trade Association (EFTA), Japan and, potentially, with the US.

India-Japan Comprehensive Economic Partnership Agreement

Talks on the India-Japan Comprehensive Economic Partnership Agreement (CEPA) started with the 'Report of the India-Japan Joint Study Group' in 2006.[24] The report identified Japan's interest in intellectual property enforcement and increasing investor protection as Japan and India had not signed a BIT. In 2007, formal negotiations were launched. A total of 14 rounds of negotiations were held before the CEPA was formally signed by both sides on 16 February 2011 in Tokyo and came into effect on 1 August 2011. During the negotiations, the IP chapter of the FTA negotiations was leaked and indicated that Japan's interests lay in streamlining of administrative matters and in IP enforcement though not to the extent that was reflected in ACTA that Japan is a key signatory and proponent of.

EU-India Broad-based Trade and Investment Agreement

Since 2007, India and the EU, through the European Commission (EC) have been negotiating an FTA that has attracted global concern over its potential impact on the manufacture, supply and distribution of generic medicines in and from India. Till recently, the EU has not featured among the aggressive developed nations that pursue TRIPS-plus measures. However, leaked negotiating texts of the IP Chapter and the Investment Chapter in 2009, 2010 and 2011 show that the EU in a stark departure from its traditional model of trade negotiations is now demanding ambitious TRIPS-plus measures of developing countries.[25] After 11 rounds, negotiations are now being held in smaller groups instead of full rounds of negotiation. Both sides have announced that a Ministerial level meeting is planned for November 2012 and that the FTA would be signed and concluded by then.[26]

EFTA—India Free Trade Agreement

EFTA is an intergovernmental organisation established by Iceland, Liechtenstein, Norway and Switzerland to promote free trade and economic integration for the benefit of these four countries. They negotiate FTAs with developing countries separately from the EU. EFTA-India talks commenced with the 'Report of the Joint Study Group on the EFTA-India FTA' in 2007[27] which identified intellectual property as an area that could be included in the negotiations. The report stated that both sides recognised that the TRIPS Agreement does not prevent parties from adopting higher levels of IP protection indicating that TRIPS-plus measures may be up for negotiation. A leaked version of the IP chapter under negotiations also indicates this. At the time of writing this chapter, 11 rounds of negotiation had taken place, the most recent in March 2012.

Potential US-India Free Trade Agreement

Over the past few years, the US and Indian governments have made regular public announcements signaling their interest in pursuing closer trade ties. In 2006 and then later in 2009, the USPTO and the Department of Industrial Policy and Promotion (DIPP) of the Indian Ministry of Commerce and Industry signed memorandums of understanding on intellectual property.[28] India and the US have been in discussions over the signing of a BIT between the two governments.[29] The negotiations would likely be based on the 2012 model BIT published by the United States Trade Representative (USTR).[30] Although a US-India FTA is not currently under negotiation, pressure from US law makers and from industry has becomes more public in the recent past. However, other trade agreements that the US is actively negotiating or promoting such as the TPPA and ACTA would have an impact on India and particularly on the health safeguards in the Indian law even though India is not party to these negotiations.

FTAS AND ACCESS TO MEDICINES: KEY CONCERNS

There are three distinct areas of concern in the already concluded and in ongoing FTA negotiations that could adversely impact India's generic production capacity and consequently the ability of patients in India and across the developing world to access safe, effective and affordable generic medicines from India. These are the *Intellectual*

Property provisions, the *Investment provisions* and the *Regulatory Standards provisions*.

INTELLECTUAL PROPERTY PROVISIONS

The IP chapters proposed by developed countries in FTA negotiations are comprehensive and cover a broad range of IP issues including copyright, geographical indications, and patents (including as they impact agro-chemicals and seeds). However, this chapter focuses on some key demands as they relate to access to medicines.

Patent Term Extension

Since 2005, India has been granting 20-year patents on products and processes as required by TRIPS. Also known as 'supplementary protection certificates,' patent term extensions would require India to extend the patent term beyond 20 years if there is any delay in the granting of a patent or in obtaining marketing approval for the medicine. A longer patent term would mean a delay in the entry of generic medicines.

A study by the Korean National Health Insurance Corporation concluded that the extension of patent term (demanded by the US in the South Korea-US FTA negotiations) could cost it $529 million if drug patents were extended for three years and $757 million for a four year patent term extension.[31] A study on the impact of patent term extension proposed in EU FTA negotiations with the Andean Community countries found that an extension of the effective patent period by four years could result in an increase of $159 million in 2025 or a 9 per cent decrease in consumption.[32] Using the methodology, a study of the impact of patent term extension in Thailand (if the demands in the US-Thai FTA negotiations were accepted) estimated that the economic impact of a five year patent term extension would be $821 million over five years and $4,039 million over 15 years.[33]

In addition, such a mechanism could place undue pressure on the patent office to grant a patent or on the drug regulator's office to grant marketing approval without due consideration. Delays in the grant of a patent or marketing approval can arise from a number of reasons including delays by the applicant. Provisions demanding patent term extensions feature in EU,[34] EFTA[35] and US[36] FTA negotiations. In India, patent term extension was demanded by the EU in the EU-India negotiations but may have been dropped now after considerable civil society pressure.[37] Although the current leaked EFTA-India IP chapter does not contain a provision on patent term extension, it is likely that it may have been demanded in earlier negotiations.

Data Exclusivity

Generic manufactures, when seeking marketing approval for their products do not have to conduct clinical trials on medicines already introduced in the market. Duplicate clinical trials on human populations for a medicine whose safety and efficacy is already proven are considered unethical. They would also add considerably to the cost of generic production. Instead under the regulatory laws of most developing countries, generic manufacturers have to show that their generic versions are 'bio-equivalent' to the medicine already approved and on the market. Data exclusivity as demanded in FTA negotiations would require generic manufacturers to conduct their own clinical trials to get marketing approval or wait till a specified exclusivity period is over (5 to 11 years) before a generic product is approved. This measure creates exclusivity over medicines separate from patents and applies even to medicines that are off-patent or where a compulsory licence is issued.

TRIPS and data exclusivity: Developed countries often argue that data exclusivity is required by the TRIPS Agreement and cite Article 39.3 which states, 'Members, when requiring, as a condition of approving the marketing of pharmaceutical or of agricultural chemical products which utilize new chemical entities, the submission of undisclosed test or other data, the origination of which involves a considerable effort, shall protect such data against unfair commercial use. In addition, Members shall protect such data against disclosure, except where necessary to protect the public, or unless steps are taken to ensure that the data are protected against unfair commercial use.'

The question of whether Article 39.3 requires data exclusivity or not is often based on the interpretation of 'unfair commercial use'.

Developed countries and MNCs argue that when a drug regulator relies on information submitted by originator companies on the safety and efficacy of a medicine to approve the generic version of the medicine, this amounts to unfair commercial use. Whether these actions of a regulator amount to unfair commercial use was settled in a 1990 House of Lords decision where it was held that, 'it is the right and duty of the licensing authority to make use of all the information supplied by any applicant for a product licence which assists the licensing authority in considering whether to grant or reject any other application, or which assists the licensingauthority in performing any of its other functions under the Act of 1968. The use of such information should not harm the appellants, and even were it to do so, this is the price which the appellants must pay for cooperating in the regime designed by Parliament for the protection of the public and for the protection of the appellants and all manufacturers of medicinal products from the dangers inherent in the introduction and reproduction of modern drugs.'[38]

In addition, the negotiating history of Article 39.3 shows that the original proposal for data exclusivity moved by the US was rejected in favour of the present provision quoted above that requires only data protection.[39]

In India, the government established an Inter-ministerial Committee to examine India's obligations under Article 39.3. The 2007 report that emerged from the deliberations of this Committee is also known also as the Satwant Reddy report (named for the bureaucrat who wrote the report) and is widely considered to be the opinion of only one Ministry i.e. the Ministry of Chemicals and Fertilizers which oversees the pharmaceutical industry. The Ministry of Health and Family Welfare and other ministries are known to have objected to the conclusions of the report[40] which, though it finds that TRIPS does not require data exclusivity, recommends that India adopt it to attract foreign investment. In addition, the report emphasises that data exclusivity would be one way to promote research and development in traditional medicines.[41] Although the Report has not been taken on board by the Indian government, it is often quoted by developed countries and MNCs citing support for the imposition of data exclusivity in India.[42]

Impact of data exclusivity on prices of medicines: Data exclusivity was originally imposed in several developing countries through the earlier US FTAs. Evidence of the impact of the imposition of data exclusivity is now emerging from these countries. In Guatemala, a study found wide variations in prices of medicines in the same therapeutic class because of data exclusivity.[43] In Jordan, a 2006 study by Oxfam showed that of the 103 medicines registered and launched since 2001 that had no patent protection in Jordan, at least 79 per cent had no competition from a generic equivalent as a consequence of data exclusivity.[44] Both Jordan and Guatemala impose data exclusivity as a result of their FTAs with the US. The Thai study discussed above found that the economic effect of data exclusivity over five years could be $2400 million.[45]

Impact of data exclusivity when a medicine is not patented: Data exclusivity applies regardless of the patentability of a medicine. In India, the application of this measure would, therefore, directly undermine the health safeguards in the Indian law including those preventing evergreening. The impact of data exclusivity on access to medicines in India can be better understood through the use of an illustration. *Valganciclovir* is an important medicine not only for organ transplants but also for the treatment of cytomegalovirus or CMV. CMV is an opportunistic infection that affects people living with HIV but is often ignored as the price of the medicine is too high or the older version of the medicine is so traumatic for patients (an injection directly in the eye) that treatment is usually not provided for it. After a protracted legal battle, in a post-grant opposition decision which included networks of people living with HIV, the Indian Patent Office agreed with patients groups that as a new form of a known substance (pro-drug of ganciclovir) and as a form that was obvious, the patent on *valganciclovir* had been wrongly granted to Roche in India.[46]

However had data exclusivity existed in India, Roche would still have enjoyed exclusive rights over the medicine. In the EU-India FTA negotiations, there was also a specific demand for data exclusivity on new indications of existing medicines. Section 3(d) of the Patents Act, 1970 excludes entirely new uses of known medicines. As noted in the Report of the Commission on Intellectual Property, Innovation and Public Health (CIPIH Report):[47]

If the patent period has expired, or there is no patent on the product, this sui generis data exclusivity may act independently of patent status to delay the entry of any generic companies wishing to enter the market. This is because the regulators cannot use the data in the period of protection to approve a product, even if the product is demonstrated to be bio-equivalent, where required. The only alternative for a generic company would be to repeat clinical trials, which would be costly and wasteful, and would raise ethical issues since it would involve replicating tests in humans to demonstrate what is already known to be effective. These sui generis regimes, which provide for data exclusivity need to be clearly differentiated from the TRIPS agreement's requirement for data protection.

Impact of data exclusivity when a medicine is patented: Where there is a patent, data exclusivity renders meaningless the key safeguards in India's law for access to medicines after a patent has been granted. Specifically, the patent law has a Bolar provision that allows generic competitors to have all the regulatory data filed and regulatory approval ready so they are ready to launch the generic medicine as soon as the patent is no longer blocking them. This could happen when the patent expires, when a compulsory licence is issued on it or when it is revoked. Revocation proceedings can also be launched to counter infringement suits and generic companies often launch medicines they believe have been wrongly patented and then challenge the patent through the infringement proceedings. This is an important and essential manner in which generic companies challenge patents on medicines. With data exclusivity, however, they would not get marketing approval during the exclusivity period and would be unable to launch the generic version. Launching patent challenges to counter infringement charges is recognised under the Indian Patents Act, 1970.

Data exclusivity, even if waived in the case of a compulsory licence, would still delay generic entry as only at the point of the waiver will the approval process commence. Marketing approval for a generic medicine requires the scrutiny of the Drugs Controller

General of India (DCGI) to ascertain that they are bioequivalent, safe and effective. This scrutiny requires time. Data exclusivity could also impact exports of generic medicines from India. In the future if the DCGI requires marketing approval before export or the importing country requires proof of marketing approval in India, data exclusivity would hamper exports. This could also impact on the working of another key provision of Indian law which incorporates the 30 August 2003 decision i.e. Section 92A of the Indian Patents Act, 1970. The 30 August decision (also known as the Para 6 solution) attempts to solve the problem of developing countries and LDCs with little or no manufacturing capacity in accessing generic medicines from another country where there is a patent on a medicine.[48] The problem here is posed by a requirement in the TRIPS Agreement that generic supply under a compulsory licence must be predominantly for the supply of the domestic market. The 30 August decision waives this requirement as long as certain, as experience has shown, onerous[49] procedural requirements are met. The Indian government needs to analyse whether other developing and least developed country governments also take into account the marketing approval given by India as an indication of the safety and efficacy of the medicine (particularly where their own drug regulatory systems are weak and particularly given the misplaced and false hype over India exporting fake medicines) before allowing a drug to be imported from India. If this is the case, again data exclusivity would impact the use of Section 92A of the Patents Act as well.

Data exclusivity and traditional medicines: As noted above, one of the grounds cited by the Satwant Reddy Report in support of data exclusivity was the promotion of R&D in traditional medicines. The Indian patent law does not permit the patenting of products based on traditional knowledge. The impact of data exclusivity on the availability of traditional medicines can be seen through the example of *colchicine* in the US. Like other traditional medicines, *colchicine* cannot be patented as it has been in use and known for 3000 years. It was also available in generic form in the US since the 19th century. Under US law, exclusivity over a medicine can be granted if it is for a rare disease. One company provided trial data for one week of the medicine to show its use also in debilitating fevers and abdominal pain (which was already known) and got exclusivity over this traditional medicine. As a result, other manufacturers of the medicine were forced to leave the market and the drug price rose 50 times from \$0.09 to \$4.85.[50]

Demands for data exclusivity feature in EU,[51] EFTA[52] and US[53] FTA negotiations while Japan[54] requires the reproduction of Article 39.3 of the TRIPS Agreement in its FTAs. When developing countries resist pressure on implementing data exclusivity, the EU may also offer to only quote the provision from the TRIPS Agreement. The impact of this is discussed below.

Patent Linkage

At present when India's drug regulator, the DCGI, registers a medicine, whether it is patented or not is irrelevant to the assessment of safety, efficacy and quality. These are the main areas of work for the DCGI or the drug regulator in any country. A patent linkage system would require the DCGI to inquire as to the patent status of a medicine and refuse to register generic versions of patented medicines. A patent linkage system undermines several of the health safeguards in the Indian law. For instance, the Bolar exception allows generic companies to take all actions necessary to comply with regulatory requirements so that a generic medicine can be launched immediately on patent expiry, if the patent is revoked or if a compulsory licence is issued. By contrast the patent linkage system prevents generic companies from completing all regulatory requirements and instead delays the launch of a generic medicine and would also delay the implementation of a compulsory licence.

A patent linkage system also places considerable financial and administrative burden on the drug regulator's office to determine the patent status of a medicine. In 1994, the US Food and Drug Administration stated, 'FDA does not have the expertise to review patent information. The agency believes that its resources would be better utilized in reviewing applications rather than reviewing patent claims.'[55]

This system originated in a US law known as the Hatch-Waxman Act. Senator Waxman, one of the authors of the Bill has famously stated in relation to the imposition of this mechanism through US FTAs in developing countries:

I think it goes without saying that the U.S. faced nothing like these kinds of problems when Hatch-Waxman was enacted here. We did not face a situation where only a tiny percentage of the population was receiving the medicines that they needed to survive. We did not face a situation where a very large percentage of the young people in our society had already contracted diseases that would swiftly and almost certainly kill them if they did not receive such medicines. If we had, the solution would certainly not have looked like Hatch-Waxman, which delays market entry of low-cost generic drugs for years after a life-saving drug becomes available. That system works in this country because most people in the U.S. have health insurance that pays for essential drugs and because we have a health care safety net to assure that the poorest in our society are not left without medical care and treatment. But to impose such a system on a country without a safety net, depriving millions of people of life-saving drugs, is irresponsible and even unethical. In developing countries, we must do everything in our power to make affordable drugs for life-threatening diseases available now.[56]

The CIPIH Report has noted that 'in both Canada and the United States, there remain provisions whereby a brand-name company can trigger a stay of generic entry, irrespective of the merits of the claim of the generic company to be non-infringing. Thus these types of rules provide, in effect, for additional periods of exclusivity, offered by the regulatory authority, rather than the patent system.'[57]

The observations of the CIPIH Report were confirmed by the report on the pharmaceutical sector of the European Competition Directorate-General, which found that despite patent linkages being illegal in the EU, patent holders have launched multiple actions against drug regulators in the EU that approve generic versions of their medicines. In the actions based on patent linkages, the report notes, patent holders 'pursue deliberate actions, including litigation, creating administrative difficulties for generic companies which might result in delays in generic entry.'[58] These actions by EU companies extend beyond the borders of the EU. As noted above, Bayer sued the Indian drug regulator to try and enforce a patent linkage system in India. The case filed in 2008 was heard by a single judge of the Delhi High Court and was dismissed in August 2009 with the judge holding that *'Bayer's argument of inferring drug agencies' role in patent policing or enforcement is unacceptable'.*[59] Appeals by Bayer to a division bench of the Delhi High Court[60] and then finally before the Supreme Court of India were unsuccessful.[61]

Patent linkage provisions appear primarily in US[62] FTAs. Curiously, though patent linkage is not employed in the EU, it is in the EU-South Korea FTA[63] while the leaked negotiation text of the EU-India FTA stated that should either country adopt this measure it would be applicable to the companies of the other country.[64]

IP Enforcement measures

A key area that recent FTA negotiations have highlighted is the interest of developed countries in aggressive IP enforcement, widely considered the latest front in the IP battle between the North and the South. Best reflected in the secretly negotiated ACTA, IP enforcement entails measures that significantly alter how IP holders like multinational pharmaceutical companies can use public resources, public money and public authorities to enforce their private rights.

A notable feature of the debate around IP enforcement is the deliberate attempt to couch the pressure for the adoption of such measures in public health terms. Referred to as anti-counterfeiting measures, the rhetoric around IP enforcement uses the different meanings of counterfeit (i.e. fake in everyday parlance and trademark violation under the TRIPS Agreement) to argue that such measures are required to ensure that patients have access to safe and good quality medicines. However, IP enforcement cannot ensure the safety and quality of a medicine which requires investment in drug regulatory frameworks.[65] In fact, there is increasing evidence that aggressive IP enforcement hampers access to medicines.

The clearest impact of aggressive IP enforcement measures has been seen in 2008 and 2009 when generic medicines on their way from India to Africa and Latin America were seized at European ports.[66] Under the EU Customs Regulations, customs officials did not require proof of patent infringement or even that the generic medicines would enter the European market before they took these actions.[67] The result of the seizures has been the filing of a WTO dispute by India against the EU on the grounds that its seizure of generic medicines in transit through Europe based on allegations of patent infringement created a barrier to the freedom of transit recognised under WTO rules.[68] India was joined by Brazil in the filing of the dispute while several other developing countries like China joined the dispute as observers. In 2011, the Indian government announced that it had reached an 'understanding' or 'informal settlement'. This is based on the condition that the EC would reflect India's position that goods in transit and which are patented in the EU should not be detained unless there is adequate evidence that the medicines may enter the EU market.[69] Although the EC released their proposal for a new Customs Regulation, several concerns remain about the powers of customs officials in relation to the enforcement of intellectual property.[70] In addition the dispute with the EU did not address the issue of seizure of medicines based on allegations of trademark violations (discussed below).

Like the substantive provisions in TRIPS, the enforcement provisions are also areas where developing countries can ensure that they adopt TRIPS in a manner that meets the needs of public health. Indeed, IP enforcement is a key area in the Development Agenda set by developing countries at the World Intellectual Property Organization (WIPO).[71] However, IP enforcement provisions in FTAs being negotiated by the EU, EFTA, US and Japan are TRIPS-plus and could create barriers in the production and supply of generic medicines.

Changing how courts and judges balance public interest and intellectual property rights: In India, the judiciary has played a key role in balancing access to medicines with intellectual property rights. For instance, in a case related to a cancer medicine, where the patent holding company tried to get an injunction against the generic version of the cancer medicine from reaching patients, the court laid down a four step test including public interest to be fulfilled before such an injunction could be granted.[72] The EC is seeking to empower patent holding companies to seek injunctions not just against generic manufacturers but also third parties and even before an infringement actually takes place. The IP holders could seek an injunction at all stages of a legal proceeding thus endangering the delicate balance that Indian judges are seeking to achieve.[73]

Border measures and medicine seizures: Border measures refer to provisions for the enforcement of intellectual property at borders and entail giving customs officials powers to seize or detain goods alleged to be infringing intellectual property. Under TRIPS, border measures are required to be applied only in the case of imports and in the cases of trademark counterfeiting and copyright violations. However, there has been an increasing push to cover all forms of intellectual property with border measures. The impact of including patent infringement in border measures has been seen through the case of the Indian generic medicine seizures. With the revelation of the seizures of generic medicines at EU ports, border measure provisions in ACTA, the TPPA and the EU-India FTA have been scaled back considerably. While ACTA[74] specifies that border measures would not apply to patents or undisclosed information, the TPPA[75] applies to trademark and copyright violations while the EU-India FTA will reportedly abide by the understanding between the EU and India.

Discussions on allowing the detention of medicines for trademark violations however continue to be of concern for production and supply of generic medicines across borders. The EU appears to be pushing for the inclusion of border measures for export and for transit for trademark violations. This is a concern as both originator companies and generic companies use part of the international non-proprietary name (INN)[76] of medicines in their brands making allegations of trademark infringement very complicated and a matter that only courts should direct actions for and not customs officials who act on complaints of trademark holders. Indeed, one of the seizures of medicines in Germany was due to concerns over trademark infringement related to the medicine amoxicilan which customs officials were concerned violated the trademark 'amoxil' of GSK.[77]

Catching treatment providers in the net: Known also as third party liability, new IP enforcement provisions would allow a patent holder to drag nearly all actors in the supply and distribution of generic medicines into litigation and to have legal measures taken against them. This could, for instance, seriously hamper the work of treatment providers who, at times, procure and distribute medicines by requiring them to provide information or by allowing injunctions to be issued against them.[78]

Chilling effect on generic producers: Several IP enforcement provisions in ACTA, the TPPA and those proposed in the EU-India FTA are designed to have a chilling effect on generic producers. The provisions empower patent holding companies to seek several measures against generic companies that are not limited to damages—freezing bank accounts, seizing properties and documents and several other harsh measures are proposed for adding to the arsenal of patent holders. In addition, provisions are also proposed that would drag the whole supply and distribution chain of generic medicines into litigation creating a strong disincentive for pharmacies to stock generic medicines, truckers to transport them or even those building machines for generic companies to continue working with the generic industry. There are several reasons that such harsh measures that are usually invoked in criminal matters should not be allowed in civil cases of infringement. Not the least of which are the multiple patents held by patent holding companies on the same products. The European Union's Competition Authority in its investigation of the pharmaceutical industry found that this approach of multiple patents on single medicines was quite common and was a method of thwarting generic competition by creating patent thickets. In one case, it found 1300 patents and patent applications on one medicine alone.[79] This is part of the strategy of patent holding companies to prevent generic competition as a competitor often will not be in a position to determine whether a medicine is still protected by a patent. As noted above, the Indian law accounts for such situations through a provision restricting evergreening while Indian courts have sought to balance public interest with the enforcement of IP rights. These provisions would however, tilt this balance towards IP holders.

The IP enforcement measures feature in EU, EFTA, US and Japan FTAs. The IP enforcement measures demanded by Japan during the India-Japan CEPA negotiation were not agreed to in the end by the Indian government. However, these provisions feature prominently in the EU-India FTA and are an area that the EC is placing considerable emphasis on in the negotiations.

Quoting TRIPS provisions and other existing IP agreements in FTAs

Under TRIPS, dispute resolution is at a multilateral, transparent level with binding terms and conditions and safeguards of the TRIPS Agreement. However when TRIPS provisions are quoted in FTAs, it would shift the dispute resolution forum to that between two countries. This is a crucial issue as often developing countries that refuse to entertain TRIPS-plus provisions in FTAs will agree to having the TRIPS provisions quoted instead. Not only does this create an alternative dispute settlement mechanism, the selective quoting of TRIPS provisions may also imply that the safeguards in the TRIPS Agreement are no longer applicable. In addition, several FTAs include the TRIPS-plus IP agreements that India is party to but that are non-binding and have no enforcement or dispute resolution mechanisms such as the Patent Co-operation Treaty. Including these agreements in the FTAs may have the effect of making India's actions in relation to those treaties subject to the dispute resolution mechanism of the FTA.

INVESTMENT (OR INVESTOR PROTECTION) MEASURES

Investment provisions in BITs or in FTAs can impact access to medicines and the use of the health safeguards in India's patent law in several ways. Investment rules typically define investment to include intellectual property rights and prohibit the 'expropriation' of such investments by the government or require 'fair and equitable treatment' for investors of the foreign country. Where a company alleges a violation of investment protection they can sue the Indian government in secret, private international arbitration instead of local courts. Such provisions are justified on several grounds including that they are necessary to attract foreign investment. But the justifications for investment treaties or provisions are increasingly being questioned even as the manner in which these provisions have been used by multinational companies to challenge health, environment and other laws and policies have come to light.[80] Investment provisions in FTAs can have the following impacts in relation to health and access to medicines:

Preventing pro-health policies and regulations: The attempts by various countries, both developed and developing, to regulate tobacco for instance, have met with aggressive legal actions under investment provisions. The cases filed by US cigarette manufacturer, Philipp Morris, against Uruguay[81] and more recently Australia[82] are well known. Philipp Morris has alleged that tobacco warnings on cigarettes or rules for plain packaging amount to infringements of their trademarks which are considered to be 'investments'. Investment provisions have also been used to challenge Poland's attempts to prevent the privatization of its public health insurance company[83] and the ability of Canada to regulate chemicals that can cause health problems.[84] Experience has shown, that regardless of the soundness of these legal actions, the fact that they are in private international arbitration and the exorbitant compensation awarded to investors has had a chilling effect on government regulations and often governments opt for settlements that inevitably the favour foreign investor. Moreover, these private arbitration panels do not consider human rights or constitutional obligations of governments in making their decisions.

Creating a TRIPS-plus forum for TRIPS dispute settlement: Investment provisions in FTAs would also create a TRIPS-plus enforcement mechanism. At present if there is a dispute between two countries over the implementation of the TRIPS Agreement, this has to be argued out in public proceedings at the WTO Dispute

Settlement Body. Investment provisions that define IP as investment allow companies to sue countries in private arbitration over so called 'expropriation' or 'fair and equitable treatment' related to their IP and are effectively challenging countries in their implementation of TRIPS. For instance where a country issues a compulsory licence, a company could argue this to be expropriation. Some countries have started including specific exemptions stating that compulsory licences are not 'expropriation.' However, these provisions apply so long as the compulsory licenceis in accordance with TRIPS. This means that companies can still challenge compulsory licences by trying to claim that they violate TRIPS—something that under TRIPS only another government can do and that only in a public proceeding before the WTO Dispute Settlement Body. This would mean that an ad-hoc panel that is unlikely to follow precedent would determine the interpretation and application of TRIPS between the two countries.

Investment measures in FTAs are more extensive than those in BITs that India has signed: The existence of BITs between some developed countries and India has led some to wonder whether the inclusion of investment provisions in India's FTAs would alter the current situation. While reports and studies are increasingly showing that companies are using these BITs to prevent governments from implementing key policies related to development, health, and environmental protection, the fact that some BITs already exist is not a sufficient argument that the investment provisions in India's FTA are not of concern.

It should be noted that the Indian government does not have BITs with all developed countries. In fact, before the India-Japan CEPA was signed, India did not have a BIT with Japan. However, now investment measures have been introduced through this FTA. In addition, India does not have BITs with several EU member states. The investment provisions in India's FTAs would dramatically broaden the scope and reach of investor protections against the Indian government.

A key concern with including investment provisions in FTAs as opposed to stand alone BITs is the link this creates between trade and investment. Where a developing country like India finds that the abuse of investor protections in these BITs is significant enough to warrant that they be revoked, they would be unable to revoke investment provisions in an FTA as that would involve the revocation of the entire FTA. They also create an additional layer of enforcement of investment provisions. A dispute over investment protection under an FTA would provide the developed country with greater avenues to enforce the award including through retaliation on matters covered by the FTA like increasing tariffs etc.

In addition investment provisions in FTAs include so-called 'market access' or 'performance requirements' that essentially prevent governments from imposing conditions or restrictions on foreign investors. In the case of companies producing essential products like medicines this is a cause of concern. To ensure the certain medicines continue to be produced or that there is no shortage of raw materials, the Indian government, especially one with such an extensive generic industry that not only Indians but developing countries rely on, would need the flexibility to impose such requirements. The market access provisions in the investment provisions proposed by the EU in the EU-India FTA would make this very difficult for the Indian government.

There are now increasing calls for the rejection or the overhaul of the global investment treaty framework. In South Korea, judges have openly objected to investor-state dispute mechanisms highlighting its impact on the sovereignty of the country and on the judiciary.[85] Australia's new trade policy clearly states that the government would no longer sign any trade agreements which include investor-state dispute mechanisms.[86]

The India-Japan CEPA contains an investment chapter which includes intellectual property in the definition of investment. Article 92(5) of the investment chapter states that the provisions would not be applicable to compulsory licences issued in accordance with TRIPS. The limitations of this exception have been noted above. In 2011, the EC received a mandate from the European Council to include an 'investment' chapter in EU-India FTA negotiations. The investment chapter would contain provisions designed to protect the interests of European investors in India and would be similar to provisions contained in bilateral investment treaties or BITs.[87] Resolutions passed by the European Parliament in April and May of 2011 directed the European Commission to ensure that these investment provisions do not hamper generic production or the use of TRIPS flexibilities or other health policies.[88] The EFTA-India FTA will also likely have an investment chapter as previous EFTA FTAs indicate.[89] In addition, the US-India BIT will include several of the provisions discussed above. News reports indicate that due to a series of legal notices by foreign telecom firms, the Indian government is re-considering its approach to investment treaties and provisions.[90]

REGULATORY HARMONIZATION

The appearance of regulatory standards in FTAs seems to be a relatively recent phenomenon. In February 2011, news reports suggested that the EC was demanding that India harmonize its drug regulatory standards with the standards set by the International Conference on Harmonization of Technical Requirements for Registration of Pharmaceuticals for Human Use (ICH).[91] The ICH emerged from secret negotiations between the EU, US and Japan in the 1990s and its secretariat is hosted by the International Federation of Pharmaceutical Manufacturers and Associations (IFPMA). The EC demands would essentially require the Indian drug regulator to enforce standards similar to those enforced by the USFDA or the European Medicines Agency (EMEA).

Developing countries (also known as the non-ICH countries) have argued against the adoption of ICH standards as they are too burdensome and expensive not only for developing country regulators but also for companies in these countries. According to critics of the ICH standards, 'public health is the first concern in non-ICH countries, where the level of technical standards has to be justified by public health needs, not by the state-of-the-art technology.'[92] More vocal critics of the attempts by developed countries and the multinational pharmaceutical industry to promote the upwards harmonization of regulatory standards argue that such standards are designed only to be met by well-resourced companies and would ultimately squeeze generic companies out of production.[93]

GOVERNMENT OF INDIA'S POSITION

The FTAs being negotiated by India with developed countries would overturn or severely undermine several of the health safeguards in India's patent regime. A free trade agreement is a legally binding legal instrument and the Indian Parliament would have to amend India's laws while the government would have to make changes in policies to implement trade agreements domestically. A change in India's patent laws that prioritizes the interests of the multinational pharmaceutical industry over the right to health and access to medicines will impact millions not just in India but across the developing world who rely on Indian generic medicines not just for HIV, but also for cancer, heart disease, blood pressure, mental illness, etc. What developed countries are demanding of the Indian government jeopardizes the hard fought for balance between public interest and intellectual property rights that the Indian Parliament sought in 2005. The patent system is already having an impact on the availability of generic medicines from India and the TRIPS-plus demands of the developed countries threaten to make a bad situation worse.

It is unclear whether the Indian government always had a clear stand against TRIPS-plus provisions in these FTAs but this is now a public position that the government has arrived at. The final signed version of the India-Japan CEPA does not include the TRIPS-plus provisions that Japan originally demanded. The resolution of the Indian government's negotiators and of the government in general appears to have been more sharply challenged in the EU-India FTA negotiations with the EC adopting a far more aggressive negotiating strategy with the Indian government.

In April 2011, the Indian Prime Minister's Office issued a press release stating that nothing in the EU-India FTA would go beyond TRIPS or India's domestic law.[94] Sources indicate that the EC has now shifted negotiation tactics to argue that several of their demands are within the TRIPS framework or are already present in Indian law. For instance, the EC's position on whether data exclusivity is required by the TRIPS Agreement has been vague and any attempt to replicate the provisions of the TRIPS Agreement in the EU-India FTA may be used by the EC at a later stage to argue that TRIPS requires data exclusivity. Under the WTO framework, one of the European countries would have to take the Indian government to the WTO's dispute settlement body to settle this issue in a public dispute. But under the FTA, these discussions would be subject to secret arbitration between the EU and India. In addition, the EC also appears to be arguing that the IP enforcement measures it is demanding are within the scope of Indian legislation.

In February 2012, the 11th EU-India Summit was held in Delhi. One of the key areas identified by the EC to be discussed at the Summit was to speed up negotiations on the FTA. According to news reports from the Summit, it appears that both India and the EC stuck to their stands on various contentious issues in the FTA.[95] Among the specific TRIPS-plus demands of the EC that are of concern, the EC claims that it is no longer demanding patent term extension or EU-style data exclusivity. However, as the negotiation texts continue to be secret, it is difficult to ascertain the actual shift in the position of the EC. Also as noted above, even if the EC drops its demand for EU-style data exclusivity, it may still argue that data exclusivity of some sort is required by the TRIPS Agreement. The European Parliament has repeatedly issued resolutions directing the European Commission to ensure that access to medicines is not affected by the FTA. In May 2011, the European Parliament specifically asked the EC not to demand data exclusivity of the Indian government and recognised the importance of the use of TRIPS flexibilities by India.

FTAS, TRIPS AND THE RIGHT TO HEALTH

Several of the health safeguards included in the Indian patent regime are at risk of being overturned or undermined by TRIPS-plus provisions being demanded in FTAs with developed countries. These demands, if accepted, would have an impact not just on patients in India but those across the developing world. As a result, India's FTA negotiations have sparked global protests. Several other developing countries are also negotiating FTAs with the EU and the FTA with India is widely considered to be the template for these negotiations. For developing countries, India's ability to resist the EU's TRIPS-plus demands would create an important precedent. Protests against the EU-India FTA have taken place across the globe, kick-started by local networks of people living with HIV in India.[96] Health and public interest groups across the developing world have also been protesting other FTA negotiations by the EU, EFTA, the US and Japan.

The EU-India FTA has attracted particular concern from global health agencies. According to Jorge Bermudez, Executive Secretary of UNITAID,[97] 'already today, in the pre-EU-India FTA era, there are concerns around the price of new World Health Organization-recommended first-line regimens. As of 2008, the Indian generic global median price for newly recommended tenofovir-based regimens ranged from $246 to $309 per person per year, notably three to four times higher than the price of the most commonly used older regimen (3TC/NVP/d4T30). However, identical regimens, comprised of non-Indian generic and innovator ARVs, are considerably more expensive than the Indian generic versions. If the Free Trade Agreement introduces TRIPS-plus measures many of the people on medicines today will not be able to access vital second-line treatment when they become resistant to the medicines they are taking now.'

As other developing countries become increasingly embroiled in FTA negotiations, UN agencies are encouraging countries to ensure that the provisions in the FTAs do not undermine access to medicines. A joint UNDP, UNAIDS and WHO press release stated;[98] 'In 2009, funding for HIV was lower than in 2008. This is putting current treatment programmes under increased strain because of reduced budgets and competing priorities. In addition, proposed bilateral and regional free trade agreements could limit the ability of developing countries to use the TRIPS flexibilities. Governments in both developed and developing countries should ensure that any free trade agreements comply with the Principles of the Doha Declaration.'

But even as current debates rage around FTAs and TRIPS-plus measures, the debate over the trade agreement that started it all, the TRIPS agreement, also continues to rage. On the radar of human rights bodies within a few years of being signed, there has been an ongoing discussion about whether the TRIPS Agreement provides the appropriate legal framework required to ensure research and development (R&D) in medicines and access to medicines. Like India, more and more developing countries are now grappling with the adverse impact of the TRIPS Agreement and the calls for its review are getting louder. The impact of generic medicines on HIV treatment has been discussed above. That scenario probably holds true for many other diseases. A report on childhood medicines by the WHO and UNICEF demonstrates the importance of generic manufacturers for child friendly formulations of medicines.[99] Similarly, a study of accessibility of malaria medicines once again showed the impact of generic competition in lowering prices.[100] The case of diagnostics and medicines for TB shows a different side of the problem with TRIPS and that is the lack of investment in so-called neglected diseases. For decades countries in the South have had to rely on a century old diagnostic and four decades old medicines. Alternative investment routes are now resulting in R&D for TB diagnostics and medicines.

The original call for a human rights approach to the TRIPS Agreement and intellectual property from UN human rights bodies came within a few years of the TRIPS Agreement being signed. In 2000, the Sub-Commission on Human Rights of the United Nations High Commissioner for Human Rights passed a resolution on 'Intellectual Property Rights and Human Rights'. The resolution declared that, 'since the implementation of the TRIPS Agreement does not adequately reflect the fundamental nature and indivisibility of all human rights, including the right of everyone to enjoy the benefits of scientific progress and its applications, the right to health, the right to food and the right to self-determination, there are apparent conflicts between the intellectual property rights regime embodied in the TRIPS Agreement, on the one hand, and international human rights law, on the other.'[101]

By 2003, at the WHO, the CIPIH process commenced and resulted in the 2006 CIPIH Report which found that, 'there is no evidence that the implementation of the TRIPS agreement in developing countries will significantly boost R&D in pharmaceuticals on Type II, and particularly Type III diseases. Insufficient market incentives are the decisive factor.' Based on the report, member states of the World Health Assembly negotiated the Global Strategy and Plan of Action on Public Health, Innovation and Intellectual Property. This was perhaps the first formal review of the TRIPS Agreement, even though it was outside the WTO framework. Its principles attempted to provide solutions to the R&D crisis as well as clear recommendations on the use of TRIPS flexibilities to ensure access to medicines. However, the same period has witnessed a sharp increase in FTA negotiations between developed and developing countries begging the whole question of the implementation of the Global Strategy. Now, the high level Global Commission on HIV and the Law has crystallized the debate by calling for a suspension of the TRIPS Agreement in relation to medicines.[102]

CONCLUSION

In 2009, a small group of protestors from networks of people living with HIV and other groups stood with banners outside the office of the European Union Delegation to India in New Delhi. As they chanted against the FTA and the demands being made of India by the EC, they were detained by the police. In 2010, people living with HIV continued to gather and protest outside the offices of the Indian Ministry of Commerce and Industry. In 2011, over 3000 people from across India were joined by colleagues from South East Asia to march through New Delhi to voice their objection to the TRIPS-plus provisions of the EU-India FTA. In 2012, as thousands marched through Delhi once more, protests against the EU-India FTA were also held in Asia, Africa, Latin America and the EU.

The global movement against these FTAs has built into a powerful coalition that has seen some critical successes emerge from their ability to ensure that this issue remains in the public domain. To a large extent they have also succeeded in defining the terms of the debate around the impact of FTAs on access to medicines. In India, campaigning and pressure by local groups has seen India take public positions on the TRIPS-plus demands in its FTA negotiations. With reference to the EU-India FTA, the shift in the government position of denying that anything in the agreement would affect access to medicines to a public statement that India would not accept data exclusivity to a press release from the Prime Minister's Office directing negotiators that all provisions must be within TRIPS/domestic law has taken some years. In all the law and policy discussion and debate on India's FTAs or indeed its compliance with TRIPS, there remains a strong narrative of peoples' protest and peoples' movements that are shaping and forcing the debate on TRIPS and the right to health. In 2005, it was networks of people living with HIV along with several other groups working on health, mental illness, cancer and so on that marched through Delhi protesting the change in the Indian patent regime. It is many of these groups that continue to use the key health safeguards in India's patent law to file oppositions often using Section 3(d) provisions. And now, it is the same organisations that are campaigning against the adoption of FTAs that have provisions going beyond TRIPS. Their counterparts in other countries have been hard at work as well. The European Parliament has recently rejected ACTA in a significant setback to this particular trade agreement.

Looking back at a decade of highs and lows in access to generic medicines indicates more and more that the arrival of generic ARV medicines was an aberration in the slow but seemingly inexorable push of the global economic framework towards monopolies in medicines. The question for many governments and public interest groups now is that if a country like India with a strong international stature, remarkable generic industry and vibrant civil society cannot counter the adverse impacts of TRIPS, what hope is there for other countries. In the end, the Indian experiment may only show that no amount of patchwork, band aids and use of 'flexibilities' can counter the systemic bias in the international economic system, stacked as it was from the beginning against the South. The FTAs being negotiated by developed countries are pushing the global IP system towards its most extreme form that currently exists in developed countries.

Notes

1. Sub-Committee on Antitrust and Monopoly, Administered Prices, Drugs, 27 June 1961, (Report submitted by Mr. Kefauer from the Committee on the Judiciary), Senate, 87th Congress, 1st Session, Report No. 448, p. 112 available at http://babel.hathitrust.org/cgi/pt?id=mdp.39015006699972

2. Ayyangar, Rajagopal N, Report on the Revision of the Patents Law, Government of India, September 1959.

3. Section 53, Patents Act 1970 (before it was amended in 2005)

4. UNAIDS and WHO, Report on the Global HIV/AIDS Epidemic, June 1998 available at http://www.unaids.org/en/media/unaids/contentassets/dataimport/pub/report/1998/19981125_global_epidemic_report_en.pdf

5. In 2000, various UN agencies set up the Accelerating Access Initiative (AAI) with top multinational pharmaceutical companies. The AAI's 2002 report noted, 'despite the major reductions in ARV prices, the annual cost of ARV treatment for a person living with HIV still exceeds the annual per capita gross domestic product of many least developed countries.' WHO and UNAIDS, Accelerating Access Initiative Widening access to care and support for people living with HIV/AIDS, Progress Report, June 2002.

6. Medecins Sans Frontieres (MSF), Untangling the web of antiretroviral price reductions, July 2012, 14th edition, available at http://utw.msfaccess.org/

7. UNAIDS, Together We Will End AIDS, 2012, available at http://www.unaids.org/en/media/unaids/contentassets/documents/epidemiology/2012/20120718_togetherwewillendaids_en.pdf

8. Waning, B. et al., 'A lifeline to treatment: the role of Indian generic manufacturers in supplying antiretroviral medicines to developing countries,' *Journal of the International AIDS Society*, 2010, 13: 35, available at http://www.ncbi.nlm.nih.gov/pmc/articles/PMC2944814/

9. Amendments to India's patent regime to comply with TRIPS started with the Patents (Amendment) Act, 1999 which introduced the exclusive marketing rights or EMR mechanism and set up the mailbox system to hold patent applications that would be examined only after 2005. This was followed by the Patents (Amendment) Act 2002 which, among other things, extended the patent term to 20 years, reflected the requirements of the Patent Cooperation Treaty, included several exclusions from patenting, amended the chapter on compulsory licensing and included several amendments related to procedures. The final set of amendments was made in 2005 in the Patents (Amendment) Act 2005 which introduced the product patent regime in India as well as key health safeguards. See Patents (Amendment) Act, 1999, No.

17 of 1999 available at http://ipindia.nic.in/ipr/patent/patact_99.PDF, Patents (Amendment) Act, 2002, No. 38 of 2002 available at http://ipindia.nic.in/ipr/patent/patentg.pdf and Patents (Amendment) Act, 2005, No. 15 of 2005 available at http://ipindia.nic.in/ipr/patent/patent_2005.pdf.

10. See Letter from Nafis Sadik, M.D. Special Envoy of the UN Secretary-General HIV/AIDS in Asia and the Pacific and Stephen Lewis, Special Envoy of the UN Secretary-General HIV/AIDS in Africa U.N. Special Envoys for HIV/AIDS to the Prime Minister and President of India, 11 March 2005; Letter from Achmat Dangor, UNAIDS to Minister of Commerce and Industry, 23 February 2005; and Letter from Jim Yong Kim, HIV/AIDS Director of the World Health Organization to Minister of Health and Family Welfare, 17 December 2004 (on file with author).

11. World Trade Organisation (WTO), Declaration on the TRIPS agreement and public health, WT/MIN(01)/DEC/2, 14 Doha, November 2001, available at http://www.wto.org/english/thewto_e/minist_e/min01_e/mindecl_trips_e.htm

12. Section 3(d) of India's Patents Act, 1970 reads: 'The following are not inventions within the meaning of this Act ... the mere discovery of a new form of a known substance which does not result in the enhancement of the known efficacy of that substance or the mere discovery of any new property or new use for a known substance or of the mere use of a known process, machine or apparatus unless such known process results in a new product or employs at least one new reactant. *Explanation*: For the purposes of this clause, salts, esters, ethers, polymorphs, metabolites, pure form, particle size, isomers, mixtures of isomers, complexes, combinations and other derivatives of a known substance shall be considered to be the same substance, unless they differ significantly in properties with regard to efficacy.'

13. Office of the Controller General Of Patents, Designs, Trade Marks and Geographical Indications, *Annual Report 2009–10*, Department of Industrial Policy and Planning, Ministry of Commerce and Industry, Government of India, 2010, p. 35 available at http://ipindia.gov.in/cgpdtm/AnnualReport_English_2009_2010.pdf

14. There are two versions of pegylated interferon that have been patented in India. Pegylated interferon alpha 2a is patented by F. Hoffman-La Roche Ltd. who sells it as *Pegasys* and Pegylated interferon alpha 2b by Schering Plough Ltd (merged in 2009 with Merck and Co. and known by the latter name) who sells it as *Pegintron*. As the medicines are largely imported by the patent holders and not available through retail pharmacies, prices are difficult to ascertain. The Indian government procures pegylated interferon alpha 2a between Rs 6,000 and Rs 6,300 per vial (depending on

dosage) for government employees. See Central Government Health Scheme (CGHS), 'Life Saving Medicines as on 10th September 2010,' available at http://cghs.nic.in/Life Saving Medicines.htm. However patients have reported paying Rs 14,000 per vial for treatment in the private sector. See Priyanka Golikeri, 'Patents drive up treatment costs of Hepatitis C', *Daily News and Analysis* (DNA), 10 September 2010.

15. See CIPLA tells Merck your anti-AIDS drug too costly in India, CNBC-TV18, 4 April 2011 available at http://www.moneycontrol.com/news/business/cipla-tells-merck-your-ant-aids-drug-too-costlyindia_533783-1.html

16. Medecins Sans Frontieres (MSF), Untangling the web of antiretroviral price reductions, July 2012, 14th edition, available at http://utw.msfaccess.org/

17. NATCO Pharma Limited v. Bayer Corporation, Compulsory Licence Application No. 1 of 2011 (Before the Controller of Patents, Mumbai; Date of Decision: 9 March 2012).

18. At an exchange rate of $1 = Rs 55.

19. In May 2012, CIPLA announced lower prices for sorefanib tosylate after the compulsory licence was granted to Natco. CIPLA, initially the first generic company in the market with this medicine was charging Rs 30,000 per person per month and then announced a new price of Rs 6780 per person per month to compete with Natco's price. See Cancer drugs to cost less, CIPLA slashes prices, CNN-IBN, 5 May 2012 available at http://ibnlive.in.com/news/cancer-drugs-to-cost-less-cipla-slashes-prices/254837-17.html

20. Bayer Corporation and another v. Union of India, Special Leave Petition No. 6540 of 2010, Supreme Court of India.

21. F.Hoffman-La Roche Ltd. and Anr. v. CIPLA Ltd. 2009 (4) PTC 125 (Del) (DB).

22. Chaudhari et al., Five Years Into The Product Patent Regime: India's Response, UNDP, December 2010 available at http://www.undp.org.in/sites/default/files/reports_publication/UNDP_IndiaStudy.pdf

23. 'Patent Pool: Legitimising Big Pharma's Practices?,' *ACCESS* (A newsletter from the Lawyers Collective HIV/AIDS Unit), Vol III, Issue No. 1, February 2012, available at http://www.lawyerscollective.org/files/Access%20-%20Vol%20III,%20No_%201.pdf

24. Report of the India-Japan Joint Study Group, June 2006 available at http://www.mofa.go.jp/region/asia-paci/india/report0606.pdf

25. Bilaterals.org, Texts of Free Trade Agreements: EU, available at http://www.bilaterals.org/spip.php?rubrique52

26. India-EU Ministerial summit in November, *The Hindu*, 27 June 2012.

27. Report of the India-EFTA Joint Study Group, 2007 available at http://www.efta.int/~/media/Documents/legal-texts/free-trade-relations/india/Report-studygroup-India.pdf

28. Memorandum of Understanding on Bilateral Co-operation between The Office of the Controller General of Patents, Designs and Trade Marks, Department of Industrial Policy and Promotion, Ministry of Commerce and Industry of the Republic of India and the United States Patent and Trademark Office, U.S. Department of Commerce, 23 November 2009, available at http://dipp.nic.in/English/International_cooperation/MOU's/MOU_IPR/MOU_of_bilateral_cooperation_with_usa.pdf

29. Ministry of Commerce and Industry, 'India US Bilateral Investment Treaty Discussion Nearly Complete: Anand Sharma, Chicago Mayor and Former Obama Chief of Staff to Lead Trade Mission to India,' Press Information Bureau, Government of India, 21 September 2011 available at http://pib.nic.in/newsite/erelease.aspx?relid=76118

30. '2012 U.S. Model Bilateral Investment Treaty,' available at http://www.ustr.gov/sites/default/files/BIT text for ACIEP Meeting.pdf

31. U.S. FTA may cost drug industry $1.2 billion: gov't, The Hankyoreh, 18 October 2006 available at http://english.hani.co.kr/art/english_edition/e_business/165065.html

The Report is available at: 'Impact of the EU-Andean Trade Agreement on Access to Medicines'. (ICTSD) http://www.haiweb.org/11112009/11Nov2009ReportIFARMAImpactStudyPeru(EN).pdf

32. IFARMA, Impact of the EU-Andean Trade Agreements on Access to Medicines in Peru, Health Action International (Europe), October 2009, available at http://www.haiweb.org/11112009/11Nov2009ReportIFARMAImpactStudyPeru(EN).pdf

33. Kessomboon et al., Impact on Access to Medicines from TRIPS-plus: A Case study of Thai-US FTA, *South Asian Journal of Tropical Medicine and Public Health*, Vol 41, No. 3, May 2010, available at http://www.tm.mahidol.ac.th/seameo/2010-41-3/23-4785.pdf

34. See Article 17.3, *Preliminary Consultation Draft on IPR Chapter of India-EU Broad-based Trade and Investment Agreement*, April 2010, Leaked Text, available at http://www.bilaterals.org/spip.php?article17290&lang=en

35. However not all EFTA FTAs mandate patent term extensions and some leave it to the developing country to decide whether or not to provide such extensions. See Article 6.9(5), *Free Trade Agreement between the Republic of Colombia and the EFTA States*, 25 November 2008 (entry into force: 30 June 2011).

36. See Article 8(6), Trans-Pacific Partnership Intellectual Property Rights Chapter (Selected Provisions), Leaked Text, September 2011 available at http://infojustice.org/download/tpp/tpp-texts/U.S. Proposed Text on IP and Medicines, dated September 2011, leaked October 2011.pdf

37. European Union Delegation to Thailand, '*The EU fully recognizes India's right to issue compulsory licensing for medicines and has no intention of weakening India's capacity to manufacture and export medicines to other developing countries, including Thailand,*' Press Release, 10 February 2012, Bangkok available at http://eeas.europa.eu/delegations/thailand/documents/news/20120210_01_en.pdf

38. R v. Licensing Authority ex p Smith Kline (H.L.) [1990] 1 A.C. 64.

39. ICTSD-UNCTAD, *Resource Book on TRIPS and Development: An authoritative and practical guide to the TRIPS Agreement*, 2005 available at http://www.iprsonline.org/unctadictsd/ResourceBookIndex.htm

40. Differences scuttle Satwant Reddy Committee Report, *The Financial Express*, 21 May 2007 available at http://www.financialexpress.com/news/differences-scuttle-satwant-reddy-committee-report/199680/

41. Satwant Reddy and G.S. Sandhu, *Report on Steps to be taken by Government of India in the context of Data Protection Provisions of Article 39.3 of TRIPS Agreement*, 31 May 2007 available at http://chemicals.nic.in/DPBooklet.pdf

42. See for e.g., Embassy of the United States New Delhi, Data Protection—IPR Toolkit, available at http://newdelhi.usembassy.gov/iprdataprot.html

43. *A Trade Agreement's Impact On Access To Generic Drugs: The Impact Of CAFTA in Guatemala on Access to Medicines*, 2009, available at http://www.cpath.org/sitebuildercontent/sitebuilderfiles/cpathhaonline8-25-09.pdf

44. *All Costs, No Benefits: How TRIPS-Plus Intellectual Property Rules in the US-Jordan FTA affect access to medicines*, Oxfam, 2007, available at http://www.oxfam.org.uk/resources/issues/health/downloads/bp102_trips.pdf

45. Kessomboon et al., 'Impact on Access to Medicines from TRIPS-plus: A Case study of Thai-US FTA', *South Asian Journal of Tropical Medicine and Public Health*, Vol 41, No. 3, May 2010, available at http://www.tm.mahidol.ac.th/seameo/2010-41-3/23-4785.pdf

46. 'Patent Office rejects Roche claim on eye drug', *Business Standard*, 6 May 2010 available at http://www.business-standard.com/india/storypage.php?autono=393974

47. 'Public Health, Innovation and intellectual property rights', *Report of the Commission on Intellectual Property Rights, Innovation and Public Health*, World Health Organization, 2006, p. 125 available at http://www.who.int/intellectualproperty/documents/thereport/ENPublicHealthReport.pdf

48. See Para 6, World Trade Organisation (WTO), Declaration on the TRIPS agreement and public health, WT/MIN(01)/DEC/2, 14 Doha, November 2001, available at http://www.wto.org/english/thewto_e/minist_e/min01_e/mindecl_trips_e.htm

49. Kanga Raja, Members discuss implementation of TRIPS 'Para 6' solution, SUNS #6864, 16 February 2010 available athttp://www.twnside.org.sg/title2/wto.info/2010/twninfo100212.htm

50. Kesselheim and Solomon, *Incentive for Drug Development—The Curious Case of Colchicine*, N Engl J Med 2010; 362:2045-2047, 3 June 2010 available at http://www.nejm.org/doi/full/10.1056/NEJMp1003126

51. See Article 18 (EU), *Preliminary Consultation Draft on IPR Chapter of India-EU Broad-based Trade and Investment Agreement*, April 2010, Leaked Text, available at http://www.bilaterals.org/spip.php?article17290&lang=en

52. See Article 6.11, *Free Trade Agreement between the Republic of Colombia and the EFTA States*, 25 November 2008 (entry into force: 30 June 2011)

53. See Article 9, Trans-Pacific Partnership Intellectual Property Rights Chapter (Selected Provisions), Leaked Text, September 2011 available at http://infojustice.org/download/tpp/tpp-texts/U.S. Proposed Text on IP and Medicines, dated September 2011, leaked October 2011.pdf

54. See Article 137, Agreement between Japan and the Kingdom of Thailand for an Economic Partnership, 3 April 2007.

55. 59 fed. reg. § 50338, 50343 (Oct. 3, 1994) c.f. United States House of Representatives Committee on Government Reform—Minority Staff, Special Investigations Division, 'Trade agreements and access to medicines under the Bush administration,' June 2005.

56. Statement of the Honorable Henry A. Waxman, a Representative in Congress from the State of California, House Committee on Ways and Means, 10 June 2003.

57. *Report of the Commission on Public Health, Innovation and Intellectual Property Rights* (CIPIH), pp. 150–51.

58. EU Directorate-General for Competition, *Pharmaceutical Sector Inquiry—Preliminary Report*, 28 November 2008.

59. Bayer Corporation and another v. Union of India and others, Writ Petition (Civil) No. 7833/2008, Delhi High Court.

60. Bayer Corporation and another v. Union of India and others, LPA 443/2009, Delhi High Court.

61. Bayer Corporation and another v. Union of India, Special Leave Petition No. 6540 of 2010, Supreme Court of India.

62. See Article 9, Trans-Pacific Partnership Intellectual Property Rights Chapter (Selected Provisions), Leaked Text, September 2011 available at http://infojustice.org/download/tpp/tpp-texts/U.S. Proposed Text on IP and Medicines, dated September 2011, leaked October 2011.pdf

63. See Article 10.35, Free Trade Agreement between the European Union and its Member States, of the one part, and the Republic of Korea, of the other part, 6 October 2010, available at http://eur-lex.europa.eu/LexUriServ/LexUriServ.do?uri=OJ:L:2011:127:0006:1343:EN:PDF

64. See Article 18(4), *Preliminary Consultation Draft on IPR Chapter of India-EU Broad-based Trade and Investment Agreement*, April 2010, Leaked Text, available at http://www.bilaterals.org/spip.php?article17290&lang=en

65. Oxfam, 'Eye on the Ball: Medicine Regulation—Not IP enforcement—can best deliver quality medicines,' February 2011, available at http://www.oxfam.org/en/policy/eye-ball

66. Health Action International et al., *Another Seizure of Generic Medicines Destined for a Developing Country, this Time in Frankfurt*, Press Release, 5 June 2009 available at http://www.haiweb.org/19062009/5%20Jun%202009%20Press%20release%20Seizure%20of%20generic%20medicines%20in%20Frankfurt.pdf

67. Council Regulation (EC) No 1383/2003, Concerning customs action against goods suspected of infringing certain intellectual property rights and the measures to be taken against goods found to have infringed such rights, 22 July 2003, available at http://eur-lex.europa.eu/LexUriServ/LexUriServ.do?uri=OJ:L:2003:196:0007:0014:EN:PDF

68. 'India, Brazil drag EU to WTO', *Business Standard*, 13 May 2010.

69. Ministry of Commerce and Industry, *India EU Reach an Understanding on Issue of Seizure of Indian Generic Drugs in Transit*, Press Information Bureau, Government of India, 28 July 2011 available at http://pib.nic.in/newsite/erelease.aspx?relid=73554

70. Baker, Brook K. 2012. 'Settlement of India/EU WTO Dispute re Seizures of In-Transit Medicines: Why the Proposed EU Border Regulation Isn't Good Enough'. PIJIP Research Paper no. 2012–02 American University Washington College of Law, Washington, D.C.

71. See Recommendation 45, The 45 Adopted Recommendations under the WIPO Development Agenda, 2007 available at http://www.wipo.int/ip-development/en/agenda/recommendations.html

72. F.Hoffman-La Roche Ltd. and Anr. v. Cipla Ltd. 2009 (4) PTC 125 (Del) (DB).

73. See Sub-Section 3, Enforcement of Intellectual Property Rights, *Preliminary Consultation Draft on IPR Chapter of India-EU Broad-based Trade and Investment Agreement*, April 2010, Leaked Text, available at http://www.bilaterals.org/spip.php?article17290&lang=en

74. Article 13, Anti-Counterfeiting Trade Agreement, available at http://www.mofa.go.jp/policy/economy/i_property/pdfs/acta1105_en.pdf

75. Article 14, Trans-Pacific Partnership Intellectual Property Rights Chapter—Draft, Leaked Text, February 2011, available at http://keepthewebopen.com/tpp

76. K.M. Gopakumar and Nirmalya Syam, A Study on the Use of International Nonproprietary Names in India, CENTAD, 2007 available at http://www.searo.who.int/LinkFiles/Reports_NonproprietaryNames.pdf

77. Health Action International et al., *Another Seizure of Generic Medicines Destined for a Developing Country, This Time in Frankfurt,* Press Release, 5 June 2009 available at http://www.haiweb.org/19062009/5%20Jun%202009%20Press%20release%20Seizure%20of%20generic%20medicines%20in%20Frankfurt.pdf

78. MSF, Blank Cheque For Abuse: ACTA and its Impact on Access to Medicines, 2012, available at http://www.msfaccess.org/content/acta-and-its-impact-access-medicines

79. EU Directorate-General for Competition, *Pharmaceutical Sector Inquiry—Preliminary Report*, 28 November 2008.

80. 'Sleeping Lions: International investment treaties, state—investor disputes and access to food, land and water', Oxfam Discussion Paper, Oxfam, May 2011 available at http://www.oxfam.org/sites/www.oxfam.org/files/dp-sleeping-lions-260511-en.pdf

81. Matthew C. Porterfield and Christopher R. Byrnes, Philip Morris v. Uruguay: Will investor-State arbitration send restrictions on tobacco marketing up in smoke?, Investment Treaty News, International Institute for Sustainable Development, 12 July 2011, available at http://www.iisd.org/itn/2011/07/12/philip-morris-v-uruguay-will-investor-state-arbitration-send-restrictions-on-tobacco-marketing-up-in-smoke/

82. Philip Morris sues Australia over cigarette packaging, BBC News Asia, 21 November 2011 available at http://www.bbc.co.uk/news/world-asia-15815311

83. Marinn Carlson (Partner) and Peter Kasperowicz, Sidley Austin LL, Dutch insurer Eureko, Polish government settle investment dispute, setting up IPO for Poland's state-owned insurer, available at http://arbitration. practicallaw.com/6-500-6640

84. Public Citizen, *Another Broken NAFTA Promise: Challenge by U.S. Corporation Leads Canada to Repeal Public Health Law—Ethyl Wins $13 million Settlement and Repeal of Ban on Controversial Gasoline Additive*, 2000 available at http://www.citizen.org/trade/article_redirect. cfm?ID=5479

85. 'Judges debate KORUS FTA task force', *The Hankyoreh*, 3 December 2011.

86. Public Statement On The International Investment Regime, 31 August 2010 available at http://www.osgoode.yorku.ca/public-statement/ documents/Public%20Statement%20%28June%202011%29.pdf

87. EU-India FTA: proposed EU negotiating mandate on investment, 2011, available at http://www.bilaterals.org/spip.php?article18960

88. See Para 11, European Parliament resolution of 6 April 2011 on the future European international investment policy (2010/2203(INI)) and Paras 21 and 22, European Parliament resolution of 11 May 2011 on the state of play in the EU-India Free Trade Agreement negotiations (2011/2620(RSP)).

89. See for e.g. See Chapter 5, Free Trade Agreement between the Republic of Colombia and the EFTA States, 25 November 2008 (entry into force: 30 June 2011).

90. 'Foreign investors can claim damage under certain condition: AG', Zeebiz.com, 14 August 2012.

91. Joe Mathew, 'India-EU FTA: Tough Negotiations Over Healthcare Norms', *Business Standard*, 21 February 2011 available at http://www. business-standard.com/india/news/india-eu-fta-tough-negotiations-over-healthcare-norms/425921/

92. 10th International Conference of Drug Regulatory Authorities, Jointly organized by the World Health Organisation and the Government of the Peoples Republic of China, 2002, available at http://apps.who.int/ medicinedocs/pdf/s4923e/s4923e.pdf

93. 'Global Harmonization and the ICH', *Essential Drugs Monitor*, Issue No. 30, World Health Organisation, 2001 available at http://apps. who.int/medicinedocs/en/d/Jh2977e/4.html

94. Prime Minister's Office (PMO), Trade Negotiator's Given Guidelines, Press Information Bureau, Government of India, 30 April 2011 available at http://pib.nic.in/newsite/PrintRelease.aspx?relid=71881

95. Alexander J., 'India, EU stick to Earlier Stands on Health Sector as High Level Summit gave Momentum for FTA', *Pharmabiz*, 14 February 2012 available at http://pharmabiz.com/NewsDetails.aspx?aid=67520&sid=1

96. Delhi Network of Positive People (DNP+), 'EU-India FTA negotiations: DNP+ protest', December 2011, available at http://www.bilaterals.org/spip.php?article20741

97. Press release dated 3 March 2011, http://unitaid.eu/en/resources/news/320-unitaid-concerned-over-future-of-medicines-access-after-eu-india-fta.html

98. UNAIDS/UNDP/WHO concerned over sustainability and scale up of HIV treatment http://www.unaids.org/en/resources/presscentre/pressreleaseandstatementarchive/2011/march/20110315prtrips/

99. WHO and UNICEF, Sources and Prices of Selected Medicines for Children, 2nd edition, 2010 available at http://www.unicef.org/supply/files/SOURCES_AND_PRICES_2010(2).pdf

100. Suerie Moon et al., 'A Win-win Solution?: A Critical Analysis of Tiered Pricing to Improve Access to Medicines in Developing Countries', *Global Health*. 2011; 7: 39, available at http://www.ncbi.nlm.nih.gov/pmc/articles/PMC3214768/

101. Intellectual Property Rights and Human Rights, Sub-Commission on Human Rights, United Nations High Commissioner for Human Rights, Resolution 2000/7, available at http://www.unhchr.ch/Huridocda/Huridoca.nsf/0/c462b62cf8a07b13c12569700046704e?Opendocument

102. *Global Commission on HIV and the Law 2012, Regional Issues Brief: Intellectual Property Rights and Access to Medicines*, United Nations Development Programme, New York, available at http://www.hivlawcommission.org/

7   At any Price? Boehringer Ingelheim, Bayer HealthCare and Baxter in India

Christiane Fischer and Claudia Jenkes

This chapter presents the results of a study of three foreign multinational pharmaceutical companies and their activities in India. Two of these are German, Boehringer Ingelheim and Bayer HealthCare, and one, Baxter, is a US-headquartered company. The study was undertaken by the German organization BUKO Pharma-Kampagne and the Institute of Public Health (IPH) in Bangalore, India, and was first published in German in March 2011 (Fischer et al. 2011). The research focused on the effects of business activities on Indian patients in terms of the quality of drugs sold by these companies in India. Every single drug was classified in the categories 'rational', 'rational and essential' or 'irrational'. Our special interest was the proportion of essential drugs sold by the examined companies, and also the access to and availability of these very important drugs. As well as quantitative methods qualitative methods like interviews were used to increase the validity and reliability of the study results. From a literature review we gained additional information about clinical trials undertaken by Bayer, Baxter and Boehringer Ingelheim as well as about their advertising, partnerships and disease awareness programs. The evaluation of business practices was based on the Declaration of Human Rights of the United Nations, the Helsinki Declaration of the World Medical Association as well as the companies' own codes of Corporate Social Responsibility.

Quantitative data was collected between February and September 2009 through a search of the Monthly Index of Medical Specialties India MIMS (Gulhati 2010) and the Current Index of Medical

Specialties CIMS (Anitha et al. 2010). We also used the online version of CIMS. From these sources we were able to provide information on the availability of the companies' branded medicines. Clinical pharmacologists then classified every single drug as rational or irrational according to scientific criteria for rational drug therapy. Each decision was made on the basis of acknowledged international specialist literature that provides reliable information on the current state of the international scientific debate. This process allowed us to determine the proportion of rational and irrational products in the portfolio of each company. The Model List of Essential Medicines of the World Health Organization was used to identify essential drugs. The second part of the study was undertaken between August and November 2010 and examined a selection of 63 medical drugs in five institutions in the public, private and NGO sector, each in two federal Indian states, Karnataka and Tamil Nadu (30 institutions altogether). We examined whether the prices were affordable for the poor and compared them to the official product prices as given in MIMS, CIMS or throughcompany information. In order to gain a deeper understanding of the matter beyond facts andfigures, 30 semi-structured interviews were held between September 2010 and January 2011 in Karnataka and Tamil Nadu. An open questionnaire served as a conversation guide. Six doctors, 6 pharmacists and 6 patients (3 poor and 3 well-to-do) from the public, private and NGO sectors were interviewed, and in addition one representative of a company. Strict confidentiality was guaranteed and written records of the interviews were made immediately afterwards from memory. This method made it possible to record relevant information in condensed form. At the same time, the fact that no sound storage medium was used represented an important prerequisite to gaining the interviewees' trust and to guaranteeing their anonymity. This qualitative data allowed us to determine the consequences of company activities for doctors, pharmacists and patients. It also showed whether sick, poor people had access to necessary therapies marketed by the firms and whether prescription patterns of doctors differed depending on the economic means of patients. Patients were considered poor when they self-identified as such or were considered poor by the interviewer. Proxy indicators (gas instead of kerosene, television set) were also taken into account.

THE EXAMINED COMPANIES

Bayer HealthCare

This company belongs to the big global players in the pharmaceutical market. It sells its pharmaceutical products in more than 100 countries and in 2010 achieved a turnover of approximately 11 billion Euros (Bayer 2012a). Like other major pharmaceutical multinationals, it reports investments in research and development (R&D) of 15–17 per cent of revenue (Wild 2008). 'Science for a better life' is Bayer's motto. The company is seeking to significantly expand its presence in the growing Indian market. It expects to reach a turnover there of one billion Euros by 2015. In 2011 its revenue in this market was around 400 million Euros (CHE 2011). Bayer in January 2011 announced the establishment of a joint venture company, Bayer Zydus Pharma, with the major Indian pharma company Zydus Cadila. The new entity, headquartered in Mumbai, is reported to combine Zydus Cadila's 'strong Indian marketing and sales expertise as well as excellent distribution and industry network with Bayer HealthCare's expertise in successfully commercializing novel products and sophisticated administration and sales processes according to international standards' (Bayer 2011). Bayer's contraceptive pills Yaz, Yasmin and Yasminelle (drospirenone and ethinylestradiol) are the company's blockbusters with a turnover of 1.2 billion Euros (2008) together worldwide. Yasmin is also sold in India. In third place on their bestseller list is the cardiac preparation Adalat (nifedipine) (626 million Euro) and in tenth place is their preparation for lowering the blood sugar levels, Glucobay (acarbose) (304 million Euros), both sold in India (Wild 2008). Regarding patent matters Bayer has tried to accuse different countries (e.g. South Africa in 2001) of violation of patent rights. In most instances, Bayer abandoned the lawsuits or lost the cases. In India Bayer tried to prevent the approval of aproduct imitating their cancer drug, Nexavar (sorafenib). The Indian authorities had accepted for consideration an application for approval by the company, CIPLA, eleven years prior to the expiry of the patent protection, because the approval of a drug is not coupled with patent protection in India. Indian manufacturers of generics are therefore allowed to produce patented products and export them to countries where there are no patent protection laws. The suits filed by Bayer were rejected in several instances and the Indian Supreme Court confirmed that there was no patent linkage under Indian law.

Boehringer Ingelheim

This is a German family business and a research based pharmaceutical manufacturing company, which in 2009 generated a global turnover of 12,721 billion Euros. It reported that 17.4 per cent of revenue was invested in R&D. 'Value through innovation' is the company's motto (Boehringer Ingelheim 2012). By far the largest proportion of Boehringer Ingelheim's turnover is generated by prescription drugs. Among its products are drugs for cardio-vascular diseases such as Micardis (telmisartan), also sold in India, and drugs for high blood pressure and HIV/AIDS. The drug Micardis (telmisartane), essential for the treatment of high blood pressure, generated proceeds of 1,123 million Euros and a growth of about 23 per cent in local currency in the year 2007. Aggrenox (dipyridamole/ASS), used for secondary prevention of apoplexies, is likewise sold in India, generating proceeds of 278 million Euros (derStandard.at 2008). Boehringer Ingelheim, which does not yet have a major presence in India, plans expansion through its alliance with Zydus Cadila (Boehringer Ingelheim 2008). In 2006 Boehringer Ingelheim tried to hinder Indian companies from selling cheap generic versions of the important AIDS-drug nevirapine to African countries. The firm threatened African pharmacists and wholesalers with lawsuits and also tried to obtain a patent in India on the children's version of nevirapine. But no patent was granted by the Indian authorities. In recent years Boehringer Ingelheim has followed a new policy and opened access to its AIDS drug for poor countries through a voluntary Non Assert Declaration.

Baxter International

This company is principally in the business of developing, manufacturing and marketing drugs for the treatment of hemophilia, immune-deficiencies, infectious diseases, cancer and renal damage.

It is the world's largest manufacturer of infusion solutions and systems for intravenous administrations. Baxter supplies products to more than 100 countries, with manufacturing in 27 countries including three production sites in India with about 700 employees. The Indian plants produce for the local market as well as for export (Baxter 2012). Baxter's global turnover was roughly $12.8 billion in 2010. The company reports R&D investments of $915 million in 2010 (Baxter 2010). Its best-selling product is Advate, a drug produced by recombinant technology to substitute blood in the treatment of hemophilia. This drug generated worldwide sales of more than $1.7 billion in 2009. It is also sold in India under the name Recombinate (Vectura 2010).

HOW GOOD ARE THE DRUGS SUPPLIED BY THESE COMPANIES?

To evaluate the quality, i.e. the efficacy and safety as well as the medicinal use, of each company's portfolio, each pharmaceutical underwent a uniform evaluation process. Medicinal drugs which are not essential may still be safe, harmless and of therapeutic value. Pharmaceuticals which are effective and harmless according to current scientific knowledge, were graded as rational (r), the rest as irrational (i). Our evaluation used the scientific criteria for rational drug therapy, which are based on clinical evidence. The pharmaceutical industry claims that their products meet these criteria. The criteria used in the evaluation process which eventually resulted in the classification into positive and negative drugs is documented in the diagram below. Pharmaceuticals deemed effective and safe according to current scientific knowledge (first line treatment, second line treatment, prescribed by specialists) are rational drugs. Drugs included on the WHO 2010 model list of essential medicines are classified essential. The list contains about 350 active agents essential for health care. All essential drugs are seen as rational (WHO 2010). The most important reasons for classifying drugs as irrational are:

They involve irrational combinations

They are ineffective

POSITIVE	Drug of first choice	Drugs of proven efficacy and with an adequate risk-benefit-ratio, thus representing the best treatment for most patients in specific fields of application.
	Drug of other choice	Products for a smaller number of patients not benefiting from a first-choice medicinal product. The risk-benefit-ratio is often more unfavorable than for the drugs of first choice.
	Drugs for specialists	Drugs whose use has particular prerequisites, e.g. a special diagnostic, apparatus or special therapeutic experience. If they are used without supervision, they bear a high potential risk (e.g. anti-cancer drugs).
NEGATIVE	Irrational combinations	Combinations of different active agents are problematic on principle since it is not possible to predict how the individual substances will interact or to calculate the desirable as well as the undesirable effects of such interactions. Different substances moreover have different profiles as regards bio-availability and pharmacokinetics: one substance is often more rapidly reabsorbed or decomposed than the other. In addition, the dosage of one of the active agents cannot be individually adapted without changing the dosage of all other substances as well. It is not only the desired effects of the medicinal agents which are combined, but also their side effects and risks. Combination preparations are evaluated as irrational if they contain more than three active agents, if they contain an ineffective or incorrectly dosed active agent, or if the active agents have mutually exclusive efficacy profiles.
	Ineffective drugs	Drugs the efficacy of which could not be proven even though they have been subjected to several trials.
	Controversial effectiveness	Controversial data has been provided on these drugs. As long as no unequivocal data is provided, these drugs should not be used but be replaced with a reliable drug.
	Insufficient testing	This drug has not been tested sufficiently and should be replaced by a better tried and proven drug.
	Alternative with fewer risks available	Although these drugs are effective, they also include a higher risk than others and thus a worse risk-benefit ratio than alternative products.
	More effective alternative available	There is no justification for using drugs which are less effective than alternative products. Patients have the right to receive the most effective medicine.
	Wrong amount of active agent	These medicinal products contain active agents in an amount that is either too large or too small. They should therefore not be used.

Their effectiveness is controversial
They have been insufficiently tested
Alternatives with fewer risks are available
More effective alternatives are available
They contain wrong amounts of the active agent
The wrong dosage is recommended.

Classification of the drugs surveyed according to evaluation criteria

Boehringer Ingelheim had 13 different preparations in 27 different recommended dosages and formulations on the Indian marketat the time of the investigation. The company offered no drugs for neglected diseases. None of their products was on the essential list, 8 (30 per cent) were deemed rational and 19 (70 per cent) irrational. Of the three companies, Boehringer Ingelheim had the worst product portfolio on the Indian market. For example, some rational products were evaluated as irrational because of their formulations: examples includehyoscine butylbromide (Buscopan) in the form of tablets or hyoscine butylbromide in combination with paracetamol (Buscopan plus). Likewise the combination of clonidine and chlorothalidone (Catapres DIU) had to be negatively evaluated as irrational. Moreover, many of its irrational products were very expensive and clearly marketed only to the affluent middle class. But we also found very costly rational products: Alteplase (actilyse) for an acute cardiac attack is sold at a price of Rs 37,500 for 1 ampoule of 50 mg. Prescribing this drug would blow the budget even of a well-off middle class household. Indicative of the average monthly income of many Indians is the income of a teacher who typically earns between Rs 10,000 and Rs 20,000 Rs, while a domestic servant may earn only Rs 3,000 to Rs 10,000.

Bayer marketed 39 different preparations in a total of 77 recommended dosages and formulations. Of these, 9 (12 per cent) drugs were on the essential list, 40 (52 per cent) were rational and 28 (36 per cent) irrational. The product portfolio of Bayer was better than that of Boehringer Ingelheim, though Bayer had more serious problem drugs on market. The essential drugs were mostly old preparations likethe antimalarial chloroquine (Resochin) which is of little use because of frequently occurring resistance. For want of alternatives, it is still frequently used in India, particularly by the poor. An Indian doctor working in a public hospital reported:'Two weeks ago I was treating a patient suffering from malaria with chloroquine. Thank God it worked since other drugs are hardly available!' None of the newer Bayer products which have come on the Indian market since 1995 was classified as essential. Furthermore several rational Bayer drugs blow the budgets of the majority of Indian households: the cost of the x-ray contrast agent Ultravist is Rs 2,667 for 20 ml, and the multiple sclerosis drug interferon beta costs Rs 116,300 for 15 pre-filled syringes. Bayer's anti-cancer drugs are likewise unaffordable: Nexavar (sorafenib) costing Rs 2,80,430 for 120 tablets of 200 mg and the anti-leukemia drug fludarabine (fludara) costing Rs 33,315 for 20 tablets. Moreover, in tablet form this preparation was deemed irrational. A total of 10 (13 per cent) products were classified as expensive.

Particularly striking is the marketing of the disputed and irrational contraceptives Diane 35 and Yasmin. Interviews with Indian doctors confirmed that medical sales representatives promoted Bayer's contraceptive pills intensively in private hospitals. The combination of cyproterone acetate and ethinylestradiole (Diane 35) is no longer approved as a contraceptive pill in Germany since the Federal Institute for Drugs and Medical Devices came to suspect that it might be associated with liver tumors in 1994. The approved indications of this agent have since been severely restricted. The only two uses for which it remains approved are first as a substitute in case of androgen-induced disorders in women, and second as a treatment of severe acne (*arznei-telegramm* 1994). The active agents also bear an increased risk of thrombosis (*arznei-telegramm* 2002). In contrast, the online version of the Indian Compendium of Medicines, CIMS India, clearly listed DIANE 35 as a contraceptive at time of the study (Anitha et al. 2010). The combination of drospirenone and ethinyl estradiol (Yasmin) is approved as a contraceptive pill in Germany also and is becoming increasingly popular among young women. However, the independent German specialist journal *arznei-telegramm* advises against the use of the pill. In comparison with other contraceptives, the risk of thrombosis is significantly higher (*arznei-telegramm* 2009). Indian women who take Bayer's Yasmin and Diane 35 are deceived twice since the contraceptive pills cannot only damage their health but are also very expensive. The preparations cost Rs 231 or 360 Rs per menstrual cycle and take money out of the women's pockets unnecessarily. The contraceptive pills levonorgestrel and ethinyl estradiol, which have significantly fewer side effects, can be obtained free-of-charge (as Mala N) in the public health system. They are manufactured by the government-owned company Hindustan Latex Limited (Hindustan Latex Limited 2012).

Highly problematic is also the vitamin mixture, Bayer's Tonic. It is relatively cheap but does not have proven benefits for patients. Our Indian partners confirmed that the tonic is purchased and consumed mainly by poor people, mostly women and children. Bayer's Tonic is not approved for children in India but Indian pharmacists still recommend it as a tonic for children since the preparation has been recommended for decades by the German manufacturer as a restorative tonic and appetite stimulant for children. In addition to liver extracts, yeast and sugar, Bayer's Tonic also contains much alcohol (10 per cent). It is above all malnourished children who are in danger of developing fatal liver cirrhosis if they take the tonic on a regular basis. The Rs 85.65 which this useless and harmful preparation costs could be otherwise used to provide a large family with healthy food for at least one day.

Irrational diabetic preparations such as acarbose (Glucobay) are also questionable. Diabetes is an increasing problem in India affecting about 40 million people. In urban areas, its prevalence has reached 9 per cent. The availability of affordable rational preparations is essential. Bayer tried to prove the benefits of acarbose (Glucobay) in its comprehensive STOP-NIDDM survey. However, this was not successful. Bayer employees participated in the administration of the survey, which resulted in conflicts of interests and contradictory data in the medical journals *Lancet* and *JAMA*. The journal *arznei-telegramm* concluded:'It has not been proven that acarbose (Glucobay) is beneficial for lowering the risk of cardiovascular diseases in patients with an increased blood sugar level. The alleged published proof of benefits by the STOP-NIDDM study is based on a data manipulation to the advantage of acarbose' (*arznei-telegramm* 2003).

Baxter sells 38 preparations in India in a total of 80 recommended dosages and formulations. Thirty-five products (43.75 per cent) were graded as essential and rational and 10 (12.5 per cent) as irrational. The product portfolio comprises few irrational and many essential products. The pricing however suggests that Baxter (as Bayer and Boehringer Ingelheim) focuses on the private sector and the Indian middle class. Many of the products have no generic alternative, such as an antibiotic infusion solution, and the pricing is therefore largely monopolistic. This excludes the poor from access to important drugs. Baxter sells numerous essential drugs in India, among them important antibiotics, anti-cancer drugs and infusion solutions such as dextrose. As in other countries, Baxter primarily focuses on infusion solutions. However, in the case of antibiotics in particular, tablets could often be used instead. These are generally produced as generics and thus offered at a lower price. In India, intravenous solutions are seen as the more potent medicine in particular among the poor. The company has introduced 10 drugs in India since 1995. None of these preparations, however, can be considered essential. Of these, 6 preparations are irrational, 4 rational.

WHAT ABOUT ACCESS?

Prices and availability of the companies' drugs were determined on the basis of the established WHO/HAI methodology (HAI 2008): 63 medical drugs were selectedfrom the Bayer, Boehringer Ingelheim and Baxter ranges, including rational, irrational and essential drugs as well as low, middle and high priced drugs. The availability and prices of these drugs were examined in five institutions in the public, private and NGO sectors in the federal Indian states of Karnataka and Tamil Nadu (30 institutions altogether). We examined whether their prices were affordable to the poor and compared the realprice of the institutions to the official price we found in MIMS, CIMS and in communication with the companies.

The selection of drugs and the company sales strategies point to the conclusion that the firms focus their business strategies on the private and NGO sectors. None of the companies' drugs is used in the public sector. Only two of Baxter's products are listed in the tender for public clinics in Tamil Nadu (TNMSC 2012). It is astonishing that many of the NGO clinics (church institutions as well as secular ones) differ only slightly from the private sector. The tendency towards originator brands was evident in both sectors but is even more pronounced in the private sector. Notably, high priced originator brands are offered by clinics which run a small intensive care unit or by a university hospital. More than 80 per cent of the examined products were sold at the maximum price allowed.

Different types of drugs are used in the different sectors, though the patients' problems are the same. Interviews with doctors from the private, NGO and public sector showed that they all treated a similar range of conditions: high blood pressure, malaria, pneumonia, dehydration after diarrhea, fungal infection or amoebic dysentery. But the prescription and and choice of drugs for treatment differs a lot according to the patients' financial situations. In the private and the NGO sectors, patients usually have to pay the full cost of medical consultations, hospitalization, food and drugs themselves since fewer than 20 per cent of the population have health insurance. In the public institutions, drugs and treatments are free of charge but high costs are often incurred for transport to the hospital. In addition, patients lose their daily income. If poor patients have to switch to NGO hospitals, the bill quickly exceeds their monthly wage. As one malaria patient explained: 'I urgently need medical and financial help. When the public health service was not able to help me, I came here (note: into an NGO hospital)'. In the course of his treatment, debts of Rs 20,000 had rapidly accumulated—at a monthly income of Rs 6,000 which is barely enough for him and his wife to live on.

Newer, innovative pharmaceuticals, which have come on the market since 1995, are not available to the poor in India. Neither compulsory licences nor non-obligatory licences have been granted on existing rational innovations of the three companies at the time of the study. Moreover, the innovative preparations produced by the companies in our survey do not correspond to the Indian need for pharmaceuticals for treating neglected diseases. In the case of malaria, this has a grave effect. When resistances develop in the treatment with chloroquine, newer and more effective preparations are not available to the poor. Likewise, tuberculosis and other diseases of the poor do not lie within the research interest of the companies.The most important innovation is the anti-cancer drug sorafenib (Nexavar). Bayer owns the patent,[1] but lost a patent suit against the company CIPLA, in which the linkage of the patent to the drug's production was on trial (patent linkage). The Indian High Court denied a connection. CIPLA is permitted to produce sorafenib as a generic, but not to sell it in India as a result of the patent protection existing there (dpa 2010). CIPLA intends to produce sorafenib at a tenth of the Bayer price. The market price of Rs 2,80,000/120 tablets is presently a massive obstacle to access. However, in August 2011 Natco Pharma Ltd applied for a compulsory licence for sorafenib tosylate (Nexavar) (*Official Journal of the Patent Office* 2011). On 12 March 2012, Natco was successful in gaining a compulsory licence for the production and supply of this product. The licence was issued essentially on the grounds that Bayer's price is exorbitant. It also doesn't manufacture the drug in India and imports in such small volumes that only a tiny fraction of potential patients could benefit.

DRUG TREATMENT IN THE NGO, PRIVATE AND PUBLIC SECTORS

The private and the NGO sectors use a largely identical range of drugs. The main emphasis is on the medium price range with many irrational products such as Bayer's Tonic. NGO clinics also distribute dubious third generation oral contraceptives such as Diane 35. Eight of the NGO hospitals included in our survey used 39 of the three companies' drugs in a total of 82 recommended dosages and formulations. Two houses used 14 or 16 products, respectively, the other clinics 8–11. Two clinics offered a costly product with human albumin. One of the houses, a university clinic, also used sorafenib (Nexavar) as well as alteplase (Actilyse). Two NGO hospitals did not use any original preparations since they generally purchased cheap rational generics from the Indian non-profit company LOCOST. Private clinics additionally offer Yasmin.

Since Bayer sponsors information campaigns on family planning and contraception, a connection has to be suspected. The World Contraception Day was staged by Bayer and the Family Planning Association of India (FPAI) on 26 September 2010 (India Blooms 2010). A comprehensive website on this day, sponsored by Bayer, offers information on the pill and about contraception in general. All private hospitals used the drugs of the companies included in the survey. We found 37 drugs in 141 different recommended dosages and formulations. Among them was one costly preparation (human albumin 5 per cent), vancomycine n (Vancomate) and cetirizine (Incid), two preparations in the medium price range. One clinic used 33 products, another 22; four houses had 14 to 16 products from Bayer Schering Pharma, Baxter and Boehringer Ingelheim on offer. Four other private clinics used 5–9 products of the three companies. In interviews, the frequent use of the original preparations in our survey was confirmed.

In the public sector, new and improved drugs, including the drugs examined, are generally not tendered for, and are often not available. Grave problems follow when patients cannot access needed drugs. Nevertheless all patients stated that they were more than satisfied with the treatment received. All had a very high opinion of doctors; one patient said: 'They are my saviours!' This evaluation of very high patient satisfaction was shared by all persons interviewed. Patients with little education, and poor patients, often preferred injections to tablets. For cultural reasons, injections are seen as stronger medicine than capsules or tablets. If a doctor did not comply with this wish, dissatisfaction was the result. In the main, poor patients initially go to a non-registered practitioner in case of an illness. Only some non-registered medics, however, have a medical degree. They are favoured by pharmaceutical company representatives. Dr Roopa Devadasan explained in an interview with BUKO Pharma-Kampagne that many small medical practices followed the golden rule of receiving the first three such representatives. Accordingly, when the practice opens, several representatives of pharmaceutical companies are already waiting at the surgery. As our interviews confirmed, poor patients only made use of public (and sometimes NGO) institutions when they could not find help in a non-registered medical practice. Their relationship to physicians in all sectors is characterized by great authority. The therapies prescribed are rarely questioned. As a rule, this relationship of confidence also exists in the case of more affluent and better educated patients who turn immediately to a private or NGO clinic in case of sickness.

RESEARCH AND PATENTS

We identified the research activities of the three companies through public databases like http://clinicaltrials.gov/as well as by correspondence with the firms, their websites and by correspondence with Indian authorities. Research undertaken by the companies is strongly focused on profitable markets and new areas of use of already bestselling products. Of the trials financed by the companies we surveyed, none is concerned with neglected diseases such as TB, malaria, chikungunya or dengue fever. Although Bayer and Boehringer Ingelheim only offer a limited pharmaceutical portfolio, they use the Indian market for numerous research projects focused on their blockbusters. In addition to a large pool of patients and highly trained specialists, India offers modern and well-equipped hospitals and comparatively low research costs.

Boehringer Ingelheim is undertaking 38 clinical trials at varying phases, including 13 trials relating to type II diabetes which is common in India. Twenty-four of Bayer's pharmaceutical trials have reached varying phases. These include a large double-blind, multi-centre trial of moxifloxacine, an antibiotic which is tested for application in children suffering from a complicated intra-abdominal infection. The drug is also tested by the Tuberculosis Research Centre together with the National Institutes of Health (NIH) in tuberculosis therapy. Bayer is not financing this trial but they emphasize in their sustainability report (Bayer 2008) that they are participating in research for a new tuberculosis drug: 'Bayer is working together worldwide with the Global Alliance for TB Drug Development, or TB Alliance for short, to develop a tuberculosis drug that significantly reduces the duration of treatment'. Baxter does not carry out any clinical trials in India.

Baxter has filed 248 patent applications, 48 of which have been granted. Only one patent application refers to a drug contained in our survey. Boehringer Ingelheim has filed 519 patent applications in India, of which 99 have been granted. For our survey, 14 applications and four patents are relevant. The Bayer Group has filed 2314 patent applications (all business areas) in India, 363 of which have been granted. The majority, however, does not refer to the pharmaceutical area. Bayer has filed 7 patent applications on the drugs included in this survey; 4 have been granted, 3 of them on moxifloxacin (Avalox)[2], one on sorafenib (Nexavar)[3]. The Bayer Group in particular does everything to aggressively assert their patent rights, as exemplified by the Nexavar case (dpa 2010), where Bayer lost a patent suit against the company, CIPLA, in which the linkage of the patent to the drug's production was on trial (patent linkage) (dpa 2010). Boehringer Ingelheim also asserts its patent rights but, in the case of AIDS, allows fairer access to their two HIV drugs, nevirapine and tripanavir, through a voluntary Non Assert Declaration. In Africa and India, these important drugs may be produced as generics without the company asserting their patent rights—an important step in the right direction (Boehringer Ingelheim 2007). Baxter is following another route: the company produces numerous rational pharmaceuticals which have no alternative treatments. So they can determine the price for many products without competition.

MARKETING AND BUSINESS BEHAVIOUR

Since 1955, direct marketing of pharmaceuticals to the general public has been prohibited in India and only permitted in professional circles (Ministry of Law and Justice 1955). Information campaigns for family planning, health care and disease awareness are, in fact, permitted. The companies therefore focus their promotional activities on the sponsoring of campaigns or they use social networks such as Facebook and Twitter, which attract, in particular, the young and affluent middle classes. Doctors and pharmacists are also intensively courted. The website www.glucobay.com is linked to the Indian Bayer page. It contained in 2011 scientifically unproven claims in its advertising to doctors: 'Glucobay delays the progression of diabetes and provides additional cardiovascular benefits'. The link to the Indian web page cleverly evades the ban on advertising to the public; the advertisement is freely accessible after a click confirming status as a healthcare professional.

In an interview in 2010, a leading Indian pharmaceutical representative from German Remedies explained: 'Lay advertising is largely without interest for us. We focus on doctors. As a rule-of-thumb: any doctor has to yield 10 times as much as we invest in them. We often put rupees five million per year into a doctor and now you can calculate how much we earn through them'. In interviews the doctors and pharmacists emphasized that the medical representatives primarily focus on the clinic pharmacists since they decide which drugs are handed out to the patients. In private hospitals, promotion is also directed at doctors. In addition, the confusing mass of unregistered doctors seems also to be the target of industry promotion since their practices are the first approached by the majority of patients. Despite downplaying its importance, the industry is lobbying to have direct advertising to consumers legalized in India as it is in some other countries (Mack 2007). Another Bayer strategy is to discredit Indian companies by implying that they market counterfeit drugs or goods of a substandard quality; whereas Bayer's name is always equated with quality medicine (Bayer 2012b). Baxter also follows this strategy by praising its products as being of a particularly high quality.

As a freely accessible space which is difficult to control, the internet offers the possibility of directing customers to international websites not subject to Indian regulations, and thus to draw their attention to branded products. For example, on their website relating to the World Contraception Day held in India, Bayer employed a subtle strategy in its product placement: the ambassadors introduced on the start page 2010 were called Claire and Diana, the same names as Bayer's contraceptive pills (Diane 35, Qlaira).

Facebook is used by all companies for promotion. 'Yes I can India' is a page sponsored by Bayer, which claims to provide information on contraception to young people and is promoted via Facebook.[4] Boehringer Ingelheim is in the lead on Twitter. In 2011, the company had 2658 followers. But Baxter and Bayer have also discovered Twitter (Mack 2009). It is possible for Indians to register via a special country code. Moreover, patients' discussion forums such as e.g. the Cancer Compass are cleverly used. There, a friendly medical representative gives the information that the anti-cancer drug Nexavar is available in India, naturally without stating the price.[5]

Bayer seeks to strengthen its corporate image through numerous partnerships such as that with the India Diabetes Educator Project. Consistent with their product portfolio of antidiabetics such as acarbose (Glucobay), Bayer trains diabetes health care professionals (Max Healthcare 2012). In addition, there are freely accessible films in which the name Bayer is mentioned and which purport to be educational (YouTube.com 2010). In the state of Karnataka, Biocon and Bayer have a partnership to enhance the public awareness of diabetes and Bayer's products (Anthra News 2010). Moreover, Bayer sponsors educational campaigns for family planning and contraceptives, a clever method to place the company in a favorable light as market leader in the contraceptive field.

Consistent with its product portfolio, Baxter sponsored the World Haemophilia Day on 17 April 2010, jointly with health care institutions in Mumbai, Chennai, Kolkata, Lucknow, Delhi, Trivandrum and Jaipur (Baxter 2010b). The company prides itself on support for the reputed Pulse Polio Program of the Indian government, in which every child under five is to be vaccinated annually (!) against polio no matter if s/he had already been vaccinated or not (Baxter 2012b). Despite this vigorous vaccination campaign, the number of polio infections has risen. The cost effectiveness of this vertical program is questionable.

In addition to their sponsoring of health events, all three companies invest in donation programmes. Bayer finances doctors and nurses in areas with tsunami victims, supports schools and children, environmental projects, projects against child labor and has an emergency fund. Similar donation programs are financed by Baxter via the Baxter International Foundation. The foundation supports the training of street children, maintains an emergency fund for tsunami victims (in which infusion solutions are donated) and finances a project for AIDS education as well as a house building project. Responsibility for many of the Baxter initiatives is borne by their employees and it is not clear whether their work is voluntary (Baxter 2012b). These projects have to be evaluated as measures which do help individuals, but which are primarily aimed at improving the company's image. Boehringer Ingelheim supports an HIV and workplace project in India. With its Non Assert Declaration, the company permits all WHO prequalified producers in India and Africa to manufacture nevirapine and tripranavir as generics (Boehringer-Ingelheim 2007). The Non Assert Declaration reaches far beyond the customary company commitment. It improves access to AIDS drugs in Africa. The access to medicine index therefore places Boehringer's patent policy in second place on a list of 20 pharmaceutical companies examined, whereas Bayer is placed at 14. Baxter was not examined (Access to Medicine Foundation 2010).

The WHO's ethical criteria for pharmaceutical promotion states: '... "promotion" refers to all informational and persuasive activities by manufacturers and distributors, the effect of which is to induce the prescription, supply, purchase and/or use of medicinal drugs'. In this sense, sponsoring of events or of patient support groups has to be understood as promotion and, even more so, a clever product placement, as in the case of Bayer's contraceptive pills. Likewise, the partnerships entered into by the companies seem primarily to serve to cultivate the companies' images.

CONCLUSION

Bayer, Baxter and Boehringer Ingelheim aim exclusively at the Indian middle and upper classes with their pricing policies. Bayer and Boehringer Ingelheim distribute many expensive drugs which serve patients poorly. In the public health care system, not one of the examined companies' drugs is being used. It is only private and NGO hospitals which use their products. Important drugs such as the cancer drug Nexavar from Bayer are not available to poor patients. On the other hand, these companies extract money from the pockets of the poor for irrational vitamin mixtures such as Bayer's Tonic. Bayer and Boehringer Ingelheim carry out numerous research projects in India and profit from the low cost of clinical trials, which are only half as expensive as similar trials in Europe (SOMO 2011). Despite that, this research is exclusively focused on profitable medical fields and at possible new applications of already established blockbusters. No trials for neglected diseases are financed by the companies in India. Instead, Bayer in particular engages in subtle product placement to promote the sale of their products. Clever marketing of third-generation contraceptive pills is the more questionable as the pills are not only more expensive but also riskier than the generic preparations offered free of charge in the public health system.

The patent system does not provide an incentive for companies to direct their research at servicing real worldwide needs. Thus the time has come for trying new ways, as is also demanded by the WHO. Research projects supported by the state, public invitations to tender for research projects or patent pools are conceivable models to boost the research of neglected diseases.

Access to important essential drugs is better ensured by the Indian generic companies than by brand-name companies. Stricter patent protection could be fatal because it results in significantly reduced access to medical health care not only in India, but also in other poor countries around the world. However, the Indian government needs to ensure, by an effective approval procedure, that patients receive safe pharmaceutical products of high quality. Germany and the EU could support this process and refrain from associating generics with counterfeit drugs. They should support the governments of poor countries such as India in strengthening and making more effective their regulatory authorities.

Notes

1. Patent number 215758
2. Patent numbers 214010, 214011 and 185805
3. Patent number 215758
4. www.facebook.com/yesicanindia?v=app_7146470109 (19.5.2011)
5. www.cancercompass.com/message-board/message/all,19295,0.htm (19.5.2011)

References

Access to Medicine Foundation, 2010. The Index 2010, Access to Medicine Index http://www.accesstomedicineindex.org/content/index-2010–0

Anitha, B., K., Asif, P., Asma, P., et al. (eds), 2010. *Current Index of Medical Specialties Asia (CIMS)*, Sri Sudindra Offset, Bangalore.

Anthra News, 2010. 'Biocon and Bayer Join Hands to Create Awareness for Self Monitoring in Diabetics', www.andhranews.net/India/2010/February/4-Biocon-Bayer-54461.asp

arznei-telegramm, 1994. 'Die Geschichte des Wirkstoffs Cyproteronaze-tat (in Diane u.a.) ... Von der "Pille für den Mann" zum "Hautpflegemittel mit Empfängnisschutz"', *arznei-telegramm*, 9: 84–6

arznei-telegramm, 2002. 'Höhere Thrombogenität von Diane', *arznei-telegramm,* 33: 130

arznei-telegramm, 2003. 'Stop-NIDDM-Studie mit Acarbose ... Schlamperei, Manipulation, Irreführung', a*rznei-telegramm,* 34: 73–74

arznei-telegramm, 2009. 'Thromboembolierisiko Drospirenon-haltiger Kontrazeptiva (Yasmin u.a)', *arznei-telegramm,* 40: 100

Bayer, 2008. Nachhaltigkeitsbericht, Leverkusen.

Bayer, 2011. 'Bayer stärkt Pharmageschäft in Indien durch Joint Venture mit Zydus Cadila', Press Release, Leverkusen.

Bayer, 2012a. 'Unternehmensprofil—Bayer HealthCare Pharmaceuticals', http://www.bayerpharma.com/de/unternehmen/ueber-uns/unternehmensprofil/index.php#top

Bayer, 2012b. 'Beware of Counterfeits—Bayer HealthCare Pharmaceuticals', http://www.bayerpharma.com/en/therapeutic-areas/products/beware-of-counterfeits/index.php

Baxter, 2010. *Annual report 2010,* Baxter International Inc. Deerfield, USA

Baxter, 2010b. World Hemophilia Day 2010, http://www.baxter.com/press_room/features/2010/04_17_10_world_hemophilia_day.html

Baxter, 2012. 'Baxter India—Global presence', http://www.baxter.in/about_baxter/company_profile/global_presence.html

Baxter, 2012b. 'Baxter India—Sustainability', www.baxter.in/about_baxter/sustainability/index.html

Boehringer Ingelheim, 2007. 'Boehringer Ingelheim further intensifies fight against AIDS', Press Release, http://www.boehringer-ingelheim.com/news/news_releases/press_releases/2007/15_may_2007.html

Boehringer Ingelheim, 2008. 'Boehringer Ingelheim Finally Increases Presence', Pharma and Healthcare Insight. July.

Boehringer Ingelheim, 2012. Unsere Version, http://www.boehringer-ingelheim. de/unternehmensprofil/unsere_vision.html

CHE, 2011. 'Bayer peilt Milliardenumsatz in Indien an', CHEManager-online.com, January.

derStandard.at, 2008, 'Boehringer Ingelheim wächst 2007, wieder schneller als der Markt SPIRIVA(R), MICARDIS(R) und FLOMAX(R) die größten Produkte', *derStandard.at*, April.

dpa, 2010. 'Bayer unterliegt im Nexavar-Patentstreit in Indien auch bei Berufungsklage', *Handelsblatt*. February.

Fischer, C., Schulz, I., Zimmermann, H., Jenkes, C., 2011. *Um Jeden Preis: Untersuchung des Geschäftsverhaltens von Boehringer Ingelheim*, Bayer und Baxter in Indien, *Pharma-Brief Spezial*, Nr. 1, BUKO Pharma-Kampagne, Bielefeld.

Gulhati C., M. (ed.), 2010. *Monthly Index of Medical Specialty India (MIMS)*, Indraprasha Press, New Dehli.

Health Action International (HAI), World Health Organization (WHO), 2008. '*Measuring medicine prices, availability, affordability and price components*' 2nd edition, HAI, WHO, Geneva.

Hindustan Latex Limited, 2012. 'Mala-D-Combination hormonal contraceptive', http://www.hlfppt.org/images/mala-d.pdf (accessed Jan 18, 2012).

India Blooms, 2010. 'World Contraception Day launched in India', India Blooms. September.

Mack, J., 2007. 'High time to Permit Pharma DTC in India?', Pharma Marketing Network Forums. April.

Mack, J., 2009. 'Pharmaguy's Twitter Followers. What Do They Want and How Is It Relevant to You?', *Pharma Marketing News*, 8(8).

Max Healthcare, 2012. 'Project HOPE—India Diabetes Educator Project', http://www.maxhealthcare.in/services_facilities/our_departments/endocrinology/pdfs/project_hope_faq.pdf.

Ministry of Law and Justice, 1955. 'The Drugs and Magic Remedies (Objectionable Advertisements) Act', New Delhi.

Official Journal Of The Patent Office, 2011. 'PUBLICATION U/S. 87(1) The Compulsory licence Application No. C.L.A. No.1 of 2011 from M/S. Nacto Pharma Ltd. In Patent No. 215758 is hereby published', *The Patent Office Journal* 12/08/2011.

SOMO, 2011. 'Putting Contract Research Organizations on the Radar An exploratory study on outsourcing of clinical trials by pharmaceutical companies to contract research organizations', http://somo.nl/publications-en/Publication_3615/view.

TNMCS, 2012. 'Finalized Rates and Suppliers for the Tender for the Supply of Speciality Drugs to TNMSC for the Year 2010–11', http://www.tnmsc.com/tnmsc/new/html/pdf/spldrug.pdf.

Vectura, 2010. *Annual Reports and Accounts 2009/10,* Vectura, Wiltshire.

Wild, H., 2008. Bayer Schering Pharma's Approach to R&D. Internal and external sourcing of innovation, Lecture at India Pharma Summit 2009, Bayer Schering Pharma, Mumbai.

World Health Organization (WHO), 2010. *WHO Model List of Essential medicines 16th list,* Geneva.

Youtube.com, 2010. 'Yes I can India—World Contraception Day 2010', www.youtube.com/watch?v=OkQwfPZwZB0.

8 Trends and Prospects for India as a Global Generic Player

Deepak Kumar Jena and Poduri Balaram

INTRODUCTION

This chapter presents an analysis of the strategic presence of Indian pharmaceutical firms in the global generics market. It draws on a comprehensive study of product registrations and filings in several countries as well as export and import data.[1]

The pharmaceutical sector is the undisputed champion among Indian industries and a major global producer and exporter of generic medicines. The industry has evolved over three phases in the past 60 years. In the period prior to the 1970s, the industry was relatively small in terms of production capacity. The second phase spanned the early 1970s through 1990, a period during which government policy induced rapid growth. In its third phase, from the beginning of the 1990s to the present, much of the policy framework and regulatory structure of the previous two decades was dismantled in the context of broad changes in general economic policy orientation. The success that this industry experienced, however, continued to build on a foundation laid in the 1970s. The period since the 1990s witnessed the consolidation and continued growth of a viable industry with significant participation by Indian entrepreneurs. In the financial year 2008–09, the pharmaceutical industry contributed 11.77 per cent to India's manufacturing sector Gross Domestic Product (GDP) and 1.86 per cent to the country's total GDP (Analysis based on data from Centre for Monitoring Indian Economy 2010; Government of India 2010). With promulgation in April, 2005, of the amended

India Patents Act, 1970, Indian companies have had to shift their focus from reverse engineering to more innovative activities.

In recent years, there has been a sharp rise in pharmaceutical exports to the highly regulated markets of the US and the European Union (EU) as well as to developing and least developed countries (Chadha 2009; Chittoor and Ray 2007). India's exports of fine chemicals, APIs and finished products reached $10.39 billion in 2010–11, recording a 5-year compounded annual growth rate (CAGR) of 15.01 per cent. According to the Directorate General of Commercial Intelligence and Statistics (DGCIS), pharmaceuticals were the fifth largest category of exports in 2009–10. In 2010–11, however, it slipped to the sixth position. Nevertheless, the value of pharmaceutical exports in that year was nearly 46 per cent of agricultural exports. With a positive trade balance of over $6 billion, the sector is among the top five with a positive trade balance. It is remarkable that the Indian pharmaceutical industry, in just a few decades, evolved from almost nonexistent to one of the world's leading suppliers of affordable and quality generic medicine (William 2007). It is estimated that Indian firms now produce 20 per cent of global generics (PricewaterhouseCoopers 2010) and that 70 per cent of patients from 87 developing countries receive medicines procured from India ('t Hoen 2009). Medicine Sans Frontiers (MSF) purchases 80 per cent of its antiretroviral drugs (ARVs) from India. That Indian drugs exported around the world are of high quality is demonstrated by the oft repeated fact that India has the highest number of United States Food and Drugs Administration (U.S. FDA) approved facilities outside the US (IHS Global Insight 2007). With significant advantages of low cost innovation and operating costs, low capital requirements, well-established manufacturing processes and R&D infrastructure, India is strategically well positioned as the 'health keeper' of the world.

REGULATORY STATUS OF INDIA IN WORLD GENERICS MARKETS

Generic drugs are medicinal compounds not protected by patents. Generics are identical to brand name drugs in dosage, safety, strength, method of administration, quality, performance, and intended use. That is, a generic product is a bioequivalent alternative to the originator brand with the same active ingredient. Generics can be legally launched upon final expiration of all pending intellectual property rights.

In the US, approvals for the production and supply of generic drugs are granted by the FDA through Abbreviated New Drug Applications (ANDAs). Following the Hatch-Waxman Act of 1984, an ANDA can be approved without its sponsor having to submit clinical studies establishing safety and efficacy, upon submission of evidence that its active ingredient is bioequivalent to a previously approved drug (U.S. FDA 2010). A Type II Drug Master File (DMF) is a document filed with the FDA for drug substances, drug intermediates and materials used in the preparation of generics. The DMF is a confidential, proprietary asset containing complete information about an API, usually containing information regarding Chemistry, Manufacturing and Controls (CMC) of a component of a drug product. It is a submission to the FDA, and is not approved or disapproved, but plays a crucial role when applying for regulatory approvals and market authorization. The information contained in the DMF may be used to support an Investigational New Drug Application (IND), a New Drug Application (NDA), an Abbreviated New Drug Application (ANDA), another DMF, an Export Application, or amendments and supplements to any of these.

India in the Active Pharmaceutical Ingredients Market

In 2010, firms from 58 countries filed Type II DMFs with the U.S. FDA. India was the leader in terms of total number of filings, and second only to the US in number of molecules for which these DMFs were filed. India had a share of 31.37 per cent of the total number of DMF filings and approximately 26.71 per cent of the total number of molecules (International Nonproprietary Name (INN)). Foreign companies accounted for nearly 38 per cent of all companies with DMFs based on Indian facilities, and the number of foreign companies in this category increased significantly in 2009.

The Israeli Teva Group was the top FDA filer of DMFs in 2010, but eight of the top 10 companies were from India. Among these, Dr Reddy's ranked first followed by Aurobindo and CIPLA. Of a total of 608 molecules filed by Indian firms as of 23 June 2010, 193 molecules (31.74 per cent) have four or more DMFs, resulting in intense competition. For example, 21 out of 30 DMFs filed with the FDA for atorvastatin, the largest selling molecule in the world in 2010, were from India. Similarly, over 80 per cent of the DMFs for several top molecules such as clopidogrel, lamivudine, sertraline, ramipril, sildenafil, zidovudine, fluvastatin, tadalafil, and citalopram, are filed from Indian facilities. For 137 molecules, including esomeprazole, escitalopram, celecoxib, lopinavir, naratriptan, salmeterol, and tenofovir, only Indian firms have filed DMFs.

In spite of its strong presence in generics and API approvals, India is mostly absent in fermentation products, controlled substances and steroids. For example, Indian firms do not have any DMFs for important fermentation products such as penicillin G, clavulanate, fludarabine, heparin, and acarbose. Similarly, Indian firms in 2010 had no DMFs for controlled substances such as morphine, fentanyl, amphetamine, propoxyphene, codeine, dronabinol, hydromorphoneand also for corticosteroids like cortisone, hydrocortisone, fludrocortisone, prednisone, and methylprednisolone (U.S. FDA data).

India is the leader in the number of Certificate of Suitability of Monographs of the European Pharmacopoeia (CEP) granted by the European Directorate for the Quality of Medicines (EDQM). EDQM grants CEPs to manufacturers or suppliers of pharmaceutical substances on the basis of demonstrated compliance with the monographs of the European Pharmacopoeia. CEPs are the means by which marketing authorisation applicants submit data on most pharmacopoeia active ingredients prepared by synthesis, fermentation or semi-synthesis, in order to satisfy licensing authorities regarding CMC (chemistry, manufacturing, control) and stability requirements. The CEP is a centralized procedure at EDQM and valid for 36 countries around the world. It guarantees that all the impurities and potential contaminations related to the manufacturing process are satisfactorily controlled, and that the quality of the substance is appropriate for use in medicine. As of 2010, India accounts for 24 per cent of CEPs and over 18 per cent of the companies are from India, which accounts for nearly 31.86 per cent of the molecules with EDQM. India leads in top categories of anti-microbials, CNS, CVS, analgesics and drugs acting on GI tract. But Indian firms are completely absent in biological, anti-cancer and corticosteroids.

India might be losing a significant advantage by lagging behind in these areas. Biologics represent the most pioneering and successful category of drugs in the decade from the year 2000, and now account for 20 per cent of all blockbuster drugs. In 2007, global biotech sales increased by 12.5 per cent, whereas global pharmaceutical sales rose by only 6.4 per cent (IMS Health 2008). China, India's foremost competitor, holds advantages in this area through manufacturing of products such as interferon series, interleukin series, colony stimulating factors, epidermal growth factors, fibroblast growth factors, recombinant insulin and human growth hormone.

Indian Firms in Generic Prescription and OTC Markets

India is currently one of the top countries in terms of number of regulatory approvals granted by the FDA for generics. In 2010,

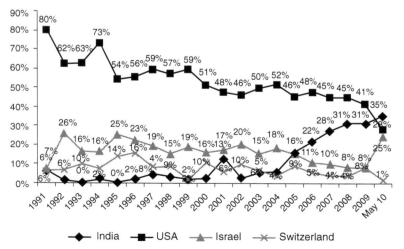

Figure 8.1: Percentage Share of Top Four Countries in Prescription
Generic Products (1991-May 2010)

India accounted for 14 per cent of approved prescription generic products (refer table 8.1). However, these were granted to only 27 Indian companies compared to 211 USA companies granted such approvals. FDA approvals to Indian firms for generic prescription products increased significantly in the five year period from 2005 to 2009 (refer figure 8.1). Indian firms were granted a total of 1,077 product approvals in this period compared to the meagre 171 approvals before 2005. Indian firms have 1,278 prescription generics product approvals out of 9,079 total granted by the FDA, making it second largest in prescription generic product approvals after the US (4,741). Israel (1,189), Switzerland (620) and Canada (370) occupy third, fourth and fifth positions. These numbers confirm the role of India as a global hub for generic products.

Teva is the leader in prescription generics with 623 products followed by the Mylan and Watson, both headquartered in the US. Among 60 companies with product approvals in OTC sector, Perrigo with a share of 21.75 per cent is the leader, followed by Watson and the Indian firm Dr. Reddy's. The top 15 companies account for over 72 per cent of the total prescription generic product approvals, that is, the majority of such approvals are held by a small group of major companies. For nine molecules including cefixime, desloratadine, amifostine, lithium carbonate, piperacillin sodium and tazobactam sodium, India is the only country with prescription ANDAs. In some ARVs and antibiotics molecules, such as zidovudine, rivastigmine, stavudine, didanosine, cefotaxime, ciprofloxacin, and cefepime, Indian firms have more than a 50 per cent share in prescriptions ANDA approvals in each product category. In molecules having more than 20 prescription approvals such as diltiazem HCL, gentamicin sulfate, amitriptyline HCL, lorazepam, clonazepam, diazepam, acyclovir, fentanyl, benazepril HCL and hydrochlorothiazide combination, morphine, theophylline, and meperidine HCL, Indian firms do not have any approvals. Several of these molecules pertain to corticosteroids, controlled substances and fermentation based products.

It must be noted that these figures do not include 265 prescription and OTC generic products belonging to erstwhile Indian companies Ranbaxy, Matrix, Dabur Oncology and Minrad (subsidiary of Piramal Healthcare), which have been acquired

Table 8.1: Regulatory Compliance Status of
India with Regulatory Authorities

Authority	Regulatory compliance	Approvals to Indian firms out of total granted	Rank of India	Status as on
U.S. FDA, USA[a].	Number of prescription and OTC generic product approvals granted[+]	1,321/9,387	Second	11 May 10
	Molecules for which prescription and OTC generic products have been granted	226/774	Second	
	Companies having prescription and OTC generic products[+]	27/314	Second	
	Total Number of Type II active DMFs filed	2,234/7,121	First	23 Jun 10
	Companies filed Type II active DMFs	340/1,082	First	
	Molecules for which DMFs have been filed	608/2,276	First	
EDQM, Europe[b].	Total number of Valid CEPs	687/2,858	First	22 Jun 10
	Companies having CEP approvals.	139/776	First	
	Molecules for which CEPs have been granted	255/800	First	
MHRA, UK[c].	Number of market authorizations (MAs)	531/11,756	N.A.	Oct. 2009
DACA, Ethiopia[d]	Number of market authorizations	485/2,843	First	25 Aug 09
	Companies having approved market Authorizations	51/238	First	
TFDA, Tanzania[e]	Number of market authorizations	1,315/3,387	First	26 Mar 10
	Companies having approved market Authorizations	74/258	First	
AECCFM, Azerbaijan[f]	Number of market authorizations	308/3,663	Third	Feb. 2010

Source: Authors' Research
[a]. United States Food and Drug Administration. [b]. European Directorate of Quality Medicine [c]. Medicines and Healthcare products Regulatory Agency [d]. Drug Administration and Control Authority, [e]. Tanzania Food and Drugs Authority [f]. Analytical Expertise Center for Medicines
[+]excluding discontinued and tentative approvals

by foreign companies, but include 90 product approvals held by Indian subsidiaries abroad. When the number of approvals for a single generic drug increases with the participation of additional companies, the result is lower prices of that particular drug due to increased competition. Thus by having more competing vendors per molecule India is playing a significant role in lowering the cost of generic medicines, thereby improving the affordability of generic medicines by the public in developed markets such as the US. Despite these impressive figures, in 2010 Dr Reddy's was the only Indian company ranked in the top 10 list of global generics companies. Teva ranked first, followed by Mylan, Sandoz, Watson, Green Stone, Par Pharmaceutical, Hospira, Apotex, Mallinckrodt, and finally Dr Reddy's was tenth (Fierce Pharma 2010).

India's Status in various Therapeutic Categories

Indian firms have the highest number of FDA approvals acting on the Central Nervous System (CNS) with a share of 35 per cent of all the approvals, followed by a 20 per cent share of approvals for drugs acting on the Cardiovascular System (CVS), Anti-infectives (16 per cent) and drugs acting on Gastrointestinal tract (GIT) (6 per cent) (see Figure 8.2). Indian firms are comparatively stronger in number of approvals of Anti-retrovirals, Anti-microbials, CVS, anti-diabetics, CNS and dermatologicals. However, India has a much lower share in corticosteriods, anti-cancer drugs and diagnostics categories. As noted, Indian firms are relatively weak in biotechnology products including fermentation products, complex chemistry, advanced dosage formulations and specialty formulations. Moreover, India does not have any approvals for nutritional supplements, dermatologicals and ophthalmics.

The absence of India in the ophthalmics and dermatologicals categories is indicative of a lack of sophisticated and advanced technology required in these areas. The weakness in biologicals, metabolic disorders, steroids, anti-cancer drugs could become a major hurdle for the continued growth of the Indian pharmaceutical industry, due to increasing prevalence of these disorders and the emergence of biologicals and nutraceuticals as therapeutically and commercially expanding product areas.

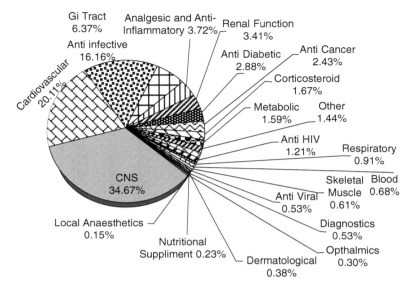

Figure 8.2: Therapeutic Category-wise Approvals of India
by U.S. FDA (as on 11.5.2010)

Drug Registrations in Selected Regulated and Semi-regulated Markets

Indian firms occupy first place in the number of market authorizations for formulation products in most African countries (Table 8.1). Analysis of product approvals granted by the Tanzania Food Drug Administration (TFDA) shows that a total of 3,400 product approvals to 258 companies from 42 countries. Indian firms ranked first in the number of approvals, accounting for nearly 39 per cent. It leads in almost all therapeutic categories. In Ethiopia, India leads in the number of market authorizations as well as in the number of companies with such approvals. In Azerbaijan India holds the third position in the number of market authorizations after Germany and the Russian Federation. India is also among the top filers in several CIS (Commonwealth of Independent States) countries. However, in the UK, Indian firms have a low share, of only 4.5 per cent of market authorizations.

These figures point to the strength of Indian firms in many highly regulated and semi-regulated pharma markets across the globe.

India is not only a major supplier of generic products to developed countries, but is also a major supplier of drugs in developing countries, where drug availability and affordability play a very important role in public health. Especially in Least Developed Countries such as Tanzania and Ethiopia, Indian firms make a major contribution to public health through supply of low cost medicines. India is the largest supplier of generic ARVs to low- and middle-income countries, providing 80 per cent of donor-funded ARVs to low and middle income countries (Waning et al. 2010).

INDIA'S BILATERAL TRADE IN PHARMACEUTICAL PRODUCTS

Trade balance and pharmaceutical exports

The value of India's total exports of pharmaceuticals and fine chemicals in 2010–11was approximately $16,529.50 million (refer table 8.2). If medical equipment, devices and surgicals are included, the figure stands at $17,391.07 million. The sector (excluding medical equipment, devices, surgicals) grew at a compounded annual growth rate (CAGR) of 14.76 per cent between 2006–07 to 2010–11. In this 5-year period, annual total imports were approximately $13,293.63 million,with this figure increasing to $2,067.32 million with the inclusion of medical equipment, devices and surgicals. Thus in this period, India had a positive trade balance of $3,225.88 million in this sector (excluding medical equipment, devices and surgicals).

Exports of formulations including biologicals constitute approximately 39.37 per cent of total pharmaceutical exports. This category is followed by bulk drugs, intermediates and excipients (25.16 per cent), fine chemicals (29.15 per cent) and herbals (Ayurvedic, Unani, Siddha and Homeopathy products, 6.1 per cent) (refer figure 8.3). A majority of imports are fine chemicals with a share of 68.70 per cent, followed by bulk drugs, intermediates and excipients (21.26 per cent), formulations including biologicals (9.11 per cent), and herbal products (0.69 per cent) (refer figure 8.4). During 2008–09, India exported to 213 countries/territories around the world and received imports from 147 countries/territories.

Asia is the largest export destination (excluding medical devices and fine chemicals) followed by North America and Europe. Asia

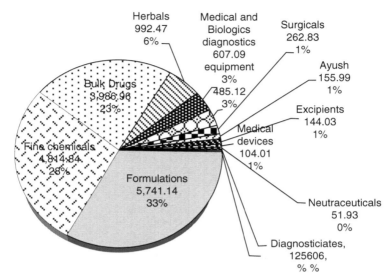

Figure 8.3: Composition of India's Pharmaceutical Sector Exports
(2010–11) (figs. in %)

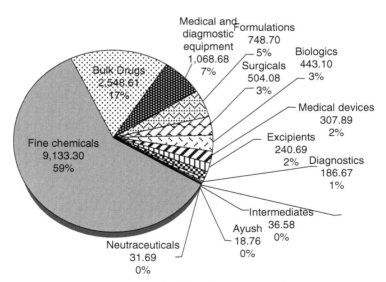

Figure 8.4: Composition of India's Pharmaceutical Sector Imports
(2010–11) (figs. in %)

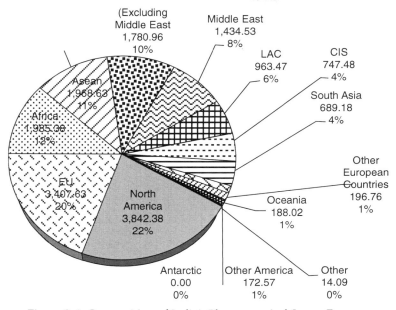

Figure 8.5: Composition of India's Pharmaceutical Sector Exports
(2010–11) (figs. in Rs Crores and %)

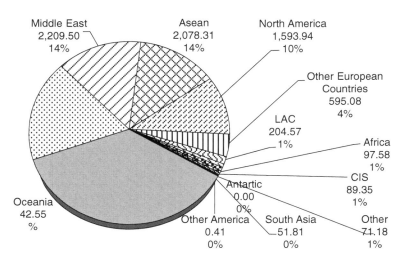

Figure 8.6: Composition of India's Pharmaceutical Sector Imports
(2010–11) (figs. in Rs Crores and %)

is also the largest sourcing region for imports followed by the same countries (refer figures 8.5 and 8.6).

Formulations are the most important exports to North America, with a share of 46.43 per cent, followed by fine chemicals and herbals. For bulk drugs and intermediates, the European Union (EU) is the most important destination with exports valued at $947.48 million in 2010. The EU is also among the important destinations for India's fine chemicals exports. An estimated 34.31 per cent of pharmaceutical product exports to this region are fine chemicals, followed by bulk drugs, intermediates and excipients at a share of 30.34 per cent. Africa is the second most important destination for formulation exports, valued at nearly $1.40 billion, growing at a 5-year CAGR of 23.96 per cent. Exports of bulk drugs and intermediates, biologicals and excipients to this region have also been increasing gradually. To the CIS region, India mainly exports formulations. In Asia, the major importers of bulk drugs and intermediates from India are China, Singapore, Israel, Turkey, South Korea, and Bangladesh. Approximately 42.52 per cent of the exports to Latin America are also bulk drugs and intermediates. India's export potential to the Oceania region is largely untapped.

Pharmaceutical Imports

In 2010–11, India imported over $2,825.88 million worth of bulk drugs and intermediates, with China contributing over 60 per cent at around $1,700.38 million. Imports from China grew at a CAGR of 20.47 per cent over the five year period from 2006–07 to 2010–11. The EU and North America are also among the important source regions for India's import of bulk drugs and intermediates. The US with an import share of 5.70 per cent is followed by Germany (4.88 per cent), Japan (2.91 per cent) and Italy (2.50 per cent). Six of the top 10 supplier countries are from Europe. Formulation imports from Switzerland and USA grew at 14.69 per cent and 21.83 per cent during this period respectively. Imports of biologicals from North America and China have also been growing at a very high rate. That Indian firms are weak in fine chemicals is evident from imports of nearly $9,133.30 million, of which China alone contributed $1,686.79 million. Imports from China grew at a CAGR of 22.4 per cent in the five year period. Saudi Arabia, Singapore, Republic of Korea, and the US are the other top suppliers of fine chemicals to India.

While India on the whole has a positive trade balance in formulations, bulk drugs, and herbals, it has negative trade balances in fine chemicals, excipients and intermediates. In medical diagnostic equipment, devices, diagnostic reagents and surgicals, India has a negative trade balance of $1,195.75 million (refer table 8.2).

OUTLOOK FOR THE INDIAN PHARMACEUTICAL INDUSTRY

As evident from the data presented, Indian firms have gone from strength to strength in the generic drug sector. India is the location for the largest number of facilities from which DMFs for Active Pharmaceutical Ingredient (APIs) have been filed with the FDA. This enables cost effective sourcing of APIs required for production of generics. The number of DMF filings by Indian firms and foreign firms based in India, based on production facilities in India, confirm that these facilities meet global regulatory standards. India has several other advantages that can further strengthen its role as a global manufacturing hub in the next decade.

Indian firms have a strong presence in generics in almost all developing and least developed countries where the need is great for low cost essential drugs. With the population expanding in most developing countries, Indian firms should remain focused on volume. India with its large installed manufacturing capacity, high number of product registrations, and low manufacturing costs, is well positioned to tap this opportunity. With largest number of vendors per molecule, India helps in increasing the affordability of medicines across many markets. Through exports to developing and least developed countries, India is also helping the poor through supply of affordable essential medicines. The rapid expansion of registrations in major markets such as the US, and forthcoming patent expiries, will add to the number of molecules that can be

Table 8.2: Region-wise Sector-wise Analysis of Exports of India's Pharmaceutical Sector (2010–11) ($ million.)

Region	Biologics	Bulk Drugs	Diagnostics	Excipients	Fine chemicals	Formulations	Herbals	intermediates	Medical & diagnostic equipment	Medical devices	Neutraceuticals	Surgicals	2010-11 Total	% Share
North America	146.13	734.10	2.76	6.60	583.49	1,710.11	464.94	10.25	113.94	16.08	27.34	26.63	3,842.38	22.09%
EU	35.14	947.48	3.61	40.29	1,121.39	903.18	212.80	3.82	53.76	23.58	4.32	58.27	3,407.63	19.59%
Africa	176.12	179.40	4.11	15.86	100.90	1,404.83	24.92	0.15	12.16	15.56	0.71	50.66	1,985.38	11.42%
Asean	46.98	364.63	1.16	11.38	948.07	310.20	46.72	0.01	186.72	6.36	5.02	41.36	1,968.63	11.32%
Asia (Excluding Middle East)	12.55	462.77	0.91	4.64	1,003.34	73.90	119.11	10.35	71.59	2.17	11.42	8.21	1,780.96	10.24%
Middle East	33.14	500.23	1.46	54.89	480.77	256.68	33.26	0.01	20.16	21.54	1.75	30.64	1,434.53	8.25%
LAC	43.85	389.83	0.87	1.56	183.35	269.92	31.71	0.08	13.09	11.20	0.06	17.95	963.47	5.54%
CIS	44.18	32.45	0.12	0.42	16.34	617.28	31.17	0.01	0.98	2.27	0.22	2.04	747.48	4.30%
South Asia	62.45	130.85	3.97	7.39	249.34	195.75	8.43	0.03	9.86	3.81	0.23	17.08	689.18	3.96%

(contd...)

(*Table 8.2: contd...*)

Region	Biologics	Bulk Drugs	Diagnostics	Excipients	Fine chemicals	Formulations	Herbals	intermediates	Medical & diagnostic equipment	Medical devices	Neutraceuticals	Surgicals	2010-11 Total	% Share
Other European Countries	0.63	92.65	0.44	0.22	74.85	16.34	4.13	0.34	1.60	0.85	0.53	4.17	196.76	1.13%
Oceania	2.26	29.37	0.12	0.55	18.81	118.91	11.04	0.01	0.70	0.48	0.30	5.46	188.02	1.08%
Other America	2.60	120.32	0.01	0.10	33.37	15.69	0.21		0.08	0.09	0.00	0.10	172.57	0.99%
Other	1.05	2.89	0.06	0.12	0.83	4.34	4.05		0.48	0.02	0.00	0.25	14.09	0.08%
Antartic					0.00		0.00						0.00	0.00%
Grand Total	607.09	3,986.96	19.61	144.03	4,814.84	5,897.13	992.47	25.06	485.12	104.01	51.93	262.83	17,391.07	100.00%
% Share	3.49%	22.93%	0.11%	0.83%	27.69%	33.91%	5.71%	0.14%	2.79%	0.60%	0.30%	1.51%	100.00%	
Trade Balance	163.98	1,438.35	-167.06	-96.66	-4,318.46	5,129.66	900.28	-11.52	-583.57	-203.87	20.24	-241.25	2,030.13	

produced in India. There is every possibility that these factors will continue to fuel the growth of the Indian pharma industry in coming years.

At the same time India has to overcome several hurdles to reach its full potential in the global pharmaceutical industry. Growing dependence on imports for bulk drugs and intermediates, and a weak presence in the biotechnology sector, are major challenges. India depends on imports of anti-protozoalsand anti-ulcerants, antibiotics (especially penicillin and its derivatives), analgesics, vitamins and hormones from China. India is also the most important export destination for Chinese bulk drug industry.

The weak position of Indian firms in the bulk drug industry in general and the fermentation industry in particular can be attributed to lack of production incentives due to high costs. Moreover, high formulation growth and stagnating bulk drug manufacturing has resulted in growing dependence on imports. Approximately 45 to 47 per cent of the domestic market for bulk drugs is currently met through imports.

In formulations, there is a need for Indian firms to upgrade into the next technological level through incremental research in areas such as dosage forms, composition, route of administration, new formulations and combination of individual approved molecules (Jena et al. 2009). It is well known that commodity generics have low barriers of entry and low profit margins due to competitive pricing, while specialty and super generic drugs have higher margins (Sawant 2010). ('Super generics' is a term for products which represent a technological upgrading of existing drugs, for example through new modified release dosage forms). Indian firms needs to enhance their production capacities in complex molecules and advanced dosage forms.

Secondly, even though India has a large number of manufacturing facilities, capabilities in international marketing, contract manufacturing, and high regulatory standards remain concentrated within a small group of top companies. The rapid growth of DMFs by foreign companies using Indian facilities, and growing bulk drug imports from regulated markets, point to the increased attraction of contract manufacturing. This in turn is often the prerequisite for acquisition of Indian companies or facilities by foreign MNCs. The top 15 companies account for nearly half the size of India's pharmaceutical industry size and around 62.24 per cent of pharmaceutical product exports. The industry is therefore highly susceptible to changes in the demand for products supplied by these top companies.

So far the focus of the MNCs in India has been to capture domestic market share. But in the recent past, US, Japanese and German MNCs have acquired a number of the top companies including Piramal Healthcare, Ranbaxy, Shantha Biotech and DaburPharma (Chaudhuri 2012).The acquisition trend appears to be aimed at tapping India's global regulatory and low cost manufacturing capabilities. Such acquisitions may have serious consequences for India and may result in rising prices in the domestic as well as foreign markets. Acquisitions may also lead to the transfer of critical intangible assets, both current and future, to foreign firms. On the positive side, acquisitions may also result in higher level chemistry and advanced formulations/technologies through technology transfer.

Thirdly, biopharmaceuticals is a rapidly growing segment in the global healthcare industry, as already noted. Several of the most successful and pioneering drugs of the past decade are biologics. These include adalimumab, bevacizumab, etanercept, infliximab and rituximab which have more than $5.5 billion global annual sales (Evaluate Pharma 2010). Patents on several biopharmaceuticals such as neupogen, novolin, protropin, activase, epogen, nutropin, avonex,and humulin have already expired, creating opportunities for biogenerics. In 2012, nearly half of all newly approved products by the FDA were expected to be biopharmaceuticals (Generic Pharmaceuticals Association 2010). The sales of biologicals are estimated to approach $150 billion by 2015 (Desheh 2010). The production of biopharmaceuticals requires high technology skills and offer higher profit margins. India is currently largely dependent on Chinese imports for most biotechnology and fermentation based products, as noted. China has strategically concentrated onthe biotechnology segment, molecular biology, gene therapy, genomics and proteomics research. The landscape of the Indian pharmaceutical industry could change rapidly through development of technologically focused biotech companies with customized manufacturing.

A study of India-manufactured approved products showed that 83 per cent were oral, mostly conventional tablets and capsules. India has little presence in advanced formulations which account for just 3 per cent of its total products. Yet, the Novel Drug Delivery Systems (NDDS) market is a fast growing and highly dynamic market segment (Jena et al., 2009). Upcoming patent expirations and the urgent need for life cycle management facing current drugs, are some of the factors contributing to this growth. It is commonly held that the introduction of NDDS is likely to improve compliance and reduce side effects and enable better patient management for physicians. They also offer a competitive edge through enhanced market penetration, brand image, extension of patent exclusivity, and allow companies to target new patient populations.

Finally, India has only recently embarked on drug discovery. However, the balance sheets of the domestic companies do not, in any significant way, permit R&D investments of the magnitude required for drug discovery projects. Yet Indian firms have made a simple beginning through alternate pathways of drug approvals in USA such as 505(b)(2), strategic international tie-ups. Through the 505(b)(2) process, an NDA can be granted for an innovative modification of existing drugs never before approved by the FDA, based on studies conducted previously and one or more investigations referenced from Reference Listed Drugs (RLD) or published literature. This is also known as hybrid NDA and contains more data than an ANDA but less compared with a stand-alone NDA. Between 1999 and 2009, there was a steady growth in 505(b)(2) approvals. A total of 175 products were approved through 505(b)(2) till 2008. An analysis of 75 approvals received in the last 3 years shows that more than 50 per cent of 505(b)(2) get market exclusivity for a period of 3–7 years based on their chemical type. Further, modification in the formulation of paranteral formulation is not permitted in ANDA and therefore 505(b)(2) is the preferred route to by-pass the formulation patent of the innovator company. In special circumstances ANDAs could also act as RLD to carryout bioequivalence study (e.g. Luxiq). Our research also shows that multiple RLDs (Reference Lead Drug) could be referred for a 505(b)(2) NDA (e.g. Olux). Further, even discontinued products can act as RLDs (e.g. Ammonul) providing opportunity for drug repositioning. It is noted that three biogenerics approved with FDA (Omnitrope, Glucagen, and Hylenex recombinant) have come through 505(b)(2) process. There is enormous opportunity for 505(b)(2) approval pathway especially in the light of generic cliff and bio-generics.

Strategic alliances between MNCs and Indian companies for preclinical, development and discovery research have also played a major role. Most companies have tied up with specialist research companies for development of new drugs in disease areas such as cancer, diabetes, malaria and nervous system disorders. For example, the US company Merck has collaborated with the Indian company Advinus Therapeutics on early-stage development of drugs for metabolic disorders (*Business Standard* 2006). Dr Reddy's has partnered with ClinTec International, UK for clinical trials and co-development of its anti-cancer drug (Palnitkar 2008). Similarly, drug giant Eli Lilly and Indian company Suven Lifesciences entered into a deal focusing on pre-clinical development of molecules for CNS disorders (Chu 2006). Other strategic alliances between Indian firms and foreign multinationals for discovery, preclinical research, and development include Ranbaxy-GSK for malaria, Jubilant-Eli Lilly, Orchid-Merck, GVK Bioscience-Wyeth, and Aurigene-Novo Nordisk (Gupta 2010).

There are several challenges before India to tap its full potential and move into the next level of discovery research. Indian firms have been mostly active in generic formulations which make up only a $90 billion in a global market of $808.2 billion (IMS Health 2008). As noted, there are many important categories such as monoclonal antibodies and peptides where Indian firms are not present. Several technologies such as sustained release/controlled/modified release, lyophilized pharmaceuticals, bio-pharmaceuticals and specialty generics are not attempted in India. India's penetration into 36 regulated markets which occupy nearly 80 per cent of world pharma imports, has been almost negligible with the exception of USA. The Indian pharma industry also requires consolidation to progress into drug discovery.

TRIPS AND THE FUTURE OF THE INDIAN PHARMACEUTICAL INDUSTRY

The success story of the Indian pharmaceutical industry is explained significantly by the favorable process patent regime introduced in the 1970s (Chaudhuri 2005). In subsequent decades the industry has developed into the largest pharmaceutical manufacturer and supplier in the world of generics. With the formation of the World Trade Organization (WTO) in 1995 came the era of multilateral trade negotiations and economic liberalization, and the door was reopened for pharma MNCs to invest and prosper in India. As a founder member of the WTO, India was obliged to introduce domestic IPR legislation compliant with the Trade Related Aspects of Intellectual Property Rights (TRIPS) Agreement. For this purpose, India amended the Patent Act of 1970 in 1999, 2002 and finally in 2005, when the product patent regime was introduced. The new IPR regime forbids the production and marketing of generic versions of patented drugs. This means that reverse engineering is no longer available as the principal avenue of growth, and product innovation is at a premium.

With the passing of the 2005 amendments to the Patents Act, there was speculation of rising medicine prices, and the affordability of life saving drugs became a major issue. As detailed elsewhere in this volume, in 2006, Novartis filed a case in the Madras High Court when it was denied a patent on the new salt from an existing drug which Novartis claims is more efficacious than the old one (Mueller 2007). The Novartis lawsuit was the first legal challenge to section 3(d) of the Patent Act, the ultimate outcome of which has implications not only for the Indian pharmaceutical industry but for the affordability of medicines globally. Section 3(d) of India's Patents Act forbids the patenting of derivative forms of known substances (e.g., salts, polymorphs, metabolites, and isomers) unless proven therapeutically more effective than the known substance. This is seen as a safeguard against 'evergreening' of patents. Evergreening, in one common form, occurs when the brand-name manufacturer 'stockpiles' patent protection by obtaining separate 20-year patents on multiple attributes of a single product through small modifications, thereby extending the period of monopoly pricing.

But neither the Indian patent statute nor its implementing rules define 'efficacy'. If Novartis' suit is successful, it will open the gate for similar claims from other companies resulting in evergreening and delay of generic entry that will affect the domestic industry and limit the affordability of life saving drugs, with dire implications for poor people globally.

The Indian pharmaceutical industry can flourish under the new IPR regime if it succeeds in utilizing a mix of technical and man power skills for research and innovation. At the same time the industry will still be able to market older out-of-patent drugs. The culture nurtured by 35 years of prohibition of pharmaceutical product patenting will not change overnight. The effects of the new IPR regime can only be ascertained when there is greater clarity about the implementation of the new IPR legislation.

Section 92A of the new Patents Act permits Indian industries to manufacture and export patented medicines to other countries that do not have local manufacturing capacity of their own. This Section represents India's own version of the framework set forth in the WTO's 2003 Implementation Decision of the Doha Ministerial on TRIPS and Public Health (Mathur 2008). Natco Pharma was India's first company to explore this clause and applied for compulsory licence for permission to manufacture Roche's patented cancer medications erlonitib (trade name 'Tarceva') and Pfizer's Sutent for export to Nepal (Subramanian 2008). The application made under Section 92A was the first of its kind. The outcome of this application can open the gate for other pharmaceutical companies to apply for compulsory licences for exports (Mondaq 2008). However, since that year, compulsory licensing has been scarcely utilized by India. In the recent years (2009) in the light of onslaught of acquisition of domestic companies by multinationals, to stem the same Department of Commerce has floated a discussion document which discussed the option of imposing of compulsory licensing against MNCs. However, very few cases of such action have been taken since then.

CONCLUSION

Notwithstanding considerable achievements, there are several untapped business segments and market opportunities for the Indian pharmaceutical industry. Sophisticated chemistry capabilities, lateral thinking in developing non-infringing processes, a disciplined approach to adherence to stringent guidelines, and dedication to manufacturing excellence, make India a favoured destination for sourcing or outsourcing of various components of the pharmaceutical value chain. Government institutions such as the Department of Commerce, the Department of Pharmaceuticals, Drug Controller General of India and Pharmaceuticals Export Promotion Council of India (Pharmexcil) are working with great zeal to boost the industry, but still multi-departmental issues arising out of globalization and challenges outlined in this chapter need to be addressed.

The chapter has documented India's emergence as a global pharmaceutical manufacturing hub. Particularly striking is the growing number of DMFs filed by foreign firms from India and the growth of imports of raw materials from USA and the European Union. India is strong in drug registrations in developing countries, and is also rapidly expanding exports of generics to major regulated markets. The strong presence of Indian firms in many developing countries with growing populations, large installed production capacities, and forthcoming patent expiries provide a base for sustaining India as a major generics producer and exporter. However, weaknesses in bulk drugs and intermediates, biotechnology, complex chemistry, and drug discovery present significant challenges. This is an opportune time for Indian pharmaceutical firms to diversify their exports to exploit niche or specialty generics in international markets. The future for India's pharmaceutical industry lies in flexibility, speed and supply chain strengths. Neither innovation nor generics on their own but only a 'compelling total offer' will put India and Indian companies close to the very top.

Notes

1. For this study, data was collected on markets for Active Pharmaceutical Ingredients (API) using Type-II Active Drug Master Files (DMFs) in the USA and Certificates of Suitability (CEP) in Europe. We considered all New Drug Applications (NDAs) and Abbreviated New Drug Applications (ANDAs) approved for marketing in the US by the US Food and Drug Administration (U.S.FDA) and all marketing authorizations by the UK Medicines and Healthcare Product Regulatory Agency (MHRA), as well as data on finished formulations in several other countries. We used Center for the Indian Economy (CMIE) databases 'Prowess' and 'India Trades' for the trade analysis.

References

Business Standard, 2006. 'Advinus, Merck establish drug discovery collaboration', 16 November. <http://www.business-standard.com/india/news/advinus-merck-establish-drug-discovery-collaboration/265005/>

Center for Indian Economy (CMIE) database 'Prowess' and 'India Trade'.

Chadha, A., 2009. 'Product cycles, Innovation, and Exports: A study of Indian Pharmaceuticals', *World Development*, 37(9): 1478–83.

Chaudhuri, S., 2012, 'Multinationals and Monopolies: Pharmaceutical Industry in India after TRIPS', *Economic and Political Weekly*, 47(12): 46–54.

Chittoor, R. and Ray, S., 2007. 'Internationalization Paths of Indian Pharmaceutical Firms—A Strategic Group Analysis', *Journal of International Management*, 13(3): 338–55.

Chu, W.L., 2006. 'Eli Lilly and Suven enter CNS research deal', Outsourcing-Pharma, 1 September,<http://www.outsourcing-pharma.com/Preclinical-Research/Eli-Lilly-and-Suven-enter-CNS-research-deal>

Department of Commerce, Ministry of Commerce and Industry, Government of India. Report of the Task Force, 2008. 'Strategy for Increasing Exports of Pharmaceutical Products'. http://www.commerce.nic.in/publications/Report%20Tas%20Force%20Pharma%2012th%20Dec%2008.pdf?id=16

Desheh, E., 2010. 'Teva Pharmaceutical Industries Ltd. UBS Global Specialty Pharmaceuticals Conference', London, 2 June. <http://www.teva.co.il/pdf/UBSSpecialtyPharmaConference010610.pdf>

Doug Long, 2009. 'U.S. Pharmaceutical Market Trends: A Picture of Increasing Trends', IMS Health. <http://www.imshealth.com/portal/site/imshealth/menuitem.a46c6d4df3db4b3d88f611019418c22a/?vgnextoid=b523257373a96210VgnVCM100000ed152ca2RCRD&vgnextfmt=defaul>

Drugs@FDA Data Files. U.S. FDA. 2010. <http://www.fda.gov/Drugs/InformationOnDrugs/ucm079750.htm

Evaluate Pharma, <http://www.evaluatepharma.com/Universal/View.aspx?type=Entity&entityType=Product&componentID=1002&id=1244&lType=modData>

Fierce Pharma, 2010. 'Top 10 Generic Drug Companies 2010, 10 August 2010', <http://www.fiercepharma.com/special-reports/top-10-generic-drug-companies-2010/teva-top-10-generic-drug-companies-2010>

Generic Pharmaceuticals Association 2010.http://www.gphaonline.org/issues/biogenerics

Gupta, J.B., 2010. 'Drug Discovery and India—A Force Reckon With', Pharmafocusasia. http://www.pharmafocusasia.com/ShowEbook.asp?PageFrom=magazineindex&Url=/strategy/drug_discovery_india_force_to_reckon.htm

Home Page, EDQM website.<http://www.edqm.eu/en/Homepage-628.html>

IHS Global Insight 2007. 'Increasing Demand for Indian Drugs Prompts Calls for Permanent U.S. FDA Presence in India, 18 Jun 07'. <http://www.ihsglobalinsight.com/SDA/SDADetail9647.htm>

IMS Health, 2008. 'Intelligence.'360—Global Pharmaceutical Perspectives 2007'. IMS Health.<http://www.imshealth.com/portal/site/imshealth/menuitem.c96f97d74b76899c33a004f0 9418c22a/?vgnextoid=b04e51dd68585110VgnVCM 10000071812ca2RCRD&vgnextfmt=default>

Industry Trends, Nasscom, (National Association of Software and Service Companies), 2010. <http://www.nasscom.in/Nasscom/templates/NormalPage.aspx?id=56966>

Jena et al. 2009. 'Presence of Indian Pharmaceutical Industries in US Market: An Empirical Analysis', *Journal of Generic Medicines*, 6: 333–44.

Krishnan V., 2011. 'Affordable Medicines Access Threat'. <http://www.soci.org/Chemistry-and-Industry/CnI-Data/2011/20/Affordable-medicines-access-threat>

Mathur H., 2008. 'Compulsory Licensing Under Section 92A: Issues and Concerns', *Journal of Intellectual Property Rights*, 13: 464–72.

Ministry of Statistics and Programme Implementation, Government of India. <http://mospi.nic.in/Mospi_New/site/home.aspx>

Mondaq., 2008. 'Contemplating compulsory licensing: A comparison between the components'. <www.mondaq.com/article.asp?articleid=65424>

Mueller, J., 2007. 'Taking TRIPS to India: Novartis, Patent Law, and Access to Medicines', *New England Journal of Medicine*, 356: 541–43

Nattrass, N., 2010. 'Government Leadership and ARV Provision in Developing Countries. Centre for social science research AIDS and society research unit'. <http://www.aids2031.org/pdfs/working%20paper%2014.pdf>

Nevrivy, D. and Bakin, R., 2009. 'China Gets Serious About Biotech'. <http://www.fiercebiotech.com/special-reports/chinas-rise-poses-challenges-opportunities-biopharma-industry>

Palnitkar, U., 2008. 'Drug Discovery in India-Trends and Challenges', *Express Pharma*, pp. 16–31, May 08.<http://www.expresspharmaonline.com/20080531/research02.shtml>

Pharmaceuticals, 2011.<http://www.ibef.org/industry/pharmaceuticals.aspx>

PricewaterhouseCoopers, 2010. 'Global Pharmaceutical Companies Need To Take An Even Closer Look At India'. <http://www.pwc.com/gx/en/pressroom/2010/global-pharma-cos-need-to-take-closer-look-at-India.jhtml>

Sawant M., 2010. 'Opportunity for India in the World Generics Market', Frost and Sullivan, <http://pharmalicensing.com/public/articles/view/1144147543_44324e57b031f/opportunity-for-india-in-the-world-generics-market>

Shaw, A.B., Drug Master Files, DIA Webinar 19 March 2007; Revised 7 November 2008. <http://www.fda.gov/downloads/AboutFDA/CentersOffices/CDER/ucm103534.pdf>

Subramanian, D., 2008, 'TRIPS and Compulsory Licensing: The Natco Nuance' SSRN, <http://ssrn.com/abstract=1289992>

't Hoen, E., 2009. *The Global Politics of Pharmaceutical Monopoly Power: Drug Patents, Access, Innovation and the Application of the WTO Doha Declaration on TRIPS and Public Health*, AMB Publishers, Diemen.

U.S. FDA, 2010. FDCA Section 505(j)(8)(B). <http://www.fda.gov/regulatoryinformation/legislation/FederalFoodDrugandCosmeticActFDCAct/FDCActChapterVDrugsandDevices/ucm108125.htm>

U.S. FDA, 2010. FDCA Section 505(j), codified at 21 U.S.C. Section 355 (j). <http://www.fda.gov/regulatoryinformation/legislation/Federal FoodDrugandCosmeticActFDCAct/FDCActChapterVDrugsandDevices/ ucm108125.htm>

Waning, B. et al., 2010. 'A Lifeline to Treatment: The Role of Indian Generic Manufacturers in Supplying Antiretroviral Medicines to Developing Countries', *Journal of the International AIDS Society*. 13:35.

Wierer, M. and Pouget. C., 2007. 'Introduction to the Certification Procedure and Inspections', Helsinki. 3 October.

William, G., 2007. 'The Emergence of India's Pharmaceutical Industry and Implications for the U.S. Generic Drug Market'. U.S. International Trade Commission. May.

9

The Indian Patent Law and Access to Antiretroviral Drugs in Sub-Saharan Africa

Christiane Fischer

Of the 33 million people estimated as HIV positive, 23 million live in sub-Saharan Africa. Despite the United Nation's target of universal access by 2010, only 6.6 million (47 per cent) of 14.2 million people in need of life-prolonging antiretroviral drugs can access such medicines (UNAIDS 2011). Beyond 2015 a dramatic rise is expected in the number of HIV-positive people in need of treatment, due to earlier commencements of therapy and longer durations of treatment as HIV-positive people stay alive longer. Fifty-five million HIV-positive people will need antiretrovirals by 2030 (All-Party Parliamentary Group on AIDS 2009).

To assure access to antiretrovirals, sub-Saharan African countries depend on Indian generics: more than 80 per cent of first-line antiretrovirals and almost all active pharmaceutical ingredients used in sub-Saharan African countries are produced and exported by 14 Indian generic companies (Chien 2007; t'Hoen 2009; Waning et al. 2010a). Therefore both the Indian generic industry and Indian patent law play a crucial role in assuring access to antiretrovirals in sub-Saharan Africa.

Current World Health Organization (WHO) treatment recommendations suggest more extensive use of more tolerable first-line regimes including tenofovir and the phasing out of stavudine (WHO 2009a). However, these medications are still more expensive, and consequently the vast majority of the 5.3 million people receiving treatment remain on the older toxic stavudine-based regime, which is available for $61 per person per year (ppy). The cost of the cheapest less toxic generic regime, tenofovir, is a minimum of $173 ppy. A switch to lopinavir/ritonavir-based second-line regimes increases treatment costs to a minimum of $620 ppy. Médecins Sans Frontières (MSF) and others are starting to replace this with atazanavir/ritonavir-based second line combinations, which are available for a minimum of $442 ppy; third and fourth-line drugs are far more expensive (MSF 2006b). In countries where these critical drugs are patent-protected, the price increment is even larger. This goes some way to explain why only 3–4 per cent of patients who receive antiretroviral therapy are treated with second-line drugs, while third- and fourth-line drugs are virtually inaccessible (All-Party Parliamentary Group 2009). This situation allows Ford et al. (2007a: 1810) to conclude: 'The battle to start antiretroviral therapy in developing countries has been won. The battle to provide the best care we can is just beginning'. Any denial of access to antiretroviral therapy for the poor must be considered unethical as access to life-saving drugs is a fundamental human right, as per articles 12 and 15 of the International Covenant on Economic, Social and Cultural Rights (UN 1966; UN 2006). Governments have an obligation to protect health and this includes achieving universal access to antiretroviral therapy (Grover 2009). This obligation must be considered of higher value than the economic interests of individual companies.

TRIPS AND PUBLIC HEALTH

The Agreement on Trade Related Aspects of Intellectual Property Rights (TRIPS) was adopted in 1994 with the foundation of the World Trade Organization (WTO). It is binding for all WTO members and mandates minimum 20 years patent protection on all products and processes including antiretrovirals for all WTO member countries (WTO 1994). This was a major policy change for many developing countries, including India and many sub-Saharan African countries, which, pre-TRIPS, did not recognize product-patents on pharmaceuticals. Indeed, 49 of the 98 member countries of the Paris Convention (the first multilateral intellectual property agreement signed in 1883 in Paris) had excluded pharmaceutical products from patentability. That had allowed developing countries to circumvent paying high prices for essential drugs including antiretrovirals, until the advent of recent legislation to achieve TRIPS compliance. Affordable medicines could be provided by the purchasing or manufacturing of generic products for a small fraction of the market price of the originator products (Smith et al. 2009; Straus 1996). India prohibited product patents from 1970 to 2004, allowing Indian companies to prosper through the production of affordable generics based on reverse engineering (t'Hoen 2009).

Though TRIPS does not translate directly into domestic law, it is a pivotal international agreement. The WTO members are required to implement the TRIPS-required minimum protective intellectual property standards into their national laws. But TRIPS includes important flexibilities which balance the demands of patent holders with the human right of access to essential medicines. How countries implement TRIPS and how they make use of its flexibilities, and whether additional TRIPS-plus provisions (data exclusivity, patent linkages) are implemented, determines access to essential antiretroviral drugs.[1] The following TRIPS flexibilities potentially protect public health safeguards by limiting intellectual property rights in circumstances of a health emergency or preventing anti-competitive behavior (Bhattacharya 2008).

COMPULSORY LICENSING

'Compulsory licensing is when a government allows someone else to produce the patented product or process without the consent of the patent owner' (WTO 2006) or issues a licence for its own use (government use licences). The use of compulsory licences is regulated under Article 31 of the TRIPS Agreement (WTO 1994). Compulsory licences are an important public health tool which can enhance access to patented antiretrovirals. They allow cheaper production of patented antiretrovirals, create market competition, and enable healthcare providers to gain access to newly developed patented antiretrovirals and other patented essential medicines (t'Hoen 2009).

The Doha Declaration on TRIPS and Public Health adopted in 2001 at the WTO ministerial conference in Doha, reaffirms both the priority of public health over commercial interests and the legality of TRIPS flexibilities, including governments' rights to use and determine the reasons for granting a compulsory licence:

We agree that the TRIPS Agreement does not and should not prevent Members from taking measures to protect public health. ... We affirm that the Agreement can and should be interpreted and implemented in a manner supportive of WTO members' right to protect public health and, in particular, to promote access to medicines for all (WTO 2001: § 4).

However a health emergency such as HIV/AIDS is only one reason for granting a compulsory licence; under TRIPS, countries are at liberty to determine the appropriate grounds for such licences. Before granting a compulsory licence, governments are obliged to negotiate a voluntary licence and even with a compulsory licence a royalty must be paid to the patent holder (WTO 2001, WTO 1994).

After the Doha Declaration reaffirmed the right of governments to use and determine reasons for granting a compulsory licence, several of the larger least developed countries (LDCs), and middle income countries with pharmaceutical manufacturing capacities such as Thailand, Indonesia, Brazil, Zambia, Mozambique and Zimbabwe, issued such licences for the production of antiretrovirals (CPT 2012; Grover 2009; Reichman 2009). At times the mere threat of compulsory licences impelled the originator industry to grant a voluntary licence (Orsi et al. 2007; see also de Mello e Souza in this volume). This happened in South Africa where Boehringer Ingelheim and GlaxoSmithKline were threatened with a compulsory licence after being accused under the Competition Act (see Nguyen in this volume) of excessive prices for essential antiretrovirals resulting in avoidable deaths (Avafia et al. 2006; t'Hoen 2009).

But the Doha Declaration notwithstanding, compulsory licences are virtually unused by smaller sub-Saharan African countries to achieve lower prices for patented antiretrovirals. Countries which use TRIPS flexibilities often face pressure from the rich countries where multinational drug companies are headquartered (Grover 2009). Two further reasons for not using compulsory licences relate to TRIPS Article 31 which limits the use of compulsory licences 'predominantly' to the domestic market:

First, Article 6 of the Doha Declaration recognizes that LDCs with 'insufficient or no manufacturing capacities in the pharmaceutical sector could face difficulties in making effective use of compulsory licensing under the TRIPS Agreement' (WTO 2001). On 30 August 2003, the WTO found a compromise allowing these LDCs to import drugs under a compulsory licence. In December 2006, this was incorporated into TRIPS through an amendment but only one country (Rwanda) has ever used this provision. In the perspective of Médecins Sans Frontières (MSF 2006a) and others, this compromise is too burdensome and therefore unworkable (MSF 2006a; WTO 2003).

Second, lack of economies of scale in many small sub-Saharan African countries with some manufacturing capacity make it impractical for local companies to produce under a compulsory licence, as the domestic market it is too small for commercial supply (Wonderling et al. 2005).

PARALLEL IMPORTS

With different prices for the same branded antiretrovirals in different markets (HAI 2009, MSF 2006b), parallel importing can induce price competition between the importer of low-cost antiretrovirals and the manufacturer of the same products. This can have positive effects on access to branded antiretrovirals. In Kenya parallel imports were effectively used by MSF and later by the public sector (Lewis-Lettington and Munyi 2004; Oxfam 2006).

TRIPS Articles 6 and 8 allow the 'exhaustion of rights'(WTO TRIPS 1994). This term refers to the situation where the patent holder has exhausted its rights by selling the product in the first country ('first sale') and is therefore not allowed to control further sales in other countries. It follows that the implementation of parallel imports provisions of TRIPS depends on the national laws of the relevant country regarding exhaustion of rights. Where international exhaustion is allowed, these parallel import provisions enable the importation of patented products from another country without the authorization of the patent holder (WTO 2006). However the original manufacturer can counter the effects of invoking these provisions by either refusing supply of the relevant drugs to potential exporting countries or by raising the price to those countries (Wonderling et al. 2005). Overall, parallel imports are poorly used in sub-Saharan Africa. Sibanda (2009) concludes that this suboptimal use is mainly due to a lack of political will and external pressures.

THE SCOPE OF PATENTABILITY

To understand why TRIPS makes it possible for countries to limit the scope of patentability, one needs to understand what a patent is. Patents, as time limited monopolies, provide exclusive rights to patent holders to produce or sell patented products. Monopoly rights, since they exclude competition from alternative versions of the same products, assure maximization of profit to holders of those rights (Barton and Emanuel 2005). Consumers and prescribers, having been conditioned to using the branded product during the patent period, tend to persist in preferring it to the generic alternative even after the expiry of patent protection when the latter becomes cheaper than the branded product.

Multi-country studies have confirmed the following findings. Most generic antiretroviral drugs are cheaper than branded products (exceptions in case of lopinavir/ritonavir do exist) (Waning et al. 2010b), and prices on off-patent first-line antiretrovirals are significantly lower than (often patented) second-line antiretrovirals. The number of manufacturers is directly associated with lower prices for antiretrovirals (Orsi et al. 2007, WHO 2008). Monopolies on drugs can lead to scenarios where the vast majority of the sale price of the drug is patent rent. For example, for some antiretrovirals such as the 3TC/d4T/NVP triple-therapy, patent rents drive the cost of a $61 sold by Indian generic companies, to more than $10,000 when sold by the branded industry (Waning et al. 2010b; Wonderling et al. 2005; MSF 2006b).

The professed rationale for patents is that they provide incentives for research and development (R&D) with the inventor being rewarded for innovative activity through the patent rent, leading to an increase in public welfare (Barton et al. 2005; VFA 2007; VFA 2009). However, due to patents producing indirect negative societal effects (decreased supply, higher prices), developing countries, where the pre-patent pharmaceutical market was characterized by competition, may suffer welfare losses (Barton et al. 2005; James 2009; Smith et al. 2009). Additionally, James (2009) and Grover (2009) argue that stronger intellectual property rights slow down technological progress by excluding competition that would otherwise force companies to be the first on the market and bring pressure on them to develop more cost-effective technologies.

Pharmaceutical companies and some economists advocate differential pricing to increase global welfare by charging lower prices in LDCs with a highly elastic demand and high prices in industrialized countries with a less elastic demand (Havlir and Hammer 2005). This could increase affordability of innovative antiretroviral drugs in sub-Saharan African countries by reducing the dead-weight loss (allocative inefficiencies), while allowing pharmaceutical companies to realize high profits (Wonderling et al. 2005; Gilead Sciences 2010). However, a necessary condition for such a pricing arrangement to succeed would be a pharmaceutical market that is strictly segmented into non-interconnected markets so there can be no reverse flow of low price antiretrovirals. But since parallel importation is permitted under TRIPS, it is difficult to prevent thereverse flow of low price antiretrovirals that such importation makes possible (Reichman 2009). Moreover, differential pricing does not assure affordable prices for the poor in middle income countries: the access program of the MNC Abbott for lopinavir/ritonavir charged $440 in LDCs, but $4119 in Chile in 2005 (Orsi et al. 2007). This has been confirmed by multi-country studies which found greater price variations of patented antiretrovirals within middle income countries than within LDCs

(Waning et al. 2010a; Waning et al. 2010b). For second-line antiretrovirals, middle income countries paid up to nine times the price charged in LDCs (Orsi et al. 2007; WHO 2008).

Furthermore, putative benefits from patents on innovative activities and public health are uncertain:

Existing studies on patent benefits have focused mainly on industrialized countries, while there is little evidence of benefits flowing to developing countries.

There is insufficient evidence to suggest that higher intellectual property protection levels stimulate innovation, or that the level of intellectual property rights protection in a developing country is causally linked to the number of innovations being made available. Only 20 of the 1556 new chemical entities (just 1.3 per cent) that entered the market between 1975 and 2004 were for neglected diseases including TB, which are responsible for 12 per cent of the global disease-burden (Oxfam 2006; Reichman 2009; Westerhaus and Castro 2006).

A possible explanation for the decrease in the number of radical innovations in this period is that research was driven by profit maximizing rather than medical needs (Barton and Emanuel 2005).

It is well established that patents on antiretroviral drugs and other essential medicines reduce availability and affordability. It is therefore crucial that countries take advantage of the right under TRIPS to limit the scope of patentability in order to help protect public health. National patent offices grant patents for products (absolute monopolies) or processes (relative monopolies) that are 'new, involve an inventive step and are capable of industrial application' (WTO 1994; Wonderling et al. 2005). However what is to count as an 'inventive step' as a necessary condition to grant a patent is not defined in TRIPS itself. This allows countries to avoid patents on products not recognized as inventive (Amin et al. 2009; Amin 2011; Grover 2009). Thus Indian patent law excludes from patentability 'the mere discovery of a new form of a known substance which does not result in the enhancement of the known efficacy...'(Indian Patents Act 2005).

INDIAN PATENT LAW

Product patents were banned in India from 1970 to 2004, allowing Indian companies to prosper by producing affordable generics through reverse engineering. Since 2005, Indian patent law has been TRIPS compliant. Pre-1995 drugs cannot be patented; drugs with market approvals granted between 1995 and 2005 can continue to be produced. If a patent is granted for such products, generic companies must pay a 'reasonable royalty' (section 11A Indian Patents Act 2005). The term 'reasonable royalty' is not defined and therefore open to interpretation (Dhar and kopakumar 2006; India Patents Act 2005). The majority of first-line antiretrovirals entered the Indian market before 2005, and more than 80 per cent of first-line antiretrovirals, and almost all active pharmaceutical ingredients used in sub-Saharan Africa countries, are produced and exported by 14 Indian generic companies (Chien 2007; t'Hoen 2009; Waning et al. 2010a). Therefore both the Indian generic industry and Indian patent law play crucial roles in assuring access to antiretrovirals in sub-Saharan Africa.

Indian patent law includes the following important flexibilities, which have not been proven to contravene TRIPS, notwithstanding the ongoing Novartis case (Mudur 2007), which enable the generic production of important drugs such as antiretrovirals to continue (Bhattacharya 2008; Lalitha 2008).

Compulsory Licences

Indian patent law provides a legal basis for compulsory licences both within the country and for export. The first licence for production for the domestic market was granted only in March 2012, when Hyderabad-based Natco Pharma was issued with a licence for manufacturing of a generic version of Nexavar (sorafenib tosylate), which is used to treat liver and kidney cancer. Bayer is the holder of the patent 215758 (*Official Journal of the Patent Office* 2011). Amin (2011) sees the limited use of compulsory licensing as partly due to political pressures on India and other countries not to use this provision.

Section 3(d)

Section 3(d) of the Indian Patent Act limits the scope of patentability of incremental innovations to prevent 'evergreening'. As noted above, this Section excludes 'the mere discovery of a new form of a known substance which does not result in the enhancement of the known efficacy...' (Amin et al. 2009; Indian Patents Act 2005; James 2009). Khader (2008) describes making enhanced efficacy a condition for a patent as a relative exception to patentability. The resulting restriction in the number of patents issued is understood by most authors as a safeguard to public health.

Section 3(d) has been used to reject patents on marginally innovative antiretrovirals such as tenofovirdisoproxilfumerate (TDF) or lopinavir/ritonavir (see below). Criticism of section 3(d) by Novartis and other brand companies is summarized in the USIB-report (US-India Business Council 2009). Most independent authors,

Table 9.1: Arguments Pro and Contra Section 3(d)

Pro (US-India Business Council 2009)	Contra (James 2009)
Incremental innovations can produce a range of similar products, which could lead to price reductions through competition.	No evidence has been found for such price reductions; instead patents on incremental innovations lead to price increases.
Since 2005, Indian companies have applied for such patents in other parts of the world.	These patents cannot justify a change of the Indian patent law.
Section 3(d) is not TRIPS compliant because it excludes the majority of incremental innovations from patentability; eligibility criteria are too strict.	Patent laws differ in their interpretation of what constitutes an inventive step; section 3(d) is effective in preventing frivolous patents.
Incremental innovations can be patient beneficial and have an economic value for the generic industry.	The United Nations sees the human right to access to affordable antiretrovirals as having higher value than the economic value of such drugs to the industry; beneficial effects are better recognized through other mechanisms such as tax reductions.
Patents on incremental innovations encourage R&D.	Limiting second-use patents to enhanced efficacy can lead to more needs-driven R&D.

including the United Nations, reject the corporate arguments (All-Party Parliamentary Group 2009; Amin et al. 2009; Amin 2011; James 2009; Reichman 2009; Patenting the poor 2005; Shasderi 2009; TAC 2010; t'Hoen 2009; UN 2006; WHOb 2008). The different views can be summarized as in Table 9.1 above:

In a case brought by Novartis the Chennai High Court confirmed section 3(d) to be constitutional and remarked that only the WTO can define TRIPS conformity. This court case and the TDF-case (see below) are seen by many observers (Love 2007; Mudur 2007; Swamy 2007) as:

supportive of continued access to affordable antiretrovirals,
setting high standards for enhanced efficacy,
preventing frivolous patents.

The United Nations resolution on HIV/AIDS (Point 43) has reinforced the view that TRIPS is 'supportive of the right to protect public health and... to promote access to essential medicines for all including the production of generic antiretroviral drugs...' (UN 2006).

Pre- and Post-grant Opposition

The legislation gives any group or individual the right to question a patent's validity before a decision is taken on whether a patent is granted—the right to 'pre-grant-opposition'. It also allows post-grant opposition: a granted patent can be challenged by interested groups, who will have to present evidence that the reasons for granting the patent were invalid. The legislation permitting such opposition not only makes it possible for outside experts to present relevant evidence to the patent office, but also recognizes the need in assessing patent applications for the kind of evidence they bring, evidence otherwise not easily obtainable by the office (Amin et al. 2009; Amin 2011; Indian Patents Act 2005; Khader 2008). The filing of such opposition cases has already decreased prices or resulted in the withdrawal of patent applications (Ford et al. 2007b).

Production before a Patent is Granted

Companies can continue generic antiretroviral drug production while a patent application is pending. An example is CIPLA's generic version of lopinavir/ritonavir which continued to be marketed while Abbott's application was pending (Bhattacharya 2008). That patent application (application No: 339/MUMNP/2006) having been rejected in January 2011 (Taylor 2011), the generic version of the drug can continue to be produced. A further price reduction is expected, but MSF and others are increasingly replacing lopinavir/ritonavir with the equally effective atazanavir/ritonavir. The latter drug is cheaper than the former and its substitution complicates the patent situation less (MSF 2006b).

AFRICAN PATENT LAWS

Accessibility of antiretrovirals for sub-Saharan African patients depends also on whether the patent laws of their countries allow for the import of off-patent antiretroviral drugs. Thirty-seven of 39 reviewed sub-Saharan African countries already provide pharmaceutical patents despite the transition period for LDCs ending only in 2016. None fully uses TRIPS flexibilities; only six allow parallel imports; only four allow restricted second-use patents and only one (Rwanda) has ever used the 30 August decision. In spite of the fact that the laws of all these countries permitted compulsory licences, their actual use of the laws to grant such licences was very limited. Musungu (2007) argues this failure to use these laws to grant such licences results in high prices. Reasons for this dismal picture would probably include a lack of expertise in poor LDCs combined with external pressures, both from the pharmaceutical industry generally and from countries hosting substantial pharmaceutical manufacturers, to implement stricter patent laws than required by TRIPS.

THE IMPACT OF THE PATENT STATUS IN INDIA ON ACCESS IN SUB-SAHARAN AFRICA

The impact of the TRIPS-compliant 2005 Indian patent legislation on access to antiretrovirals in sub-Saharan Africa depends on the patent status of the respective drug and/or of its active pharmaceutical ingredients in India (for its ability to export). It also depends on the patent laws of importing sub-Saharan African countries and the availability of such drugs from local manufacturers.

Access to Off-patent Drugs

Indian patent law has no impact on off-patent antiretrovirals since it allows Indian generic companies to produce and export generic versions which sub-Saharan African countries may import. Generic antiretrovirals serve public-health needs as they increase availability (quantity) and accessibility (price). The cost in the year 2000 of first-line antiretroviral therapy was $15,000 ppy. As product patents were not required in India then, CIPLA was able to start generic production and supply for $350 in 2001, decreasing the cost to $61 ppy (MSF 2006b). The price decrease of more than 99 per cent demonstrates that low-cost generic antiretroviral-production on a large scale is possible under conditions of free competition when products are not patented. Supply by CIPLA and other Indian companies has resulted in increased access to antiretrovirals in sub-Saharan Africa (Amin 2011; Bhattacharya 2008; Grover 2009).

Limited Access to Incremental Innovative Antiretrovirals

Incremental innovative antiretrovirals such as 'the mere discovery of a new form of a known substance' without enhanced efficacy are not seen as innovative enough to qualify for patent protection (Indian Patents Act 2005). As generics of these incremental innovative antiretrovirals (without enhanced efficacy) can be produced in India, Indian patent law has only a limited impact on access to them. The TDF-case and the lopinavir/ritononavir case illustrate two different aspects of such impact.

There was clear clinical evidence from 2001 justifying the inclusion of TDF in first-line treatment in US and Europe. This treatment could not however be extended globally as long as TDF remained unaffordable (Ford et al. 2007a). However, as a result of the supply of generic TDF by Indian firms and to a limited extend by Aspen/South Africa, the price decreased. The cheapest generic once-daily fixed dose combination (TDF/3TC/EFV) is available now for $173 ppy, having come down by over 70 per cent in the period 2008–11. Over the same period, the branded product, available through Gilead's global access-program, remained at the same price of \$613 ppy in the 125 eligible LDCs (MSF 2006b; Amin et al. 2009). Even though tenofovir was first discovered in 1985, Gilead filed a patent application in India (first filed in 1997, assessed after the enactment of the 2005 Patent Act amendment) arguing that its development of this drug's ester-derivative and salt was an inventive step (Amin et al. 2009). This argument ignored the specific exclusion of esters and salts from patentability by section 3(d) of the India Patents Act (2005). After pre-grant opposition India rejected Gilead's patent application in September 2009 (India refuses 2009). The TDF-case demonstrates that most incremental innovations are ineligible for patenting under section 3(d) (James 2009).

The emergence of alternative sources of TDF, aided by patent denial in India, has brought down the price in many markets and has enabled the WHO in 2009, and subsequently sub-Saharan African countries, to include TDF in new first-line antiretroviral drug recommendations (WHO 2009). The extent to which voluntary licences contributed to this process remains unclear. In South Africa TDF was exclusively marketed by Aspen through a voluntary licence from Gilead for \$613 ppy which enabled only 0.5 per cent of those accessing antiretroviral therapy to be treated with TDF. This might change, as affordable generics can now be imported from India (TAC 2010). But there are concerns about Gilead's 11 voluntary licences to Indian generic companies (Amin et al. 2009; Amin 2011; Afavia et al. 2006). Thus, in spite of the rejection of Gilead's patent application, increased access to TDF could still be hindered if the export limitations specified in these licences prove to be valid (Amin et al. 2009; Amin 2011; Gilead Sciences 2010; TAC 2010).

It is indisputable that worldwide, an increasing number of patents are being applied and/or granted for incremental innovations (US-India Business Council 2009; WHO 2008; James 2009) but assessments of the implications vary significantly as illustrated in Figure 9.1.

While the USBIC report could be seen to argue plausibly that allowing the patenting of incremental innovation should lead to price decreases, there is little evidence to suggest that this is indeed

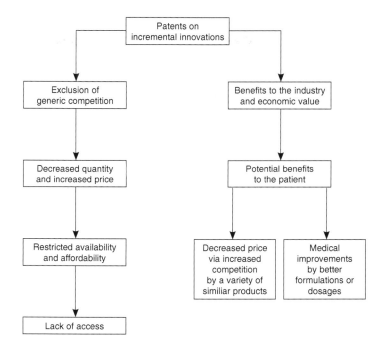

Figure 9.1: Patents on Incremental Innovations: Contradictory Assessments

happening. To the contrary, there is strong evidence to suggest that patents on incremental innovations restrict access, while patent-denial results in rising generic competition, decreased price and increased access. Limiting the scope of patentability, including pre-grant opposition, is therefore clearly shown to be a crucial TRIPS flexibility, which can prevent frivolous patents.

It must be conceded, however, that incremental innovations such as once-daily formulations can be advantageous for patients. Since these innovations may still fall below the line of 'enhanced efficacy', the criterion for granting a patent, it might be argued, may discourage companies from developing such advantageous formulations. But other methods, such as tax reductions (Dhar and Gopakumar 2006), which do not, as patents do, restrict access to the relevant drugs, can be used to encourage incremental innovations. 'Enhanced efficacy' in section 3(d) of the Indian patent law should remain a high-level criterion for patents being granted on incremental innovations. The burden of proof must stay with the applicant.

Generic production while a patent application is pending: the lopinavir/ritonavir case

A different situation pertains with the essential second-line antiretroviral drug lopinavir/ritonavir, for which a patent application (application No: 339/MUMNP/2006) was rejected in January 2011 (Taylor 2011). Lopinavir/ritonavir is marketed by Abbott, which does not grant any voluntary licences and therefore remains the only supplier in most sub-Saharan African countries. Indian generic companies already produced heat-stable lopinavir/ritonavir, which was legal while the patent-application was pending (Big Patents India 2012, Shasderi 2009). Indian firms cannot however export this product to countries such as South Africa, where lopinavir/ritonavir is patented (Patent No. 96/10475).

Abbott's tiered price for LDCs at $410 ppy was lowered from $500 ppy after the Indian firms CIPLA and Matrix undercut this price, which shows that even limited competition leads to price reductions (MSF 2006b; Shasderi 2009). With a patent application pending, however, generic production in India was not expanded widely (Mudur 2007). The recent patent rejection under section 3(d) is considered to have had a major influence on access to the relevant antiretroviral drug. Currently Indian generic companies can export lopinavir/ritonavir to all LDCs and middle income countries, where no patent exists, offering a large price advantage to middle income countries. A price increase could happen if countries such as South Africa, where the drug is under patent, are switched by Abbott to the second category. Then these countries would have to pay $1000 ppy.

LACKING ACCESS TO PATENTED RADICAL INNOVATIVE ANTIRETROVIRALS

There are several Indian patents for radical innovative antiretrovirals which do not fall under section 3(d) such as for raltegravir (Patent

No: IN212400). Patenting in India precludes competition and this means antiretrovirals become unaffordable and unavailable there. But since patents on these drugs are granted also in sub-Saharan Africa including South Africa, the drugs become unaffordable and unavailable in those regions too. In these circumstances access to these medicines in sub-Saharan Africa can be considered negligible. This is already a problem for patients needing to switch to second or third-line treatment in order to sustain treatment (Havlir and Wammer 2005). In future this situation is expected to apply to an increasing number of antiretrovirals. There is the risk of a gap of up to 20 years until the poor can access radically innovative essential antiretrovirals (All-Party Parliamentary Group 2009; Bhattacharya 2008; James 2009; Smith et al. 2009).

Compulsory licences, parallel imports and/or voluntary licences are the only means of ensuring access in India and sub-Saharan Africa to patented radical innovative antiretrovirals. Yet compulsory licences involve a burdensome process and sub-Saharan African countries without sufficient manufacturing capacity are de facto prevented from importing compulsory licenced antiretrovirals notwithstanding the 30 August decision (Love 2007; MSF 2006a). While most sub-Saharan African patent laws include provisions for compulsory licences, their use remains very limited due to external pressures as exemplified by Novartis' challenge to section 3(d) of the Indian Patent Act and free trade agreements which restrict such licences. Voluntary licences rely to a large extent on the good will of brand companies or are granted under a threat to use compulsory licences (Grover 2009; Oxfam 2006).

PATENTS MATTER

While the Indian patent law does not impact on off-patent antiretrovirals, affordable access to both marginal and radical innovative antiretrovirals is dependent on how countries make use of TRIPS flexibilities and on whether additional TRIPS-plus provisions (data exclusivity, patent term extensions) apply as a result of free trade agreements. The brand industry argues that patents do not impact negatively on access, which, they say, depends mainly on levels of poverty, lack of infrastructure, and the political will of sub-Saharan African countries (VFA 2007; VFA 2009). While weak political will, poverty, and a lack of infrastructure surely play a role, Deiss (2007) demonstrated that the number of patents in a sub-Saharan African country is positively correlated to HIV prevalence, and that more patents are found in countries where they are easier to file. South Africa, with 13 patents on antiretrovirals, is the sub-Saharan African country with the highest number of such patents (Deiss 2007).

By providing the opportunity for countries to balance rights and legal obligations under TRIPS, the Doha Declaration encouraged India to introduce crucial safeguards into its patent laws.However, owing to the persistence of power imbalances between pharmaceutical multi-nationals and poor countries, neither the Doha Declaration nor the 30 August decision has solved the antiretroviral access problem for sub-Saharan Africa (Chien 2007; Lalitha 2008). The safeguards introduced to Indian patent law are likely to reduce the restrictions imposed by patents on access to *incremental* innovative antiretrovirals in sub-Saharan Africa. It is doubtful, however, whether the scope provided by those provisions, and by the international agreements on which they are based, will be used to mitigate the negative impact of patents on access to *new radical* innovative antiretrovirals.

Notes

1. Data exclusivity: clinical test data is protected for a certain time and therefore not available in this period for generic manufacturers to prove bio-equivalence, which is necessary for market approval. This results in an extension of the period of monopoly pricing. Patent linkage refers to a legal situation, where the market approval of a generic is linked to its patent status.

References

All-Party Parliamentary Group on AIDS, 2009. 'The Treatment Timebomb', All-Party Parliamentary Group on AIDS, London.

Amin, T., 2011. 'Re-Visiting the Patents and Access to Medicines Dichotomy: An Evaluation of TRIPS Implementation and Public Health Safeguards in Developing Countries' in O. Aginam, J. Harrington, P. Yu (eds.), *Global Governance of HIV/AIDS: Intellectual Property and Access to Essential Medicines,* Edward Elgar Publishing, Cheltenham, Northampton.

Amin, T., Rajkumar, R., Radhakrishnan, P., Kesselheim, A.S., 2009. 'Expert Review of Drug Patent Applications: Improving Health in the Developing World', *Health Affairs,* 28(5): w948–w956.

Avafia, T., Berger, J., Hartzenberg, T., 2006. 'The ability of select Sub-Saharan African Countries to Utilise TRIPs Flexibilities and Competition Law to Ensure a Sustainable Supply of Essential Medicines: A Study of Producing and Importing Countries', Trade Law Centre for Southern Africa.

Barton, J.H., Emanuel, J.E., 2005. The Patents-Based Pharmaceutical Development Process: Rationale, Problems, and Potential Reforms', *Journal of the American Medical Association,* 294: 2075–82

Bhattacharya, R., 2008. 'Are developing countries going too far on TRIPS? A closer look at the new laws in India', *American Journal of Law Medicine,* 34(2–3): 395–421.

Big Patents India, 2012. [http://india.bigpatents.org].

Chien, V.C., 2007. 'HIV/AIDS Drugs for Sub-Saharan Africa: How Do Brand and Generic Supply Compare?', *PLoS ONE,* 2(3): e278

Consumer Project on Technology, 'Examples of Health-Related Compulsory Licences', [http://www.cptech.org/ip/health/cl/recent-examples.html].

Deiss, R., 2007. 'Intellectual property organizations and pharmaceutical patents in Africa', *Social Science and Medicine,* 64(2): 287–91.

Dhar, B., Gopakumar, K.M., 2006, 'Post-2005 TRIPS Scenario in Patent Protection in the Pharmaceutical Sector: The Case of the Generic Pharmaceutical Industry in India', Geneva: ICTSD and UNCTAD, Ottawa: IDRC.

Ford, N., Mills, E., Calmy, A., 2007. 'Rationing Antiretroviral Therapy in Africa: Treating Too Few Too Late', *New England Journal of Medicine,* 360(18): 1808–10.

Ford, N., Wilson, D., Costa Chaves, G., Lotrowska, M., Kijtiwatchakul, K., 2007. 'Sustaining Access to Antiretroviral Therapy in the Less-Developed World: Lessons from Brazil and Thailand', *AIDS Review,* 21(Suppl 4): 21–29.

Gilead Sciences, 2010, *Advancing Sustainable Access to HIV/AIDS:*

Medicines in the Developing World, Gilead Sciences, Foster City. pp. 395–400

Grover, A., 2009. 'Promotion and Protection of All Human Rights, Civil, Political, Economic, Social and Cultural Rights, Including the Right to Development: Report of the Special Rapporteur on the Right of Everyone to the Enjoyment of the Highest Attainable Standard of Physical and Mental Health', UN Human Rights Council Eleventh session Agenda item 3 A/HRC/11/12. p. 79.

Havlir, D.V., Hammer, S.M., 2005. 'Patents versus Patients? Antiretroviral Therapy in India', *New England Journal of Medicine,* 353(8): 749–51.

Health Action International Africa, 2009. 'Prices and Availability Affect Access to Medicines', HAI Africa, Nairobi.

'India Refuses Patent Protection for Two Key HIV Drugs', 2009. *HIV AIDS Policy Law Review,* 14(2): 28–29.

James, T.C., 2009, 'Patent Protection and Innovation Section 3(d) of the Patents Act and Indian Pharmaceutical Industry', Indian Pharmaceutical Alliance, Mumbai.

Khader, F.A., 2008. 'Transcending Differences: The Challenge for Pharmaceuticals in the Post-TRIPS Indian Patent Regime', *Journal of Intellectual Property Rights,* 13(5): 424–31.

Lalitha, N., 2008. 'Doha Declaration and Public Health Issues', *Journal of Intellectual Property Rights,* 13(5): 401–13.

Lewis-Lettington, R., Munyi, P., 2004, 'Willingness and Ability to use TRIPs Flexibilities: How will WTO Patent Rules affect Kenyan Legislation and Policy?', DFID Health Systems Resource Centre, London.

Love, J., 2007. 'Straight talk from ... James Love', *Nature Medicine,* 13(9): 101.

Médecins Sans Frontières, 2006a. 'Neither expeditious, nor a solution: The WTO's 30th August decision is unworkable',Médecins Sans Frontières, Geneva.

Médecins Sans Frontières, 2006b. 'Untangling the Web of Antiretroviral Price Reductions', [http://utw.msfaccess.org].

Ministry of Law and Justice, 2005. 'The Patents (Amendment) Act No. 15 of 2005', New Delhi.

Mudur, G., 2007. 'Court Dismisses Novartis Challenge to Indian Patent Law', *British Medical Journal,* 335(7614): 273.

Musungu, S.F., 2007. 'Access to ART and Other Essential Medicines in Sub-Saharan Africa: Intellectual Property and Relevant Legislations', UNDP Regional Service Centre for Eastern and Southern Africa, Johannesburg.

Official Journal of the Patent Office., 2011. 'PUBLICATION U/S. 87(1) The Compulsory licence Application No. C.L.A. No. 1 of 2011 from M/S. NactoPharma Ltd. In Patent No. 215758 is hereby published', *The Patent Office Journal* 12/08/2011

Orsi, F., D'Almeida, C., Hasenclever, L., Camara, M., Tigre, P., Coriat, B., 2007. 'TRIPS post-2005 and Access to New Antiretroviral Treatments in Southern Countries: Issues and Challenges', *AIDS*, 21: 1997–2003.

Oxfam, 2006, *Patents versus Patients: Five Years after the Doha Declaration*, Oxfam International, London.

2005. 'Patenting the poor' *Lancet Oncology*, 6(4): 191.

Reichman, J.H., 2009. 'Comment: compulsory licensing of patented pharmaceutical inventions: evaluating the options', *Journal of Law Medicine & Ethics*, 37(2): 247–263.

Republic of South Africa, 1998. *Competition Act No. 89 of 1998*, South Africa.

Republic of South Africa, 2009. *Competition Amendment Act No. 1 of 2009*, South Africa.

Republic of South Africa, 1978. *Patents Act No. 57 of 1978*, South Africa.

Shasderi, R., 2009. 'Indian Patent Law and ARV', in Action Against Aids Germany (ed.), pp. 12–14, *Indian Generics and AIDS*, Action Against Aids Germany, Tübingen.

Sibanda, O., 2009. 'Parallel Importation and Compulsory Licensing in Kenya and South Africa as measures to access HIV/AIDS medicine', *Acta Academica*, 41(1): 183–206.

Smith, R.D., Correa, C., Oh, C., 2009. 'Trade, TRIPS, and pharmaceuticals' *Lancet*, 373(9664): 684–91.

Srinivasan, S., 2012. 'The Compulsory Licence for Nexavar: A Landmark Order', *Economic and Political Weekly*, 47(14): 10–3.

Straus, Josef, 1996, 'Implications of the TRIPS Agreement in the Field of Patent Law' in Beier, F.K., Schricker, G. (eds.), pp 160–215, *From GATT to TRIPS: The Agreement on Trade-Related Aspects of Intellectual Property Rights*, VHC, Weinheim.

Swamy, M., 2007. 'India: Court Upholds Patent Law Denying Patents for Slightly Modified Versions of Existing Drugs', *HIV AIDS Policy Law Rev*, 12(2–3): 50–51.

Taylor, L., 2011. 'India Rejects Abbott Patent on Kaletra', *Pharma Times online*.

t'Hoen, E., 2009. *The Global Politics of Pharmaceutical Monopoly Power:*

Drug Patents, Access, Innovation and the Application of the WTO Doha Declaration on TRIPS and Public Health, AMB Publishers, Diemen.

Treatment Action Campaign (TAC), 2010. 'Tenofovir: An explanation of why we need TDF-based fixed-dose combinations and the steps to bring them to the market in South Africa', Treatment Action Campaign, South Africa.

UNAIDS, 2011. 'Factsheet World Aids Day Report', UNAIDS, 2011.

United Nations (UN) General Assembly, 1966. 'International Covenant on Economic, Social and Cultural Rights', United Nations General Assembly Resolution 2200A (XXI).

United Nations (UN) General Assembly, 2006. 'Political Declaration on HIV/AIDS', United Nations General Assembly Resolution A/RES/60/262.

US-India Business Council, Coalition for Healthy India, 2009. *The Value Of Incremental Pharmaceutical Innovation: Benefits For Indian Patients and Indian Business,* Gale Group, Farmington Hills, Michigan.

Verband Forschender Arzneimittelhersteller VFA 2009: *Forschung ist die beste Medizin,* 2009.

Verband ForschenderArzneimittelhersteller VFA 2009: *Setting the correct course for combating AIDS in Africa,* 2007.

Waning, B., Diedrichsen, E., Moon, S., 2010. 'A Lifeline to Treatment: The Role of Indian Generic Manufacturers in Supplying Antiretroviral Medicines to Developing Countries', *Journal of the International AIDS Society,* 13: 35.

Waning, B., Kaplan, W., Fox, M.P., Boyd-Boffa, M., King, A.C., Lawrence, D., 2010. 'Temporal Trends in Generic and Brand Prices of Antiretroviral Medicines Procured with Donor Funds in Developing Countries', *Journal of Generic Medicines,* 7: 159–75.

Westerhaus, M., Castro, A., 2006. 'How do Intellectual Property Law and International Trade Agreements Affect Access to Antiretroviral Therapy?', *PLoS Med,* 3(8): e332

Wonderling, D., Gruen, R., Black, N., 2005. *Introduction to Health Economics,* Open University Press, Berkshire, New York.

World Health Organization, 2008. 'A Summary Report from the Global Price Reporting Mechanism on Antiretroviral Drugs', World Health Organization, Geneva.

World Health Organization (WHO), 2009. 'Rapid advice: therapy for HIV infection in adults and adolescents', World Health Organization, Geneva.

World Health Organization (WHO), UNAIDS, 2009. 'AIDS epidemic update', World Health Organization, Geneva.

World Health Organization, UNDP, 2008. 'Workshop on the Examination of Pharmaceutical Patents: Developing a Public Health Perspective', 30–31 Oct, World Health Organization, Cape Town.

World Trade Organization (WHO), 2006. 'Compulsory licensing of pharmaceuticals and TRIPS: TRIPS and Health Frequently Asked Questions', World Trade Organization, online [http://www.wto.org/english/tratop_e/trips_e/public_health_faq_e.htm].

World Trade Organization (WTO), 2001. 'Declaration on the TRIPS agreement and public health', World Trade Organization, Doha: Ministerial Conference WT/MIN(01)/DEC/2.

World Trade Organization (WTO), 2003. 'Implementation of paragraph 6 of the Doha Declaration on the TRIPS Agreement and public health', World Trade Organization, Cancun: General Council WT/L/540 and Corr.1.

World Trade Organization (WTO), 1994. 'Marrakesh Agreement Establishing the World Trade Organization Annex 1C: Agreement on Trade-Related Aspects of Intellectual Property Rights (TRIPS)', World Trade Organization, Marrakesh.

10 Accessing Medicines in Developing Economies

Tu Thanh Nguyen

As recognised in the TRIPS Agreement, the protection and enforcement of intellectual property rights (IPRs) should contribute not only to 'the promotion of technical innovation' but also 'the transfer and dissemination of technology'; it should benefit both innovators and innovation users 'in a manner conducive to social and economic welfare' by creating balanced rights and obligations among stakeholders (WTO 2010, TRIPS Agreement: Art. 7).[1] WTO members have therefore increasingly emphasised 'the need for the effective use of the IP regime and of the flexibilities in the TRIPS Agreement' (Lamy 2010) at both national and international levels to address public health problems and, particularly, to gain access to medicines. One such flexibility is the use of competition law.

Competition provisions in the TRIPS Agreement, including Articles 8.2, 31(k) and 40[2] provide broad discretion for WTO members to enact and apply domestic competition law in addressing both anti-competitive unilateral abuses of right holders and anti-competitive contractual restraints in contractual licences provided consistency and appropriateness requirements are satisfied. In addition, compulsory licensing and other sanctions may be ordered by members' relevant authorities to correct such anti-competitive conduct (Nguyen 2010: 42–52). Developing countries, however, have rarely applied domestic competition law to promote access to medicines. There are many reasons for this, but perhaps most important are the underdevelopment of competition law and the complexity of the interface between IPRs and competition law in such countries. This is not likely to remain the case, however, because appropriate competition policy in general, and IPR-related competition law in particular, are not just a luxury to be enjoyed by rich countries but a real necessity for countries striving to create democratic market economies (Stiglitz 2001).

Consequently issues concerning the use of competition law to promote access to medicines have recently gained considerable attention in developing economies and international forums. There is growing awareness of the adverse effects of IPR-related anti-competitive practices on these economies' technological and economic development and, more specifically, on their populations and public health. They are increasingly recognising the potential benefits derived from IPR-related competition law enforcement. At the international level IPR-related competition issues were addressed in the WIPO Development Agenda (WIPO 2007), resulting in a project to promote a better understanding of the interface between IP and competition law and policy, and to foster technology transfer to developing countries (WIPO 2009). Issues concerning technical cooperation and assistance in the area of IPR-related competition law were raised for discussion in the WTO by Brazil in the TRIPS Council meeting of June 2008 (WTO 2008) and are presently under discussion in this Council.

In the context of IPRs and public health, the WHO adopted its global strategy and plan of action on public health, innovation and IP in May 2008, encouraging and promoting the use of competition law and policy to improve the availability and affordability of medicines. One of the actions WHO recommended to developing countries was that countries take appropriate actions consistent with the TRIPS Agreement to prevent IPR abuse 'by right holders or the resort to practices which unreasonably restrain trade or adversely affect the international transfer of technology, in the field of health products' (WHO 2008). In addition, it is worth noting that, from a human rights perspective, the United Nations Commission on Human Rights (UNCHR) has encouraged 'States to consider the elaboration of competition laws that prevent abuses of IPRs that lead to violations of the right to health in particular restrictive licensing practices or the setting of high prices for essential drugs' (UNCHR 2001).

In practice, it appears that the developing world is trying to use public health–related flexibilities, which are, exceptions and limitations permitted in the TRIPS Agreement and regulated in domestic IP law, to increase access to medicines (WTO 2010: Arts. 30–3; Doha Declaration of TRIPS Agreement and Public Health 2001). These limited flexibilities alone, however, cannot solve all of the issues relating to access to medicines. This can be illustrated by the fact that IPR-related anti-competitive practices in the pharmaceutical sector are now subject to intensive competition or antitrust law scrutiny in both the European Union (EU) and the United States (US). In July 2009, the European Commission (EC) released the final report of its inquiry into the pharmaceutical sector dealing with the alleged obstacles to market entry for generic and innovative pharmaceutical products. The report's main conclusion was that competition law enforcement, among other things, can be used to improve the competitive functioning of the pharmaceutical market (EC 2009: paras 1563–77). This finding was also reflected in the AstraZeneca judgement delivered by the EU General Court in July 2010 (*AstraZeneca v. Commission* 2010). In this case, AstraZeneca was fined for abuse of the patents system and of the system for authorising medicines, intending to delay competition with a blockbuster drug from generic and parallel-imported pharmaceuticals. In the US, antitrust authorities have been very active in antitrust law enforcement in the field of health care services and products (FTC 2009). One of the most timely and prominent issues in US antitrust law today is how to assess settlements of patents disputes involving payments from innovative to generic drug manufacturers, the so-called pay-for-delay settlements or reverse payments.[3] The goal of such antitrust enforcement is to ensure access to innovative, safe and affordable medicines.

This chapter will investigate—through a number of relevant cases and an examination of Indian competition law—whether or not and to what extent developing economies can adopt and enforce domestic competition law to promote access to medicines with the support of the international community. To establish the background for this discussion it is necessary to review the intersection between IPRs and competition law.

INTERSECTION BETWEEN IPRS AND COMPETITION LAW

Exclusive rights granted by IP law seek to protect IPRs. In doing so the IP system 'permits owners to raise price above marginal cost, creating deadweight losses by raising the price to consumers, potentially limiting competition' (Lemley 2005:1059). Thus, IP protection may be criticised for creating monopoly rights that undermine consumer interests. In contrast competition law generally reflects the premise that consumer welfare is best served by removing impediments to competition. From the IP perspective competition law may be considered an interventionist instrument that infringes right holders' entitlements and, thereby, affects the very foundations of IP law. Consequently IP law may be considered to conflict with the aims of competition law, and vice versa.

From the perspective of economic efficiency,[4] the relationship between competition law and IP law can be seen in the difference between static efficiency and dynamic (or innovation) efficiency. Respectively, these forms measure the efficiency of the market at a particular point in time, and over time. Static efficiency refers to the reduction of costs and prices, and the increase of quantity (and quality to some extent) at given prices. It consists of productive efficiency and allocative efficiency.[5] Dynamic efficiency involves the increase of novelty and improvement through new products, processes, services or ways of doing business.

Competition law protects static efficiency by eliminating artificial restraints (for example, collusion and abuse of a company's dominant position) and promoting the entry of new competitors in order to leave more benefits and surplus in the hands of consumers. Static efficiency alone is not sufficient to ensure economic efficiency or competition welfare.[6] The major impetus to growth and welfare comes from dynamic efficiency, which refers to the gains that result from entirely new ways of doing business through investments in innovation, aimed at both creating new or improved products and reducing the cost of existing ones (Masoudi 2006; Rosch 2010). Innovation furthers economic efficiency more than any policy that drives prices to marginal cost or reduces production costs. Many risky investments, however, must be made to achieve dynamic efficiency—developing a new drug takes more than ten years and can cost $800 million (WHO 2006: 17–18).When competitors rapidly 'free-ride' on a new innovation, driving production costs and prices to their lowest levels, innovators and investors are less likely to recoup their capital expenditure or benefit from their investment. Consequently growth and competition welfare are impaired. Dynamic efficiency, therefore, cannot be gained without limited exclusivity, which may nevertheless lead to static efficiency losses.

The meaning of 'monopoly' conferred on a right holder under IP law, however, is merely the right to exclude others. It is analogous to a purely legal monopoly and not equivalent to an economic monopoly, that is, a dominant position, under competition law, where a firm gains power enabling it to 'behave, to an appreciable extent, independently on the market' (*AstraZeneca v. Commission* 2010, para. 265). Accordingly, a short-term approach has been replaced by a longer term one, which acknowledges some restrictions on competition today in order to promote competition in new products and processes tomorrow. Rather than being in conflict, the goals of IP law and competition law are complementary and mutually reinforcing. They share the common purpose of promoting competition, innovation and commercialisation and of benefiting consumers, as well as efficiently allocating economic resources (Carrier 2009; Nguyen 2010).

The US and EU competition authorities have followed this view. The US Antitrust Guidelines for the Licensing of IP (DOJ and FTC 1995) state:

The [IP] laws and the antitrust laws share the common purpose of promoting innovation and enhancing consumer welfare. The [IP] laws provide incentives for innovation and its dissemination and commercialization by establishing enforceable property rights for the creators of new and useful products, more efficient processes, and original works of expression ... The antitrust laws promote innovation and consumer welfare by prohibiting certain actions that may harm competition with respect to either existing or new ways of serving consumers.

In other words, the two systems 'work in tandem to bring new and better technologies, products, and services to consumers at lower prices' (DOJ and FTC 2007: 1). The European Commission Guidelines on the application of Article 81 EC (now Article 101 TFEU) for technology transfer agreements (EC 2004: para. 7) similarly state that:

Both bodies of law share the same basic objective of promoting consumer welfare and an efficient allocation of resources. [IPRs] promote dynamic competition by encouraging undertakings to invest in developing new or improved products and processes. So does competition by putting pressure on undertakings to innovate. Therefore, both [IPRs] and competition are necessary to promote innovation and ensure a competitive exploitation thereof.

Although IP and competition laws aim to promote innovation, they will discourage it if they are pursued either too strongly or too weakly. From the IP perspective, too much IP protection 'can produce costly monopolies or exclusive rights that others must either licence or innovate around' (Hovenkamp 2005: 249). Additionally it should be noted that in practice many firms, especially in the pharmaceutical sector, maintain and use patents to 'block the development of a new, competing product rather than for protecting' their own products (EC 2009: paras 1117–18). On the other hand, from the competition perspective, if competition law enforcement is pursued so aggressively that companies are permitted easy access to their competitor's innovation, there will be few incentives to invest in or to commercialise innovation (OECD 2005: 17–18).

The fact that IP law grants exclusive rights of exploitation, however, does not imply that IPRs are immune from the intervention of competition law (EC 2004). IPRs do not confer a privilege to violate competition law. The existence of legal monopoly rights conferred by IP law does not in itself infringe competition law; but such rights may be exercised and exploited in such a way, and to such an extent, that competition law could be infringed. Competition law should be applied to ensure that consumers benefit from the best quality products at the lowest prices. That is why, despite the fact that the exercise of IPRs is already extensively regulated under IP law by way of scope and duration rules and various exceptions,[7] an extra filter of regulation is provided by competition law. This second filter aims to ensure that the grant of exclusivity by IP law is not abused or misused by anti-competitive licensing agreements or that monopolistic conduct takes place that would deny parties access to the market and harm consumer welfare. Competition law, nevertheless, must not be a substitute for bad IP law, which is to say IP law that cannot establish a balance within itself as the first filter.

Briefly, IPRs should be regarded as being in themselves pro-competition unless unilateral or concerted practices have transformed them into an anti-competitive tool. From the competition law perspective, IPRs are considered private property rights that could be abused. Both IP law and competition law—the first and second filters respectively—should operate together to control and prevent IPR-related abuses. They should both be regarded as part of competition and innovation policy in which IP law creates the market for innovations and their commercialisation, while competition law controls and corrects malfunctions of that market (Nguyen 2009).

REFUSAL TO LICENCE PHARMACEUTICAL PATENTS IN SOUTH AFRICA

Intellectual property rights provide holders rights to exclude others from exploiting their IP. Refusal to licence cannot by itself be in breach of competition or IP law. However, if refusal to licence by an innovator pharmaceutical firm holding a dominant position constitutes an IPR abuse under a country's competition law, the TRIPS Agreement permits that country to grant compulsory licensing to remedy such anti-competitive conduct (WTO 2010, TRIPS Agreement: Art. 31(k)). It is worth reiterating that refusal to licence patents and excessive pricing of patented medicines may be considered two sides of anti-competitive conduct.

Hazel Tau v. GSK and BI

In September 2002, a group of individuals and organisations led by the Treatment Action Campaign (TAC) initiated a complaint against GlaxoSmithKline (GSK) and Boehringer Ingelheim (BI) with the South African Competition Commission (SACC).The complainants alleged that these two pharmaceutical companies, which were dominant firms in the anti-retroviral medicine (ARV) market for HIV/AIDS in South Africa, engaged in excessive pricing of ARV to the detriment of consumers, in violation of Section 8(a) of the South Africa's Competition Act 1998, amended in 2009 (Nguyen 2009; Flynn 2010).

This competition case provided the basis for a larger public campaign, which attracted the attention of both local and international communities. After conducting its investigation. the SACC agreed with the complainants' arguments. It went even further to conclude that GSK and BI had both abused their dominance and contravened not only Section 8(a) of the Competition Act, as a result of excessive pricing, but also Section 8(b), relating to refusal to supply an essential facility, and Section 8(c), regarding exclusionary conduct. The SACC argued, in particular, that although competitive supply of the medicines was feasible, patented products of both GSK and BI were being sold at prices five to fifteen times higher than those of generic equivalents available outside South Africa and were unaffordable for almost all South Africans living with HIV/AIDS. This conduct was deemed to be illegal excessive pricing. Also, GSK and BI had refused competitors access to their patents on the basis that they were non-duplicable resources, although it was economically feasible to make them available. This constituted a refusal to grant access to an essential facility. Finally, without a legitimate business justification, GSK and BI had impeded generic suppliers from entering the South African market for ARV by refusing to grant them licences at reasonable royalty rates. The anti-competitive effects of the refusal significantly outweighed any potential technological, efficiency or other pro-competitive gains, and it was deemed an illegal exclusionary act (Nguyen 2009; Flynn 2010).

Faced with these judgements GSK and BI requested negotiation between the parties, and in December 2003, agreed to grant voluntary licences of their ARV-related patents to generic manufacturers (Nguyen 2009; Flynn 2010).

TAC v. Merck/MSD

At the end of 2007, the TAC filed a competition complaint with the SACC against Merck, a pharmaceutical company based in the US, and its South African subsidiary, MSD. The TAC alleged that Merck/MSD abused their dominant position in the market for efavirenz (EFV) (an ARV branded as Stocrin) by refusing to licence generic producers to manufacture, import or sell the medicine, a generic version of it, or co-formulated or co-packaged generic products containing EFV and at least one other ARV, on reasonable and non-discriminatory terms in the South African market. Instead of focusing on excessive pricing as the consequence of refusal to licence as in *Hazel Tau v. GSK and BI*, the TAC regarded the two types of refusal to licence by Merck/MSD as exclusionary conduct in which the anti-competitive effects outweighed any pro-competitive gains—actions prohibited under Section 8(c) of the Competition Act (Nguyen 2009).

To prove an infringement under Section 8(c), a complainant has to prove two conditions: first, that the alleged infringer has a dominant position; and second, that (i) its conduct is exclusionary, (ii) this conduct has anti-competitive effects, and (iii) such effects outweigh any pro-competitive justifications. Regarding the question of dominant position, the TAC contended that, as in *Hazel Tau v. GSK and BI*, because ARVs are generally not substitutable,[8] EFV constitutes its own market in respect of manufacturers, marketers and consumers. The TAC showed that, with respect to the relevant therapeutic class (non-nucleoside reverse transcriptase inhibitors), MSD's South African market share was over 45 per cent in terms of both turnover and units sold (Nguyen 2009).

In respect of the second condition, the TAC argued that Merck/MSD's refusal meant no firm (except Aspen and Adcock, two licencees of Merck/MSD) could import into, manufacture, use, offer to dispose of or dispose of generic EFV products in South Africa; and no firm (including Aspen and Adcock) could import into, manufacture, use, offer to dispose of or dispose of co-formulated or co-packaged generic products containing EFV and at least one other ARV in South Africa. The refusal, therefore, impeded and prevented a generic producer from entering not only the generic EFV market but also the co-formulated and co-packaged product market (the fixed dose combination ARV market) in South Africa (Nguyen 2009).

Regarding anti-competitive effects, the TAC argued that Merck's refusal to licence additional generic producers unreasonably harmed consumer welfare and prevented development of new products for which there was potential customer demand. It contended that consumers in South Africa suffered unreasonable harm not only in terms of prices but also in terms of access to new products. In addition, consumer welfare was harmed by shortages in supply of EFV as well as other ARV. Merck/MSD's refusal to licence was thus alleged to be anti-competitive (Nguyen 2009).

To weigh the anti-competitive effects and the pro-competitive justifications of the refusal, the TAC analysed US and EU case law, especially the doctrine of refusal to supply, and argued that a right holder could not justify exclusionary conduct solely on the basis of its IPRs. The TAC also noted the fundamental issues relating to the rights to property, life, dignity and access to medicines in view of the Constitution of South Africa and international law. Based on all of the reasoning, the TAC contended that Merck's refusal to licence violated Section 8(c) of the Competition Act (Nguyen 2009).

During the SACC's investigation, Merck/MSD licenced four generic drug companies, two local producers and two locally based importers to bring stand-alone patented EFV medicines into the South African market. They agreed that all four licencees were entitled to bring co-packaged or co-formulated products containing EFV into the market and waived any right to royalties. As Merck/MSD's responses met the main concerns of the TAC's complaint, on 30 May 2008, it announced that Merck/MSD was no longer acting in an anti-competitive way. There was no longer any need for the SACC to refer the case to the Competition Tribunal for adjudication (Nguyen 2009).

SOME CONSIDERATIONS

The cases discussed above demonstrate how competition law can be used to achieve a significant effect: reduction in the prices of patented medicines and gaining access to relevant patents through compulsory or voluntary licences. However, these achievements may give rise to concerns relating to the relationship between IP and competition laws in developing economies.

Effects of applying IPR-related competition law

The application of domestic competition law in a developing country may threaten the existence of IPRs and reduce innovation. That country may no longer attract investment in research and development (R&D) or foreign investment (and even be subject to WTO dispute). It should be recalled, however, that the TRIPS Agreement, although granting right holders a legal monopoly, also confirms that this must not result in abuses of IPRs, which can take various forms.

Regarding innovation and investment in R&D, the IP protected under domestic IP law in developing countries has, for the most part, been created in developed countries.[9] In general, when making their investment decisions about R&D, firms expect to make most of their profits in the markets of developed economies (Roin 2009: 547–8). The pharmaceutical sector, with its very large investments, high costs and considerable risks, is illustrative—out of approximately $160 billion per year spent globally on health R&D, only 3 per cent 'is directed at diseases that disproportionately affect developing countries' (WHO 2009: para.8). In other words, world sales of medicines are very highly directed towards markets in developed countries; North America, Europe and Japan account for 85.6 per cent of global sales. Meanwhile developing countries, accounting for more than 80 per cent of the world's population, are responsible for about only 10 per cent of global sales, and Africa only 1.1 per cent (WHO 2006: 15). Frederick M. Abbott and Jerome H. Reichman

(2007), after carefully addressing the need to preserve incentives for R&D of new medicines, conclude:

[O]riginator pharmaceutical companies based in the OECD recover the great part of their R&D expenditures in the more affluent OECD markets, and invest a small part of their R&D budgets on diseases of special relevance to developing countries. Consequently, the use by developing countries of compulsory licensing to ensure public access to affordable medicines is unlikely to have a material effect on the level of research currently undertaken in the OECD.

So reducing innovators' monopoly rents via competition law in developing countries, where markets are normally small, may not result in as large costs in lost innovation as would be the case in developed countries.[10] Further, the information disclosure function of IP systems is not as significant in developing countries. Domestic firms in developing countries, in theory, may obtain information from the patent disclosures protected in developed countries. It is true from an economic perspective that restricting the market power of patent protection by competition law in small technology-importing economies will 'lead to static gain, while the dynamic loss from discouraging innovation or less information disclosure would be close to zero' (Aoki and Small 2004: 19). Similarly, it is reasonable that poor countries 'should not have to pay as large a share of those research costs' as wealthy countries (Barton 2008).

The US and EU case law generally shows that domestic competition law can intervene where harm to consumers is derived from the anti-competitive exercise of IPRs and exceeds economic incentives for innovation (Nguyen 2010). It is unreasonable and unfair from either a legal or an economic perspective that developing countries cannot appropriately apply their competition law to remedy anti-competitive practices relating to refusal to licence, or its derivative conduct, while developed countries may do so. However, due to the complexity and difficulty of proving abuses of a dominant position by right holders, competition law should not be used where other flexibilities permitted under the TRIPS Agreement and national IP law, such as public health and public security grounds, can be. The use of competition law in IPR abuses, whether in developing or developed countries, should be a measure of last resort to protect consumer welfare, competition and innovation. For all that, in these cases, any adverse effects on foreign investment (if any) appear to be minimal.

Dominant position of a right holder

As is generally accepted in the US and the EU, it should not be presumed that IPRs create (or even increase) market power.[11] On this basis it might be argued that the way in which the complainants and the SACC defined the relevant product market and dominant position in the two cases cited above posed a threat to right holders. The position might be taken that in the patented product market the mere holding of a patent confers a monopoly on the patent holder. But any such view would not be accurate. The SACC and complainants in these cases followed the view that each active ingredient or substance formed a relevant market in its own right on the basis of the lack of substitutability between the various ARV active ingredients, rather than on the fact that each active ingredient was the subject of a patent. Similarly the US Supreme Court in the Eastman Kodak Case (*Eastman Kodak Co. v. Image Technical Services* 1992: 481–2) held that a single brand of a product or service can be a relevant product market on the basis of lack of interchangeability available to consumers. It is indeed correct for competition authorities to use the principle that a product market definition depends on the substitutability (or interchangeability) of the relevant product with other comparable products from the consumer perspective, regardless of whether or not a product is subject to IP protection. This is illustrated in the EU AstraZeneca judgement (*AstraZeneca v. Commission* 2010: paras 147–221 and 239–94).[12]

IPR-related excessive pricing and refusal to licence under competition law

Many developing countries, and even the EU (Nguyen 2010: 78–82), stipulate in their domestic competition and IP law that excessive pricing of IPR-embodied products is detrimental to consumers and therefore constitutes an IPR abuse. From the consumer perspective, excessive pricing may be regarded as one of the most blatant abuses of a dominant position because wealth is transferred from consumers to dominant firms, creating inefficiency. However there are three reasons why competition authorities may not wish to intervene in cases of excessive pricing. First, prohibition of excessive pricing may reduce the incentive to innovate and invest in R&D *ex ante*. Second, prohibition is difficult to implement because it is difficult to identify excessiveness. It is not easy for antitrust courts to directly police price issues, and there is no safe harbour for the pricing practices of firms.[13] Third, prohibition may be redundant because excessive pricing is self-correcting by the invisible hand of the market (Ezrachi and Gilo 2009: 249–51).

But one might raise various objections against these. As to the first point, application of competition law in the pharmaceutical sector in developing economies hardly affects innovation in general. As to the third point, Ezrachi and Gilo (2009) have recently argued that the self-correcting nature of the market cannot be taken as given. As to the second, there is still controversy over the criteria determining the anti-competitive conduct of excessive pricing. However, if the competent authorities can prove that the price of a patented medicine in the domestic market of a developing country is unreasonably higher than the price of a like product in a developed country or in any other developing country with similar economic conditions, then it is clear that the right holder is engaging in excessive pricing. In such a case, in addition to permitting parallel imports, which would be decided under domestic legislation,[14] competition authorities, together with IP authorities, can require the right holder to reduce the price or grant compulsory licences. If unreasonable price difference between the two countries is not proved, then competition authorities can combine a cost-based and a demand-side approach to determine economic value, and compare this with the market price. In any event innovation costs should be fully taken into account.

Excessive pricing is an exploitative practice constituting an abuse of dominant position and thus violates competition law. In contrast mere high pricing violates neither competition law nor IP law. IPRs granted under domestic IP law provide right holders the opportunity to 'tax the economy' so as to maximise their profits; but if right holders hold a dominant position in the relevant market their profit maximisation should not extend to 'private avarice' (Carstensen 2006:1079). Instead pricing should reasonably relate to public policy goals in a context of balancing social costs and innovations.

Briefly, IPR-related competition cases in South Africa show that developing countries can properly use domestic competition law to promote access to medicines. If local firms do not have the capacity to use compulsorily licenced patents, the Paragraph 6 system of the Doha Declaration, or the proposed Article 31*b is* of the TRIPS Agreement, may well fix the problem.

ABBOTT'S WITHDRAWAL OF MEDICINE REGISTRATION APPLICATIONS IN THAILAND

Thailand has taken advantage of the public health-related flexibilities of Article 31 of the TRIPS Agreement to authorise compulsory licences for pharmaceutical patents in order to increase access to medicines (Nguyen 2009). In January 2007, Thailand granted compulsory licensing on the grounds of public use for a patented ARV (a combination of lopinavir and ritonavir) owned and sold by Abbott Laboratories under the trade name Kaletra. In March 2007, in response to the compulsory licensing, Abbott withdrew registration of seven different medicines (including Aluvia, a new heat-stabilised version of Kaletra) from the Food and Drug Administration of Thailand. In April 2007, HIV/AIDS treatment activists lodged a complaint with the Competition Commission of Thailand, alleging that Abbott's withdrawal of registration applications for medicines, especially Aluvia, was a violation of the Thailand's Competition Act 1999, in particular Sections 25(3) and 28. However, in December 2007, the Competition Commission concluded that the withdrawal did not violate the Competition Act (Nguyen 2009 and Flynn 2010).

The Competition Commission found that Abbott's turnover in the Thai market was below the threshold of holding a dominant position. Moreover Abbott had not yet obtained the required certificate of product registration, which was what made its products unavailable in the market. Abbott's conduct was therefore considered not to have constituted a refusal to supply. In addition, the Commission found that Abbott's withdrawal was not intended to cause harm to Thai consumers, arguing that medicine registration was subject to a decision of the Food and Drug Administration. Moreover due to the need for medical prescriptions Thai consumers would never directly order from Abbott's head office in the US. As a consequence, the conduct in question was regarded not to have violated Section 28 (Thai Competition Commission 2007).

Importantly, the Abbott case may reflect the relationship between the application of IP law and competition law on access to patented medicines. It should be taken into account that access to the patent held by Abbott had been achieved via compulsory licensing under Thai IP law. If the patent holder's actions had also been attacked under competition law this could have caused concern to the international community, as well as to the patent holder. The TRIPS Agreement recognises the built-in exceptions to and limitations of IPRs. A developing country, through its domestic IP law, can use those exceptions and limitations. If it is unable to apply them it can find another solution through domestic competition law, since the enforcement of competition law requires a variety of legal and economic analyses to avoid defects in enforcement. This confirms the observation that it is better for a developing country to use domestic competition law as a last resort.

EXCLUSIVE DISTRIBUTION AND THE HIGH PRICES OF MEDICINES IN VIETNAM

Under the Law on Pharmaceuticals of Vietnam 2005, the pharmaceutical industry, including the sector involved in the distribution of medicines, is heavily regulated (Law on Pharmaceuticals of Vietnam 2005). The price of medicines may be determined by pharmaceutical companies, and they have the right to compete on prices; but prices and any changes of prices must be registered with the relevant authorities. Such prices cannot be higher than those in countries with similar conditions to those in

Vietnam, and Article 9.7 of the Law on Pharmaceuticals prohibits any abuses of a dominant position for the purpose of seeking or securing unlawful profits.

Despite these protections, however, the price of medicines in Vietnam is generally very high and has continued to increase, especially for imported medicines protected by patents. A de facto monopoly in distribution is a major factor leading to price increases. The *Zuellig Pharma* case provides a useful illustration.

Zuellig Pharma is a multinational company specialising in the distribution of medicines. In 1999, the parent company established Zuellig Pharma Vietnam (ZPV), a 100 per cent foreign-owned company in Vietnam. In May 2000, the Hanoi Industrial and Export Processing Zone permitted ZPV to import, export and distribute medicines in the Vietnamese market.[15] Since then ZPV has signed exclusive distribution agreements to distribute medicines in Vietnam with many big foreign pharmaceutical companies. This is arguably the main reason for the unprecedented rise in the price of medicines in Vietnam between 2003 and 2004 (Nguyen 2009).

In 2004, when the Law on Competition of Vietnam was in the final drafting process, the Ministry of Health of Vietnam contended that ZPV's de facto monopoly was partially responsible for price rises. However, as there was no competition law operating in Vietnam at that time, so ZPV was not prosecuted.

Now excessive pricing by a dominant firm is subject to the Law on Competition but neither the Ministry of Health nor the competition authorities have instituted any official response to the increase in prices, despite the continued existence of a network of exclusive distribution of medicines, particularly patented ones. In a report on anti-competitive practices in the distribution of medicines in the Vietnamese market (VCAD 2009), ZPV and a few foreign-owned pharmaceutical distribution companies were alleged to have abused their exclusivity in the distribution (through Vietnamese partners) of imported medicines by imposing excessive prices. But the report did not analyse relevant product markets. It merely indicated that it was very difficult to determine whether or not these companies had, in practice, a dominant position (Nguyen 2009).

In brief, not only innovative or generic drug companies but also pharmaceutical distributors (or any other set of entities in a supply chain) can employ anti-competitive practices. If anti-competitive conduct in national pharmaceutical distribution systems is not appropriately controlled by competition authorities (in cooperation with pharmaceutical regulators) consumers will not have access to affordable medicines.

INDIAN PERSPECTIVE

Vigorous but responsible domestic competition law enforcement will be an important component in the creation of a more pro-competitive environment for access to medicines in developing economies. However it is neither easy to apply in practice, nor is it a panacea, for reasons related to the complicated intersection between IPRs and competition law.

Section 3.5(i) of India's Competition Act 2002, amended in 2007, states that the anti-competitive agreements section of the Act shall not restrict an IPR holder to 'impose reasonable conditions, as may be necessary for protecting any of his rights which have been or may be conferred upon him' under India's IP legislation (Competition Act 2002). In light of this exemption it is unclear how the Act would treat IPR-related anti-competitive practices in the pharmaceutical sector. Cases directly relating to this issue have not been found in India. However, in a trademark misrepresentation case *(Vallal Peruman and Dileep Singh Bhuria v. Godfrey Phillips (India) Ltd* 1994), the Monopoly and Restrictive Trade Practices Commission—the predecessor of the current Competition Commission of India—analysed the impact of IPRs on competition noting the distinction between the existence of IPRs and their exercise as elaborated by the Court of Justice of the European Union. It concluded that competition law 'would be attracted only where there is an abuse in the exercise of the rights protected and granted' under IP statutes (*Vallal Peruman and Dileep Singh Bhuria v. Godfrey Phillips (India) Ltd* 1994: paras 14–17). Consequently an abuse of IPRs may fall under the Competition Act, at least under Section 4 (prohibition of abuse of dominant position), although the Act contains a provision exempting the normal exercise of IPRs.

Moreover, as noted in an advocacy booklet on IPRs published by the Competition Commission of India, it seems that Section 3.5(i) does not automatically include the right to exercise monopoly power (Competition Commission of India 2008). The Competition Commission will scrutinise any unreasonable conditions incorporated into licensing agreements or any IPR abuse. This booklet also lists sixteen practices with respect to licensing agreements that are regarded as adversely affecting competition in markets and, therefore, per se, unreasonable under competition law (Competition Commission of India 2008). This strict approach is supported by India's Patents (Amendment) Act 2002 (Section 84) and Patents (Amendment) Act 2005 (Section 90(1)(ix), in which certain practices, namely excessive pricing, refusal to licence (affecting downstream markets), tying, exclusive grantback, non-challenge and package licensing are subject to compulsory licensing.

In addition to the control of anti-competitive agreements and abuse of dominance in the pharmaceutical industry, merger and acquisition in this sector should also be scrutinised, under Section 5 of the Competition Act. The takeover of generic companies by global pharmaceutical companies in the Ranbaxy/Daiichi Case, for instance, or consolidation of Indian generics companies may give rise to concerns from the perspective of competition law as they may lead to dominance in the generic or branded medicine market and abuse of such dominance (Dahiya 2010).

In any case, when enforcing the Competition Act to promote access to medicines, India's relevant authorities should balance the rights and benefits of IPR holders and consumer welfare taking into account allocative, productive and dynamic efficiencies. As the Indian Supreme Court ruled in *Steel Authority of India Ltd and Anr*, these efficiencies 'by and large have been accepted all over the world as the guiding principles for effective implementation of competition law' (*Competition Commission of India v. Steel Authority of India Ltd and Anr*, 2010).

CONCLUDING REMARKS

It is not easy to adequately balance the interests of IPR holders, competitors and the public at large but it may be possible to achieve if IP law, competition law, or a combination of both, is appropriately applied: the 'relatively perfect triangle' of such interests might be figured out. Each developing country, including India, should find an approach that best suits its own locale. In that process it should be noted that competition law is antitrust—it is neither anti-IPRs nor anti-trade. The enforcement of domestic competition law to promote access to medicines should take into account the legitimate rights of right holders regardless of their nationality. Under the TRIPS Agreement, it must not hinder international trade liberalisation or adversely affect the minimum standards of IP protection.

In any case, India and other developing countries can and deserve to use domestic competition law in combination with domestic IP law—both of which should be interpreted in light of human rights issues—to promote access to innovative, affordable, safe and effective medicines. When enforcing competition law, close cooperation should be established among authorities in the competition law, IP and pharmaceutical fields, as well as with the relevant national authorities and international forums.

In brief, competition law can help developing countries facilitate access to medicines.

Notes

1. This chapter draws on the author's previous work, including Nguyen (2011), Nguyen (2010) and Nguyen (2009). It has been prepared strictly in the author's personal capacity.

2. Arts. 6, 31(c), and 37.2, of the TRIPS Agreement may be also regarded as competition rules.

3. See Brief Amici Curiae of 86 Intellectual Property Law, Antitrust Law, Economics, Business and Public Health Professors in Louisiana Wholesale Drug v. Bayer (cert. denied), 2011 WL 767662.

4. Economic efficiency reflects 'a decision or event that increases the total value of all economically measurable assets in the society or total welfare'

(Brodley 1987:1025). This efficiency 'is a measure of how much wealth is created in proportion to the inputs used: the more efficient a process, the more output it can create or the more inputs in can save for other uses, and the more wealth results' (Barnett 2008: 1194).

5. Productive efficiency is achieved when products are produced cost-effectively under existing technology, i.e. at the lowest possible cost level. Allocative efficiency occurs when the prices of products are driven down to a level close to production costs, i.e. marginal cost.

6. Competition welfare includes economic efficiency (dynamic, productive, and allocative efficiency), consumers' welfare, and inter-firm rivalry. Consumers' welfare may be defined as the maximisation of consumer surplus, which is reflected in lower prices, more quantity, better quality, and a wider choice of new or improved goods and services (Brodley 1987: 1023).

7. Under the TRIPS Agreement, an invention is patentable if it is new, non-obvious, and useful (Art. 27.1). Further, there are conditions on patent applicants regarding sufficiently clear and complete disclosure of an invention (Art. 29). Even if the invention meets those criteria it may be excluded from disclosure of invention on patent applicants (Art. 29). Even if the invention meets those criteria it may be excluded from patentability if it is contrary to *ordre public*, or morality, or other specific circumstances (Arts 27.2 and 27.3). The monopoly rights of the patent holder are limited to a specific period of time, but at least 20 years counted from the filing date (Art. 33), with some exceptions, and other use not needing authorisation of the patent holder (Arts 30 and 31).

8. According to standard regimens for HIV/AIDS treatment each patient must take at least three ARV simultaneously and must also be able to change to other ARV, i.e. other regimens, in case of unmanageable side-effects or treatment failure.

9. In 2007, around the world the total number of patent applications was approximately 1.85 million, and approximately 0.76 million patent were granted. Patent applicants or patent owners from Japan, the US and the EU accounted for around 70 per cent. Although there has been an increase in patent filings in developing countries, non-resident applicants accounted for the largest share of total filings in these countries. Moreover, out of around $110 billion of receipts for international licensing in 2004, the receipts going to the US, the EU, and Japan accounted for more than 90 per cent (Nguyen 2009).

10. Many originator pharmaceutical companies file patents in only a small number of the countries where they have the legal ability to do so.

The cost of patenting an initial compound—often hundreds of thousands of dollars per patent—without assurance that it will be one of the few successful compounds in clinical trials is simply too high (Silverman 2005: 157–8).

11. For the US, see *Illinois Tool Works Inc. v. Independent Ink, Inc.*, 547 U.S. 28, 45–46 [2006]. In the EU see, For example, Case 24/67, *Parke, Davis and Co. v. Probe* [1968] ECR 55, p. 72; Case 40/70, *Serena v. Eda* [1971] ECR 69, paras 5 and 16; and Case 78/70, *Deutsche Grammophon v. Metro* [1971] ECR 487, paras 11–16.

12. It should be noted that the Anatomical Therapeutic Chemical Classification System (ATC) 'classifies pharmaceutical products into different groups, according to the organs or systems on which they act and their chemical, pharmacological and therapeutic properties, and divides them into five different levels. The third ATC level groups pharmaceutical products according to their therapeutic indications, the fourth ATC level normally takes into consideration the mode of action and the fifth level defines the narrowest classes, including active substances taken individually' (*AstraZeneca v. Commission* 2010, para.154).

13. See, for example, *Pacific Bell Telephone Co. v. Linkline Communications Inc.*, 129 S.Ct. 1109, 1121 [2009]; *Verizon Communications Inc. v. Law Offices of Curtis V. Trinko*, 540 U.S. 398, 408 [2004].

14. Art. 6 of the TRIPS Agreement states: 'nothing in this Agreement shall be used to address the issue of the exhaustion' of IPRs.

15. For the Paragraph 6 system see<http://www.wto.org/english/tratop_e/trips_e/implem_para6_e.htm>; for Art. 31*b is* of the TRIPS Agreement, see <www.wto.org/english/tratop_e/trips_e/wtl641_e.htm>.

16. The Hanoi Industrial and Export Processing Zone had no power to permit ZPV to distribute medicines in the Vietnamese market. Therefore, the Prime Minister of Vietnam concluded that ZPV would only have a right to distribute imported medicines for three years from the date it started its business. See Official Letter No. 2080/VPCP-QHQT of the Government Office of 15 May 2001.

References

Abbott, F., and Reichman, J.H., 2007. 'Access to Essential Medicines: Lessons Learned since the Doha Declaration on the TRIPS Agreement and Public Health, and Policy Options for the European Union',<www.law.duke.edu/news/pdf/a-r_directorate_report.pdf>.

Aoki, R., and Small, J., 2004. 'Compulsory Licensing of Technology and the Essential Facilities Doctrine', *Information Economics and Policy*, 16(1): 13–19.

AstraZeneca v. Commission, 2010. Judgement 1 July 2010, Case T-321/05, pending appeal in C-457/10.

Barnett, T.O., 2008. 'Maximizing Welfare through Technological Innovation', *George Mason Law Review*, 15: 1191–204.

Barton, J. H., 2008. *Statement to the United States Senate Finance Committee Hearing on International Enforcement of IPRs and American Competitiveness*,<http://finance.senate.gov/sitepages/hearing071508.htm>.

Brodley, J.F., 1987. 'The Economic Goals of Antitrust: Efficiency, Customer Welfare, and Technology Progress', *New York University Law Review*, 62: 1020–53.

Carrier, M.A., 2009. *Innovation for the 21st Century: Harnessing the Power of Intellectual Property and Antitrust Law*, Oxford University Press, New York.

Carstensen, P., 2006. 'Post-Sale Restraints via Patent Licensing: A "Seedcentric" Perspective', *Fordham Intellectual Property, Media and Entertainment Law Journal*, 16: 1053–80.

Competition Act 2002, India. <www.cci.gov.in/images/media/competition_act/act2002.pdf>.

Competition Commission of India, 2008. *Intellectual Property Rights under the Competition Act*, <www.cci.gov.in/images/media/Advocacy/Awareness/IPR.pdf>.

Competition Commission of India v. Steel Authority of India Ltd and Anr, 2010. Supreme Court of India, Civil Appellate Jurisdiction, Civil Appeal No. 7779 of 2010 (D.No.12247 of 2010), 9 September 2010.

Dahiya, N., 2010. 'Competition Law as Patent Safety Net in the Pharmaceutical Industry',<www.cci.gov.in/images/media/Research Reports/NaveenDahiyaROUGHDRAFT.pdf>.

Department of Justice and Federal Trade Commission (DOJ and FTC), 1995. 'Antitrust Guidelines for the Licensing of Intellectual Property issued by the US Department of Justice and Federal Trade Commission', 6 April, <www.usdoj.gov/atr/public/guidelines/0558.pdf>.

―――― 2007. *Antitrust Enforcement and Intellectual Property Rights: Promoting Innovation and Competition*, <www.justice.gov/atr/public/hearings/ip/222655.pdf>.

Doha Declaration on the TRIPS Agreement and Public Health, WT/MIN(01)/DEC/2, 14 November 2001.

Eastman Kodak Co. v. Image Technical Services, Inc., 504 U.S. 451 [1992].

European Commission (EC), 2004. *European Commission Guidelines on the Application of Article 81 of the EC Treaty to Technology Transfer Agreements*, OJ 2004 C 101/2.

———— 2009. *Pharmaceutical Sector Inquiry: Final Report*, 8 July, <http://ec.europa.eu/competition/sectors/pharmaceuticals/inquiry/staff_working_paper_part1.pdf>.

Ezrachi, A., and D. Gilo, 2009. 'Are Excessive Prices Really Self-Correcting?', *Journal of Competition Law and Economics*, 5(2): 249–51.

Flynn, S.M., 2010. 'Using Competition Law to Promote Access to Knowledge', Washington College of Law Research Paper, no. 2010–24, <http://papers.ssrn.com/sol3/papers.cfm?abstract_id=1654023>.

Federal Trade Commission (FTC), 2009. *Overview of the FTC Antitrust Actions in Health Care Services and Products*, <www.ftc.gov/bc/0906hcupdate.pdf>.

Hovenkamp, H., 2005. *The Antitrust Enterprise: Principle and Execution*, Harvard University Press, Cambridge, MA.

Lamy, P, 2010. 'Opening Remarks: Creating Synergies Between Intellectual Property Rights and Public Health', *Access to Medicines: Pricing and Procurement Practices*, WHO-WIPO-WTO Joint Technical Symposium, Geneva, 16 July, <www.wto.org/english/tratop_e/trips_e/techsymp_july10_e/techsymp_july10_e.htm#dg>.

Law on Competition of Vietnam 2004. Law No. 27/2004/QH11, 1 December 2004.

Law on Pharmaceuticals of Vietnam 2005. Law No.34/2005/QH11, 14 June 2005.

Lemley, M.A., 2005. 'Property, Intellectual Property, and Free-riding', *Texas Law Review*, 83: 1031–68.

Masoudi, G.F., 2006. 'Intellectual Property and Competition: Four Principles for Encouraging Innovation', <www.usdoj.gov/atr/public/speeches/215645.pdf>.

Ministry of Health, Ministry of Finance and Ministry of Industry and Trade of Vietnam, 2007. Joint Circular No. 11/2007/TTLT-BYT-BTC-BCT, 31 August.

Nguyen, T.T., 2009. 'Competition Law and Access to Pharmaceutical Technology in the Developing World', *Biotechnology Law Report*, 28(6): 693–715.

———— 2010. *Competition Law, Technology Transfer and the TRIPS Agreement: Implications for Developing Countries*, Edward Elgar, Cheltenham.

_____ 2011, 'Technology Transfer and Competition Law: Options for Developing Countries', in H.H. Lidgard et al, *Sustainable Technology Transfer: A Guide to Global Aid and Trade Development*, Wolters Kluwer, Alphen aan den Rijn.

Organisation for Economic Cooperation and Development (OECD), 2005. Intellectual Property Rights', DAF/COMP(2004)24, <www.oecd.org/dataoecd/61/48/34306055.pdf>.

Roin, B.N., 2009. 'Unpatentable Drugs and the Standards of Patentability', *Texas Law Review*, 87: 503–48.

Rosch, J.T., 2010. *The Role of Static and Dynamic Analysis in Pharmaceutical Antitrust*, <www.ftc.gov/speeches/rosch/100218pharmaantitrust.pdf>.

Silverman, R., 2005. 'Patent Filing Strategies for Pharmaceutical Products: A Simple Cost-Benefit Analysis Based on Filing Costs and Pharmaceutical Sales', *AIPLA Quarterly Journal*, 33:153–8.

Stiglitz, J., 2001. *Competing over Competition Policy*, <www.project-syndicate.org/commentary/stiglitz5>.

Thai Competition Commission 2007. Decision of 27 December 2007 on the complaint against Abbott, on file with the author.

United Nations Commission on Human Rights (UNCHR), 2001. 'The Impact of the Agreement on Trade-Related Aspects of Intellectual Property Rights on Human Rights—Report of the High Commissioner', E/CN.4/Sub.2/2001/13, 27 June.

Vallal Peruman and Dileep Singh Bhuria v. Godfrey Phillips (India) Ltd, 91/92 in UTPE 180/92—Monopoly and Restricted Trade Practices Commission, New Delhi, 24 May 1994.

Vietnam Competition Administration Department (VCAD), 2009. Report on Anti-competitive Practices in the Distribution of Medicines in the Vietnamese Market (in Vietnamese), Hanoi.

World Health Organisation (WHO), 2006. 'Public Health, Innovation and Intellectual Property Rights', World Health Organisation, Geneva.

_____ 2008. 'Global Strategy and Plan of Action on Public health, Innovation and Intellectual Property', WHA61.21 (24 May), revised in WHA62.16 (22 May 2009).

_____ 2009. 'Public Health, Innovation and Intellectual Property: Global Strategy and Plan of Action—Proposed Time Frames and Estimated Funding Needs', EB124/16 Add.2, <http://apps.who.int/gb/ebwha/pdf_files/EB124/B124_16Add2-en.pdf>.

World Intellectual Property Organisation (WIPO), 2007. 'Development Agenda, adopted by the WIPO General Assembly',<www.wipo.

int/export/sites/www/ip-development/en/agenda/recommendations. pdf>.

——— 2009. 'Project on Intellectual Property and Competition Policy', CDIP/4/4 Rev., 25 September,<www.wipo.int/edocs/mdocs/mdocs/en/ cdip_5/cdip_5_ref_cdip_4_4_rev.pdf>.

World Trade Organisation (WTO), 2008. Minutes of Meeting of the TRIPS Council, 17 June, IP/C/M/57.

——— 2010. *The Legal Texts: The Results of the Uruguay Round of Multilateral Trade Negotiations*, Cambridge University Press, Cambridge.

11 The Politics of AIDS Treatment in Brazil

André de Mello e Souza

INTRODUCTION

Brazil has played a pivotal role in debates concerning the public policy of HIV/AIDS. Its National Sexually Transmitted Diseases/ AIDS Program was praised as the best of its kind in the developing world by the United Nations and has served as a model for thirty-one other developing countries as well as for the global HIV/AIDS policy adopted by the World Health Organization (WHO) since 2003 (Coordenação Nacional de DST/AIDS, 2002; Chade, 2003; d'Adesky, 2003). Brazil's widely recognized success in controlling HIV/AIDS resulted primarily from its provision of free and universal access to antiretroviral (ARV) therapies since 1996, a policy which has been the most groundbreaking and consequential aspect of the country's response to the epidemic. Notably, Brazil was the first developing nation to provide anti-AIDS therapies at no cost to all patients for whom they were prescribed. By 2010, about 200,000 patients had benefited from these therapies (Programa Nacional de DST/AIDS, 2010).

Yet AIDS treatment in Brazil has, from the outset, been challenged by the high costs of ARVs protected by patents. The country adopted a new Industrial Property Law in 1996 which, in accordance with the Agreement on Trade-Related Aspects of Intellectual Property Rights (TRIPS), recognizes patents for pharmaceutical products and processes. As result, the local manufacturing of generic ARV drugs commercialized after 1997, when this law came into force, has been jeopardized by drug patenting. Nonetheless such local drug manufacturing has thus far ensured the affordability of AIDS treatment in Brazil both by offering cheaper generic versions of ARVs that were marketed before 1997, and therefore unpatented manufacturing and by enabling the government to make credible threats of compulsory licensing, thereby successfully negotiating considerable price discounts for post-1997 patented ARVs with brand-name pharmaceutical multinationals.

However, the affordability of Brazil's AIDS treatment program has been challenged as other developing country members of the World Trade Organization (WTO)—and most notably India—began adjusting their intellectual property rights legislation in accordance with TRIPS so as to meet the Agreement's 2005 deadline for compliance, in so doing undermining the international trade of generic ARVs or their active ingredients. Impediments to drug imports are particularly worrisome because, given Brazil's lack of competency in the production of such active ingredients, the country has relied heavily on Asian generic companies to supply them.

In the following section I show how AIDS treatment in Brazil has depended on the local production of generic ARVs as a strategy to contain treatment costs. This strategy has not only reduced the import of anti-AIDS drugs but also forced brand-name pharmaceutical companies to concede large price-cuts in order to avoid having their patents' monopoly rights overrun by compulsory licensing. However, as discussed in the third section, the US government has generally acted at these companies' behest, and in response, has pressured Brazil not only bilaterally but also in and multilateral venues, and especially in the WTO to enforce stricter patent rules. The full mobilization of Brazil's government, both in its relations with the US and in international forums, as well as the support this government has received from transnational advocacy networks were critical in enabling it to resist such pressures.

The third section also shows that the Brazilian strategy of negotiating price reductions with brand-name pharmaceutical companies has ceased to be effective since 2005, when India and other suppliers of ARV active ingredients to Brazil adopted stricter patent laws in accordance with TRIPS. Indeed, the results of these negotiations have been increasingly unsatisfactory as the government's threats of compulsory licensing have become less credible. Even after resorting to the compulsory licensing of the ARV efavirenz, patented by the US-based company Merck, the Brazilian AIDS treatment program remains at risk given the country's lack of pharmaceutical manufacturing capabilities and the difficulties of importing ARVs in the wake of the implementation of TRIPS.

The fourth section discusses legal and institutional reforms implemented in an effort to restrict patent rights and thereby reduce the costs of ARVs, which enable pre-grant patent opposition by health authorities, more flexible and easier compulsory licensing and expedite post-patent generic entry. A bill that bans patents for anti-AIDS drugs altogether has also been proposed. This section argues that, while important, these reforms tend in the long-term to become palliatives and fail to ensure the sustainability of AIDS treatment in Brazil.

Finally, the chapter concludes that universal and free access to ARVs in Brazil depends crucially on further technological capacitating of the Brazilian pharmaceutical industry, without which neither transnational political support nor lax domestic patent rules will suffice in the context of TRIPS. ARV active ingredient purchases from foreign suppliers become increasingly difficult and solutions based on the 30 August 2003 WTO Agreement, which allow the importation of compulsory licenced medicines by countries that lack pharmaceutical manufacturing capabilities, do not appear to be promising in the light of the costs and complications involved. ARV production partnerships with drug multinationals may help reduce treatment costs. Still, the command over all phases of ARV production is key for Brazil to exercise bargaining and market power in face of global patent rules and strong external opposition.

THE STRATEGY OF LOCAL GENERIC PRODUCTION

The Brazilian government began offering free and universal access to ARV triple therapies in 1996 in response to the announcement of such therapies as a more effective treatment option for AIDS in the XI International AIDS Conference held in Vancouver; to lawsuits sponsored by local AIDS non-governmental organizations (NGOs) demanding free and universal access to AIDS treatment; to the 1988 Constitution which declared health a right of citizenship and duty of the state (Constituição, 1988); and, finally, to the sanctioning of a law which obligates the government to provide anti-AIDS drugs at no cost to all patients who need them (Lei 9.313, 1996; Coordenação Nacional de DST/AIDS, 1999; Mello e Souza, 2007, pp. 38–40).[1] While zidovudine had been locally produced in Brazil since 1993, the import of other high priced ARV drugs used in Brazil's HIV/ AIDS program drained the Health Ministry's resources and by 1997 accounted for almost half of this program's total expenditures. In response, the Brazilian government began capacitating public pharmaceutical labs to provide cheaper generic versions of these drugs (Cassier and Correa, 2003, p. 90; Mello e Souza, 2007, p. 41).

Largely in reaction to pressures from the US government,[2] Brazil passed a new industrial property law on 14 May 1996 recognizing pharmaceutical patents (Lei 9.279, 1996). However, all products that had been commercialized anywhere in the world before 14 May 1997, when this new law was put into effect, became forever ineligible for patent protection in the country. As result, ten anti-AIDS drugs remained unpatented in Brazil and could be legally copied (Orsi et al., 2003, p. 116).

Employing reverse engineering techniques, Brazilian government pharmaceutical labs discovered the formulas of most of these unpatented ARVs and began to produce them (Cassier and Correa, p. 91) using active ingredients imported mostly from India and China (Orsi et al., p. 132). Zalcitabine and stavudine became available by the end of 1997, didanosine the following year, lamivudine and its combination with zidovudine in 1999, and indinavir and nevirapine in 2000 (Coordenação Nacional de DST/AIDS, 2001). By 2011, nine of the nineteen existing anti-AIDS drugs were locally supplied; and this number should increase to 11 by 2016, with the expected inclusion of atazanavir and raltegravir among the ARVs produced by Brazilian government labs (see Table 11.1).

Crucially, since the Health Ministry began substituting expensive imports with local generic equivalents, the prices of unpatented ARV drugs have fallen by an average of 80.9 per cent in Brazil (see Table 11.2). Domestic producers have been able to bring down the costs of these drugs by setting profit margins much lower than those of pharmaceutical multinationals and by breaking their monopolies. In addition, bulk orders from Brazil have caused a considerable decrease in the world prices of the active ingredients of ARV drugs, which account on average for 66 per cent of the cost of these drugs[3] (see Figure 11.1).

Nevertheless, the costs of importing patented anti-AIDS drugs still represented a substantial burden on the Brazilian health budget. On 6 October 1999, President Fernando Henrique Cardoso sanctioned a decree empowering ministries to issue compulsory licences on the grounds of national emergencies (Decreto 3.201, 1999, Art. 3). In February 2001, the Health Ministry threatened to issue a compulsory licence for the drugs efavirenz and nelfinavir, which together accounted for about 36 per cent of its total expenditures with ARVs (Sá and Malavez, 2001, pp. 10–11; Far-Manguinhos, 2002, pp. 79–80); and were exclusively licenced in Brazil to American and Swiss pharmaceutical multinationals Merck Sharp and Dohme and Hoffman—La Roche.

As soon as the Brazilian federal lab Far-Manguinhos proved its capacity to import active ingredients from Asia, to use the legal

Table 11.1: Antiretroviral Drugs Distributed in Brazil (2011)

Imported	Produced Locally
1) Abacavir	1) Efavirenz
2) Amprenavir	2) Stavudine
3) Atazanavir[1]	3) Indinavir
4) Darunavir	4) Lamivudine
5) Didanosine	5) Nevirapine
6) Enfuvirtide	6) Saquinavir
7) Fosamprenavir	7) Tenofovir
8) Lopinavir/Ritonavir	8) Zidovudine
9) Raltegravir[1]	9) Zidovudine/Lamivudine
10) Ritonavir	

Source: Departamento de Doenças Sexualmente Transmissíveis (DST), AIDS e Hepatites Virais (2011).
[1]Antiretrovirals that are expected to be produced by Brazilian government labs by 2016.

Table 11.2: Antiretroviral Prices in Brazil (1996–2008)

Antiretroviral	Price per Unit ($)[1]												
	1996	1997	1998	1999	2000	2001	2002	2003	2004	2005	2006	2007	2008
Abacavir pill 300 mg	(a)	(a)	(a)	(a)	(a)	2.700	2.290	1.860	1.855	2.228	2.370	2.370	1.500
Abacavir oral sol. 20 mg/ml 240 ml	(a)	(a)	(a)	(a)	(a)	49.500	27.500	34.030	33.998	40.832	43.438	43.438	
Didanosine pill 2.5 mg	0.520	0.410	0.258	0.232	0.191	0.162	0.070	0.070	0.072	0.086	0.092	(d)	(d)
Didanosine pill 100 mg	1.850	1.390	1.023	0.760	0.501	0.487	0.290	0.310	0.307	0.369	0.392	(d)	(d)
Didanosine powder oral sol. 4 g	(a)	(a)	60.185	37.810	38.152	33.482	23.190	25.720	25.701	30.867	32.838	32.837	
Lamivudine pill 150 mg	2.900	2.700	2.390	1.512	0.812	0.341	0.220	0.230	0.230	0.276	0.293	0.293	0.314
Lamivudine oral sol. 10 mg/ml 240 ml	(a)	45.570	31.176	12.045	12.536	(b)	7.620	8.130	8.120	9.752	10.375	10.375	
Stavudine cap. 30 mg	(a)	1.750	1.032	0.465	0.211	0.097	0.080	0.090	0.094	0.113	0.121	0.121	0.131
Stavudine cap. 40 mg	(a)	2.320	1.023	0.643	0.274	0.270	0.170	0.180	0.177	0.212	0.226	0.226	
Stavudine powder oral sol. 200 mg	(a)	41.786	35.104	34.455		(b)	18.130	18.670	18.651	21.800	23.183	23.183	

(contd...)

(Table 11.2: contd...)

Antiretroviral	Price per Unit ($)[1]												
	1996	1997	1998	1999	2000	2001	2002	2003	2004	2005	2006	2007	2008
Zalcitabine pill 0.75 mg	1.550	1.080	0.580	0.180	0.080	(d)	(d)	(d)	(d)	(d)	(d)	(d)	(d)
Zidovudine cap. 100 mg	0.560	0.530	0.447	0.211	0.180	0.146	0.100	0.110	0.110	0.132	0.141	0.141	0.149
Zidovudine oral sol. 10 mg/ml 200 ml	10.220	9.170	8.469	6.298	4.469	(b)	2.670	2.960	2.958	3.553	3.779	3.779	
Zidovudine susp. inj. 10 mg/ml 20 ml	13.400	11.930	11.074	2.463	2.109	1.808	3.780	1.400	1.399	1.739	1.850	1.850	
Zidovudine+ lamivudine pill 300+150 mg	(a)	(a)	3.379	2.015	0.703	0.676	0.420	0.460	0.456	0.548	0.583	0.583	0.629
Efavirenz cap. 200 mg	(a)	(a)	(a)	2.320	2.320	0.840	0.840	(b)	(b)	0.641	0.641	–	0.237
Efavirenz pill 600 mg	(a)	(a)	(a)	(a)	(a)	(a)	(a)	2.100	1.590	1.592	1.592	1.592	0.443
Efavirenz oral sol. 30 mg/ml 180 ml	(a)	(a)	(a)	(a)	(a)	(a)	28.790	28.790	21.800	21.800	21.800	21.800	
Nevirapine pill 200 mg	(a)	(a)	3.040	3.020	1.280	1.250	0.260	0.280	0.276	0.332	0.353	0.353	0.377

(contd...)

(Table 11.2: contd...)

Antiretroviral	Price per Unit ($)[1]												
	1996	1997	1998	1999	2000	2001	2002	2003	2004	2005	2006	2007	2008
Nevirapine oral susp. 10 mg/ml 240 ml	(a)	(a)	(a)	(a)	55.87	(b)	(b)	33.330	30.940	33.400	39.575	39.575	39.575
Amprenavir cap. 150 mg	(a)	(a)	(a)	(a)	(a)	0.745	0.520	0.550	0.683	0.820	0.872	0.872	
Amprenavir oral sol. 15 mg/ml 240 ml	(a)	(a)	(a)	(a)	(a)	102.964	91.210	83.230	83.162	99.880	106.255	–	
Indinavir cap. 400 mg	2.000	2.000	1.940	1.914	1.337	0.470	0.370	0.470/0.390	0.389	0.468	0.498	0.498	0.537
Lopinavir/ritonavir cap. 133+33 mg	(a)	(a)	(a)	(a)	(a)	(a)	1.600	1.500/1.480	1.300	1.170	0.630	1.040	
Lopinavir/ritonavir oral sol. 80/20 mg/ml 160 ml	(a)	(a)	(a)	(a)	(a)	(a)	(c)	(c)	(c)	(c)	(c)	(c)	(c)
Nelfinavir pill 250 mg 1.5	(a)	(a)	1.530	1.450	1.360	1.075	0.525	0.520	0.468	0.468	0.468	0.468	
Nelfinavir powder oral susp. 7.2 g	(a)	(a)	52.400	52.400	(b)	42.100	42.100	42.100	42.100	(c)	(c)	(c)	(c)
Ritonavir cap. 100 mg	0.900	0.900	0.880	0.880	0.880	0.760	0.490	0.460	0.440	0.512	0.545	0.545	0.282
Ritonavir oral sol. 80 mg/ml 240 ml	(a)	222.410	168.943	168.943	168.940	(b)	57.010	57.010	57.010	57.010	80.426		

(contd...)

(*Table 11.2: contd...*)

Antiretroviral	Price per Unit ($)[1]												
	1996	1997	1998	1999	2000	2001	2002	2003	2004	2005	2006	2007	2008
Saquinavir cap. 200 mg	1.310	1.310	1.190	1.190	0.750	0.480	0.480	0.480	0.530	–	–	0.660	0.891
Atazanavir 150 mg	(a)	(a)	(a)	(a)	(a)	(a)	(a)	3.250	3.250	3.000	3.000	2.910	2.180
Atazanavir 200 mg	(a)	(a)	(a)	(a)	(a)	(a)	(a)	3.250	3.250	3.130	3.130	3.040	2.280
Tenofovir 300 mg	(a)	(a)	(a)	(a)	(a)	(a)	(a)	9.04/ 7.96	7.680	7.680	3.800	3.800	3.800
Talidomide 100 mg	–	–	–	–	–	–	–	–	0.064	0.120	0.128	0.128	0.128
Didanosine ec 250 mg	(a)	(a)	(a)	(a)	(a)	(a)	(a)	(a)	1.560	1.250	1.250	1.250	0.940
Didanosine ec 400 mg	(a)	(a)	(a)	(a)	(a)	(a)	(a)	(a)	2.500	1.540	1.540	1.540	1.540
Enfuvirtide (T-20)	(a)	(a)	(a)	(a)	(a)	(a)	(a)	(a)	1,422.000	1,333.130	1,333.130	1,333.130	

Notes:

(a) ARVs not yet offered by the Health Ministry during the indicated year.

(b) Acquisition not programmed during the indicated year.

(c) Donation of the manufacturer.

(d) ARVs that were no longer acquired by the Health Ministry during the indicated year.

(1) ARV acquired in Reais and converted to US dollars, using average exchange rate and price during the indicated year.

Source: Coordenação Nacional de DST e Aids/Departamento de DST, Aids e Hepatites Virais.

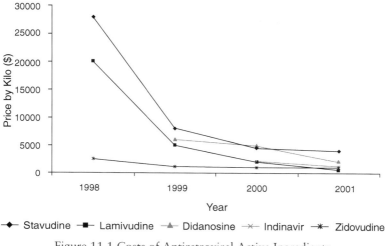

Figure 11.1 Costs of Antiretroviral Active Ingredients
Purchased by Brazil (1998–2000)

instruments afforded by the new presidential decree and, ultimately, to produce and sell these ARVs for prices far below the ones charged by the multinationals, the threat of compulsory licensing became credible. Since Merck and Roche refused to grant voluntary licences for efavirenz and nelfinavir, they needed to beat the price offered by Far-Manguinhos in order to preserve their share of the Brazilian market for anti-AIDS medicines, which is the largest in the developing world. Local generic production thus became a crucial element of empowerment of the Brazilian government with relation to the brand-name pharmaceutical sector, because it not only provided the former with a cheaper alternative supply of needed ARV drugs, but it also provided information concerning the production costs of these drugs, which allowed the government to negotiate price discounts for them more effectively (Mello e Souza, 2007, p. 44).

On 30 March Merck agreed to cut the prices of efavirenz by 59 per cent and of indinavir by 64.8 per cent[4] (see Table 11.2). These price reductions represented yearly savings of about $40 million for the Brazilian Health Ministry (Bailey, 2001, p. 9). Similarly, early in September Roche accepted a 40 per cent diminution in the price of nelfinavir. As result, the Health Ministry has saved approximately $35 million per year (Sá and Malavez, 2001, p. 11; Tribune de Genève, 2001). Concurrently, the US-based drug company Abbott reached a similar agreement with this Ministry, offering a 46 per cent discount for its patented combination of lopinavir and ritonavir.[5]

Negotiations over the prices of brand-name ARVs resumed in 2003. On 5 September, a new presidential decree on compulsory licensing issued by President Luiz Inácio Lula da Silva modified the previous one in crucial ways: it allows the importation of generic versions of compulsory licenced goods whenever local production is impractical and obliges the patentee to disclose all information needed for such production (Decreto 4.830, 2003, Art. 5° II §1°; Art. 10). This decree further increased the Brazilian government's leverage to negotiate with pharmaceutical multinationals. By means of an agreement reached with the US-based company Bristol-Myers Squibb in November, the Health Ministry achieved a 76.4 per cent reduction in the market price of the new ARV atazanavir, saving $66 million (Coordenação Nacional de DST/AIDS, 2003) (see Table 11.2). In response to additional threats of compulsory licensing from the Health Ministry, Merck agreed to further reduce the price of efavirenz by 25 per cent a week later (BBC, 2003). Similarly on 15 January 2004, it was announced that Roche and Abbott would cut the prices of nelfinavir and the lopinavir/ritonavir compound by an additional 10 per cent and 13.3 per cent, respectively.[6] Finally, US-based biopharmaceutical company Gilead reduced the prices of the new ARV tenofovir by 43.35 per cent. Table 11.2 displays the overall decrease in the costs of these drugs. Combined, these five latest discounts should have represented savings of $107 million for the Brazilian Health Ministry in 2004 (Coordenação Nacional de DST/AIDS, 2004). As a result of the discounts granted by multinational pharmaceutical companies and the increase in competition between ARV suppliers generated by Brazilian public labs, the annual cost of AIDS treatment per patient in the country dropped from $3,810 in 1997 to $1, 374 in 2004 (Mello e Souza, 2007, p. 46).

CHALLENGES TO THE SUSTAINABILITY OF AN INCLUSIVE AIDS TREATMENT POLICY

In what was widely interpreted as a reaction to the Health Ministry's intervention on the production and pricing of highly profitable ARV drugs patented by or exclusively licenced to American companies, the US government requested the opening of a panel in the World Trade Organization (WTO) against Brazil on 1 February 2001. The alleged reason was Article 68§1°—I of the Brazilian Industrial Property Law, which has generated much controversy. This article determines that compulsory licences may be issued for patented goods which are not produced locally after three years of the granting of their patents (Lei 9.279, 1996, Art. 68). US representatives claimed it violates Article 27.1 of TRIPS. Conversely, Brazil called attention to Article 2.1 of TRIPS, which states that 'in respect of Parts II, III and IV of this Agreement, Members shall comply with Articles 1 through 12, and Article 19, of the Paris Convention (1967)', which allows local working provisions (WTO, 1994; Nogueira Viana, 2002, pp. 311–12); and insisted that Article 68 of its law does not render the lack of domestic production a sufficient condition for compulsory licensing (Bailey, 2001, p. 14).[7] That same day, Brazilian authorities also started consultation procedures that could lead to a panel against the US, maintaining that Articles 204 and 209 of the US Patent Act are similar to Article 68 of Brazil's Industrial Property Law (Gazeta Mercantil, 2001a; Nogueira Viana, 2002, p. 312). Critically, it became clear that if the panel decided in favor of Brazil it would create jurisprudence and set an important precedent for many developing countries which had yet to adopt new patent laws in accordance with TRIPS (Abbott, 2001).[8]

Moreover, Brazil had mobilized the support of the media, of NGOs, and of public opinion worldwide. Letters were written to American officials and to the press, and demonstrations were held in front of US consulates and embassies.[9] In June, the Brazilian Health Ministry began publishing paid advertisements in major American newspapers which stated that 'AIDS is not a business' and explained that the local production of ARVs was not 'an act of war' on the drug industry, but rather 'an act of life' (O Globo, 2001).[10] The WTO Secretariat also received countless phone calls, faxes and e-mails backing Brazil (Gazeta Mercantil, 2001b; Valor Econômico, 2001; Nogueira Viana, 2002, p. 313). Increasingly, the WTO dispute became a public relations disaster for the US. After consulting with the American pharmaceutical industry association, the US government finally announced the withdrawal of its case against Brazil in 25 June in return for assurances that it would be notified before any products patented by or licenced to American companies are subjected to compulsory licensing in the country (Pilling, Williams and Dyer, 2001; Jornal do Brasil, 2001).[11]

Despite the successful resistance against US pressures, the initial success in price negotiations with companies that hold ARV patents, the significant price discounts obtained for these drugs and the savings generated by such discounts for the Health Ministry, the financial sustainability of the Brazilian AIDS treatment policy has been threatened since 2005. More recent negotiations between this Ministry and pharmaceutical multinationals produced less satisfactory results, indicating that the government's bargaining power has been undermined as its compulsory licensing threats have become less credible.

Most notably, after canceling an agreement reached with Abbott in June, 2005, which was endorsed by a previous Minister and denounced as being highly unfavorable to the Health Ministry, the Ministry signed another agreement with the company in October which has been similarly criticized by activists and analysts. This new agreement reduced from $1.17 to $0.63 the unit price charged by Abbott for the lopinavir/ritonavir compound (see Table 11.2), and the company pledged to donate $3 million worth in medicines of several different kinds to the Ministry in 2006. According to official estimates, the deal would generate savings of about $339.5 million to the Ministry which, in return, agreed not to compulsory licence the ARV until 2011. However, since the price of lopinavir/ritonavir was expected to fall by about $0.50 a unit in three years due to the competition of new drugs, the Ministry probably paid more than its market price by 2011.[12] Moreover, lopinavir/ritonavir was already by that time a relatively obsolete drug, and its patent would expire shortly in 2012 (Intellectual Property Working Group of REBRIP, 2005; Veja, 2006).

As result of the loss of bargaining power of the government relative to the pharmaceutical multinational companies, AIDS treatment costs in Brazil increased significantly since 2003, surmounting the increase in the number of patients treated. By 2006, ARV expenses represented 80 per cent of the Health Ministry's expenses with medicines.[13] While in 2000 half of the total of ARVs purchased by the Ministry was locally produced, by 2007 generics from national public labs represented only 20 per cent of these purchases (Milward de Azevedo Meiners, 2008, p. 1474). According to recent estimates, Brazil's GDP would need to grow at an annual rate of about 6 per cent in order to sustain the country's AIDS treatment policy without cutting expenses in other areas (Grangeiro et al., 2006, pp. 60–69).

Largely in response to its incapacity to continue obtaining satisfactory discounts in the prices of patented ARVs, and after six months of negotiation and more than seven fruitless meetings with executives from the pharmaceutical company Merck and US officials, in 2007, the Brazilian government issued a compulsory licence for the ARV efavirenz on grounds of public interest.[14] This compulsory licence was valid for five years, and renewed in 2012 for an additional five years (Decreto 7.723, 2012 ÿ). The substitution of the patented efavirenz for its generic version has led the Health Ministry to save about $30 million a year. It was also possible to extend treatment for patients of hepatitis B and C. The compulsory licence has ensured Merck remuneration in royalties of 1.5 per cent of the expenditure with the importation from India of the generic version of efavirenz. The active ingredient of this ARV is currently produced by a Brazilian private consortium,[15] but the eight month delay in its domestic production—efavirenz only began to be offered by Far-Manguinhos in 2009— constitutes evidence of the lack of investments in technological capacitating in the Brazilian pharmaceutical sector (Paduan, 2008; Fiocruz, 2009).

This was the first case of compulsory licensing of an ARV in the Americas, though Thailand had already established an important precedent by issuing compulsory licences for the same ARV, efavirenz, in November of 2006 as well as for the lopinavir/ritonavir compound in January of 2007 (ICTSD, 2007). Many NGOs and local, foreign and transnational activist groups, which had been demanding the compulsory licensing of ARVs in Brazil for about ten years, celebrated the decision. They stressed its 'legality and legitimacy', believing that the breach of the monopoly rights granted by ARV patents would pave the way for the dissemination of the practice of compulsory licensing in other developing countries, increasing the supply of cheap generics in the market and, as a consequence, the access to essential medicines.[16]

In contrast, pharmaceutical multinational companies and governments of several developed countries, and above all the United States, considered the compulsory licence unnecessary and threatened to reduce investments in Brazil (Folha de São Paulo, 2007). According to the president of the US Chamber of Commerce, Mark Smith, the licence would make it more difficult to maintain Brazil as a beneficiary of the General System of Preferences, a fiscal benefit program through which the country exports $3.5 billion annually to the US (d'Ávila, 2007).

In 2011, the Laboratory of the Ezequiel Dias Foundation (FUNED), of the Minas Gerais State Government, began to produce a generic version of the ARV tenofovir. This ARV is used by 64 thousand AIDS patients in Brazil (in addition to 15 thousand hepatitis patients), and is the second most expensive in the cocktail offered by the Health Ministry, accounting for 10 per cent of the expenditures with medicines of the National Sexually Transmitted Diseases/AIDS Program. According to estimates of the federal government, by 2016 the supply of a generic version of tenofovir should generate savings of about R$440 million.

Crucially, the local production of this generic was only made possible because tenofovir's patent application in Brazil, submitted by Gilead, was denied by the National Institute of Industrial Property (Instituto Nacional de Propriedade Industrial—INPI) on the grounds that its fumarate salt form is not an innovation, already being present in a number of other pharmaceutical agents. This denial resulted largely from the efforts of Far-Manguinhos and the advocacy group Brazilian Interdisciplinary AIDS Association (Associação Brasileira Interdisciplinar de AIDS—ABIA) in disputing the patenting of tenofovir at INPI; and of the Health Ministry, which declared tenofovir to be a medicine of public interest in 2008 (FORMENTI, 2011).

Previously that same year, ABIA also had filed an opposition against the grant of a patent for tenofovir in India, along with an Indian NGO, the Centre for Residential Care and Rehabilitation. ABIA claimed that the patenting of tenofovir in India would undermine the ability of Brazil to import, produce and distribute affordable generic versions of the ARV. This was the first time that a foreign organization filed an opposition against the granting of an ARV patent in India (RAAJ 2008).

Public-private partnerships established in 2011 should also allow the local generic production of two additional ARVs in Brazil by 2016. In particular, such partnerships involve Far-Manguinhos and Bristol/Nortec for the production of atazanavir; and the Pharmaceutical Laboratory of the State of Pernambuco (Laboratório Farmacêutico do Estado de Pernambuco—LAFEPE) and Merck/Nortec for the production of raltegravir. They may represent a promising alternative for the supply of generic ARVs and thus for ensuring the affordability of AIDS treatment in Brazil (MINISTÉRIO DA SAÚDE, 2011).

Nonetheless, even if the Brazilian government manages to secure a more cooperative rather than confrontational relationship with the pharmaceutical multinationals, the erosion of its relative bargaining power and the resulting exhaustion of its negotiation strategy is evident, largely caused by insufficient investments in the local pharmaceutical industry (Grangeiro et al., 2006). In particular, the lack of competency in the production of ARV active ingredients reduces the possibilities for compulsory licensing, since the importation of these active ingredients is jeopardized by the adoption of new patent laws compliant with TRIPS in 2005 by foreign suppliers, and especially India. As result, negotiations of the Health Ministry with the pharmaceutical multinationals—both for ARV price discounts and for ARV production partnerships—tend to be less favorable to the former.

RESTRICTING PATENT RIGHTS TO REDUCE ARV COSTS

Since 1996, the Brazilian government has been legally and politically obliged to provide free and universal access to ARV therapies, on the one hand, but also obliged by TRIPS to recognize patents for pharmaceutical products and processes, on the other. The unaffordable prices of patented ARVs led the government to adopt a series of legal and institutional measures to restrict pharmaceutical, and particularly ARV, patent rights. In particular, the acquisition of pharmaceutical patents was made more difficult, the patent law was altered to facilitate government efforts to reduce prices by means of compulsory licensing, and measures were approved by the government to encourage competition with generics.

The first of the health-oriented measures that restrict patent rights were decrees that regulate the 1996 Industrial Property Law in what concerns compulsory licensing. The decree sanctioned on 6 October 1999, empowered all ministries to issue compulsory licences on the grounds of national emergencies (Decreto 3.201, 1999, Art. 3); and the decree issued on 5 September of the same year allowed the import of generic versions of compulsory licenced goods whenever local production is impractical and obliged the patentee to disclose all information needed for such production (Decreto 4.830, 2003, Art. 5° II §1°; Art. 10). Both defined the criteria for compulsory licensing, simplified the required procedures and gave the Brazilian Health Ministry greater authority to act. As discussed in previous sections, these decrees were crucial in permitting the Ministry to make credible threats of compulsory licensing in price negotiations with the pharmaceutical multinationals.

Another health-oriented reform, introduced by decree in 1999 and converted into law in 2001, aimed to provide the Brazilian Ministry of Health with an instrument to influence the patent examination process, which it would otherwise lack on account of Brazil's National Institute for Industrial Property (INPI) being situated within the Ministry of Commerce, Industry and Development. This reform has required that all pharmaceutical applications approved by INPI be sent to the Ministry of Health for review. Pharmaceutical patents are issued only after the Ministry's health surveillance agency (ANVISA) issues 'prior consent'. This means that drug patents applications are subjected to stricter standards of 'novelty' in order to be approved. As Kenneth Shadlen (2009) explains:

Many patent applications are not for new molecular entities (NMEs) but rather revised versions of NMEs that are already patented, raising the question of how patent examiners define 'novelty.' ANVISA's health-focused examination is significantly stricter than INPI's. Whereas INPI is criticized by health activists and lawyers for adopting an overly broad definition of novelty, ANVISA denies patents to drugs that lack 'genuine' novelty and where it adjudges that providing exclusive rights would be harmful to public health. Typically, ANVISA uses its authority to prevent patents that, by its judgment, would extend the terms of existing patents.

Yet, despite being praised by several analysts, the prior consent mechanism has been under constant legal and political attack since its origins, and INPI has consistently sought to minimize ANVISA's participation in patent examination (Shadlen, 2011).

With the objective of increasing generic competition, the Brazilian government also amended the 1996 Industrial Property Law to introduce an early working provision that permits generic companies to plan for market entry in the immediate aftermath of patent expiration. Crucially, the government refuses to adjust terms for patents granted under the pipeline mechanism. This means that patents granted in Brazil through such mechanism expire on the same day as those granted originally in other countries, even if these countries afterwards extended the patent expiry date. Despite strong opposition from pharmaceutical multinational companies, this norm has not been revoked in court. The refusal to adjust patent terms offers incentives to generic producers to utilize the early working provision. Moreover, the effectiveness of this provision is reinforced by ANVISA's policy of granting quick approval for drugs that satisfy health criteria, leaving issues of potential patent violation to be disputed in courts (Shadlen, 2009: 8).

Finally, as the negotiations with Abbott were carried out, a commission of the Brazilian Chamber of Deputies approved unanimously a Bill which prohibits the registration of patents for drugs used in the prevention and treatment of AIDS.[17] This Bill was explicitly aimed at ensuring the viability of the Health Ministry's AIDS treatment program by reducing ARV prices and guaranteeing the continuation of local generic ARV production (Cassier and Correa, 2007). However, the Bill still has not been voted in the plenary of the Chamber of Deputies nor sent to the Senate.

There is no doubt that these health-oriented patent reforms were crucial in ensuring the sustainability of the Brazilian AIDS treatment program. As mentioned earlier, the two presidential decrees enhanced the credibility of compulsory licensing threats and thereby allowed the Brazilian Health Ministry to obtain, at least initially, considerable ARV price cuts in negotiations with brand-name pharmaceutical companies. The prior consent mechanism has led ANVISA to reject 53 drug patent applications from 2001 to July 2008, which represents a rejection rate of 31.1 per cent; and in 42 per cent of the applications approved the applicant first had to reduce the breadth of the patent's claims (Silva, 2008). Since most of the patented ARVs whose price were the focus of negotiations and disputes with pharmaceutical multinational companies benefited from the pipeline mechanism, the early working provision is also clearly significant as a means of reducing the patent term of these ARVs. Finally, if the bill banning ARV drug patents is approved and all of such drugs can be freely copied by local manufacturers, increased generic competition could lower their prices and make them more affordable.

Yet, for all the importance of the patent rights-restricting reforms, they are insufficient to ensure the sustainability of the AIDS treatment program in the absence of further technological capacitating in the Brazilian pharmaceutical industry. Compulsory licensing is not credible and cannot increase competition in the ARV market if there are no local laboratories capable of offering generic versions of these drugs. Importation of ARVs (or at least their active ingredients) from India and other foreign suppliers remains possible but has become more complicated, costly and uncertain after 2005, when many developing countries changed their patent laws in accordance with TRIPS. The prior consent requirement bans for the most part drug patent applications that are too broad or that contain little therapeutic innovation relative to existing drugs, but are unlikely to ban the patenting of second or third-line regimens to treat AIDS. Similarly, the patenting of newer drugs in Brazil will no longer need to resort to the pipeline mechanism, and can therefore claim a twenty-year term of protection as mandated by TRIPS. Finally, prohibiting ARV patents in the absence of alternative generic ARV suppliers and in the face of TRIPS import restrictions is a measure as innocuous as compulsory licensing.

CONCLUSIONS

The local production of generic ARVs was used strategically by the Brazilian government to contain AIDS treatment costs in the wake of TRIPS, and has thus far ensured the affordability of such treatment. Crucially, Brazilian ARV generics substituted for expensive brand-name imports that were unpatented, made compulsory licensing of patented ARVs credible, and provided important information on ARV production costs, thereby allowing the Health Ministry to achieve significant savings in ARV purchases. Without local generic ARV production, AIDS treatment would certainly have already become unaffordable in Brazil. In addition, the success of the Brazilian response to AIDS was recognized globally and gained the political support of foreign and transnational actors against the economic pressures and threats from the brand-name pharmaceutical industry and the US government.

Yet, since ARVs treat but do not cure HIV/AIDS, they need to be taken for an indefinite period; and an ever increasing number of patients need to migrate from treatment regimens as viral resistance develops. This means that the Health Ministry will increasingly need to offer second and third-line regimens based on newer drugs that are patented in Brazil. For this reason, the reproduction of unpatented ARVs through reverse engineering will no longer be a viable option for reducing AIDS treatment costs.

In addition, there is evidence that the negotiation strategy employed by the Health Ministry to convince (or coerce) pharmaceutical brand-name companies to concede significant discounts for their patented ARVs has exhausted and ceased to be effective. In particular, the agreement reached with Abbott for lopinavir and the compulsory licensing of Merck's efavirenz suggest that the Health Ministry has no longer been able to obtain satisfactory price cuts from these companies. The threat of compulsory licensing has lost its credibility largely because of insufficient investments in the Brazilian pharmaceutical industry (Grangeiro et al., 2006). Brazil's lack of competency in the production of ARV active ingredients makes it dependent on mostly Indian imports, but such imports are nowadays subject to a new Indian Patent Act as well as the provisions of TRIPS that apply to all WTO members.[18]

TRIPS states in its article 31(k) that compulsory licensing 'shall be authorized predominantly for the supply of the domestic market of the Member authorizing such use' (WTO, 1994). Paragraph 6 of the Doha Declaration on TRIPS and Public Health (WTO, 2001) has left unsolved problems of access to essential medicines arising from this article in countries that lack pharmaceutical manufacturing capabilities. The 30 August 2003 agreement aimed at solving such problems by allowing the international trade of compulsory licenced medicines. However, the requirements imposed by this agreement have been found in practice too cumbersome and costly.[19] Until 2011, there has been only one instance where countries resorted to the agreement in order to trade a compulsory licenced medicine—involving Canada as the exporter and Rwanda as the importer—and the exporters found it was too difficult to repeat, and therefore not a viable solution (New, 2009). Hence, the 30 August 2003 agreement should not be expected to facilitate the importation of ARVs into Brazil.

Fortunately, the import of ARVs or their active ingredients that are compulsorily licenced from India should not be banned by the Article 31(f) of TRIPS since, given the large size of the Indian domestic market, it would be possible for the country to satisfy the Brazilian demand and still supply the drugs predominantly for its domestic market. Nevertheless, Brazil would depend on the willingness and capacity of Indian generic producers of ARVs to issue compulsory licences.

Alternatively, Brazil could issue compulsory licences based on anti-competitive practices and thereby be exempt from TRIPS' Article 31(f). Article 31(k) of the agreement states that 'Members are not obliged to apply the conditions set forth in subparagraphs (b) and (f) where such use is permitted to remedy a practice determined after judicial or administrative process to be anti-competitive' (WTO, 1994). But this would entail further amendments to the Brazilian 1996 Industrial Property Law, and the compulsory licences threatened or actually issued in the country thus far have not resorted to claims of anti-competitive practices.[20]

Partnerships announced in 2011 between the Brazilian government and private labs and pharmaceutical multinationals to produce ARVs locally may signal a possible and promising change in the relations between the Health Ministry and these multinationals; and may contribute to the reduction of AIDS treatment costs. However, these partnerships are still highly uncertain and involve negotiations on issues that have a direct bearing on ARV costs, such as the payment of royalties, technology transfers and active ingredients purchases, among others. To the extent that the Health Ministry is losing bargaining power relative to the pharmaceutical multinationals, it will be less capable of carrying out such negotiations on favorable terms, and ARVs will not become significantly more affordable.[21]

In short, given that the importation of ARVs has become undermined by TRIPS after 2005, the sustainability of the Brazilian AIDS treatment program must depend fundamentally on local production, which requires in turn investments in pharmaceutical technology. The possibility of restricting or even overriding drug patent rights will not lead to lower ARV prices unless Brazil can rely on domestic generic ARV suppliers. Indeed, the Brazilian experience shows that local production is crucial for reducing AIDS treatment costs even when ARVs are purchased from pharmaceutical patent holders, because it allows the government to negotiate price discounts—and possible partnerships—more successfully. Accordingly, patent reforms which granted health authorities prominence in reviewing patent applications, made compulsory licensing provisions more flexible and easier to use, expedited post-patent generic entry, and which may ban ARV patents entirely are all important and in some cases have proven decisive for the sustainability of the Brazilian AIDS treatment program. However, in the long-term, as new ARVs are developed and adopted in anti-AIDS cocktails, these reforms tend to become palliatives and will not suffice unless Brazil is capable of replacing brand-name suppliers with generic ones.

Notes

1. Many in Congress and elsewhere have considered this law redundant and unnecessary in view of the health rights ensured by the Constitution.

2. With the aim of coercing Brazil into observing pharmaceutical patents, in 1988 the US imposed a 100 per cent retaliatory tariff on imports of Brazilian pharmaceuticals, paper and electronic products (Sell, 1995, p. 327).

3. Maria Fernanda G. Macedo, former intellectual property consultant of Far-Manguinhos, interview by author, Rio de Janeiro, 20 June 2002.

4. Brazilian government labs suspended the production of indinavir due to problems in the quality of its imported active ingredients. Cristina d'Almeida, former intellectual property consultant of Far-Manguinhos, telephone conversation with author, 11 August 2003.

5. Ministério da Saúde.

6. Despite previous discounts, efavirenz, nelfinavir and lopinavir/ritonavir represented 63 per cent of governmental ARV expenditures in 2003 (Athias, 2003).

7. José Marcos Nogueira Viana, a diplomat who represented the Brazilian Ministry of Health, interview by author, Brasilia, 18 July 2002.

8. Nogueira Viana, interview.

9. James Love, director of the American consumer advocacy NGO Consumer Project on Technology, interview by author, Rio de Janeiro, 4 December 2002.

10. Nogueira Viana, interview.

11. Not coincidentally, the US government backed off on the first day of the United Nations General Assembly Special Session on HIV/AIDS.

12. Abbott already sold liponavir/ritonavir for $0.23 a unit in other countries (Veja, 2006).

13. Almost 65 per cent of these expenses was devoted to the acquisition of ritonavir-boosted lopinavir (34.5%), efavirenz (17.8%) and tenofovir (12.2%) (Orsi et al., 2007, p. 2000).

14. The only concessions offered by the president of Merck's Brazilian branch were a 2 per cent discount and technology transfer to Far-Manguinhos in 2012, the year in which the ARV's patent expires. After the intervention of the US Ambassador in Brazil, Clifford Sobel, the global president of Merck presented a proposal of thirty per cent discount, reducing the price of the dose of efavirenz from $1.59 to $1.10. However, generic versions of the same ARV cost $0.65 in Thailand—where it was compulsory licenced—and $0.44 in India. The pharmaceutical company also offered to anticipate the transfer of technology to 2010, but Brazil would be obligated to purchase the active ingredient from Merck (Paduan, 2008; Fiocruz, 2009).

15. This consortium is made up of the companies Nortec, Cristália e Globe.

16. See, for instance, 'Abaixo assinado em Apoio à Emissão da Licença Compulsória do Medicamento Efavirenz', available online in http://www.rebrip.org.br/_rebrip/pagina.php?id=1496 .

17. The Bill introduces an amendment to Article 18 of the Brazilian Industrial Property Law which deals with exclusions to patentability (Projeto de Lei N° 22/03, 2005).

18. Fortunately, second-line regimens are not patented in India, but third-line regimens most likely will be.

19. These requirements include the approval by the WTO of the trade deal, the compulsory licensing of the medicine in both the importer and the exporter countries, and the packaging of medicines in clearly identifiable containers in order to avoid smuggling.

20. As Tu Thanh Nguyen notes in his contribution to this volume, developing countries in general have rarely applied domestic competition law to promote access to medicines, largely as result of 'the under-development of competition law and the complexity of the interface between intellectual property rights and competition law in these countries'. He further suggests that, due to 'the difficulty of proving abuses of a dominant position by right holders, competition law should not be used by itself where other flexibilities permitted under the TRIPS Agreement and national intellectual property law, such as public health and public security grounds, may be used'.

21. In general, negotiations between the Brazilian Health Ministry and pharmaceutical multinationals for the concession of voluntary licences have failed largely because of disagreements on issues such as these. In contrast, in South Africa local labs such as *Aspen Pharmacare* have succeeded in obtaining voluntary licences for the production of ARVs and supplied most the ARVs used in the country's AIDS treatment program.

References

Abbott, M.L., 2001. Brasil e EUA Travam 'Guerra das Patentes' *Valor Econômico.* 2 February.

Athias, G., 2003. Governo Quer Forçar Produção de Remédio. *Folha de São Paulo* 9 December.

BBC, 2003. New Anti-HIV Drug Deal for Brazil. *BBC,* [online] 18 November. Available at: <http://news.bbc.co.uk/go/pr/fr/-/1/hi/world/americas/3281683.stm>

Bailey, M., 2001. *Companhias Farmacêuticas X Brasil: uma Ameaça à Saúde Pública* [leaflet] Brasilia: Oxfam.

Cassier, M. and Correa, M., 2003. 'Patents, Innovation and Public Health: Brazilian Public-Sector Laboratories' Experience in Copying AIDS Drugs'. In B. Coriat et al., eds. *Economics of AIDS and Access to HIV/AIDS Care in Developing Countries, Issues and Challenges.* Paris: ANRS Editions.

Chade, J., 2003. OMS Vai Copiar Política contra a Aids do Brasil. *O Estado de São Paulo* 20 May.

Constituição da República Federativa do Brasil. 1988. Brasília, 5 October.

Coordenação Nacional de DST/AIDS, 1999. *Terapia Anti-Retroviral e Saúde Pública: Um Balanço da Experiência Brasileira.* Brasilia: Coordenação Nacional de DST/AIDS.

Coordenação Nacional de DST/AIDS, 2001. *National AIDS Drug Policy.* Brasilia: Coordenação Nacional de DST/AIDS.

Coordenação Nacional de DST/AIDS, 2002. 'President Cardoso Agrees to Become an International Activist on Behalf of AIDS Cause', *IP-Health.* [e-mail] Sent 27 November 2002, 6:54 PM.

Coordenação Nacional de DST/AIDS, 2003. 'Brazilian Health Ministry Obtains Record Reduction in Price of New Anti-AIDS Drug', [e-mail]. 14 November, 11:23 AM.

Coordenação Nacional de DST/AIDS, 2004. *Saúde Fecha Acordo com Laboratórios de Anti-Retrovirais.* Press Release, 15 January 2004.

d'Adesky, A., 2003. Brazil's AIDS Model: A Global Blueprint? *American Foundation for AIDS Research,* [online] Available at: < http://www.thegully.com/essays/brazil/030904_brazil_AIDS_dadesky.html>.

d'Ávila, S., 2007. Brasil se Igualou à Junta Militar da Tailândia. *Folha de São Paulo.* May 6.

Decreto 3.201 de 6 de Outubro de 1999. *Dispõe sobre a Concessão, de Ofício, de Licença Compulsória nos Casos de Emergência Nacional e de Interesse Público de que Trata o art. 71 da Lei nº 9.279, de 14 de maio de 1996*. Brasília: Diário Oficial da União, 7 October 1999.

Decreto 4.830 de 4 de Setembro de 2003. *Dá Nova Redação aos Arts. 1º, 2º, 5º, 9º e 10 do Decreto n° 3.201, de 6 de Outubro de 1999, que Dispõe sobre a Concessão, de Ofício, de Licença Compulsória nos Casos de Emergência Nacional e de Interesse Público de que Trata o Art. 71 da Lei n° 9.279, de 14 de Maio de 1996*. Diário Oficial da União, 5 September 2003.

Decreto 7.723 de 4 de Maio de 2012. Prorroga o Prazo de Vigência do Licenciamento Compulsório, por Interesse Público, das Patentes Referentes ao Efavirenz para Fins de Maio de 2007. Diário Oficial da União, 4 May 2012.

Far-Manguinhos. 2002. *Far-Manguinhos—Remédio para o Brasil*. Rio de Janeiro: Ministério da Saúde, Fundação Oswaldo Cruz, Far-Manguinhos.

Fiocruz. 2009. Farmanguinhos Entrega ao Ministério da Saúde o Efavirenz Nacional. Rio de Janeiro: Agência Fiocruz de Notícias, 19 February.

Folha de São Paulo. 2007. Governo Quebra Patente de Droga Anti-Aids; Laboratório Critica Decisão. 4 May.

Formenti, 2011. L. Genérico do tenofovir terá versão brasileira. *O Estado de S. Paulo*. 10 February.

Gazeta Mercantil. 2001a. EUA Reagem no Conflito das Patentes. 2 February.

Gazeta Mercantil. 2001b. ONGs Apóiam Brasil. 5 February.

Grangeiro, A. et al. 2006. Sustentabilidade da Política de Acesso a Medicamentos Anti-retrovirais no Brasil. *Revista de Saúde Pública* 40 (Supl): 60–9.

ICTSD. 2007. A primeira licença compulsória de medicamento na América Latina. *Pontes*, 3(3) [online] Available at: <http://ictsd.org/i/news/12456/>

Intellectual Property Working Group of REBRIP. 2005. Agreement of the Brazilian Government with Abbott Frustrates Brazilians. 13 July. [online] Available at: <http://www.rebrip.org.br/publique/cgi/public/cgilua.exe/web/templates/htm/_template01/printerview.htm?user=read er&editionsectionid=5&infoid=252>

Jornal do Brasil. 2001. EUA Recuam na Guerra das Patentes. 26 June.

Lei 9.279 de 14 de maio de 1996. *Regula Direitos e Obrigações Relativos à Propriedade Industrial*. Brasília: Diário Oficial da União, 15 May, 1996.

Lei 9.313 de 13 de novembro de 1996. *Dispõe sobre a Distribuição Gratuita de Medicamentos aos Portadores do HIV e Doentes de AIDS*. Brasilia: Diário Oficial da União, 12 November 1996.

Mello e Souza, A., 2007. Defying Globalization: Effective Self-Reliance in Brazil. In P. G. Harris and P. D. Siplon, eds. *The Global Politics of AIDS*, eds. Boulder, Colo.: Lynne Rienner Publishers, Ch. 3.

Milward de Azevedo Meiners, C. M. 2008. Patentes Farmacêuticas e Saúde Pública: Desafios à Política Brasileira de Acesso ao Tratamento Anti-retroviral. *Cadernos de Saúde Pública* 24(7): 1467–78.

Ministério da Saúde. Brasil vai produzir dois novos medicamentos para AIDS. *Comunicado à Imprensa*. Brasília: Ministério da Saúde, 2011. Available at: <http://www.aids.gov.br/noticia/brasil-vai-produzir-dois-novos-medicamentos-para-aids>

New, W., 2009. TRIPS Council Annual Report: Extension of Health Amendment Deadline Looms Again. *Intellectual Property Watch*, [online] Available at: <http://www.ip-watch.org/weblog/2009/11/18/trips-council-annual-report-extension-of-health-amendment-deadline-looms-again/>

Nogueira Viana, J.M., 2002. Intellectual Property Rights, the World Trade Organization and Public Health: the Brazilian Perspective. *Connecticut Journal of International Law* 311.

O Globo. 2001. Brasil Defende Política Anti-AIDS nos EUA. 25 June.

Orsi, F. et al. 2003. Intellectual Property Rights, Anti-AIDS Policy and Generic Drugs: Lessons from the Brazilian Public Health Program. In B. Coriat et al., eds. *Economics of AIDS and Access to HIV/AIDS Care in Developing Countries, Issues and Challenges*. Paris: ANRS Editions.

Paduan, R. 2008. Cadê o remédio? *Exame*. 21 de agosto.

Pilling, D., Williams, F. and Dyer, G., 2001. U.S. Patent Retreat Deals Fresh Setback to Drugs Groups. *Financial Times*. 25 June.

Programa Nacional de DST/AIDS, 2010. *Departamento de DST, AIDS e Hepatites Virais: Portal sobre AIDS, Doenças Sexualmente Transmissíveis e Hepatites Virais*. [online] Available at: <http://www.aids.gov.br/pagina/quais-sao-os-antirretrovirais>

Projeto de Lei N° 22/03, 2005 June.

Raaj, N. Brazilian Group Opposes Gilead's AIDS Drug Patent. *The Times of India*. 27 June 2008.

Sá, F. and Malavez, P., 2001. Briga contra Titãs. *Veja Rio 5* September.

Sell, S.K., 1995. 'Intellectual Property Protection and Antitrust in the Developing World: Crisis, Coercion and Choice'. *International Organization* 49(2): 315–49.

Shadlen, K.C., 2009. 'The Politics of Patents and Drugs in Brazil and Mexico: The Industrial Bases of Health Policies'. *Comparative Politics*, 42(1): 41–58.

Shadlen, K.C., 2011. 'The Political Contradictions of Incremental Innovation: Lessons from Pharmaceutical Patent Examination in Brazil'. *Politics and Society*, 39, No. 2: 143–74. June 2011.

Silva, H.M., 2008 *Avaliação da Análise dos Pedidos de Patentes Farmacêuticas Feita pela Anvisa no Cumprimento do Mandato Legal da Anuência Prévia*. Masters. National School of Public Health, Fundação Oswaldo Cruz.

Tribune de Genève. 2001. Sida: le Brésil Fait Plier Roche. 3 September.

Valor Econômico. 2001. ONGs Apóiam Iniciativa do Brasil sobre Medicamentos. 5 February.

Veja, 2006. Ministério da Saúde X Abbott, 7 January.

WTO. 1994. 'Agreement on Trade-Related Aspects of Intellectual Property Rights'. Marrakesh, 15 April.

WTO. 2001. 'Declaration on the TRIPS Agreement and Public Health'. Doha, 14 November.

12 Financing Pharmaceutical Research and Development
Alternatives to the Patent System
Philip Soos and Hans Löfgren

Few policies have caused as much domestic and international controversy as the patents system for pharmaceuticals. Patents comprise part of the umbrella of intellectual property rights (IPRs) that features prominently in multilateral, regional and bilateral trade agreements. Most notably, the 1994 Agreement on Trade Related Aspects of Intellectual Property Rights (TRIPS), administered and enforced by the World Trade Organization (WTO), constitutes a global system of minimum IPR standards. TRIPS resulted from lobbying by business sectors increasingly reliant on IPR portfolios, particularly the pharmaceutical industry, beginning in the 1970s and pursued with mounting vigour in the 1980s and 1990s (Drahos and Braithwaite 2002; Sell 2010). Combined with regional and bilateral free trade agreements (FTAs), TRIPS drives a process of increasingly stringent IPRs which underpin the pharmaceutical industry as a global industrial powerhouse and a formidable pressure group.

Many developed and developing countries did not allow pharmaceutical patents until relatively recently. For example, in Switzerland pharmaceutical patents were introduced only in 1977 (Boldrin and Levine 2008, ch. 9). Since 1995 countries which had not previously recognised such patents (including most developing countries) have freely adopted or been pressured to introduce pharmaceutical patents. Many FTAs entered into between developed and low-income countries have included measures designed to coerce governments into strengthening the private property rights assigned to intellectual outputs (Sell 2007). The reason for resisting strengthened IPRs is the ongoing concern over implications for domestic production and consumers, in particular for access to affordable medicines. The vast majority of pharmaceutical and other patents are held by corporations in the developed countries, and it is very likely that the benefits from IPRs also flow largely in this direction. The globalization of markets and knowledge since the 1980s, and particularly since TRIPS, proved a favourable corporate environment, but the multinational pharmaceutical companies have faced a challenge in achieving the effective enactment and enforcement of pharmaceutical patents as envisaged by the industry (Yu 2011). As detailed elsewhere in this volume, TRIPS requires national legislation for implementation. When legislating for TRIPS compliance, governments can take advantage of a range of 'flexibilities' for the purpose of protection of public health. Conflicts over TRIPS implementation have become increasingly frequent as developing countries, notably India, have sought to take advantage of such flexibilities to protect local production and supply of low-cost medicines.

The prescription pharmaceutical industry is characterised by a structure of high fixed costs (costs incurred by a firm that do not vary by production volume and revenue) but low marginal costs (the cost of producing the next good) (Perelman 2002). Research and development (R&D), as a fixed cost, is an expensive and lengthy process, costing firms hundreds of millions of dollars to identify and (in particular) develop a chemical entity into a new drug. DiMasi et al. (2003) in a much discussed and criticized estimate suggested that the cost of bringing a new drug to market was in the order of $800 million dollars (Angell 2005; Light and Warburton 2005).However, the marginal cost of manufacturing and packaging a medicinal drug is insignificant compared to its fixed costs. Policy proposals for global justice in terms of access to affordable essential medicines, as detailed below, are designed to enable market competition to achieve prices more closely approximating the low cost of production. The conventional argument in favour of patents is that market competitive prices make it impossible for firms to recoup the costs of R&D. Free and open competition would thus provide socially damaging disincentives to investments in R&D (Perelman 2002). The argument for patents as an incentive to spur pharmaceutical firms to invest in R&D is straightforward: the prospect of monopolistic market rents (above normal profits) provides the inducement for pharmaceutical, biotech and medical device firms to invest greater amounts in R&D than would be the case under competitive market conditions. Accordingly, it is generally accepted that without some form of government intervention, markets will produce a less than optimal level of R&D. If a constant pipeline of new medicines is not ensured, society will be worse off, despite the monopolistic costs levied upon consumers and taxpayers. The assumed trade-off is this: static inefficiencies (monopoly prices) are necessary to support dynamic efficiencies (R&D investment). This notion has come to form part of mainstream public policy thinking, grounded theoretically in influential papers by Robert Nelson and Kenneth Arrow (Arrow 1962; Nelson 1959).

That the patent system comprises the most economically efficient intervention to stimulate markets to produce a higher level of R&D for the purpose of economic growth and technological progress has acquired the status of common sense. As summarized by Mazzoleni and Nelson (1998: 273):

Today's conventional wisdom, among economists, lawyers, public officials, and many lay persons, is heavily weighted toward the proposition that strong and broad patent rights are conducive to economic progress. This is especially so in the United States. Through negotiations regarding GATT, and now the proceedings of the WTO, the United States has been pushing on other countries its beliefs about the economic value of strong patents. The U.S. position here is heavily freighted with national interest, but there also is honest belief in the rightness of the position. And other countries have been going along, not always simply as a reaction to the pressure, but also because of an honest belief, on the part of many parties, that in the long run strong patent protection will be good for their economic development.

In this perspective, rejecting patents is to attack economic and social progress. Yet, the patent system gives rise to serious economic and social problems. Indeed, patents may not comprise an optimal policy for stimulating private investment in R&D

(Baker and Chatani 2002; Pogge et al. 2010). That new production technologies strain the logical and feasibility of IPRs is evidenced by the rear-guard battle fought by media and software corporations to protect revenue from products readily distributed through the Internet, with marginal production costs close to zero (Boldrin and Levine 2008).

It is well understood that pharmaceutical patents have the effect of making new essential medicines unaffordable to a large proportion of the world's population. The problem will be exacerbated with more drugs becoming subject to twenty-year patents as new products enter the market, and if the tightening of the global IPR system continues. This effect, however, is accepted by the industry and most governments as collateral damage in order to spur new and innovative medicines that will benefit more people in the long run, on the assumption that public health and economic benefits of patents outweigh the costs (Gallini and Scotchmer 2002). The mainstream economic and public policy perspectives stipulate that the strengthening of IPRs is a necessary and inevitable process of economic globalization. Yet these presumed rights are in stark conflict with the obligation of states to provide for access to medicines for their citizens under international human rights law (Hestermeyer 2007).

By the mid-1990s the tightening global IPR regime appeared unassailable. Developing countries opposing pharmaceutical patents had been marginalized through the TRIPS Agreement, and unorthodox academic critics of the patent system exercised little influence. All countries seemed to be moving towards the type of strong IPR protection advocated by the pharmaceutical industry. But TRIPS provide member nations with flexibilities, as explored in the Indian context in several chapters of this volume, such as the right to define the criteria of patentability and to issue compulsory licences. These flexibilities were confirmed in the 2001 Doha Declaration on the TRIPS Agreement and Public Health. As noted, conflicts between developing nations and the pharmaceutical industry over the interpretation of TRIPS compliance has escalated since 2001. Strong pressures have been brought to bear on countries seeking to take advantage of the flexibilities available under TRIPS. Notably, there have been only a small number of cases of actual compulsory licensing, and these have met fierce objections from the multinational companies backed by the US and the European Union. In other cases, however, for example in Brazil, governments have used the threat of issuing such licences as an effective bargaining chip in price negotiations with the MNCs (Beall and Kuhn 2012).

The implementation and enforcement of TRIPS has resulted in a great deal of conflict. The stakeholders tend to coalesce into two major groups. The first may be labelled the private property/ innovation coalition, comprised of corporations, industry lobby groups, many government agencies and supranational organizations, business-oriented think-tanks, and most economists and policy analysts. The other group includes some governments or at least some government agencies, public health and medical professionals, consumer protection and lobby groups, progressive academics and think-tanks, and a plethora of local, national and international social movement organizations such as Medicines Sans Frontiers, Health Action International and the People's Health Movement.

Medicines are essential to individuals and societies and have resulted in improvements in longevity and public health. New effective drugs are associated with increased productivity and governments have long recognized the importance of R&D to bring new medicines to the market (Congressional Budget Office 2005). It is undeniable that commercially produced medicines have saved millions of lives, and alleviate the suffering of millions more, but it is now apparent that the patent system has serious shortcomings. Accordingly, this chapter highlights some of these problems and explains briefly alternative models for financing pharmaceutical R&D.

PROBLEMS WITH THE PATENT SYSTEM

There is by now a wealth of studies that examine the patent system critically. Many apply a technical economic perspective, focusing on, for example, spill over effects (externalities), public and private expenditures, and tax policy and welfare efficiencies/inefficiencies (Chaudhuri et al. 2006; Deardorff 1992; Guell and Fischbaum

1995; Mazzoleni and Nelson 1998; Wright 1983). In particular, the problems that plague pharmaceutical patents have generated powerful critiques (Angell 2005; Baker and Chatani 2002; Baker 2004; Hollis 2005; Kremer and Glennerster 2004; Love and Hubbard 2007; Perelman 2002; 2003a).

Monopoly pricing, non-innovative copycat drugs, withholding of negative clinical trial research, regulatory capture, uncompensated appropriation of public R&D, intimidation of researchers, conflicts of interest between medical professionals and industry, fraud, the tragedy of the anti-commons, endless expensive litigation, misleading high-pressure advertising, distortion of physician prescribing, anti-competitive behavior, 'astroturf' campaigning (fraudulent corporate-funded health consumer groups), corporate influence on university research, exaggerated R&D expenditures, rent-seeking, counterfeiting, and capture of medical journals are some of the issues highlighted in arguments that the patents system does not function as effectively as is commonly assumed (Angell 2005; Baker and Chatani 2002; Boldrin and Levine 2008). The following section summarizes the drawbacks of the patent system.

Monopolistic pricing. The most widely acknowledged cost to society generated by patents is that of monopolistic pricing, the intended effect of patents. Introductory microeconomics textbooks detail the inefficiencies derived from monopolistic pricing, including consumer welfare losses and the abrogation of free trade. Faloon (2002) has documented the mark-up of some popular medicines over the cost of production, which range from 2,000 to 550,000 per cent, while Baker (2004) suggests a more conservative 300 to 400 per cent. Patents constitute the leading driver of thwarting affordable access to medicines, especially in low-income countries. Millions around the world die due to the lack of timely and affordable access to medicines, and billions more on low and moderate incomes experience difficulties purchasing these medicines (MDG Gap Task Force 2009). To ameliorate this harm, most developed nations operate pharmaceutical insurance and subsidy schemes to ensure affordable consumer access, but have not tackled monopolistic pricing at its source. In developing nations, however, consumers typically have to bear the full cost of medicines.

Distortion of the R&D process. The pharmaceutical industry is loath to provide the data required for accurate estimates of the cost of drug development. The lack of this information adds to the difficulty of achieving a balance between the interests of all stakeholders, including insurers and consumers, in the design and financing of subsidy schemes. Under the patents system, the profit motive provides the incentive for R&D investment. Drug research is oriented towards areas of maximal potential returns, that is, high-income markets and not the conditions causing the greatest burden of disease globally. The result is the misallocation of R&D towards copycat and lifestyle medicines in wealthy countries rather than the diseases that cause high rates of mortality in developing countries (Moran et al. 2009). Basic research is to a large extent undertaken in the public sector, while corporations develop promising discoveries into marketable drugs. Examples abound of the industry's appropriation and misdirection of this taxpayer-funded public research (European Generic Medicines Association 2007; General Accounting Office 2003; Perelman 2002). Stevens et al. (2011) establish that '153 new FDA-approved drugs, vaccines, or new indications for existing drugs were discovered through research carried out in public-sector research institutions' between 1970 and 2009. Firms have incentives to hide negative results stemming from clinical trial testing (Baker 2008). Clinical trial outcomes that do not favour the firm performing the R&D can be manipulated or ignored. The industry increasingly outsources clinical trials to contract research organizations (CROs),which has created another set of perverse incentives as firms shop around for CROs who will provide overly optimistic appraisals (Mirowski and Horn 2005).The capture of medical journals by industry, through paid advertising, combined with ghost-written papers, has distorted health and medical science (Sismondo 2007).

Anti-social behaviour. The industryis often under the media spotlight for acts of anti-social behaviour. Firms have been known to interfere with academic appointments, engage in character assassinations of doctors, researchers and academics, suppress negative research, and abysmal treatment of whistle-blowers (Gibson et al. 2002; Olivieri 2003). Shah (2006) presents damning evidence of unethical experimentation on poor people in developing countries, including India, where poverty and illiteracy provide a plentiful supply of individuals accepting to participate in clinical trials. The result has led to thousands of avoidable deaths, with industry sidestepping protocols, regulations and laws in the pursuit of profit.

Undue influencing of university research. The industry's role in shaping the direction of medical university research is well documented (Angell 2010). The resources wielded by industry in this relationship risks undermining the norms of science such as universalism and disinterestedness (Packham 2003). Strained for funding, universities have turned to industry and have increasingly become dependent on corporate partnerships. At times, universities become the *de facto* research arm of corporations, while being funded in part by taxpayers. In an atmosphere of corporate entrepreneurialism, academics, researchers and scientists may be constrained from working within collaborative networks (Perelman 2002). Values such as respect for evidence, admission of mistakes, pursuit of truth and moral and intellectual independence are vital to science but are likely to erode where corporate objectives take centre stage.

Corruption of medical professionals. The pharmaceutical industry has an interest in health and medical professionals viewing them favourably. There is plentiful evidence detailing the methods that industry applies in pursuit of this objective. The practice begins in medical school, where students are treated to freebies and gifts, with the unstated expectation that this will be reciprocated later. Prominent professionals are targeted as thought leaders who are lavishly endowed if agreeing to promote a firm's product (Angell 2000; Moynihan 2003a, 2003b; Rogers et al. 2004). Conflicts of interest between the medical profession and industry are common with industry engaging in legalized bribery (Kassirer 2005). This practice has extended to seemingly independent grassroots patient support groups (Burton et al. 2003; Vitry and Lofgren 2011).

Patent offices. As strengthened IPRs have been enacted into law and enforced by governments, controversies have revolved around the criteria for patentability in terms of definitions of novelty and non-obviousness, as in conflicts over Section 3(d) in India's Patents (Amendment) Act, 2005. The industry has placed considerable pressure on governments to relax patenting standards, to enable so-called evergreening of monopoly pricing through new patents for trivial modifications of existing products (Ghosh and Kesan 2004; Perelman 2002). As detailed elsewhere in this volume, the multinational pharmaceutical industry consider illegitimate India's use of strict patentability criteria to prevent the patenting of new uses and new forms of known medicines.

Legal disputes. Courts must hear disputes between patent owners and alleged violators. In recent years, there has been an explosion of expensive patent infringement cases brought to court in the United States and elsewhere. As firms engage in R&D, they may inadvertently or purposefully infringe upon patents held by other parties. In effect, litigation acts like a tax on innovation (Bessen and Meurer 2008). This epidemic of litigation has resulted in academics and scientists wasting time learning and teaching themselves patent law rather than pursuing their specializations (Perelman 2003b).

Information privatization. Patents transform information into a private good, despite its economic attributes as a public good. By privatizing information, patents create an 'enclosure movement' that restricts the free dissemination of information and concentrates ownership narrowly into the hands of the corporate sector. While this form of privatization can help to partially solve the problem of sub-optimal R&D spending, it causes the 'tragedy of the anti-commons', the mirror image of the tragedy of the commons (Heller 2008). Under the tragedy of the anti-commons, ownership is so fragmented among multiple entities that it poses difficulties for firms to carry out R&D by acquiring licences for all necessary project components. This can result in gridlock: firms cannot move forward with R&D because other firms have blocked progress (Heller and Eisenberg 1998).

Advertising and marketing. Direct to consumer (DTC) marketing is banned in all developed countries with the exception of New Zealand and the US, on the ground that firms are likely to mislead and manipulate consumers. Firms compete for market share on the basis of selling medicines that are often similar to other drugs within the same therapeutic class. Consumers have little knowledge of the efficacy of specific medicines and treatments, but can be swayed by advertising.The experience of DTC marketing in New Zealand and the US has not been positive (Angell 2005; Coney 2002). A great deal of industry promotion is 'disease mongering', a ploy to convince consumers that they are sick and need medication, with promotion through television, radio, magazines, newspapers, billboards, and so on (Moynihan and Cassels 2005).

ALTERNATIVE MECHANISMS FOR FINANCING R&D

India's Patents Act, 1970, enacted in 1972, was drafted with the intention of supporting the fledgling domestic pharmaceutical industry and making medicines more affordable, as detailed elsewhere in this volume. Patents were not granted on active ingredients and firms could develop processes for the manufacturing of generics to supply domestic consumers and export markets. R&D was required to enhance manufacturing techniques and expand production volumes, though not at the level required for drug discovery. As Indian firms grew into major suppliers on the world stage, the non-granting of product patents became a focal point of critiques spearheaded by the multinationals and Western governments. Membership of the WTO ultimately compelled India to re-introduce product patents through a legislative amendment passed in 2005, with the result that monopolistically-priced medicines will increasingly diminish affordability. The strengthening of the IPR system in India and other developing nations is often seen as the only realistic option for preserving the incentive for private investment in R&D. So strong is this idea that many developing countries have moved in lockstep with their wealthier counterparts in implementing TRIPS while not fully taking advantage of available flexibilities. It would be a mistake, however, to believe that the patent system is the only conceivable mechanism for funding of the discovery and development of new medicines. Indeed, the period since around 2000 has seen aglobal debate focused on alternative R&D funding mechanisms (see for example, Pogge et al. 2010 and Expert Working Group on Research and Development 2012). Positions range from the view that only minor tinkering with the patent system is required, to arguments for less reliance on intellectual property rights within a new global framework for health research, and also to models that do away with patents altogether. All of these alternatives involve government intervention to varying degrees on the basis that in the absence of patent protection a suboptimal level of R&D will occur if markets are left to their own devices. They are also mostly premised on marginal cost pricing arrived at through market competition. The major proposals are summarized in the following.

Advance market commitments (AMCs). Kremer and Glennerster (2004) propose that coalitions of governments, international organisations and charitable funds make legally binding commitments to make large purchases of newly developed vaccines (or drugs). They consider this highly practicable since requisite institutional structures are already in place, including centralised procurement arrangements and regulatory systems. It would, they argue, be relatively straightforward to specify in contractual form the requirements that new vaccines or drugs would have to meet. In addition to safety and efficacy criteria, contracts would stipulate conditions for usability in low-income countries, and recipient governments would have to make a co-payment to demonstrate a commitment to the program. An independent adjudication committee would determine whether eligibility conditions have been met. This system would provide innovators (firms) with the incentive to invest in lines of R&D that would otherwise not be commercially viable. The AMC concept addresses the '10/90 gap', that 90 per cent of the global disease burden attracts ten per cent of research investments. It does not represent a fundamental critique of the patent system or the multinational pharmaceutical companies, but proposes a market-like mechanism to achieve a better alignment between corporate research investments and global health needs. Its basic supposition is that the self-contained big corporation provides the best framework for cutting edge vaccine and drug developments.

Kremer auction system. Michael Kremer (1998) is also associated with this model, similarly compatible with the existing patent system. The government however enacts an auction system to purchase patents from individuals and firms willing to sell them. It is argued that as auctions provide an effective mechanism for revealing the current market value of patents, governments can purchase them at an efficient price plus a constant mark-up to reflect the additional social value. This social value is reflective of the wider benefits (positive externalities) that society gains through pharmaceutical consumption and R&D spillovers stemming from both public and industry investment. For instance, consumption of a specific drug may inhibit spread of a virulent disease, preventing further infection to other parties. Given the extensive social returns to innovation, this mark-up is likely to be equal to the private value (the market price of the patent), effectively doubling the total cost of patent buyouts (Kremer 1998). Governments may occasionally let the highest bidders at auction purchase patents on the basis that if other parties know that they retain a significant chance of outbidding the government, they will have an incentive to accurately value patents. This does not prohibit the winner from then auctioning off the patent to another party. Patents purchased under this auction system are then placed in the public domain, allowing for medicines to be produced as generics at marginal cost. The other major benefit of the auction system is that patent-protected medicines that offer only marginal improvements will not command significant private value and social mark-up, thus providing incentive for investment only in lines of R&D of considerable social value. Abramowicz (2003) provides a lengthy critical analysis of the Kremer model along with similar auction and patent prize funding proposals (see also Pogge et al. 2010, ch. 7).

Health Impact Fund. The HIF is a taxpayer-financed mechanism designed by philosopher Thomas Pogge and economist Aiden Hollis, in an effort to provide industry with incentives to invest in R&D lines with high social returns but which do not offer similar financial returns (Hollis 2008; Pogge et al. 2010, ch. 5). Given the profit motive of industry, some socially beneficial lines of R&D will not be funded due to the paucity of returns, thus necessitating an intervention to ensure such developments will brought to market. Herein lies the primary benefit of the HIF: it provides a significant incentive to fund investments that result in large health impacts while pricing medicines close to marginal cost (Hollis 2008). The HIF is not a compulsory mechanism; firms can opt in if the resulting returns outweigh opportunity costs. Rewards are provided on an annual basis, on the measurable impact that a medicine has in reducing the burden of disease, for a period of ten years for new drugs and five years for existing drugs tailored to new uses. Firms rewarded under the HIF agree to allow their medicines to be sold at marginal cost. Like the AMC model, the HIF is a supplement rather than a replacement to the patent system, ultimately seeking to realign R&D investment to promote more socially beneficial outcomes.

Hollis' compulsory licensing proposal. Aiden Hollis (2005) has also advocated a novel model whereby the government uses a zero-cost compulsory licence to acquire patents and reward firms for producing medicines. While it has some similarities with current flexibilities under TRIPS allowing governments to acquire medicines deemed critical to public health, there is a major difference. In this model, compulsory licensing becomes the norm. Firms are granted patents as per usual, but the government acquires production licences and compensates firms on an annual basis according to the therapeutic value of the medicines based upon measures of improved life quality. Under current 'government use' compulsory licensing arrangements, governments can choose to either provide a paltry payment or refuse reimbursement altogether. Under the

Hollis model, however, the government draws upon a large pool of funding to ensure that firms are both compensated reasonably for their R&D investments and provided with incentives to continue to pursue productive lines of research. A cornerstone of this model is to ensure that inefficient financing of 'me-too' or copycat medicines is minimised.

Hubbard and Love trade framework. This proposal is named after Tim Hubbard and James Love, two policy experts advocating a new trade framework to finance R&D at both the international and domestic levels (Hubbard and Love 2003). On the international stage, the WHO could implement and administer a program for financing global health R&D, with signatories required to meet funding targets to avoid nations free-riding off each other. In this scenario, patents as mandated under do not have to be enforced as per TRIPS requirements which does not have to enforce patents as the primary mechanism to prevent free-riding. Under the new framework, trade rules can be modified to allow governments the freedom of choice to meet these targets by a variety of R&D mechanisms (as covered in this section) rather than relying solely upon the patent system. At the domestic level, governments can enhance R&D investments by public, academic and private R&D institutions through further public funding. A specific proposal is to mandate a contribution by employers, set by government, to finance R&D, possibly based upon the number of employees. This is done by allocating contributions to a R&D intermediary, an organization operating like a pension fund, holding assets to provide an income stream. Employers have the freedom to choose which R&D fund to finance, and R&D intermediaries have the choice to decide upon both the allocation mechanism and to which part(ies) receive funding. Competition among R&D intermediaries provides the incentive to ensure that only lines of research that are productive and profitable are funded, for they will ultimately lose out if large amounts of money are continually sunk into wasteful ventures.

Kucinich public option. Dennis Kucinich, a Democratic Party congressman and former presidential candidate, has put forward a plan to enable greater participation of the public sector in R&D investment (Kucinich 2004). The proposed legislation provides funding for an organization called the National Institute for Biomedical Research and Development (NIBRD), funded through tax revenues. It would be based on and run in collaboration with the National Institutes of Health (NIH), a collection of publically-financed organizations that has led the way in health and pharmaceutical R&D in the US over several decades. An initial ten laboratories would be established, run within the NIH. Lines of R&D would be pursed only on the expectation that a patent will be granted, though it is important to note that patents are secured on the basis of placing them in the public domain to prevent profiteering though monopolistic pricing by other entities. Thus, even as patents are still granted under this model, medicines would now be produced at marginal cost via market competition. All R&D is to be made publicly available in a timely manner free of charge through the Internet, presumably similar to the US National Library of Medicine currently run by the NIH. Although the NIBRD would be a public organization, it would retain an element of competition as the director would be authorized to perform an audit once every decade to terminate a lab deemed to be unproductive. A prize fund is also established to reward individual researchers and/or organizations for outstanding R&D discoveries (Baker 2004).

Patent pools. This is a figurative pool where two or more parties agree to share or cross-licence patents to further mutual goals. Patent pools have existed for decades, notably used during both World Wars when such arrangements were implemented to prevent aircraft and radio manufacturers from blocking each other from developing and producing critical equipment needed in the US war effort (Perelman 2003a). The same occurs within the pharmaceutical industry as firms are often blocked from pursuing promising lines of R&D (the tragedy of the anti-commons or patent thickets) and/or violate other firms' patents (Perelman 2002). This results in significant social costs for the former and triggers large legal costs in the case of the latter. In the interest of keeping the cost of doing business to a minimum, firms will often agree to share patents.

Patent pools, however, are not only used by the private sector; they are also used within the public sector and private non-profit sectors. The most notable example is the Medicines Patent Pool, a Swiss-based organization created in July 2010 that focuses upon improving access and affordability to critical medicines in the developing world. The MPP negotiates with patent holders to place their patents in the pool, thus allowing generic manufacturers to produce critically-needed medicines at vastly reduced costs. This way, licence holders still receive royalties, generics manufacturers can supply markets without fear of patent violation and lawsuits, and consumers benefit from lower pricing (Mara 2012).

Prize funds. This is an alternative to the patent system which has found advocates and been studied for decades (Abramowicz 2003). Under a prize fund system, firms engage in a race to find cures to specific diseases and ailments that the government will provide rewards for. Rewards are typically calculated on the basis of social utility, and are given to the innovator after the cure is created. Medicines invented via this system are placed in the public domain and produced at cost, thus avoiding deadweight losses (the economic loss to the consumer from purchasing at an inefficient monopolistic price) as per the other proposals discussed above. A major issue regarding prize funds is the government's ability to correctly value the future social value of an innovation, given the concerns over a lack of timely and accurate information, though rewards can be based other ex-post measures, notably reductions in disease burdens and sales (Shavell and Ypersele 2001).

Open source drug discovery. The open source model draws on the example of the successful and freely available Linux operating system within the software industry, and points to non-commercial collaborations across firms and public research agencies using IT networks and computational tools, with a particular focus on basic research. The public good nature of R&D as information and knowledge in the scientific commons extends across from the software to pharmaceutical industries. The open source movement advocates an open-ended and flexible approach to R&D without being restricted to any one mechanism. In fact, multiple mechanisms in part or whole can be used to facilitate drug discovery, across the public and private sectors whilst minimizing attempting to reduce barriers caused by patents. Promising results can then be channelled into public-private partnerships (PPPs) equipped to manage development through the pre-clinical, clinical and production stages. Participation in open source ventures is motivated by non-monetary rewards, such as personal satisfaction and commitment to the public good, skills developments, and enhancement of professional reputation (Pogge et al. 2010, ch. 10).

Global tax alternatives. The Consultative Expert Working Group (CEWG) is an organization established by the World Health Assembly in 2010. In its submission to the WHA, the CEWG commented on various taxation measures that could help to boost funding for drug R&D (Expert Working Group on Research and Development 2012). There exist a plethora of taxes related to public health, for instance, sin taxes to reduce alcohol and tobacco consumption and general goods and services taxes (VAT and GST) to provide general funding. Globally, there appears to be only one tax raised specifically to fund R&D (in Italy), and nothing at the international level. France, along with several European and Latin American countries, has led the way by implementing an airline tax to help fund UNITAID. This Geneva-based organisation, which raised two billion dollars in the five years to 2012, creates market demand and incentives for the development of new and adapted drugs. These include paediatric formulations and fixed-dose combinations that mix several ingredients into an easy-to-take once-a-day pill.While not comprising an international tax per se, it is the closest equivalent. To remedy the lack of general revenue raised to fund R&D, the CEWG suggested a number of potential options: taxes on financial transactions, patents, repatriated pharmaceutical industry profits and even military hardware. These tax proposals are not meant to be a replacement for the patent system but are proposed as supplements to bolster pharmaceutical R&D globally.

This brief review makes evident that the IPR system is not the only mechanism available to governments and the international community to stimulate and finance investment in R&D; there exist numerous other models that could complement or potentially replace patents, several of which are already in existence on a relatively small scale. The core feature of most of these alternative models is the elimination of monopolistic pricing in favour of marginal cost pricing. In one study, Baker (2004) reviews four of the above models (Hollis, Hubbard and Love, Kremer, and Kucinich) and argues that they are all superior to the patent system in terms of pricing, along with other important aspects of the R&D and production process. It cannot be readily established if one proposal is 'better' than another, given the multitude of factors that must be assessed. Wright (1983, p. 691) notes:

Though public intervention in the market for research is virtually universal, economists have paid surprisingly little attention to the choice of the form of research incentive in a given market structure. Many studies concentrate on patents, but any assumption of their superiority over other incentives has been founded on intuition rather than on formal analysis.

As most of these alternatives rely upon various forms of public funding, political interference in R&D lines remains a concern. Hettinger (1989, p. 49) explains, however, that public funding does have to imply government control:

Government funding of intellectual labor can be divorced from government control over what is funded. University research is an example. Most of this is supported by public funds, but government control over its content is minor and indirect. Agencies at different governmental levels could distribute funding for intellectual labor with only the most general guidance over content, leaving businesses, universities, and private individuals to decide which projects to pursue.

Through any of these alternatives R&D in this domain would regain its proper public good status and the tragedy of the anti-commons and associated transaction costs could be avoided. With R&D delinked from sales, combined with an open clinical trial system, firms would have little incentive to falsify and/or suppress data and results could be freely published. Without the enormous profits stemming from monopolistic rents, the ability of firms to saturate consumers with biased and misleading advertising, marketing and public relations material would be reduced, along with corruption of the medical establishment through 'gifts' and privileges. Counterfeiters will no longer be able to take advantage of the difference between market price and marginal cost, and parallel importation would become irrelevant.

Some proposals tend to focus on investment and R&D wholly within one set of institutions, whether government or private for-profit firms rather than considering the diverse number of institutions in the economy engaged in R&D. It stands to reason that all sectors of an economy's R&D intensive institutions require funding: public laboratories, universities, for-profit firms and non-profit foundations. Each has their strengths and weaknesses, and should be utilized accordingly. Of these, the for-profit industry requires the most extensive restructuring for their viability, in alternative models, depends on mechanisms such as prizes or publically-financed contracts, though little prevents universities and non-profit foundations contracting out R&D to firms. Government laboratories, universities and non-profit foundations are unlikely to have their internal operations radically altered; rather they would require expansion to take advantage of increasing funding. A five to ten year transition period would allow enough time to prepare and stabilize a new regulatory and institutional environment for managers and workers. They may allow for modification that suits particular countries' regulatory and institutional environments, where government intervention and markets can take on larger or smaller roles, performing different functions as required as Varian (1993, p. 546) clarifies:

The standard theory of public goods doesn't call for government intervention—it just says that when public goods are present, simple markets won't achieve efficient outcomes. Conventional economic theory is mute on the question of whether there is any other mechanism that will improve upon the market. Indeed, the standard theory is perfectly open to the view that some sort of hybrid mechanism may do better than direct government intervention.

Notably, several of these alternate models can operate side to side with the current patents system without adversely interfering in its operations. While this suggests that implementation may proceed in an orderly manner, it does not follow that industry will casually accept such modifications of the current patent system on the grounds that it comprises the source of monopolistic rents and hence economic power. Substituting, for instance, private finance with public funding and contracts, and monopolistic pricing with market competitive pricing, will place downward pressure on industry profits. Even the consideration of major alternatives by policy makers may create uncertainty to the point that industry may stop investing in R&D, causing significant market turmoil. Adding to this difficulty is the political and economic power of the industry, skilled in the art of rent-seeking and political manoeuvring, that would be mobilised to prevent any substantial change in the organisation of innovation and production. Indeed, the US pharmaceutical lobby is one of the most powerful business interest group in that country, and the same is likely true in many other nations. Problems of implementation are not just logistical or economic but political.

Although trade agreements and treaties, notably TRIPS, legally obligate signatories to enforce pharmaceutical patents, governments do have considerable leeway in deciding how R&D should be financed. These treaties do not force governments to grant patents, do not prevent the establishment and financing of alternate R&D systems and presumably legislation could be enacted to disallow the patenting of R&D that has been financed directly or indirectly by the taxpayer to stem the appropriation of publically-financed R&D by industry.

Baker (2004) provides a starting point for a comparative assessment of R&D systems which could be extended further to examine the intricacies of the patents system and the alternatives presented here. Determining the optimal level of R&D that requires public financing, establishing an effective balance between government intervention and markets, implementing strategies to negate the possibility of political interference in the R&D process, and implications for employment are among the factors that require careful study.

CONCLUSION

The pharmaceutical patents system is widely regarded as the most effective government intervention to motivate firms to invest in greater levels of R&D than would exist under market competitive conditions. Although patents achieve this objective to some extent, it had resulted in obstacles that prevent affordable and timely access to medicines. In particular, patents and the market system do not provide incentives for socially necessary research to address the neglected diseases of the poor. The most apparent issue is that of monopolistic pricing, raising medicine prices many multiples above the cost of production, though somewhat attenuated by insurance schemes found in higher-income countries. Poorer countries such as India, however, lack effective safety nets for consumers.

The monopolistic rents inherent in the patents system are ultimately self-defeating: while these may spur firms to create 'innovative' medicines, competitors will follow suit by investing R&D into copycats of limited to non-existent therapeutic value to cash in on economic rents. Standard economic theory confirms that patents result in distortions and misallocations of resources.It has been found that the R&D process is marred by the numerous perverse incentives firms face due to the link between R&D expenditures and sales. Under the patent system, firms have every incentive to maximize revenue regardless of the therapeutic efficacy of drugs granted marketing approval, leading to an array of anti-social behaviours. The patents system may be taken for granted by most stakeholders in the global system of pharmaceutical R&D and production, but it does not follow that this will continue to be the case, as Baker (2005, p. 6) notes:

... the key point is that the country should as a matter of public policy decide the best mechanism for financing research. It cannot continue to accept patent-financed research, with all of its known inefficiencies and flaws, simply because it worked in the Middle Ages. People should not die because of patents.

Considering that this form of state intervention has existed for centuries and forms a central part of modern economies, it is curious that the patent system and its alternatives have not been more extensively studied to determine how medical and pharmaceutical R&D can be best funded, for the greatest social benefit, at the least cost. But the tide may now be turning; the global debate on these issues suggests that major change is inevitable. Those involved in access to medicines campaigns need to advocate for alternatives to the patent system.

References

Abramowicz, M., 2003. 'Perfecting Patent Prizes', *Vanderbilt Law Review*, 56: 115–236.

Angell, M., 2000. 'Is Academic Medicine for Sale?', *New England Journal of Medicine*, 342: 1516–18.

Angell, M., 2005. *The Truth About the Drug Companies: How They Deceive Us and What To Do About It*, Random House, New York.

Angell, M., 2010. 'Big Pharma, Bad Medicine', *Boston Review*, May/June, http://bostonreview.net/BR35.3/angell.php.

Arrow, K., 1962. 'Economic Welfare and the Allocation of Resources for Invention', in H.M. Groves (ed.) *The Rate and Direction of Inventive Activity: Economic and Social Factors*, pp. 609–26, NBER Books, Cambridge, MA.

Baker, D., 2004. 'Financing Drug Research: What Are the Issues?', Center for Economic and Policy Research, Washington D.C.

Baker, D., 2005. 'Bird Flu Fears: Is There a Better Way to Develop Drugs?', *Center for Economic and Policy Research*, Washington D.C.

Baker, D., 2008. 'The Benefits and Savings from Publicly-Funded Clinical Trials of Prescription Drug', Center for Economic and Policy Research, Washington D.C.

Baker, D. and Chatani, N., 2002. 'Promoting Good Ideas on Drugs: Are Patents the Best Way?', Center for Economic and Policy Research, Washington D.C.

Beall, R. and Kuhn, R., 2012. 'Trends in Compulsory Licensing of Pharmaceuticals Since the Doha Declaration: A Database Analysis', *PLoS Medicine*, 9(1).

Bessen, J. and Meurer, M.J., 2008. 'The Private Costs of Patent Litigation', Boston University School of Law.

Boldrin, M. and Levine, D.K., 2008. *Against Intellectual Monopoly*, Cambridge University Press, New York.

Burton, B. and Rowell, A., 2003. 'Unhealthy Spin', *British Medical Journal*, 326: 1205–07.

Chaudhuri, S., Goldberg, P.K., and Jia, P., 2006. 'Estimating the Effects of Global Patent Protection in Pharmaceuticals: A Case Study of Quinolones in India', *The American Economic Review*, 96(5): 1477–514.

Congressional Budget Office, 2005. R&D and Productivity Growth, Background Paper, Congress of the United States, Washington D.C.

Coney, S., 2002. 'Direct-to-Consumer Advertising of Prescription Pharmaceuticals: A Consumer Perspective from New Zealand', *Journal of Public Policy and Marketing*, 21(2): 213–23.

Drahos, P. and Braithwaite, J., 2002. *Information Feudalism*, Earthscan, London.

Deardorff, A.V., 1992. 'Welfare Effects of Global Patent Protection', *Economica*, 59(233): 35–51.

DiMasi, J.A., Hansen, R.W., and Grabowski, H.G., 2003. 'The price of Innovation: New Estimates of Drug Development Costs', *Journal of Health Economics*, 22(2): 151–85.

European Generic Medicines Association, 2007. 'Myths and Realities of the Pharmaceutical Industry', http://www.egagenerics.com/doc/MythsRealities_03.pdf

Expert Working Group on Research and Development, 2012. 'Research and Development to Meet Health Needs in Developing Countries: Strengthening Global Financing and Coordination: Report of the Consultative Expert Working Group on Research and Development: Financing and Coordination', World Health Organization, Geneva.

Faloon, W., 2002. 'The FDA Versus the American Consumer', *Life Extension Magazine*,http://www.lef.org/magazine/mag2002/oct2002_awsi_01.html

Gallini, N. and S. Scotchmer., 2002. 'Intellectual Property: When Is It the Best Incentive System?', *Innovation Policy and the Economy*, 2: 51–77.

General Accounting Office, 2003, Technology Transfer: NIH-Private Sector Partnership in the Development of Taxol, United States General Accounting Office, Washington D.C.

Ghosh, S. and Kesan, J., 2004. 'What Do Patents Purchase? In Search of Optimal Ignorance in the Patent Office', *Houston Law Review*, 40: 1219–64.

Gibson, E., Baylis, F., and Lewis, S., 2002. 'Dances with the Pharmaceutical Industry,' *Canadian Medical Association Journal*, 166(4): 448–50.

Guell, R.C., and Fischbaum, M., 1995. 'Toward Allocative Efficiency in the Prescription Drug Industry', *The Milbank Quarterly*, 73(2): 213–30.

Healy, D., 2002. 'In the Grip of the Python: Conflicts at the University-Industry Interface', *Science and Engineering Ethics*, 9(1): 59–71.

Heller, M., 2008. *The Gridlock Economy: How Too Much Ownership Wrecks Markets, Stops Innovation, and Costs Lives*, Basic Books, New York.

Heller, M.A. and Eisenberg, R.S., 1998. 'Can Patents Deter Innovation? The Anticommons in Biomedical Research', *Science*, 280(5364): 696–701.

Hestermeyer, H., 2007. *Human Rights and the WTO: The Case of Patents and Access to Medicines*, Oxford University Press, Oxford.

Hettinger, E.C., 1989. 'Justifying Intellectual Property', *Philosophy and Public Affairs*, 18(1): 31–52.

Hollis, A., 2005. 'An Efficient Reward System for Pharmaceutical Innovation', Department of Economics, University of Calgary.

Hollis, A., 2008. 'The Health Impact Fund: A Useful Supplement to the Patent System?', *Public Health Ethics*, 1(2): 124–33.

Hubbard, T. and Love, J.,2004. 'A New Trade Framework for Global Healthcare R&D', *PLoS Biology*, 2(2): 147–50.

Kassirer, J.P., 2005. *On The Take: How Medicine's Complicity With Big Business Can Endanger Your Health*, Oxford University Press, New York.

Kremer, M., 1998. 'Patent Buyouts: A Mechanism for Encouraging Innovation', *The Quarterly Journal of Economics*,113(4): 1137–67.

Kremer, M. and Glennerster, R., 2004. *Strong Medicine: Creating Incentives for Pharmaceutical Research on Neglected Diseases*, Princeton University Press, Princeton.

Kucinich, D., 2004. 'H.R. 5155: To establish the National Institute for Biomedical Research and Development', 108th Congress 2nd Session, Washington DC.

Light, D.W. and Warburton, R.N., 2005. 'Extraordinary Claims Require Extraordinary Evidence', *Journal of Health Economics*, 24(5): 1030–33.

Love, J. and Hubbard, T., 2007. 'The Big Idea: Prizes to Stimulate R&D for New Medicines', *Chicago-Kent Law Review*, 82(3): 1519–53.

Mara, K., 2012. 'The Medicines Patent Pool: improving access to ARVs and stimulating innovationfor new medicines', *Africa Health*, January, pp. 20–23.

Mazzoleni, R. and Nelson, R.R., 1998. 'The Benefits and Costs of Strong Patent Protection: A Contribution to the Current Debate,' *Research Policy*, 27(3): 273–84.

MDG Gap Task Force, 2009. 'Strengthening the Global Partnership for Development in a Time of Crisis', United Nations, New York.

Mirowski, P. and Horn, R.V., 2005. 'The Contract Research Organization and the Commercialization of Scientific Research', *Social Studies of Science*, 35(4): 503–48.

Moran, M., Guzman, J., Ropars, A., McDonald, A., Jameson, N., Omune, B., Ryan, S. and L. Wu, 2009. 'Neglected Disease Research and Development: How Much Are We Really Spending?', *PLos Medicine*, 6(2): 137–46.

Moynihan, R., 2003a. 'Who Pays for the Pizza? Redefining the Relationships Between Doctors and Drug Companies. 1: Entanglement', *British Medical Journal*, 326(7400): 1189–92.

Moynihan, R., 2003b. 'Who pays for the pizza? Redefining the relationships between doctors and drug companies. 2: Disentanglement', *BMJ*, 326(7400): 1193–96.

Moynihan, R. and Cassels, A., 2005, *Selling Sickness: How Drug Companies Are Turning Us All Into Patients*, Allen and Unwin, Crows Nest, N.S.W.

Nelson, R., 1959. 'The Simple Economics of Basic Scientific Research', *The Journal of Political Economy*, 67(3): 297–306.

Olivieri, N.F., 2003. 'Patients' Health or Company Profits? The Commercialisation of Academic Research', *Science and Engineering Ethics*, 9(1): 29–41.

Packham, D.E., 2003, 'G.A.T.S. and Universities: Implications for Research', *Science and Engineering Ethics*, 9(1): 85–100.

Perelman, M., 2002. *Steal This Idea: Intellectual Property Rights and the Corporate Confiscation of Creativity*, Palgrave Macmillan, New York.

Perelman, M., 2003a. 'The Weakness in Strong Intellectual Property Rights', *Challenge*, 46(6): 32–61.

Perelman, M., 2003b. 'Intellectual Property Rights and the Commodity Form: New Dimensions in the Legislated Transfer of Surplus Value', *Review of Radical Political Economics*, 35(3): 304–11.

Pogge, T., Rimmer, M., and Rubenstein, K., 2010. *Incentives for Global Public Health: Patent Law and Access to Essential Medicines*, Cambridge University Press, Cambridge.

Rogers, W.A., Mansfield, P.R., Braunack-Mayer, A.J. and J.N. Jureidini, 2004. 'The Ethics of Pharmaceutical Industry Relationships with Medical Students', *Medical Journal of Australia*, 180: 411–14.

Sell, S., 2007. 'TRIPS-Plus Free Trade Agreements and Access to Medicines', *Liverpool Law Review*, 28(1): 41–75.

Sell, S., 2010. 'Business and Democracy? Pharmaceutical Firms, Intellectual Property and Developing Countries' in Porter and Ronit eds., *The Challenges of Global Business Authority: Democratic Renewal, Stalemate or Decay?*, State University of New York Press, New York.

Shah, S., 2006. *The Body Hunters: How the Drug Industry Tests Its Products On the World's Poorest Patients*, The New Press, New York.

Shavell, S. and Ypersele, T.V., 2001. 'Rewards Versus Intellectual Property Rights', *Journal of Law and Economics*, 44(2): 525–47.

Sismondo, S., 2007. 'Ghost Management: How Much of the Medical Literature Is Shaped Behind the Scenes by the Pharmaceutical Industry?', *PLoS Medicine*, 4(9): 1429–33.

Stevens, A.J., Jensen, J.J., Wyller, K., Kilgore, P.C., Chatterjee, S. and Rohrbaugh, M.L., 2011. 'The Role of Public-Sector Research in the Discovery of Drugs and Vaccines', *The New England Journal of Medicine*, 364(6): 535–41.

Varian, H.R., 1993. 'Markets for Public Goods?', *Critical Review*, 7(4): 539–57.

Vitry, A. and Löfgren, H., 2011. 'Health Consumer Groups and the Pharmaceutical Industry: Is Transparency the Answer?', in H. Lofgren, E. de Leeuw and M. Leahy (eds), *Democratizing Health: Consumer Groups in the Policy Process*, pp. 239–54, Edward Elgar, Cheltenham.

Wright, B.D., 1983. 'The Economics of Invention Incentives: Patents, Prizes, and Research Contracts', *The American Economic Review*, 73(4): 691–707.

Yu, P.K., 2011. 'TRIPS and its Achilles' Heel', *Journal of Intellectual Property Law*, 18: 479–531.

13 Post-script
Hans Löfgren

This volume aimed to contribute to a better understanding of the politics of pharmaceuticals and access to medicines in India and beyond. It does not, of course, address the full range of policy challenges. Much more could be said about the national innovation system and research into neglected diseases, the growth of clinical trials, the role of retail pharmacy, the price regulation system, and the need for broader public health reform. Moreover, any of the chapters could be usefully expanded into full-length books in their own right. For example, it would be of great interest for the stories of major companies such as CIPLA, Dr Reddy's and Ranbaxy to be told in greater detail. Business history focused on particular firms can shed much light on entrepreneurialism and innovation, interdependencies between firms, government regulators and research institutes, the role of labour, consumers and other stakeholders, and so on. Chandler's (2005) telling of 'the remarkable story of the modern chemical and pharmaceutical industries' provides a fine case in point. This post-script identifies key insights from preceding chapters and offers a few observations about global industry trends and their implications for India.

A wealth of information on India's pharmaceutical industry is readily available; hundreds of articles have appeared in refereed social science journals. The central divide in this literature is between an emphasis on entrepreneurial achievements and economic development and a concern with access to affordable essential medicines. In the terminology of the introductory chapter, analysts tend to view the industry as (principally) a source of *exchange value* for the purpose of capital accumulation ('economic development') or as a producer of *use value* to enhance public health. In this volume, Deepak Kumar Jena and Poduri Balaram have documented the success of Indian generics producers and considered the prospects and requirements for maintaining the momentum of growth and profits. In contrast, S. Srinivasan and Anant Phadke criticised the irrationality, from a social and public health perspective, of many of the innovation, production and marketing activities of the same group of firms. Most business and economic analysts are somewhat equivocal: the emergence of a large domestic manufacturing sector from the 1970s is acclaimed as a national economic success story and its unique role as contributor to public health is recognised as a fortunate consequence of this story.

The tension between capital accumulation and public health is reflected not only in the academic literature but in fragmentation and friction within governments. Policies and programs in the three core regulatory areas of (1) safety and efficacy controls for the purpose of public health, (2) access and equity, and (3) assisting industry development, are promoted by different departments and agencies, which are in turn linked to distinct groups of social and economic interests, including business associations and firms, health professionals, and consumers. Such fragmentation between agencies and interlocking advocacy coalitions is a characteristic of pharmaceutical policy in all countries, particularly those with significant local industries (Lofgren and de Boer 2004). Relations between regulatory agencies and firms present a perennial difficulty for governments, and every so often a corruption scandal erupts (Angell 2005). There has to be great concern when the industry assistance objective is allowed to override public health to the point of capture of regulatory agencies, as appears to be the case with India's Central Drugs Standard Control Organisation (Parliamentary Standing Committee on Health and Welfare 2012). It is also well recognised that regulation for access and equity through health insurance and reimbursement schemes is seriously underdeveloped in India. Recent public debates on health reform, and reports such as Planning Commission of India (2012), may suggest that change for the better is now on the policy agenda.

International public health advocates such as Médecins Sans Frontières, and Christiane Fischer in this volume, applaud the role of the Indian industry as a game-changer within global pharmaceutical markets. The upheaval caused by the supply by CIPLA and other Indian firms of low-cost HIV/AIDS and other medications, and consequent pressure on the MNCs, might indicate that it is possible to (at least partially) bridge the divide between use and exchange value. Reform of regulatory and policy frameworks could perhaps sustain the trend towards better access to affordable essential medicines that has emerged in the past decade ('t Hoen 2009). In this optimistic view, Indian firms appear as the 'good guys' within an industry renowned for wicked and too often illegal behaviour. By way of illustration of this behaviour, US regulators between 2009 and 2012 fined six of the largest pharma MNCs (Eli Lilly, Pfizer, AstraZeneca, Merck, Abbott and GlaxoSmithKline) close to $10 billion for inappropriate and in some cases illegal drug promotion (Almashat et al. 2010; Groeger 2012). For more on the industry's conduct, see for example Braithwaite (1984), Angell (2005), and recent critiques of the patent system itself, for example Hestermeyer (2007) and Boldrin and Levine (2008). Research and advocacy by public health activists and many NGOs, for example Knowledge Ecology International (see http://keionline.org/), provide similar evidence of harmful aspects of the industry's activities.

Vijay's chapter is an exception to the view that Indian pharma companies are providers of good news. He considers these firms integral to a development model in the global periphery premised on corruption, poor regulation, and extreme exploitation of labour and the environment. Local firms, as Vijay sees it, were subordinated to metropolitan capitalism through the opening up of international markets for polluting manufacturing well before recent tie-ins, mergers and acquisitions. The concept of accumulation by dispossession, as explained by Harvey (2010) and by critics of India's special economic zone policy (e.g. Levien 2011), is central to this analysis. It is a chimera, in this perspective, to believe that Indian manufacturers could ever challenge the incumbent MNCs that dominate the global pharmaceutical industry. There is also little reason to have confidence in technology, policy tinkering or better regulation, but only in social and political mobilisation for a different model of production and industrialisation. S. Srinivasan and Anant Phadke's critique of regulatory failures points towards the same conclusion—that the production of medicines to meet public health needs must ultimately overcome the market logic and be organised as manufacturing and distribution within the public sector.

Indian pharma industry entrepreneurs, however, cannot plausibly be characterised as merely comprador capitalists acting in the interest of foreign interests. Capitalist development is always uneven and fraught with contradictions and conflict between different factions of capital. The global political economy is in a state of great flux, with economic stagnation in much of the developed world and the rapid rise of China. Indian pharmaceutical firms in this context do not lack agency in designing strategies in response to changes in global markets. Moreover, Chaudhuri (2005) and others have shown that these firms carved out a relatively independent niche, supported by government policy, in the latter part of the era of Nehruvian self-reliance, even as participants in a process of accumulation by dispossession. It could be, however, that by responding to recent changes in the global political economy, major companies are accepting integration into the innovation and production networks of the MNCs. There is no longer much talk of an all-out competitive challenge to global innovation-based producers. Power politics and external pressures, such as the threat of trade sanctions and legal challenges by MNCs for alleged failures to properly enforce patent rights (as in the cases of Novartis and Bayer), and even seizures of generic drugs traded internationally, are likely to have resulted in a narrowing of the scope for autonomous business strategies (Micara 2012; Sell 2010). This turn to collaborations with the MNCs and the wave of mergers and acquisitions is reported to be of concern to some within government, which at the time of writing is considering scrutiny by the Foreign Investment Promotion Board (FIPB) of acquisitions resulting in majority foreign ownership. The aim is reported to be to 'ensure that pharmaceutical sector is not controlled by foreign companies thereby denying availability of cheaper drugs in the domestic market' (Special correspondent 2012).

This book thus appears at a defining moment for the pharmaceutical sector in India and globally. The MNC are 'in a period of rapid environmental change and intense competition, following a relatively long period of ... stability in which the same business models ... dominated for many decades' (Smith 2011, p. 100). Put more colloquially: 'The good old days of the pharmaceutical industry are gone forever' (Hunt, Manson and Morgan 2011). The industry is being reshaped due to steadily falling R&D productivity, the expiry of patents on many major products, a shift towards biological medicines, constraints on health expenditure in developed countries, mergers and acquisitions, the threat of pandemics, and political mobilisations for access to medicines for all. The now faltering MNC business model has been premised on profits from sales in developed-country markets of patent-protected so-called blockbuster drugs (those with annual sales of more than $1 billion). Concerns about 'a fundamental shift in the structure of the research-based industry' stem from the slower emergence of new such products (Kaitin and DiMasi 2011, p. 183). While R&D investments by the world's top 500 pharmaceutical and biotechnology companies are estimated to have increased by 93 per cent between 2002 and 2011, to $133 billion, the number of new drug launches in the US remained stagnant at an annual average of 25 (AstraZeneca 2011, p. 16). Due to the R&D productivity crisis and declining growth in developed markets, the industry is consolidating, closing plants, and retrenching workers. In 2011 alone, ten top pharma MNCs shed almost 25,000 staff, mostly in developed countries (IMAP 2012, p. 6). Yet the dominant trend may not be consolidation in the form of giant corporations; *McKinsey Quarterly* reports that 'the number of companies competing for the profit pool has more than doubled' (Hunt, Manson and Morgan 2011, p. 5). Instead, the MNCs are building innovation and production networks that link public research systems, smaller dedicated bio-technology firms, and various types of services providers across many locations, including many sites in India. Of particular significance is a shift of MNC business strategies to focus more on emerging economies; '[t] here is consensus that future growth in the Pharma Industry will mainly come from emerging markets, most notably China' (IMAP 2012, p. 1). The world market in 2011 grew by the historically low rate of 4.5 per cent, to $839 billion. The US and Western Europe accounted for around 62 per cent of global sales, and per-capita spending is much higher in developed countries than in emerging markets. Yet the aggregate growth rate in these markets was 12 per cent in 2011, four times that of 'established markets' at 2.8 per cent (IMS Health data cited in AstraZeneca 2011). Brian Tempest (2010, p. 116), the former CEO of Ranbaxy, observes that 'Big Pharma have become intrigued by the fact that 88 per cent of the world's pharmaceuticals is shared among only 18 per cent of the world's population. ... Here lies a business opportunity'. In particular, the expansion of markets for contract research and manufacturing services ('CRAMS') offer opportunities for India to become part of these networks. Indeed, to the extent that Indian firms undertake discovery research—and recently such research has been in decline—it is premised on the expectation of out-licensing of promising molecules to MNCs (Joseph 2011).This is a trend which does not necessarily bode well for the future of production of low-cost essential drugs for the developing world.

Overall, the generics segment is expanding across all markets; according to Pfizer (2012), '[b]y 2020, off-patent medicines and their generic equivalents are estimated to account for more than 50 per cent of global pharmaceutical sales'. As patents expire, institutional arrangements in established markets ensure that prices come down drastically. For example, in the US, generics now constitute 80 per cent of the market by volume (AstraZeneca 2011, p. 18). In the European Union and elsewhere, tender-based models of drug procurement deliver a large market share for generics (Kanavos, Seeley and Vandoros 2009). In contrast, in countries such as India, price control systems are patchy, consumers often carry the full cost of medicines, and drug markets are only imperfectly regulated for quality, safety and efficacy. Typically, high-margin 'branded generics' predominate, seen as providing quality assurance, as explained by S. Srinivasan and Anant Phadke; this creates markets quite different from the low-profit commodity generic markets of the US and Europe. While the majority of drugs in India and other emerging markets continue to be non-patented, product patenting have become a more effective and important strategic tool for the MNCs. According to Correa (2011, p. 21), 'most of patenting [in a group of five emerging economies [including India] is motivated by strategic reasons, namely to restrict generic competition, rather than to protect genuine innovations'. This follows from the global IPR regime which will have the effect, over time, of reducing the generic new product pipeline available to local companies in countries such as India which until recently did not recognise drug product patents. While middle class markets in the global South are important, there may be less capacity or commercial incentive in the medium term to produce low-value generics for the poor. For India the commercial appeal of exports to developed countries (rather than increased patenting as a consequence of TRIPS) might be the principal reason for pessimism about the future of production and supply of medicines for the global poor. Yet, pressures will continue to build for access to affordable essential medicines for all, and this book makes a modest contribution to this process.

References

Almashat, S., Preston, C., Waterman, T., and Wolfe, S., 2010. 'Rapidly Increasing Criminal and Civil Monetary Penalties Against the Pharmaceutical Industry: 1991 to 2010', Public Citizen's Health Research Group.

Angell, M., 2005. *The Truth About the Drug Companies: How They Deceive Us and What to do About it*, Random House, New York.

AstraZeneca 2011, *Annual Report and Form 20-F Information*, <http://www.astrazeneca-annualreports.com/2011/documents/pdfs/annual_report_pdf_entire.pdf >.

Boldrin, M., and Levine, D.K., 2008. *Against Intellectual Monopoly*, Cambridge University Press, New York, <http://www.dklevine.com/general/intellectual/againstfinal.htm>.

Braithwaite, J., 1984. *Corporate Crime in the Pharmaceutical Industry*, Routledge and Kegan Paul, London.

Chandler, A.D.J., 2005. *Shaping the Industrial Century: The Remarkable Story of the Evolution of the Modern Chemical and Pharmaceutical Industries*, Harvard University Press, Cambridge, MA.

Chaudhuri, S., 2005. *The WTO and India's Pharmaceuticals Industry: Patent Protection, TRIPS, and Developing Countries*, Oxford University Press, New Delhi.

Groeger, L., 2012. 'Big Pharma's Big Fines', ProPublica, <http://www.tru-rx.com/articles/share/11100/>.

Harvey, D., 2010. *The Enigma of Capital, and the Crises of Capitalism*, Oxford University Press, Oxford [England]; New York.

Hestermeyer, H., 2007. *Human Rights and the WTO: The Case of Patents and Access to Medicines*, Oxford University Press, Oxford.

Hunt, V., Manson, N., and Morgan, P., 2011. 'A Wake-Up Call for Big Pharma', *McKinsey Quarterly*, no. December, <https://www.mckinseyquarterly.com/A_wake-up_call_for_Big_Pharma_2897>.

IMAP 2012, *Global Pharma and M&A Report 2012*. http://www.imap.com/imap/media/resources/Pharma-Report-2012-FINAL-2F6C8ADA76680.pdf>.

Joseph, R.K., 2011. 'The R&D Scenario in Indian Pharmaceutical Industry', Research and Information System for Developing Countries (RIS), New Delhi.

Kaitin, K.I., and DiMasi, J.A., 2011. 'Pharmaceutical Innovation in the 21st Century: New Drug Approvals in the First Decade, 2000–2009', *Clinical Pharmacology And Therapeutics*, vol. 89, no. 2: 183–8.

Kanavos, P., Seeley, L., and Vandoros, S., 2009. 'Tender systems for outpatient pharmaceuticals in the European Union: Evidence from the Netherlands, Germany and Belgium', European Commission Brussels.

Levien, M., 2011. 'Special Economic Zones and Accumulation by Dispossession in India', *Journal of Agrarian Change*, vol. 11, no. 4: 453–616.

Lofgren, H., and de Boer, R., 2004. 'Pharmaceuticals in Australia: Developments in Regulation and Governance', *Social Science and Medicine*, vol. 58, no. 12: 2397–407.

Micara, A.G., 2012. 'TRIPS-Plus Border Measures and Access to Medicines', *Journal of World Intellectual Property*, vol. 15, no. 1: 73–101.

Parliamentary Standing Committee on Health and Welfare 2012. 'The Functioning of the Central Drugs Standard Control Organisation (CDSCO)', Government of India, New Delhi.

Pfizer 2012, *Annual Review 2011*, Pfizer <http://www.pfizer.com/investors/financial_reports/annual_reports/2011/biopharmaceutical.jsp>.

Planning Commission of India 2012, 'Report of the Steering Committee on Health for the 12th Five-Year Plan', Health Division Planning Commission, New Delhi.

Sell, S.K., 2010. 'The Rise and Rule of a Trade-Based Strategy: Historical Institutionalism and the International Regulation of Intellectual Property', *Review of Inernational Political Economy*, vol. 17, no. 4: 762–90.

Smith, B.D., 2011. *The Future of Pharma: Evolutionary Threats and Opportunities*, Ashgate, Farnham.

Special correspondent 2012. 'Expert Group on FDI in Pharma to Meet on Tuesday', *The Hindu*, no. 23 July, <http://www.thehindu.com/business/companies/article3674156.ece>.

't Hoen, EFM 2009. *The Global Politics of Pharmaceutical Monopoly Power: Drug Patents, Access, Innovation and the Application of the WTO Doha Declaration on TRIPS and Public Health*, AMB Publishers, Diemen.

Glossary

ABBREVIATED NEW DRUG APPLICATION (ANDA)

'An Abbreviated New Drug Application (ANDA) contains data that, when submitted to the [US Food and Drug Administration's] Center for Drug Evaluation and Research, Office of Generic Drugs, provides for the review and ultimate approval of a generic drug product. Generic drug applications are called "abbreviated" because they are generally not required to include preclinical (animal) and clinical (human) data to establish safety and effectiveness. Instead, a generic applicant must scientifically demonstrate that its product is bioequivalent (i.e., performs in the same manner as the innovator drug). Once approved, an applicant may manufacture and market the generic drug product to provide a safe, effective, low cost alternative to the American public' (Food and Drug Administration 2012).

ACTIVE PHARMACEUTICAL INGREDIENT (API)

'Any substance or combination of substances used in a finished pharmaceutical product, intended to furnish pharmacological activity or to otherwise have direct effect in the diagnosis, cure, mitigation, treatment or prevention of disease, or to have direct effect in restoring, correcting or modifying physiological functions in human beings' (World Health Organization 2006).

ACCESS TO MEDICINES

'Expenditure on medicines accounts for a major proportion of health costs in developing countries. This means that access to treatment is heavily dependent on the availability of affordable medicines. Although trade in medicines is increasing rapidly, most of it takes place between wealthy countries, with developing countries accounting for just 17 per cent of imports and 6 per cent of exports. It is estimated that one-third of the developing world's people are unable to receive or purchase essential medicines on a regular basis. The provision of access to medicines depends on four factors: rational selection and use of medicines; affordable prices; sustainable financing; [and] reliable health and supply systems' (World Health Organization 2012).

BIOEQUIVALENCE

'The key factor in creating a generic medicine is establishing bioequivalence. Bioequivalence means that, when compared scientifically, the generic medicine and the originator product demonstrate essentially the same rate and extent of biological availability of the active substance in the body when administered in the same dose. In simple terms, the generic medicine and the original product must be equally effective' (European Generic Medicines Association 2012).

BIOLOGICAL PRODUCT (BIOLOGIC)

'Biological products include a wide range of products such as vaccines, blood and blood components, allergenics, somatic cells, gene therapy, tissues, and recombinant therapeutic proteins. Biologics can be composed of sugars, proteins, or nucleic acids or complex combinations of these substances, or may be living entities such as cells and tissues. Biologics are isolated from a variety of natural sources—human, animal, or microorganism—and may be produced by biotechnology methods and other cutting-edge technologies. Gene-based and cellular biologics, for example, often are at the forefront of biomedical research, and may be used to treat a variety of medical conditions for which no other treatments are available' (Food and Drug Administration 2012).

BRAND NAME

'A brand name drug is a drug marketed under a proprietary, trademark-protected name' (Food and Drug Administration 2012).

BULK DRUG

See Active Pharmaceutical Ingredient (API).

CLINICAL TRIALS

'A clinical trial is any research study that prospectively assigns human participants or groups of humans to one or more health-related interventions to evaluate the effects on health outcomes. Clinical trials may also be referred to as interventional trials. Interventions include but are not restricted to drugs, cells and other biological products, surgical procedures, radiologic procedures, devices, behavioural treatments, process-of-care changes, preventive care, etc.' (World Health Organization 2012c).

COUNTERFEIT DRUG PRODUCT

'A pharmaceutical product that is deliberately and fraudulently mislabelled with respect to identity and/or source. Both branded and generic products can be counterfeited, and counterfeit products may include products with the correct ingredients, with the wrong ingredients, without active ingredients, with insufficient quantity of active ingredients or with fake packaging' (World Health Organization 2006).

DATA EXCLUSIVITY PERIOD

'Data exclusivity refers to a practice whereby, for a certain number of years, the national drug regulatory authority may not rely on the safety and efficacy data that the originator company files to get marketing approval, in order to register a generic version of the same medicine. This means that during the data exclusivity period, generic versions of a medicine cannot be registered. Thegeneric producer would have to conduct fresh clinical trials before its version of the drug can be registered (which may be difficult in practice), or will have to wait till the end of the exclusivity period. Thus, data exclusivity delays the marketing of generic medicines, through a mechanism that is different from and operates independently of patents' (World Health Organization 2012d).

DRUG (PHARMACEUTICAL PRODUCT)

'Any substance or mixture of substances that is manufactured for sale or distribution, sold, supplied, offered for sale of presented for use in: (i) the treatment, mitigation, cure, prevention or diagnosis of disease, an abnormal physical state or the symptoms thereof and abnormal physiological conditions in human or animal; or (ii) the restoration, correction or modification of organic functions in human or animal' (World Health Organization 2006).

DRUG REGULATORY AUTHORITY

'The national agency responsible for the registration of and other regulatory activities concerning pharmaceutical products' (World Health Organization 2006).

DRUG MASTER FILE

'Detailed information concerning a specific facility, process or product submitted to the drug regulatory authority, intended for the incorporation into the application for marketing authorization' (World Health Organization 2006).

ESSENTIAL MEDICINES

'Essential medicines are those that satisfy the priority health care needs of a population. They are selected with due regard to public health relevance, evidence on efficacy and safety, and comparative cost-effectiveness. Essential medicines are intended to be available in functioning health systems at all times, in adequate amounts, in the appropriate dosage forms, with assured quality and adequate information, and at a price the individual and the community can afford. These drugs are supported as safe, effective and of high quality. Efforts are focused on their correct prescription and rational use (rational use of drugs)' (World Health Organization 2012).

ESSENTIAL MEDICINES LISTS

'Essential medicines are intended to be available within the context of functioning health systems at all times in adequate amounts, in the appropriate dosage forms, with assured quality, and at a price the individual and the community can afford' (World Health Organization 2006).

EVERGREENING

'Due to a diminishing number of newly registered products and contracting product pipelines, originator companies may be tempted to unjustly prolong the patent monopoly of existing products. The result is known as the 'evergreening' of a basic patent with the help of follow-on patents to keep generic competitors off the market. These follow-on patents are often weak or trivial and, upon careful examination, it is clear that they should never have been granted' (European Generic Medicines Association 2012).

EXCHANGE VALUE

'Exchange-value is the *quantitative* aspect of value, as opposed to "use-value" which is the *qualitative* aspect of value, and constitutes the substratum of the price of a commodity. "Value" is often used as a synonym for exchange-value, though strictly speaking, "value" indicates the concept which incorporates both quantity and quality' (Encyclopedia of Marxism 2012).

FIXED DOSE COMBINATION

'A combination of two or more active pharmaceutical ingredients in a fixed ratio of doses. This term is used generically to mean a particular combination of active pharmaceutical ingredients irrespective of the formulation or brand. It may be administered as single entity products given concurrently or as a finished pharmaceutical product' (World Health Organization 2006).

GENERIC DRUG (MEDICINE)

'A generic medicine is a medicine that is developed to be the same as a medicine that has already been authorised, called the 'reference medicine'. A generic medicine contains the same active substances as the reference medicine, and it is used at the same doses to treat the same diseases. However, a generic medicine's inactive ingredients, name, appearance and packaging can be different from the reference medicine's. Generic medicines are manufactured according to the same quality standards as all other medicines' (European Medicines Agency 2012).

GOOD MANUFACTURING PRACTICE (GMP)

'That part of quality assurance which ensures that products are consistently produced and controlled to the quality standards appropriate to their intended use and as required by the marketing authorization' (World Health Organization 2006).

HIV/AIDS

Human Immunodeficiency Virus (HIV) is the retrovirus that weakens the immune system, particularly by causing the death of many CD4+T cells, which coordinate the human immune system's response to intruders. This weakening of the immune system leaves the body open to attack from opportunistic infections, eventually leading to the development of Acquired Immune Deficiency

Syndrome (AIDS). HIV/AIDS affects every country in the world and in many infection rates are increasing rapidly. Today, an estimated 42 million people live with HIV/AIDS' (World Health Organization 2012).

INNOVATOR PHARMACEUTICAL PRODUCT

'Generally, the innovator pharmaceutical product is that which was first authorized for marketing (normally as a patented drug) on the basis of documentation of efficacy, safety and quality (according to contemporary requirements). When drugs have been available for many years, it may not be possible to identify an innovator pharmaceutical product' (World Health Organization 2006).

INTELLECTUAL PROPERTY RIGHTS (IPR)

'Intellectual property rights are exclusive rights, often temporary, granted by the state for the exploitation of intellectual creations. Intellectual property rights fall into two categories: rights relating to industrial property (invention patents, industrial designs and models, trademarks and geographical indications) and those relating to literary and artistic property (copyright). The Agreement on Trade-Related Aspects of Intellectual Property Rights (TRIPS) covers the main categories of intellectual property law' (World Health Organization 2012).

LICENCE

'A licence is a contract whereby the holder of an industrial property right (patent, trademark, design or model) cedes to a third party, in whole or in part, the enjoyment of the right to its working, free of charge, or in return for payment of fees or royalties. Governments may issue a compulsory licence to allow the use of an invention (e.g. a patented drug) without the consent of the patent holder on grounds of public interest. Under the Agreement on Trade-Related Aspects of Intellectual Property Rights (TRIPS), a voluntary licence should normally be requested before a compulsory licence is issued and the patent holder must be paid adequate remuneration, even under compulsory licence conditions. A compulsory licence may be issued without prior request for a voluntary licence in cases such as national emergency, extreme urgency, or for public, non-commercial use' (World Health Organization 2012).

MARKETING AUTHORIZATION

'An official document issued by the competent drug regulatory authority for the purpose ofmarketing or free distribution of a product after evaluation for safety, efficacy and quality. Itmust set out, inter alia, the name of the product, the pharmaceutical dosage form, thequantitative formula (including excipients) per unit dose (using international non-proprietary names or national generic names where they exist), the shelf-life and storage conditions andpackaging characteristics. It also contains information approved for health professionals andthe public, the sales category, the name and address of the licence holder, and the period ofvalidity of the licence' (World Health Organization 2006).

OVER-THE-COUNTER DRUGS

'These are drugs that can be sold from licensed dealers without professional supervision and without prescriptions. These drugs are suitable for self-medication for minor diseases and symptoms' (World Health Organization 2006).

PARALLEL IMPORTS

'Parallel imports are imports of a patented or trademarked product from a country where it is already marketed. For example, in Mozambique, 100 units of Bayer's ciprofloxacin (500mg) costs US$740, but in India Bayer sells the same drug for US$15 (owing to local generic competition). Mozambique can import the product from India without Bayer's consent' (World Health Organization 2012).

PATENT OPPOSITION

'Patent oppositions are a tool used to prevent patent applications that do not fulfil the requirements in national legislation for granting the patents. According to TRIPS, inventions must be new, involve an inventive step and be capable of industrial application. Patent oppositions have been successfully used in Thailand and India to prevent the granting of questionable patents on essential medicines. Some FTAs restrict the ability of countries to provide for pre-grant patent oppositions' (UNAIDS 2012).

PATENT

'A patent is a title, granted by the public authorities, conferring a temporary monopoly for the exploitation of an invention on the person who reveals it, furnishes a sufficiently clear and full description of it and claims this monopoly. The patent owner may give permission to other parties to use the invention, or sell the right to the invention in the form of a licence. An invention must be of practical use; and it must show an element of novelty and show an inventive step that could not be deduced by a person with average knowledge of the technical field. Finally, its subject matter must be accepted as "patentable" under law' (World Health Organization 2012).

PATENT POOLS

'A patent pool is a way of facilitating access to intellectual property. Through a patent pool, two or more patent-holders agree to share their intellectual property with each other or with third parties through the negotiation of licences. Patent pools can serve different purposes: to promote competition, to facilitate innovation, and/or to set industry standards. They can be designed to benefit patent-holders, product manufacturers and/or the public interest. In the past, patent pools have been organized by patent-holders, by manufacturers, by non-profit institutions, and/or by governments. In short, there are many different purposes of patent pools, and many different ways to manage them' (Medicines Patent Pool 2012).

PRESCRIPTION-ONLY DRUGS

'These are drugs supplied only in licensed pharmacies on the presentation of signed prescriptions issued by a licensed and registered medical practitioner, licensed and/or registered dentist (for dental treatment only), and/or licensed and/or registered veterinarian (for animal treatment only), and the supply and dispensing of these drugs must be carried out by a pharmacist or under the supervision of a pharmacist. Prescription drugs are further subdivided into controlled drugs (narcotic drugs and psychotropic substances) and noncontrolled drugs' (World Health Organization 2006).

PUBLIC HEALTH

'Public health refers to all organized measures (whether public or private) to prevent disease, promote health, and prolong life among the population as a whole. Its activities aim to provide conditions in which people can be healthy and focus on entire populations, not on individual patients or diseases. Thus, public health is concerned with the total system and not only the eradication of a particular disease' (World Health Organization 2012).

RATIONAL USE OF MEDICINES

'Rational use of medicines requires that patients receive medications appropriate to their clinical needs, in doses that meet their own individual requirements, for an adequate period of time, and at the lowest cost to them and their community' (World Health Organization 2012b).

REGULATORY CAPTURE

'The tendency of regulators to identify with the interest of the industry they are supposed to regulate. This occurs when a public authority charged with regulating an industry in the public interest comes to identify the public interest with the interests of producers in the industry, rather than the interests of its customers, or the general public' (*A Dictionary of Economics* 2009).

RESEARCH AND DEVELOPMENT

'This term is typically used to describe scientific investigation and invention. Applied research and development has a commercial objective and includes the invention and design of production systems. In the pharmaceutical sector, research and development (R&D) costs are often very high and so the industry is likely to invest only in drugs with profit potential' (World Health Organization 2012).

USE VALUE

'Use-value is the qualitative aspect of value, i.e., the concrete way in which a thing meets human needs: "The utility of a thing makes it a use-value. But this utility is not a thing of air. Being limited by the physical properties of the commodity, it has no existence apart from that commodity. A commodity, such as iron, corn, or a diamond, is therefore, so far as it is a material thing, a use-value, something useful. This property of a commodity is independent of the amount of labour required to appropriate its useful qualities. When treating of use-value, we always assume to be dealing with definite quantities, such as dozens of watches, yards of linen, or tons of iron. The use-values of commodities furnish the material for a special study, that of the commercial knowledge of commodities. Use-values become a reality only by use or consumption: they also constitute the substance of all wealth, whatever may be the social form of that wealth. In the form of society we are about to consider, they are, in addition, the material depositories of exchange-value." [Capital, Chapter 1]' (Encyclopedia of Marxism 2012).

WORLD HEALTH ORGANIZATION (WHO)

'WHO is the directing and coordinating authority for health within the United Nations system. It is responsible for providing leadership on global health matters, shaping the health research agenda, setting norms and standards, articulating evidence-based policy options, providing technical support to countries and monitoring and assessing health trends' (World Health Organization 2012e).

WORLD TRADE ORGANIZATION (WTO)

'The WTO is the principal international institution for the management of international trade. It was created at the Uruguay Round of trade talks in 1994, when it was agreed to transform the General Agreement on Tariffs and Trade (GATT) into a permanent institution. The Uruguay Round was a round of GATT negotiations started in Uruguay in 1986 and designed to promote free trade. It was the origin of the WTO and a range of multilateral agreements' (World Health Organization 2012).

Sources:

Encyclopedia of Marxism (2012) http://www.marxists.org/glossary/index. htm

European Generic Medicines Association (2012), http://www.egagenerics. com/index.php/generic-medicines/introduction

European Medicines Agency (2012). Generic Medicines, http://www.ema. europa.eu/ema/index.jsp?curl=pages/special_topics/document_listing/ document_listing_000335.jsp&mid=WC0b01ac0580514d5c

Food and Drug Administration (2012). Drugs@FDA Glossary of Terms, http://www.fda.gov/Drugs/InformationOnDrugs/ucm079436.htm#A

UNAIDS (2012), The Potential Impact of Free Trade Agreements on Public Health http://www.unaids.org/en/media/unaids/contentassets/documents/ unaidspublication/2012/JC2349_Issue_Brief_Free-Trade-Agreements_ en.pdf

Medicines Patent Pool (2012). 'What is a Patent Pool?', http://www. medicinespatentpool.org/what-we-do/what-is-a-patent-pool/

A Dictionary of Economics 2009, Oxford Reference Online, Oxford University Press, http://www.oxfordreference.com/views/ENTRY. html?subview=Main&entry=t19.e2643

World Health Organization (2006). 'QAS Terminology db—List of Terms and related guidelines', http://www.who.int/medicines/services/ expertcommittees/pharmprep/TermListcategory.pdf

World Health Organization (2012a). Glossary of Globalization, Trade and Health terms, http://www.who.int/trade/glossary/en/

World Health Organization (2012b). Rational use of Medicines, http://www.who.int/medicines/areas/rational_use/en/

World Health Organization (2012c). International Clinical Trials Registry Platform (ICTRP), http://www.who.int/ictrp/glossary/en/

World Health Organization (2012d). Health Systems Development, http://www.searo.who.int/en/Section1243/Section2599_15088.htm

World Health Organization (2012e). About WHO, http://www.who.int/about/en/

For Product Safety Concerns and Information please contact our EU
representative GPSR@taylorandfrancis.com Taylor & Francis Verlag GmbH,
Kaufingerstraße 24, 80331 München, Germany

Printed and bound by CPI Group (UK) Ltd, Croydon, CR0 4YY
11/05/2025
01866594-0001